The Practice of Citizenship

THE PRACTICE OF CITIZENSHIP

Black Politics and Print Culture in the Early United States

Derrick R. Spires

PENN

UNIVERSITY OF PENNSYLVANIA PRESS

PHILADELPHIA

Published by
University of Pennsylvania Press
Philadelphia, Pennsylvania 19104-4112
www.upenn.edu/pennpress

Printed in the United States of America
on acid-free paper
1 3 5 7 9 10 8 6 4 2

Library of Congress Cataloging-in-Publication Data
ISBN 978-0-8122-5080-0

For Daisy and Nafissa

CONTENTS

INTRODUCTION

Black Theorizing

Reimagining a "Beautiful but Baneful Object"

Fellow Citizens

This book is about the questions and methodologies that emerge when we focus our analyses on the concerns black writers made foremost and on understanding these concerns in the terms they set forth. When we approach early black writing through a print culture made up of pamphlets, poems, sketches, orations, appeals, treatises, convention proceedings, letters, mastheads, gift books, petitions, autobiographies, and a host of other kinds of documents by black individuals and collectives, citizenship quickly emerges as a key term and vexed concept. A perusal of Dorothy Porter's touchstone *Early Negro Writings* (1971) reveals a collection of addresses on the abolition of the slave trade from 1808 to 1815 that begin, "Fathers, Brethren, and Fellow Citizens," or simply, "Citizens."[1] Martin R. Delany dedicates *Condition, Elevation, Emigration, and Destiny of the Colored People in the United States* (1852) "to the American People, North and South. By Their Most Devout, and Patriotic Fellow Citizen, the Author"; Frederick Douglass addresses his July 5th "Oration" to "fellow citizens," even as he positions himself outside the "nation"; and many of the collective addresses black citizens issued to various publics through colored conventions were addressed to "fellow citizens."[2] Even texts that did not argue for citizenship *in* the United States provide productive analyses *about* citizenship more broadly—what it was in the moment and what it could become. "Citizen," as the 1854 National Emigration Convention put it, was "a term desired and ever cherished" throughout early black America. While this convention argued explicitly for emigration, it nonetheless made useful claims about the meaning of citizenship, perhaps more so because it highlighted its abrogation for black Americans.[3]

These explicit and implicit invocations of citizenship throughout early black print culture suggest that citizenship was a potent concept. Yet, it is still one of the most understudied by critics of early African American literature. It's not that scholars haven't taken up questions of black citizenship—that is, whether or not black Americans were U.S. citizens, legal persons, or humans before the law; the ways they made the case for their citizenship; and the multiform ways (local and national; cultural, economic, and political) that white Americans made clear their refusal to recognize black Americans as equal citizens, if citizens at all.[4] These questions have been ably taken up and will continue to be important points of analysis. Yet, while scholars continue to recover histories of citizenship that document and analyze black activism and trace processes of racial ascription and white supremacy, we have yet to describe the degree to which black writers themselves conceptualized and transformed the meaning of citizenship in the early republic.[5] Even when studies have taken up black theoretical work, they tend to focus on Frederick Douglass's writing or conflicts between Douglass and other men (Henry Highland Garnet and Martin Delany prominent among them).[6] Overemphasizing Douglass flattens out a vibrant intellectual network of newspaper correspondents, convention goers, pamphleteers, and artists, whose key texts and forms were more often than not generated collectively. Hence, this book demonstrates the communal facets of citizenship discourse in black print culture to show that individuals and collectives were both critical to theorizing and practicing citizenship. What I demonstrate in this book stems from answering the following key questions: What happens to our thinking about citizenship if, instead of reading black writers as reacting to or a presence in a largely white-defined discourse, we base our working definitions of citizenship on black writers' proactive attempts to describe their own political work? What happens when we base our working definition of citizenship on black writers' texts written explicitly to and for black communities?

The proliferation of the phrase "fellow citizen" was more than a rhetorical device or ironic signifying. *The Practice of Citizenship* tells a story about how black writers theorized and practiced citizenship in the early United States through a robust print culture. It insists on exploring citizenship not just from the perspective of law and its framing of black people and others but also from the perspective of black Americans, who were some of the most important theorists of citizenship, both then and now. Yes, the texts I analyze here argue for black citizenship, but the citizenship for which they argue is not the same citizenship from which black Americans had been and continue to be excluded. Black writers argue for more than simple inclusion; indeed, they argue for the kind of political world in which they would not have to make such an argument. They argue for and actively seek to create a world otherwise. To understand this theory, *The Practice of Citizenship* moves beyond simply defining "citizenship" and pursues the processes by which black citizens used print to articulate and enact the citizenship they theorized. *How* black print culture imagined citizenship is therefore as central to this study as the citizenship they imagined, and by the end of this book, I hope it is clear that the process of theorizing does the work of citizenship.

I examine the parallel development of U.S. citizenship and early black print culture through key understudied flashpoints (the 1793 Philadelphia yellow fever epidemic and outbreaks of antislavery violence in 1856), movements (black state conventions and vigilance committees), intellectuals (James McCune Smith and William J. Wilson), and genres (the sketch, ballad, and convention minutes). I begin with events recorded in Absalom Jones and Richard Allen's *A Narrative of the Proceedings of the Black People* (1794) and end with Frances Ellen Watkins Harper's sketches for the last issues of the *Anglo-African Magazine* (1859–1860) just before the Civil War. Black citizenship theorizing developed over time as a collaborative, multimedia, polygeneric cultural and intellectual process for sustaining life in a fundamentally unjust society. For these writers, citizenship (and blackness itself) emerges not as a destination, an enacted identity, or static relation to a state but rather as a self-reflexive, dialectical process of becoming.

As state policies and public discourse around citizenship were becoming more racially restrictive, black activists articulated an expansive, practice-based theory of citizenship, not as a common identity as such but rather as a set of common practices: political participation, mutual aid, critique and revolution, and the myriad daily interactions between people living in the same spaces, both physical and virtual. They reject definitions of "citizen" based on who a person is, a preordained or predefined subject or subjectivity, in favor of definitions grounded in the active engagement in the process of creating and maintaining collectivity, whether defined as state, community, or other affiliative structure.[7] Citizenship, in other words, is not a thing determined by who one is but rather by what one does.[8] Law and custom shape these activities (negatively and positively), but they do not make citizenship or citizens. Practicing citizenship makes citizens.

Citizenship practices create citizens by enabling them, to quote Michel de Certeau, "to take up a position in the network of social relations" made up not only of currently recognized citizens but also of people who, by virtue of their engagement with and contribution to the whole, become citizens.[9] This "more or less coherent and fluid assemblage of elements" is simultaneously formal, performative, and open to improvisation. It is governed by rules and conventions that are nonetheless subject to misfire and therefore under constant revision and contestation on scales large and small.[10] Practices form a tradition insofar as they draw on catalogues of past activities and habits (from ways of worship and manners of speech to understandings of gender and sexuality, race and class), but they constantly respond to context and the need to make sense of the now. My sense of citizenship as a practice, then, is capacious, embracing recognizable acts, such as voting, alongside less structured acts, such as greeting others on the street. Both acts can signal membership in a political body, and exclusion or refusal (in the act of greeting) can become mechanisms of erasure or identifying those outside the bounds of "citizen." That is, citizenship and struggles for citizenship happen outside of official state institutions, in those very spaces black writers consistently cite as life sustaining. And it is through these sites that restrictive notions of belonging can be contested and in which alternate models can be theorized and practiced.

The role of spaces beyond state sanction is crucial to my argument. While it is true that the state provides one powerful structure for shaping citizenship, that does not mean that people who do not have this sanction are not theorizing and practicing citizenship.[11] Yet that is how we typically understand it. The state *sanctions* certain practices and enables those in power to limit the range of activities we come to recognize as citizenship. This book, though, recognizes the unsanctioned activities of citizenship, arguing that they are perhaps more powerful and productive than the state allows and that scholarship has adequately acknowledged. As Dana Nelson claims in terms of vernacular citizenship, these practices are "immediate, informal, and non-delegable," not individual but rather "grounded in community. Not a ritual in the sense of voting, the democratic power of the commons is both *colloquial* and *routine*: a daily practice."[12] And while, as Saidiya Hartman reminds us, such practices under conditions of domination rarely result in lasting victories, they do open new possibilities of political action and for valuing everyday activities in making community.[13]

As the chapters that follow suggest, in each reiterative instance, "citizen" invokes a civic ethos and protocols of recognition and justice that call on audiences to think about their relation to citizens and others as one of mutual responsibility, responsiveness, and active engagement, a relation in which membership and individual rights come with moral obligations to a collective. Put differently, citizenship for these writers is not reducible to individual interest nor should it be managed by racial, economic, or other forms of hierarchy. Alongside and beyond state-organized relationships, black writers linked citizenship to those actions that create and sustain relations between people, within and without formal politics. Absalom Jones's 1799 petition to the "President, Senate, and House of Representatives," for instance, claimed citizenship for his fellow petitioners, including enslaved people, "believing them to be objects of your representation in your public councils, in common with ourselves and every other class of citizens within the jurisdiction of the United States."[14] But they were not merely objects of representation; rather, they were included in the Constitution's "We, the people of the United States" and, as such, were not outsiders asking for inclusion in the body politic or for a special dispensation. Black citizens, including enslaved people, were "guardians of our rights, and patriots of equal and national liberties."[15] Thirty years later, when David Walker addressed his *Appeal* (1829) to the "colored citizens of the world, but in particular, and very expressly, to those of the United States of America," he was similarly speaking "colored citizens" into being, making a claim about their relationship to traditionally recognized citizens, and calling on them to assume the rights and subjectivity of citizenship.

Beyond overt invocations of "citizen" and claims making, *The Practice of Citizenship* is concerned with the multiple spaces—physical and in print—where black citizens theorized and enacted citizenship. As social geographer Anna Secor notes, "The everyday life-spaces of the city—its neighborhoods, parks, streets, and buildings—" function as "both the medium through which citizenship struggles take place and, frequently, that which is at stake in the struggle."[16] While Secor's work focuses on urban spatial practices, *Practice of Citizenship* demonstrates that the principle holds for spaces of all kinds, both physical and imaginary, including texts such as Absalom Jones and Richard Allen's 1794 *Narrative* or William J. Wilson's 1859 "Afric-American Picture Gallery" in which "citizen" is not the operative term in play. As my discussions of neighborliness and economic citizenship reveal, black writers often found useful models for civic practices in unlikely places, such as the early American backcountry, picture galleries, parlors, or in abstract constructs such as the republic of letters.

At their most elastic, black theories framed enslaved people as rights-bearing citizens, found inspiration and instruction in antislavery violence, and embraced parlors and picture galleries as revolutionary spaces of marronage. "Forget not that you are native-born American citizens," Henry Highland Garnet proclaims to his assumed audience of enslaved "brethren" in his "Address to the Slaves of the United States" (delivered 1843, first printed 1848), "and as such, you are justly entitled to all the rights that are granted to the freest."[17] Garnet argues that enslaved people, as citizens, had a right to refuse to labor without wages, leave the plantations if their masters did not comply, and defend themselves if their masters attempted to retain them by force. His recognition of their citizenship does not so much make them citizens before the law as it acknowledges and names a citizenship that they simply had to act on. In this sense, black theorizing insisted on and created black citizens in the act of insisting. The rest of this introduction develops the literary critical, theoretical, and historical threads subtending the arguments about citizenship that I develop more fully in subsequent chapters.

Citizenship and Early African American Print Culture

Scholars of African American literature and print culture have been drawing our attention to "early Negro writings" from a variety of collectives, including mutual aid societies, religious and fraternal organizations, sermons, confessionals, and constitutions, for decades. These texts bring to light a different set of intellectual, social, and cultural insights into what Porter describes as "the beginnings of the Afro-American's artistic consciousness . . . the first articulations of the appeal of beauty and the moral sense."[18] While we have historically treated the documents comprising Porter's *Early Negro Writings* as documentary or evidentiary in nature, Porter framed them as the institutional and cultural building blocks of a literary culture, one decidedly more collaborative and situated in ephemeral media than the texts privileged in our traditional literary historical focus on bound books and single-authored works. Carla Peterson, Elizabeth McHenry,

Frances Smith Foster, Jocelyn Moody, Eric Gardner, John Ernest, and others have begun changing this tendency and have given us a robust sense of the "early Negro writings" emanating from a variety of collectives, including mutual aid societies, religious and fraternal organizations, literary societies, and labor unions.[19] Their projects are not just about the recovery of texts or troubling the canon, nor do they seek to diminish the importance of the slave narrative or experiences of enslavement; rather, they are invested in creating a deeper understanding of the expressive print cultures black communities created out of these experiences. Black citizens did this work not simply as a response to white oppression but as a matter of course in the shaping of their own communities and in the process of meeting their own political, social, and cultural needs "to speak to and for themselves about matters they considered worthy of written words."[20] In those spaces, we still find free black Americans wrestling with issues of enslavement but also very much invested in local, everyday issues, slavery being one—though sometimes tertiary—issue among many. They meditate on ethical and deliberative notions of republican citizenship, model these paradigms through textual form and circulation, and activate them through embodied performances like conventions, vigilance activities, and everyday activities of walking, working, and loving.[21]

These narratives, then, take shape in what Gardner describes as "unexpected places": print and geographical sites including periodicals, texts from the western states and territories, black writing in languages other than English, and massive collections of poetry that have yet to be fully explored or theorized.[22] This book's attention to print sources and how writers engaged them highlights the work of intellectuals such as William J. Wilson, who, often writing as "Ethiop," featured prominently among his contemporaries but whose work is only now coming to critical light.[23] It also draws on canonical figures such as Harper from their more understudied works and genres. By thinking about citizenship beyond the laws and state relations shaping it, thinking instead about how and where black writers theorized and enacted it, I broaden the range of texts and sites where we can analyze how citizenship theorizing happened. Some of these sites are obvious in their concern with citizenship, but our emphasis on their documentary nature, the sometimes messy fights over power between men like Douglass and Garnet, and the focus on nationalist/integrationist binaries has obscured the ways they produce ideas about citizenship, both in conversation with and quite different from contemporaneous models. The black state conventions, for instance, often outlined the legal and historical basis for black citizenship as they petitioned states to restore rights taken away from them. Beyond these arguments for citizenship, however, they were also theorizing and practicing citizenship in the modes through which they made these claims: in the many gatherings and print exchanges leading to the convention, in the deliberative activities of the conventions, and in the circulation and discussion following the conventions. The circulation of ideas, documents, and civic energies these conventions organized theorizes and enacts the participatory politics from which black citizens were being excluded formally.

Even as black writing offered theoretical readings of citizenship—that is, the content of black theories—its structure, innovative use of genre and form, and modes of circulation model the theories they sought to outline both in terms of how republican institutions should look and the critical sensibilities of the citizens who would constitute and, in turn, be constituted through them.[24] Black writers' attention to and experimentation with form, style, and the relation between politics and aesthetics challenge us to rethink our narratives of early African American literary history. Their work, from Jones and Allen's 1794 *Narrative* to Harper's 1860 "Triumph of Freedom" in the *Anglo-African Magazine*, suggests this history has routes that do not lead inexorably from slave narrative to novel but rather, like early national citizenship practices, proliferate in multiple directions.

The periodical press is particularly useful for analyzing this aspect of black theorizing, precisely because its structure cultivated multivocal, dialogic narratives, and its modes of circulation often demanded communal reading and reenactment. Ernest observes, "The periodical press was uniquely suited to the task of telling the story of African American history—because the story it could tell would be marked by narrative disruption and because, in telling the story, the press could only be multivocal and multiperspectival."[25] Todd Vogel has argued similarly that the ephemeral quality of the press "made the writers nimble. They could plunge into the public conversation and get their views out immediately" and, I would add, in a way that to some degree sidestepped the policing and paternalistic behavior of other activists, both white and black.[26] While black men, Douglass in particular, have been canonized as representatives and drivers of black intellectual history, this archive offers a much wider range of voices and ideas. As "Caleb" reminds would-be leaders in "A Note on Leaders," an 1861 article in the *Weekly Anglo-African*, while being "pious or educated at a time when knowing the alphabet seemed extraordinary" may have once vaulted any man to leadership, that time had long passed; black people could and were thinking and writing for themselves.[27] Top-down (and, I would add, masculinist) notions of black leadership would work no longer, if they ever had.

As Benjamin Fagan posits, the black press forces us to think about the ways black writers constituted community outside of the nation-state form.[28] This includes acknowledging that citizenship in the United States was not always (or sometimes even) the black press's primary point of identification. At the same time, these collectives were still thinking through modes of organization and self-government, however formal or informal, that have much to teach us about citizenship as a relation created by and practiced between members of a community. The question these texts pose is less how citizenship theorizing in the black press imagined black Americans as U.S. citizens and more how black theorizing imagined citizenship practices within and without the U.S. nation-state. The black press and broader print archive, then, offers models of democratic exchange and the kinds of spaces and institutions (print, galleries, conventions, markets, etc.) that support it.

Black national and state conventions are another form to which *The Practice of Citizenship* gives special attention. These events and the texts they produced were by nature dialogic. They included the back and forth of debates before and during conventions along with the rendering of the physical events in print form for distribution and further commentary. The printed minutes have traditionally been objects only of historical and not literary analysis, though the Colored Convention's Project's dedication to chronicling the conventions as a cultural movement is quickly changing that. While the national colored convention movement that began with the 1830 "National Convention of Free People of Colour held in Philadelphia, PA," has dominated critical discussions about black nationalism and political strategy, the myriad state conventions held across the country from 1840 through the 1890s demonstrate the vast variety in black political thought and strategy and reveal the degree to which U.S. citizenship was functionally state based, not national, particularly before the Civil War.[29] As I discuss in Chapter 2, these documents manifest materially what literary critics have described as "double-voiced discourse," often speaking simultaneously to black citizens and white voters. Most visibly, the New York and Pennsylvania conventions I analyze issued addresses to "colored fellow citizens" and "to the people of the state," often printed in the same document. These addresses mixed defiance with deference politics as convention delegates, on one hand, entreated black citizens not to lose faith in their advocacy and to continue working for their own uplift as proof of civic worth and, at the same time, excoriated white voters for demanding arbitrary proofs for rights that by law and principle should belong to black citizens as a matter of course. At the same time, these addresses could hint at, if not outright announce, calls to revolution and/or separation if white voters refused to heed delegates' reasoned arguments. Often, convention addresses made these moves simultaneously, sometimes within the same sentence.

Other forms, such as the sketches, short fiction, and poetry published in black and antislavery periodicals and newspapers, did equally important theoretical work. Many of the pieces in the *Anglo-African Magazine*, the short-lived magazine founded by Thomas and Robert Hamilton in 1859, were not explicitly about (concerned with) citizenship in the sense that they made arguments for black citizenship or challenged particular laws (though some did that). Yet they were about citizenship in the sense that they interrogated and modeled citizenship practices. When Wilson introduced Ethiop in the "Afric-American Picture Gallery" as someone meditating on U.S. and black American history through art and through his writing about art, he also introduced readers to a mode of critique essential to citizenship. Harper's Jane Rustic, the pseudonymous narrator of her "Fancy Sketches" series, similarly models a mode of citizenship-as-critique when she consistently interrupts the "tomfoolery" of the men who engaged in discussions about black liberation as an elite rhetorical pastime.

Reading black print as a space where citizenship was both theorized and practiced—that is, as both archive and repertoire—reveals the degree to which black theories of citizenship unfold through a highly creative and diverse community of letters, not easily reducible to representative figures or genres. I borrow from Diana Taylor's *Archive and Repertoire* (2003) not to expand the meaning of "repertoire" to the point of incoherence or to erase the distinction between archive and repertoire but rather to think through how print, when read less as an end point or a medium that fixes meaning and more as one element among several at the time of production, becomes a space where writers engaged in processes that created citizenship, knowledge, and power in a nation that denied both their citizenship and print culture. Though the texts black writers produced are an archive insofar as they record thoughts, events, and proceedings, black print culture—the creation, circulation, and consumption of these texts—constitutes an ongoing performance that we can read as a repertoire. These texts were not static documents, as the convention proceedings reveal most clearly; instead, they involved, among other things, public gatherings, oral delivery, recording, public debate in print and in person, and varying vectors into print and into variously constituted print publics. Insofar as the black state conventions were a performance, to stay with this one example, this performance extended beyond the meetings themselves to include conversations about the conventions in print and in local gatherings, the choreographed presentation of convention documents to the public in the form of proceedings, and the ongoing discussion of the convention and its documents, again, in print and in local gatherings. This complex interaction between print and embodied action constitutes a unique performance that is different in each instance.

In this sense, these texts, when taken as part of a larger cultural formation, belong to those practices "rehearsed and performed daily in the public sphere" that include, for Diana Taylor, "civic obedience, resistance, citizenship, gender, ethnicity, and sexual identity."[30] In the context of black theorizing, writing and publication are part of the "cultural practices" Taylor cites alongside "embodied practice" that offer "a way of knowing," a way of theorizing.[31] I extend Taylor's thinking to situate black theorizing as a practice depending on both embodied expression and print. This is not to say that one is consistently privileged over the other or that the distribution of work between print and embodied performance is even, but rather to highlight how the two were always enmeshed. Other kinds of embodied culture—street fashion, slave escapes, acts of civil disobedience, antislavery violence, storytelling, and so on—that were happening remain crucial lines of inquiry. At the same time, this study is interested in how black theorizing mobilized and conceptualized print as a site of knowledge production and a site of resistance that could destabilize white supremacist citizenship. By thinking of individual instances of black theorizing as a repertoire and the aggregate as an archive, I mean to signal each moment as a unique complex of textual production, circulation, and reception (imagined and actual) and at the same time to acknowledge my own position as an observer collecting and shaping a narrative out of these sites, a position I share with the writers I'm analyzing insofar as we are both engaged in the theorizing process.

"Can These Dry Bones Live?" Reading Citizenship Reparatively

Throughout this book, then, I emphasize theorizing over conclusive definitions, seeking forms rather than identifying a singular tradition, and articulating citizenship practices instead of defining formal citizenship status.[32] Black writers and activists saw great potential in U.S. framing ideals—its civic republicanism, the comingling of peoples and ideas, and shared sovereignty—but they also recognized that these same ideals could and did accommodate systems of oppression as readily as they did egalitarian polity. U.S. citizenship was a "beautiful but baneful object": beautiful in its potential realization of "*E pluribus unum*" and baneful because enslavement and other exclusionary practices not only limited the capacity to imagine this potential but also were integral to conceptions of citizenship's beauty.[33] In this sense, black theories of citizenship were both critical—defamiliarizing the ostensible naturalness of what citizenship was becoming—and reparative in their articulation of what might have been and what could still be. In calling these theories "reparative," I draw on Eve Kosofsky Sedgwick's description of reparative reading: "[a] position from which it is possible in turn to use one's own resources to assemble or 'repair' the murderous part-objects into something like a whole—though not, and may I emphasize this, *not necessarily like any preexisting whole.* Once assembled to one's own specifications, the more satisfying object is available both to be identified with and to offer one nourishment and comfort in turn."[34] While the "more satisfying object" —that is, a just and equal citizenship—may never be achieved, the point is to identify and reconstruct (or, in some cases, construct anew) methods for working toward it. Hortense Spillers articulates this point from a slightly different angle directly connected to the twinned acts of speaking and writing and in the context of a larger black feminist project. "In order for me to speak a truer word concerning myself, I must strip down through layers of attenuated meaning," she notes. This stripping down is not an end, and the outcome is not given; rather, it is the necessary preparatory work that will allow her/us to "await whatever marvels of my own inventiveness."[35] The power of this stance is in the energies black theorizing marshals and the "room" it creates "to realize that the future may be different from the present" and that the past could have happened differently.[36]

This stance finds its expression in speech and print as a collective imaginative enterprise that strips down to make anew. Early black writers remind us again and again that the past as we have received it did not have to unfold in the ways it did. Black theorizing breaks down and exposes the ravages of white supremacist citizenship in the name of creating and recreating a more affirming world. As I argue throughout this book, this seeking does not point to a messianic ending or a return to some founding ideal. The seeking itself enacts the citizenship for which black theorizers sought.

Scholarship has begun asking versions of this question in terms of "the human," personhood, and belonging. Jeanine DeLombard's analysis of black civic presence in *In the Shadow of the Gallows* asks, "How could the black majority ever achieve political membership in the form of citizenship" in a republic that attempted to remove them from "both the public sphere and the liberal state through their enslaved or outlaw status?"[37] Alexander G. Weheliye has asked, "What different modalities of the human come to light if we do not take the liberal humanist figure of Man as the master-subject but focus on how humanity has been imagined and lived by those subjects excluded from this domain?"[38] Following Weheliye, Lloyd Pratt adds a formalist dimension: "What does the human look like when we attend not only to how it is 'imagined and lived by those subjects excluded from' the major lines of liberal humanist thought, but also to the formal and institutional structures that facilitate and constrain that imagining?"[39] The question itself is not necessarily a new one if we consider critical work from black literary studies that interrogated the relation between black writing and contemporaneous discourses such as sentimentalism or paradigms such as the public sphere.[40] Yet these recent iterations of the question and the print culture methodologies through which we have begun examining it place renewed emphasis on black writing's work as simultaneously critical and creative and operating in forms and genres (conventions, pamphlets, periodical literature, and sketches) that remain understudied.

Rather than ask how black citizens could achieve citizenship or had achieved citizenship as a destination defined by the state or white recognition, *The Practice of Citizenship* asks how black citizens defined citizenship themselves, claiming their everyday activities as doing the work of citizenship, often outside of or despite dominant political frameworks. The question for me is less how the state constructed citizenship or black citizens or how texts about black people produced a black civic presence or black (in)humanity and more how black theorists thought about and mobilized citizenship within and without legal constructions through their own collaboratively developed texts and spaces. In this sense, *The Practice of Citizenship* expands on Walter Johnson's call to attend to how "enslaved people theorized their own actions and the practical process through which those actions provided the predicate for new ways of thinking about slavery and resistance."[41] Johnson's observation about scholarship on enslavement also applies to studies of black print culture, where we often have more direct access to accounts from black citizens themselves about citizenship.

My interest in taking up this inquiry through citizenship comes from the term's equal ubiquity in black writing and its lack of a stable definition anywhere in the antebellum United States. Black citizenship theorizing developed in an era of proliferating, overlapping, contradictory, and improvisational definitions of citizenship from constitutional ratification through passage of the Fourteenth Amendment.[42] Conceptions of citizenship were legion. Beyond taking my cue from black print, my interest in citizenship comes from a determination to not cede key political concepts—citizenship, civility, deliberation, and so on—to those who would use them to restrict freedom, access, and reparative justice. I am fully aware that these concepts carry with them the racist, imperialist, sexist, heteronormative, and Eurocentric traces of Enlightenment humanism, a humanism that was framed around and through white supremacy from its inception. Lauren Berlant, Russ Castronovo, Hartman, and others have described this dominant mode of citizenship as a process of subjection and a state apparatus "that narrows subjects to mere shadows of once embodied and engaged persons."[43] It encourages citizens to cede politics to specialized classes and spaces in the name of consensus, impoverished civility, and moral innocence.

At the same time, black citizens needed to be even more vigilant against the trappings of liberal citizenship and its logics of ahistorical individual responsibility. As Hartman has traced, a version of citizenship as "burdened individuality" enacted during Reconstruction served to subjugate newly freed black people under the guise of formal equality. Hartman notes, "The ascribed responsibility of the liberal individual served to displace the nation's responsibility for providing and ensuring the rights and privileges conferred by the Reconstruction Amendments and shifted the burden of duty onto the freed. It was their duty to prove their worthiness for freedom rather than the nation's duty to guarantee, at minimum, the exercise of liberty and equality, if not opportunities for livelihood other than debt-peonage."[44] The "gift" of freedom erased any obligations on the part of the state to the past and made individual freepersons solely responsible for their present condition and future prospects. Hartman and others—and, as we shall see, early black theorizers—warn against a kind of cruel optimism in which the citizenship struggled for and won becomes the means for reconstructing modes of subjection, a bait-and-switch in which giving up on a more critically engaged citizenship and claims for reparative justice are the price for admission.[45]

Even so, citizenship remains a potent concept. Despite critical turns to transnational, international, Atlantic world, and other frameworks that decenter the nation-state, "despite," as Ayelet Shachar notes, "jubilant predictions by post-nationalists of the imminent demise of citizenship, the legal distinction between member and stranger is, if anything, back with a vengeance."[46] Citizenship can in fact be a powerful mode for grounding and organizing a more liberatory politics based in a "commitment to public debate, an insistence on grappling with material conditions, a refusal to absorb embodied differences under consensus."[47] Black theorizing foregrounded these messy processes, arguing for a more radical citizenship even as it sometimes became trapped in its limits, particularly in terms of gender as the black state conventions demonstrate.[48] While we should continue critiquing citizenship's exclusions and while we should continue looking for other modes of affiliation, we should also attend to the ways excluded people have reconceptualized and worked through citizenship as a productive social, political, and economic arrangement.

More than challenge who is or is not a citizen or who can and cannot become a citizen under already recognized frameworks (birthright, property, gender, race, ethnicity, class, etc.), then, black theorizers redefined what citizenship meant. They weren't looking to join the politically dead, and they were even less interested in acceding to their own political and social deaths. Like the Hebrew God confronting Ezekiel, they ask, "Can these dry bones live?" And like Ezekiel, they evince a faith that dry bones can indeed live, but they must first receive the word.[49] This "faith in the performative power of the word—both spoken and written" that Peterson highlights in black women's writing recurs throughout black theorizing.[50] The word "agitates": it disturbs complacency, upends commonsense logics, and confronts us with the limits of our own perceptions in a way that cultivates a higher awareness and compels action.

These interruptive and intrusive acts constitute what I discuss in Chapters 4 and 5 as citizenship's critical and revolutionary functions insofar as they challenge and redistribute the range of ideas and actions that are thinkable, knowable, sayable, and doable and the range of people who can think, know, say, and do them.[51] The power of the creative word, as Jacques Rancière notes, is in its ability to "widen gaps, open up space for deviations, modify the speeds, trajectories, and the ways in which groups of people adhere to a condition, react to situations, recognize their images."[52] This last point is crucial. Black citizenship theorizing and early black print more broadly produced a different "angle of vision," new "conditions of possibility for the political," in its constant saying of the unsayable from people whose exclusion was increasingly framed as the precondition for American political union.[53] Black print offers narratives of an expanding universe, not a contracting one, in which citizenship is less about membership in a predefined group, less about granting and withholding privileges, and more about creating structures that maximize human potential and what they saw as the benefits of republican governance.

Citizenship should enliven, not deaden. This vision of citizenship eschews neoliberal fantasies of a citizenry composed of abstractly equal disembodied individuals in favor of critically and collaboratively constructed citizenship practices. From the perspective of black theorizing, states do not make citizens—active and involved individuals and collectives create citizens. Or, as I argue in my discussion of neighborly citizenship, neighbors do not look for a good neighbor; they make neighborhood. Black writers argued that the state and civic institutions should work to strengthen the "social intercourse" that enables people to practice citizenship rather than allowing "private" racial, gender, or economic interests to create artificial barriers. Like the human body, the body politic could only grow stronger when power circulated evenly among its members, and like the human body (a potent metaphor in early Republican political discourse), it would suffer if this circulation were blocked.

We see this emphasis on citizenship as enlivening and circulatory throughout black print. Hosea Easton's *A Treatise on the Intellectual Character, and Civil and Political Condition of the Colored People of the U. States* (1837), for instance, theorizes citizenship as a commons (rather than a private possession) essential to the functioning of any society and the livelihood of individuals within that society. "A withholding of the enjoyment of any American principle from an American man," Easton asserts, "either governmental, ecclesiastical, civil, social or alimental is in effect taking away his means of subsistence; and consequently, taking away his life."[54] We might extrapolate from Easton and others to think about citizenship as a kind of political commoning. As Nelson notes, commoning is "a communal labor in communication, sharing, and meaning-making. It is about the sharing of work and materials: not just the bounty of nature but also the bounty of what people can produce together in local community."[55] In a similar vein, Easton posits citizenship as the process through which communities make meaning and distribute resources, material and immaterial, in a republican government. Easton is not suggesting that lacking citizenship equals a lack of personhood or humanity but rather that citizenship, for him, was the most robust access point for constituting social, political, and economic collectives.[56] Enclosing access to this commons, like enclosing access to water, arable land, or an affirmative culture, has very real material effects not just to the individuals or groups excluded but also to the republic as a whole. Refusing access to these networks constitutes an act of violence that makes the perpetrator, in Easton's words, a "murderer of the worst kind" because such restrictions—for current and potential citizens—create the very material inequalities that were paradoxically used to justify them, stripping individuals and groups of the means of political, material, and social existence.[57]

And yet, an archive of black writing testifies that attempted murder could result in new forms of living and of articulating life. "Not all subjects lie still in democracy's graveyard," Castronovo notes, and Joanna Brooks asks us to consider how the world looks "to one who," like the biblical Lazarus, "has faced and survived death."[58] Just as Vincent Brown's *Reaper's Garden* invites us to see the political and "social connections and communities of memory" that enslaved people "created through struggle," black theorists draw our attention to a "purposeful will and action" that didn't simply index the loss of rights associated with citizenship but rather actively worked to generate new ways of understanding citizenship and being citizens outside rights discourse even as, paradoxically, they argued for rights.[59] This legacy included underground economies, vigilance committees, mutual aid societies, institutionalized shadow politics, and myriad informal and ad hoc cultural practices that often supplemented or replaced official citizenship frameworks.[60] These citizenship acts help us uncouple citizenship from the state institutions that are the most recognized but not the only medium for organizing them.

Early U.S. Citizenship: Inverse Causality and Denization

By centering early African American print culture, I offer a take on citizenship from the perspective of those our studies often frame as the objects of legislation, excluded, or occupying a position of negation—those whose texts we often place in conversation with dominant discourses in ways that frame them as primarily responding rather than creating. Contrary to this narrative, the writers I study here claimed citizenship as their own. They called white America's bluff in ways that forced individuals, states, and the federal government to articulate exactly how black Americans were not (supposed to be) citizens. As I discuss in this section, this process required constant forgetting and definitional revisions that were never sufficient. Black citizens simply did not go away.

Before the Fourteenth Amendment established birthright citizenship as the federal standard, the United States did not have an explicit or uniform definition of "citizen."[61] In the decades before the Fourteenth Amendment made birthright citizenship the national standard, experiences of citizenship were more state based than federal, and citizens in the early republic were identified more by a shifting catalogue of what they could and could not do within states (e.g., vote, own land, marry) and between states (e.g., freedom of movement and inhabitance) than by categorical federal statute.[62] Each state had its own criteria for these rights, privileges, and protections involving gender, inhabitance, economics, age, native status, and increasingly race among the cadre of qualifications. On the federal level, the Constitution's Privileges and Immunities Clause knit these disparate rules into a patchwork approximating national citizenship.[63] By the passage of the Fugitive Slave Law in 1850, however, popular consensus, if not the law itself, saw black Americans as not fully citizens, neither in the rights-bearing sense nor in the eyes of most of the white citizenry. While individual states might have granted black Americans citizenship rights—the right to vote, for instance—these rights did not travel with them across state lines.

This was not always the case, nor was it an inevitable outcome of the Revolution. The Articles of Confederation defined citizenship explicitly and broadly: "The free inhabitants of each of these States, paupers, vagabonds, and fugitives from justice excepted shall be entitled to all privileges and immunities of free *citizens* in the several states."[64] The 1787 federal constitution, however, was silent on the subject, in part because slavery and the status of American Indians, women, and others were minefields for the Constitutional Convention but also because the distribution of power between federal and state governments, to the extent that it was settled, was weighted in favor of the states. When the Constitution used the word "citizen," it did so without definition. The Privileges and Immunities Clause, Article IV, Section 2, was the closest the Constitution came to defining citizens: "The Citizens of each State shall be entitled to all Privileges and Immunities of Citizens in the several States."[65] The document refers to citizens in the requirements for office holding and in defining the role of the judiciary but not in a way that gives insight into who is or can be a citizen or who was or was not a citizen at ratification.[66]

The Naturalization Act of 1790 attempted to fill in some of the gaps as it clarified whom Congress believed could become a citizen, restricting naturalization to "free white persons." But it did nothing to clarify the status of those already in the country, at least not in law. Instead, as historian Douglass Bradburn explains, it, along with a similar restriction in the 1792 Militia Act, clearly demonstrated "an awareness" on the part of the federal government "of the type of citizens the act expected to create" and placed people of color in the double bind of not being accepted as native-born citizens and not having a clear institutional way to secure full citizenship.[67] Where the Naturalization Act of 1790 "guaranteed that Indians and blacks would not be welcomed as future equal citizens," the Militia Act of 1792 "effectively ratified" this guarantee by restricting militia service, "one of the most potent symbols of male citizenship in the new American republic," to white men.[68]

Against this backdrop, black writers invoked British and U.S. legal history and histories of black civic activity and cited ongoing citizenship practices, noting that changes in law were more akin to gross fraud than a clarification of some original plan. In this sense, documents such as the 1837 "Appeal of Forty Thousand Citizens, Threatened with Disfranchisement, to the People of Pennsylvania" were both part of and intervening in a developing but as yet unestablished consensus about who citizens were and what they did. The document itself exemplifies the kind of content we tend to focus on when analyzing black citizenship. The "Appeal," drafted by Robert Purvis, outlines the legal and historical basis for black citizenship in Pennsylvania with a blistering critique of justifications for black disenfranchisement given during that state's constitutional convention in 1837–38. They cite black military service during the Revolution and War of 1812, black office holding and taxpaying, moments during the framing of the Articles of Confederation when delegates struck down attempts to affix "white" as a modifier of freeman or free inhabitant, black passport holding, and passages from the *Journal of Congress* that confirm black citizenship from the nation's founding not simply as a rhetorical mishap but rather as a deliberate and deliberative decision on the part of the framers.[69]

The "Appeal" points to an important strain of black theorizing as textual criticism, one hearkening back to Benjamin Banneker's critique of Jefferson's *Notes on the State of Virginia* and Jones and Allen's "refutation" of Matthew Carey's *Short Account* (1793), which I will discuss in more detail in Chapter 1. Purvis and others were especially attentive to records like the *Congressional Journal*, convention proceedings, and records of debates as sources for and objects of interpretation as they theorized citizenship, developing in the process a robust archive. In particular, they note a reference to "*citizens of the United States*, as *are free persons of color*" in a December 21, 1803, resolution on "American seaman."[70] Over twenty years later, in the wake of the *Dred Scott v. Sandford* decision (1857), James McCune Smith would return to these documents along with their roots in Roman citizenship. "[I]n the absence of any definition of the word [citizen] in the Constitution," Smith argues, "the word must bear the meaning which language itself attaches to it . . . when it expresses the relation of the individual to the general government." He enumerates the rights associated with Roman and U.S. citizenship, noting that free black citizens exercised them all. He, like the Pennsylvania appealers before, then sets out to define citizens by way of the rights they exercise and the responsibilities they hold: "the possession of all or any of" these rights "constituted citizenship on the part of the individual holding them."[71] Readings such as the 1837 petitioners and Smith's engaged historical and contemporaneous legal writing to expand, rather than contract, citizenship's parameters and to refuse the calculus by which white whim gained the force of timeless law.

Like many of the texts in this book, the 1837 "Appeal's" materiality —its circulation and literal presence on the table at the convention—was key to its intervention. The "Appeal" was read during Pennsylvania's Reform Convention in 1837, sparking a prolonged debate among delegates (almost twenty pages), first over printing and distributing the "Appeal" to the convention and then over questions including the petitioners' status as citizens, what some delegates saw as the "Appeal's" "injurious" language, and the implications of accepting the "Appeal" for Pennsylvania's relation to slaveholding states. Some delegates took issue with the document's tone, calling it "a mere argumentative paper" with "nothing in its character which entitled it to receive any special attention," a document that contained language "not very courteous . . . indeed, for petitioners."[72] These comments prompted Thaddeus Stevens (Adams County) to counter, "When a petition was couched in language respectful to the body to which it was presented, they were bound to receive it. Was this memorial, then, to be rejected? He would never give his vote for that. Such a memorial, coming from white men, would not be considered offensive."[73] For Stevens, it seemed clear that to some of his fellow delegates, the document's "respectful" nature hinged on the racial identity of the petitioners, which itself was under question and admittedly artificial, as "probably many of those who signed the memorial are as white as many of us, although they do not rank according to the technical terms of 'white' and 'black.'"[74] The debate highlights the degree to which notions about racial hierarchy colored the reception of political acts and even whether or not an act would be received as political at all. The convention eventually decided at least to print and distribute the petition (fifty-six for, forty-five against), though it kept the language restricting voting rights to white men.

This moment of claims making through print circulation, like so many instances on scales small and large, was a civic and textual act that called those in power to recognize and admit how central black citizens and their claims were to national politics and the very definitions of republicanism and freedom.[75] As one delegate to Pennsylvania's constitutional convention put it, the "Appeal" "involved questions of the utmost importance not only to the character of our deliberations, but to that of the State, and to the Union itself, of which it forms an important part."[76] While the "Appeal's" content articulated the sham of Pennsylvania's disenfranchisement of black citizens, debates over its formal status as a petition, appeal, or memorial, as well as the debate over how the convention should accept it, if at all, had ramifications for the nature of representation and the relation between government and the governed more broadly.[77] The stakes involved not just whether or not black men could vote on the same terms as white men but also the meaning of citizenship altogether.

In contrast to the histories and practices that documents such as the "Appeal" and Smith's "Citizenship" excavated, some of the earliest attempts to define U.S. citizenship quickly began linking those rights and social markers that identified the citizen to white men, in principle if not yet in law, through historical amnesia and outright fabrication. David Ramsay's 1789 *A Dissertation on the Manners of Acquiring the Character and Privileges of a Citizen*, for instance, used "Negroes" as a foil for differentiating between sovereign citizens and mere inhabitants:

> Negroes are inhabitants, but not citizens. Citizenship confers a right of voting at elections, and many other privileges not enjoyed by those who are no more than inhabitants. The precise difference may be thus stated: The citizen of a free state is so united to it as to possess an individual's proportion of the common sovereignty; but he who is no more than an inhabitant, or resident, has no farther connection with the state in which he resides, than such as gives him security for his person and property, agreeably to fixed laws, without any participation in its government.[78]

Ramsay builds on a generally understood connection between citizenship and the specific set of rights and social practices associated with sovereignty and collective governance: citizens were sovereign, voting was a sign of sovereignty, and, therefore, anyone who voted was implicitly a U.S. citizen. But he does so in a way that fixes the range of people who could conceivably perform these practices, suggesting that "Negroes" (along with women, children, and American Indians) were and could only be inhabitants without a share in collective sovereignty. The fact that at the time Ramsay was writing, free black people ("Negroes") *could* and *were* legally voting in every state except Georgia and his own South Carolina, and so were *in fact* citizens by Ramsay's own definition, was less important in practice than the conventional wisdom that black people, a priori, were not "original citizens" and were, in fact, the negative against which citizenship gained clarity.[79] Being "Negro," free or otherwise from Ramsay's perspective, precluded them from being part of the original contract, so citizenship was something they would have to be given with the consent of and always contingent on white sovereigns' sufferance.

These assumptions were codified as historical fact, as the definition of "citizen" developed in subsequent texts such as the United States' first legal dictionary, John Bouvier's *A Law Dictionary, Adapted to the Constitution and Laws of the United States of America* (1839). In 1839, Bouvier's *Dictionary* defined citizen without racial ascription: "One who, under the constitution and laws of the United States, has a right to vote for representatives in congress and other public officers, and who is qualified to fill offices in the gift of the people." The entry distinguished between "natural born" and "naturalized" citizens only in that the latter could not become president.[80] The central change to the dictionary's definition over the next decades was a racial qualification: "under the word citizen, are included *all white persons born in the United States*, and naturalized persons born out of the same, who have not lost their right as such. This includes men, women, and children."[81] The 1854 edition then devotes the entire third entry to explaining birthright citizenship's limits: "All natives are not citizens of the United States; the descendants of the aborigines, and those of African origin, are not entitled to the rights of citizens. Anterior to the adoption of the constitution of the United States, each state had the right to make citizens of such persons as it pleased. That constitution does not authorize any but white persons to become citizens of the United States; and it must therefore be presumed that no one is a citizen who is not white."[82] Texts such as Bouvier's attempted to prescribe a particular understanding of white citizenship as much as, if not more than, they described citizenship in practice.[83] Like Ramsay's definition, these revisions neglected the Articles of Confederation, the Constitution's silence on citizenship in general, and other proofs of black citizenship. The revisions demonstrate how racializing citizenship required consistent acts of historical revision, amnesia, and counterfactual narration but also, particularly in the decades when states were revising their constitutions, how racialized citizenship was codified in law only in the wake of black citizens asserting their position as citizens and as white powerbrokers were attempting to consolidate their own positions.

Ramsay's *Dissertation* and changes to Bouvier's *Dictionary* map a trajectory that first linked citizenship to political rights generally assumed to be restricted to white men but then increasingly linked citizenship to white manhood itself, eliding rights as the third term in the metonymic chain in a way that produced race—whiteness and blackness.[84] As states revised their constitutions to restrict political rights to white men and as new states adopted constitutions with even more restrictive black codes, Ramsay's, Bouvier's, and others' assumptions became reality and took on the timeless character of what had always already been. The state of Connecticut's argument against black citizenship in *Crandall v. State of Connecticut* (1834), for instance, argued that since voting rights had "been denied to the coloured race generally, it is evidence, that that race were not embraced by the framers of the constitution, in the term citizen."[85]

This argument, as the defense for Crandall pointed out, ignored black voting "in Pennsylvania and New-York, (as well as in Maine, New-Hampshire, Massachusetts, Vermont, New-Jersey, Delaware, Maryland, North-Carolina and Tennessee)."[86] The defense also attempted to unlink voting and citizenship by citing instances in which people could not vote (naturalized citizens, women, and children) but were nevertheless recognized as citizens. At the same time, their list of states where black citizens could and did vote shows how readily black citizenship practices could be ignored or erased in argument and memory even in the face of historical records.

Other states and attorneys general, following *Crandall*, argued that because black Americans did not exercise *all* of the rights of white citizens (never mind that all white men did not exercise all the rights of their fellow citizens across all states), they should not be considered citizens of the United States or, if citizens, a special kind of second-level citizen whose rights other states were not obligated to respect. Instead, these courts and legislatures read claims for black people under the Privileges and Immunities Clause as one state's encroaching on the jurisdiction of another. Georgia, for instance, justified its detention of black sailors based on both disenfranchisement across several states and laws explicitly preventing marriage between black and white people in states such as Massachusetts. Free black people did not have a claim to all the privileges and immunities of federal citizenship, the state of Georgia argued, because they did not enjoy all the privileges of citizenship in their home states. South Carolina similarly justified the imprisonment of free black seamen through the states' police powers, arguing that such men would be disruptive to state and national security.[87]

Definitions like Ramsay's and Bouvier's and subsequent legislation and court decisions would seem to confirm Barbara Welke's assertion that from the ratification of the federal constitution, the "law privileged able white men's ownership of self, according full personhood and belonging only to those who were able, white, and male."[88] And there's strong evidence for this characterization, as Welke's study bears out. Yet, black theorists rarely conceded this assumption as fact. Indeed, black writers from Absalom Jones to Frances Harper would take the absence of racial designations in law literally, forcing states to make presumptions of white citizenship explicit in law.[89] If, from the outset of the new republic, white men assumed citizenship as their private domain, black citizens (men and women) would continually argue and act in ways that suggested they assumed otherwise.

When viewed from this position, these "official" delineations of citizenship were neither static nor definitive in this era but rather participated in a broader process seeking to fix these categories and to do so, at least in part, in a way that explicitly curtailed or foreclosed access for all except Anglo-Saxon Protestant men. As the century wore on, whiteness began trumping even property as an indication of citizenship. Bradburn has described this process as "denization," a procedure that "extended only *some* rights and privileges of citizens" to black people without considering them "part of the body politic." Black Americans were not "aliens," as such, but the state increasingly treated them as partial citizens only, denizens, and their status "remained conditional, and privileges once extended could be revoked."[90] The facts of black citizenship gave way to tragi-comic commonsense assertions that such could never have been the case. Where Ramsay argued in 1789 that since "Negroes" could not vote, they must not be citizens, Chief Justice Roger Taney and Senator Stephen A. Douglas (Ill.), backed by revisionist history, racial science, and popular opinion, would argue in 1857 that black people could not be and were never intended to become citizens; they could never be more than inhabitants because they were not white. And, to riff off Taney, even if they had rights, no white man was "bound to respect" them.

Ramsay's *Dissertation*, myriad federal and state judicial decisions, and the 1787 Federal Constitution demonstrate that the codification of white citizenship was a long political and economic process of selective inclusion and exclusion requiring constant institutional and cultural maintenance. This narrative is a familiar one, filled with the duplicity, willful ignorance, and betrayal that characterize the "racial contract's" institutionalized and "iterative" privileging of white interests at the expense of all others.[91] It can fit neatly within contemporary scholarship placing blackness as the negative against which the West defines humanity and can serve as a prelude to a narrative of black agency and resistance.[92] And this book at times offers a bit of both.

At the same time, this book's overarching trajectory suggests a narrative of inverse causality. Neither black reaction nor protest as we've generally used the term, inverse causality suggests a dynamic in which white citizens (1) stripped rights away in response to or fear of black citizenship practices and aspirations; (2) structurally created conditions that led to material inequality; and then (3) retroactively used the resultant "condition" to argue that black Americans were never citizens because they did not, could not, and could never have exercised the rights from which white Americans had (just) barred them.[93] Reading early citizenship restrictions through inverse causality and denization reorients the action-reaction model we tend to follow that frames black activism as responding to racist policy. Bradburn notes this dynamic in the eighteenth-century context: "As more and more free blacks clamored for access to power, more and more restrictions were placed upon their citizenship." "Unlike subjecthood," Bradburn concludes, "citizenship demanded equality—and equality was out of the question."[94] In this sense, U.S. citizenship cannot be untangled from the tensions gradual emancipation wrought across northern states. Though I hesitate to draw a direct causal relation between specific black texts and shifts in documents like Bouvier's *Dictionary*, his and others' revisions did not happen in a vacuum—he, in fact, practiced law in Pennsylvania during the ratification of that state's 1838 constitution. His editions and the discourse of U.S. citizenship must be considered in relation to the political movements occurring in the intervening years (women's rights, workers' rights, and the focus of this book, the black state and national conventions) that forced representatives of the law to clarify, again and again, a restrictive definition of citizenship and associated concepts and to deny, again and again, the histories and practices that Purvis and others kept in circulation.

Chapter Outline

Using the interpretive insights of Absalom Jones and Richard Allen, the black state conventions, Frances Ellen Watkins Harper, and the countless contributors to the black press as guides, *The Practice of Citizenship* is organized around five interrelated citizenship practices and the stylistic and perspectival schemas each practice cultivates: neighborly contact, the free circulation of civic energy, economic representation, critique, and revolution. This listing is not meant to be comprehensive but rather suggestive of key concepts that emerge from the archive I've assembled. Together, these chapters offer a diachronic and synchronic narrative of black theories and practices as each chapter takes up a specific site that constitutes black theorizing's repertoire. It argues for the specificity of each moment in terms of historical context, geographic scale, and the exigencies of needing to persuade a wide range of audiences, from hostile white auditors to ambivalent black citizens to fellow black activists with opposing views. At the same time, black theorizers often thought of these practices as scalable. Neighborly citizenship, for instance, is not just about local interactions but rather models an ethics for institution building and for how institutions should facilitate citizenship's work.

Though each chapter focuses on a specific citizenship practice, these practices are mutually constituting and always simultaneously in play. One requires the other to create a viable polity: neighborliness depends on circulation and critique to give it boundaries; economic citizens should behave not as individual agents in an ostensibly liberal market but ethically, as participants in a collective neighborhood. Yet writers emphasize one approach over another in response to political and historical moments of crisis and change. There were more possibilities for citizenship when Jones and Allen formed the Free African Society in 1787 than when Robert and Thomas Hamilton founded the *Anglo-African Magazine* in 1859, and black theorists' tactical shifts reflect that declension. The black state conventions emphasized voting rights as crucial to citizenship in the 1840s in the wake of multiple states ratifying constitutions restricting voting to white men. Many of these same writers continued advocating for formal rights into the 1850s, but they also shifted focus to the need for more dramatic political reconstruction in light of states rejecting their claims and after passage of the Fugitive Slave Law (1850) and the Kansas-Nebraska Act (1854). Jones and Allen's foregrounding of neighborliness—what I define in Chapter 1 as the ability of fellow citizens to engage each other on terms of mutual responsibility and good faith through "real sensibility"—in the 1790s speaks to their sense of hope that the young nation could hold to the promises of equality and commonwealth they saw articulated in the Declaration of Independence, the Constitution, and abolitionism. The rapidity with which the two former slaves rose to prominence in Philadelphia gave them an attenuated hope in a generally progressive trend, despite many setbacks. But the moment did not last, not in Jones and Allen's day and not across subsequent decades. By 1860, calls for neighborly citizenship might have seemed misplaced in light of an ascendant capitalist citizenship and the sense that the current world would need to be dismantled completely before any kind of democratic society could be constructed. And yet, this is precisely when Harper returns our attention to the potential power of "real sensibility" and the power of the word—spoken and written—to spark substantive and revolutionary realignments.

Many of the texts and scenes I draw from constellate around Philadelphia and New York as the setting or point of origin, in part as a reflection of the two cities' status as print centers. And yet, as Gardner has noted, periodicals such as the *Christian Recorder*, *Douglass's Paper*, and the *Anglo-African Magazine* might have been produced in Philadelphia and New York, but their correspondents and circulation went well beyond these confines.[95] Indeed, though the *Anglo-African Magazine* was based in New York City, contributors such as Harper were not. At the same time, my selection of these texts is not an argument for a cohesive or homogeneous black print public.[96] Instead, it reflects my sense that citizenship theorizing was always simultaneously local and contextual in nature and at the same time aware of and pointed toward larger audiences that, as I discuss in Chapter 3, McCune Smith invoked in terms of the "Republic of Letters."[97] By focusing tightly on specific literary historical flashpoints, *The Practice of Citizenship* does the necessary work of providing context for understanding both the continuities and differences in what comes after. My approach here has been shaped by Elizabeth McHenry's work on black readers in *Forgotten Readers* (2002), an interest in micro-history, and how lessons learned from micro-histories of black texts might be applied at varying spatial and temporal scales. By drawing attention to theorizing as a process, rather than a goal, to citizenship as constantly under construction, rather than something possessed, *The Practice of Citizenship* nevertheless also offers a model for thinking across multiply configured periods without losing this specificity.[98]

I end with 1861, because the moment just before the Civil War represents a time of intense theorizing that often gets overshadowed by what comes after in much the same way that *Dred Scott v. Sanford* overshadows events of 1856, including "Bleeding Kansas" and Margaret Garner's killing of her daughter. Indeed, while a potential Thirteenth Amendment that explicitly prevented Congress from interfering with state enslavement laws was on its way to ratification, a literary explosion was occurring in black periodicals, where writers were producing fiction, poetry, and essays at a blistering pace. I want to capture the tensions between possibility and disappointment from this prewar perspective—as if emancipation and the Reconstruction amendments had not and perhaps would never happen—and from a moment when all signs pointed toward the permanence of enslavement and increasing racism.[99] Chapter 1 examines competing accounts of Philadelphia's 1793 yellow fever epidemic to outline neighborliness as the ethical foundation for the citizenship practices articulated throughout *The Practice of Citizenship*. Building on the notion of an "expressive language of conduct," Jones and Allen's 1794 *Narrative of the Proceedings of the Black People* clarifies neighborliness as a form of sensibility made material through concrete actions. The neighborly focus on being a good neighbor rather than on identifying the good neighbor creates fellow feeling independent of other forms of association—familial, racial, economic, national, and so on. *Narrative*'s vignettes in the style of the parable of the Good Samaritan flesh out neighborliness as a citizenship practice robust enough to promote mutual aid yet open enough to promote more democratic engagement.

Jones and Allen published *Narrative*, in part, as a direct response to Matthew Carey's *A Short Account of the Malignant Fever, Lately Prevalent in Philadelphia* (1793, 1794), which accused black Philadelphians of theft during the epidemic. Yet, Carey's *Account* provided not only an occasion to go to print but also a foil against which to stage their account of black citizenship practices. The two restage scenes from and in the style of *Account* as a way to narratively dismantle its racial and economic assumptions. More than a response to Carey's immediate claims, however, Jones and Allen's articulation of neighborly citizenship provides the grounding for their plan for emancipation, an "experiment" in institutional neighborliness that would educate the children of slaves as full citizens.

Chapter 2 positions the black state conventions of the 1840s as central to our understanding of citizenship and the operation of participatory politics as a citizenship practice more generally. Through readings of convention proceedings from New York (1840), Pennsylvania (1841, 1848), and Ohio (1848, 1849, 1851), I trace a shift in U.S. political culture from potentially more direct and public forms of political participation, like extra-governmental conventions, to more managed and proprietary forms of representation. To counter arguments that black people were either too irredeemably inferior or too dependent on waged and manual labor to warrant full citizenship, convention addresses built on natural rights theory and contemporaneous physics to suggest a circulatory model of civic power. Fellow citizens, they suggest, are not linked by common ancestry or political agreement but rather by their faith and participation in a republican style of government. Just as blocking access to major waterways could destroy a city, blocking the free circulation of civic power could result in either civic and social deterioration or explosive revolt among those disenfranchised.

While the male delegates to these conventions often made these claims in explicitly masculinist terms, black women nevertheless made use of the conventions to stake their own claims to participatory politics and citizenship. They lobbied for recognition in official convention spaces and were key to the convention's material contexts, including providing the means for circulating documents for some conventions and forming auxiliary committees. The conventions allow us to track not only the arguments black activists made for citizenship but also the tensions within black collectives around gender and access to political space.[100] Moreover, the printed documents associated with these conventions—the calls, debates, actual proceedings, and subsequent responses—evince a robust print culture that put the theoretical concerns about the relation between political participation and citizenship into practice.

My discussions of neighborly citizenship and the circulation of civic power reveal that citizenship practices and economics were inextricably linked. Chapter 3 turns to pseudonymous correspondences in *Douglass's Paper* during the early 1850s—James McCune Smith's "Heads of the Colored People" series and William J. Wilson's "Letters from Our Brooklyn Correspondent"—to excavate changing understandings of citizenship in the wake of midcentury market revolutions. Both Wilson and Smith read the United States as tending toward economic citizenship, a structure in which the market displaces civil society as the privileged space of citizenship practices and civic identity. Yet, where Wilson argues pragmatically for the cultivation of a "black aristocracy," economic representatives for what he saw as a solidifying U.S. oligarchy, Smith valorizes the "best average colored" person as the embodiment of a new urban republicanism, the foundation for a strong democratic polity of laboring folk.

Wilson and Smith use their pseudonymous narrators, "Ethiop" and "Communipaw," and the generic flexibility of the sketch to lay out the kinds of fluid subjectivities best suited to navigate the new civic-economic terrain, the former offering a street-savvy businessman viewing the economic landscape from the "heights" and the latter a "whitewasher," a skilled laborer who transgresses boundaries and insists on a horizontal configuration of politics. Rather than a precursor to the Washington–Du Bois debates that have become standard to our narrative of black intellectualism, however, these two collaborated to create a culture of engagement through literary expression. Their collection of fictionalized case studies, ethnographic observations, and flâneur-like urban narratives highlights the degree to which black conceptions of citizenship unfolded not just in speeches, conventions, and pamphlets but also through communities of letters engaged in explicitly literary discussions about representation.

The writers and collectives I examine throughout this book did not separate politics, citizenship, and critique. They did not restrict politics to voting or specialized spaces, and while the state conventions often restricted or did not credit women's participation, as I discuss in Chapter 2, these restrictions themselves became a matter of critique from within the conventions themselves. While the chapters on neighborliness, circulation, and economics are all also concerned with practices of critique and revolution, this book's final two chapters take up critical and revolutionary citizenship explicitly. Separating the two allows me to distinguish between two fronts: (1) how black writers analyzed and critiqued the framing of public thought and citizenship and (2) how black writers analyzed and represented the violence—cognitive, physical, and aesthetic—of breaking that framing and found in antislavery violence, be it fugitive rescues or insurrections, sites of knowledge production. In this sense, while slave rebellions are certainly moments of critique, characterizing them as revolution emphasizes not just their physicality but also the way they created new worlds and, even in failure, reaffirmed a sense of potentiality.

Chapter 4 examines the meaning of critique and the means for cultivating a critical sense among a diverse citizenry. Through the *Anglo-African Magazine* (1859–1860), I outline a collective and participatory project of building different idioms of citizenship and peoplehood as a counter to the "limitation of humanity and human rights" and "truth," following editor Thomas Hamilton and Frederick Douglass, that national fantasies of white citizenship authorized.[101] Critique under white citizenship allows deliberation within the structural confines of the racial contract but punishes discourse operating outside those confines. No matter how acrimonious Abraham Lincoln and Stephen A. Douglas became in 1858, for instance, both candidates cultivated a taste for white supremacist citizenship. Each performance reaffirmed whiteness as foundational and set this reaffirmation as the linchpin that would maintain the Union and that would get either Lincoln or Douglas elected.[102] By contrast, critical citizenship is at its core concerned with identifying, probing, and challenging these frameworks and taste regimes. The work in the *Anglo-African Magazine*—serialized fiction, scientific and historical treatises, and polemics—cultivates readers' tastes for understandings of history, the constitutional "we the people," and politics more broadly as messy, sometimes contradictory, and always in process. Through William J. Wilson's "Afric-American Picture Gallery" series, the chapter examines how the "thrillingly sublime courage" of slave resistance catalyzes this disruptive process and serves as a warning that critique, without a concomitant impulse to action, risks reproducing the very closures it is meant to defy.

Taking up the question of consciousness raising, revolutionary violence, and literary representation, Chapter 5 uses Harper's writing, speaking, and activism in the years before the Civil War to explore the cultural work that could sustain a prolonged battle for emancipation, even if, or perhaps especially when, violent conflict seemed not only imminent but also necessary.[103] These writings—letters, poetry, sketches, and short stories—offer an overview of black political rhetoric and citizenship practices from the past decades and analyze their grounding ethos. They argue that this work should be focused through the fight against enslavement and the greater dissemination of freedom. Harper theorizes the generative power of the word and the connections between theory and practice and word and deed perhaps more clearly than any other writer this book examines. Her work from the months between John Brown's execution and the first shots of the Civil War use the sublime—identified as sublime, agitation, soul energy—to reinvigorate sensibility, to reconnect it to a sense of possibility in a moment of uncertainty and pessimism. The retrospective and reflexive nature of Harper's work also occasions a critique of the previous chapters, a warning that even if the principles I outline here are consistent in nature, their application must adapt to the contingencies of context. In a broader sense, her meditations on the sublime—identified as sublime, agitation, soul energy, and the like—raise questions about the relation between revolution, righteous violence, and citizenship and prompt us to ask, "What happens after critique?"

While still active today in movements such as Black Lives Matter, environmental justice actions, and advocacy for refugee communities, we know in hindsight that these versions of citizenship have yet to become common practice. Formal recognition of black citizenship in the shape of the Fourteenth Amendment brought with it new forms of subjection in part by nationalizing the racial restrictions that had been in force in northern states for decades. And the amendment did nothing to include Native Americans, Chinese immigrants, or others.[104] To the extent that *The Practice of Citizenship* tells a story, then, it is a story about the tension between black citizens' creative struggle for a just society based on the promises they saw in republican self-governance set against the developing national predilection to foreclose such possibilities through increasingly restrictive legal and social practices. The continued pressure of such a volatile landscape forced black theorists to rethink and rearticulate their relation to the state continually, resulting in a body of literature that offers some of the most incisive analyses of citizenship available today.

CHAPTER 1

Neighborly Citizenship in Absalom Jones and Richard Allen's *A Narrative of the Proceedings of the Black People During the Late and Awful Calamity in Philadelphia in the Year 1793*

> With regard to the emigration to Africa you mention, we have at present but little to communicate on that head, apprehending every pious man is a good citizen of the whole world.
>
> —Reply of the Free African Society (Philadelphia, Pennsylvania) to the Union Society of Africans (Newport, Rhode Island), October 1789

The 1789 response from the Free African Society (FAS) to the African Union Society of Rhode Island's proposal for a settlement in Africa projects a sense of optimism at the close of the eighteenth century. Rather than cite the new federal Constitution or the spread of "republicanism," the FAS sees a cosmopolitan citizenship manifesting in the "expressive language of conduct" of those "persons who are sacrificing their own time, ease and property for us, the stranger and the fatherless, in this wilderness."[1] More than an article of faith, however, the FAS provides a statement about citizenship practices by way of what the good citizen *does* and, as important, how the good citizen views and engages others, stranger and friend alike. The pious citizen does not identify fellow citizens based on "worth," nor can we identify the pious citizen outside this citizen's actions. Rather, pious citizens reach out to those in need according to an ethic of neighborliness suggested in the golden-rule injunction to, as the FAS puts it, "do unto all men as we would they should do unto us."[2] The pious may be citizens of the world, but they demonstrate this citizenship through concrete local, everyday interactions.

Though formal citizenship was in flux for black citizens, accounts of citizenship such as the above statement from the FAS provide key critiques and interventions within contemporaneous paradigms. Even as federalists and antifederalists debated the nature of the bonds between citizens in a republic, the role of human interests in maintaining and/or disrupting those bonds, and the kinds of institutions best suited to managing those (particularly economic) interests, black citizens were forming citizenship practices based on their own experiences and understandings of political and religious texts. Even as civic republican and liberal versions of citizenship took shape in the late eighteenth-century United States, other civic schematics were not only possible but also concurrently being developed and enacted.

This chapter takes up one such account, Absalom Jones and Richard Allen's *A Narrative of the Proceedings of the Black People During the Late and Awful Calamity in Philadelphia in the Year 1793 and A Refutation of Some Censures, Thrown upon Them in Some Late* (1794), to develop a social theory of citizenship as a practice of neighborliness.[3] Written partially in response to Matthew Carey's accusations of black theft and extortion during Philadelphia's 1793 yellow fever epidemic in his *A Short Account of the Malignant Fever, Lately Prevalent in Philadelphia* (1793), *Narrative* draws on the image of the pious citizen of the world, Christian ethics, civic republicanism, and the notion of an "expressive language of conduct" to theorize neighborly citizenship as the proactive engagement with the suffering stranger out of what *Narrative* calls "real sensibility."[4] This active principle and Jones and Allen's articulation of it through black citizenship pointedly critique and revise emergent notions of civic republican citizenship and fellow feeling.

Carey's *Account* provided Jones and Allen with a distillation of early U.S. citizenship. This rendering of citizenship, outlined in this chapter's first section, attempted to assuage fears that republican citizenship failed during the yellow fever epidemic by (1) drawing attention to "respectable citizens" whose virtue led them to assume responsibility for the faltering city and (2) noting that the massive flight during the epidemic did not signal the failures of fellow feeling but rather the freedom of republican governance. Jones and Allen reveal that the ethics subtending this reading encouraged a more passive approach to fellow citizenship that depended less on what citizens did on the ground and more on the power of narration to justify these activities. Indeed, this chapter's second half, following Jones and Allen's own critical strategies, highlights the ways the form and point of view *Narrative* takes model the kinds of bonds and citizenship practice Jones and Allen were theorizing. In contrast to Carey's emphasis on the virtues of a managerial elite, *Narrative* reproduces some of *Account*'s key scenes from the perspective of the citizens *on the ground*, very ordinary "poor black" men and women, whose actions were otherwise unnoted or vilified.

Narrative's vignettes describe specific encounters among strangers in the style of the parable of the Good Samaritan, fleshing out neighborliness as a citizenship practice robust enough to promote mutual responsibility yet open enough to promote more democratic engagement. Just as the parable uses narrative inversion to critically reevaluate the terms of the question "Who is my neighbor?" *Narrative* interrogates late eighteenth-century theories about the ethical relation between citizens by thinking about the kinds of relations the good citizen should actively produce rather than the inverse, how to produce or identify the good citizen.[5] This shift in perspective suggests that fellow citizenship did not fail during the crisis; rather, early national narratives such as Carey's sought it in the wrong places, ignoring the citizenship practices and potential fellow citizens right in front of them.

The pamphlet's main thrust, then, was not simply refuting Carey's charges. As I argue throughout this chapter, Jones and Allen's *Narrative* provides a positive vision of citizenship that exceeds the goals stated in the title and that have preoccupied criticism on *Narrative*. I am not suggesting here a call-and-response model in which *Narrative* responds to *Account*'s provocation. Rather, *Account* provided a convenient and widely read medium for arguments already developing in black political thought through institutions such as the Free African Society and Church and from individuals including Benjamin Banneker. They appropriate the occasion of responding to Carey and use his text as a substrate—a widely circulating articulation of a common understanding of citizenship—for ideas that the two men and the collectives they represented had been working through over the past decade, as suggested in the Free African Society's response to their Rhode Island counterparts.

Responding to Carey allowed Jones and Allen to use the style of public "*Refutation*" to make claims against Carey and the nation more broadly. As I discuss in this chapter's final section, the appended "Address to Those Who Keep Slaves, and Approve of the Practice," in turn, uses the proceedings of the black people as a case study that justifies and provides a framework for further "experiments": emancipation, abolition, and the full incorporation of black citizens after slavery. In the moments characterized by Myra Jehlen as "history before the fact" or, in this case, citizenship before the fact, the terms of fellow citizenship were unsettled not just in Philadelphia in the immediate aftermath of the epidemic but also across a new republic still unsure of its federal compact.[6] Even as Jones and Allen recounted events in recognizably republican terms, their narrative structure represents an attempt to reshape the discourse of citizenship in the messy moments when the city and the nation were trying to make sense of what seemed to be wholesale civic failure during the crisis.

Seizing the Moment: Jones and Allen's Print Politics

Published in January 1794 after the third edition of Carey's *Account*, *A Narrative of the Proceedings of the Black People* provides a chronology of black work during the epidemic, beginning with Jones, Allen, and William Gray's voluntary efforts and the FAS and Free African Church's (FAC's) response to Mayor Matthew Clarkson's call for assistance and ending with an accounting of the group's expenditures and disposal of beds.[7] Jones and Allen contest "kind assurances" of black immunity that were widely accepted as fact at the time, detail their management of relief works (black convicts among them), and set out to counter "partial, censorious" accounts of the black workers as a response to not only Carey but also, in Jones and Allen's words, "the many unprovoked enemies who begrudge us the liberty we enjoy, and are glad to hear of any complaint against our colour, be it just or unjust."[8] In part owing to the strength of this defense of black Philadelphians, much of the scholarship on *Narrative* has examined how its authors distinguish black virtue and sensibility from white inhumanity to carve out space for black citizenship. Sarah Knott, for instance, notes Jones and Allen "understood, as Carey perhaps did not, that social belonging *depended* on the claim to sensibility; it did not just easily flow from it." Where Knott sees mastery, Philip Gould suggests Jones and

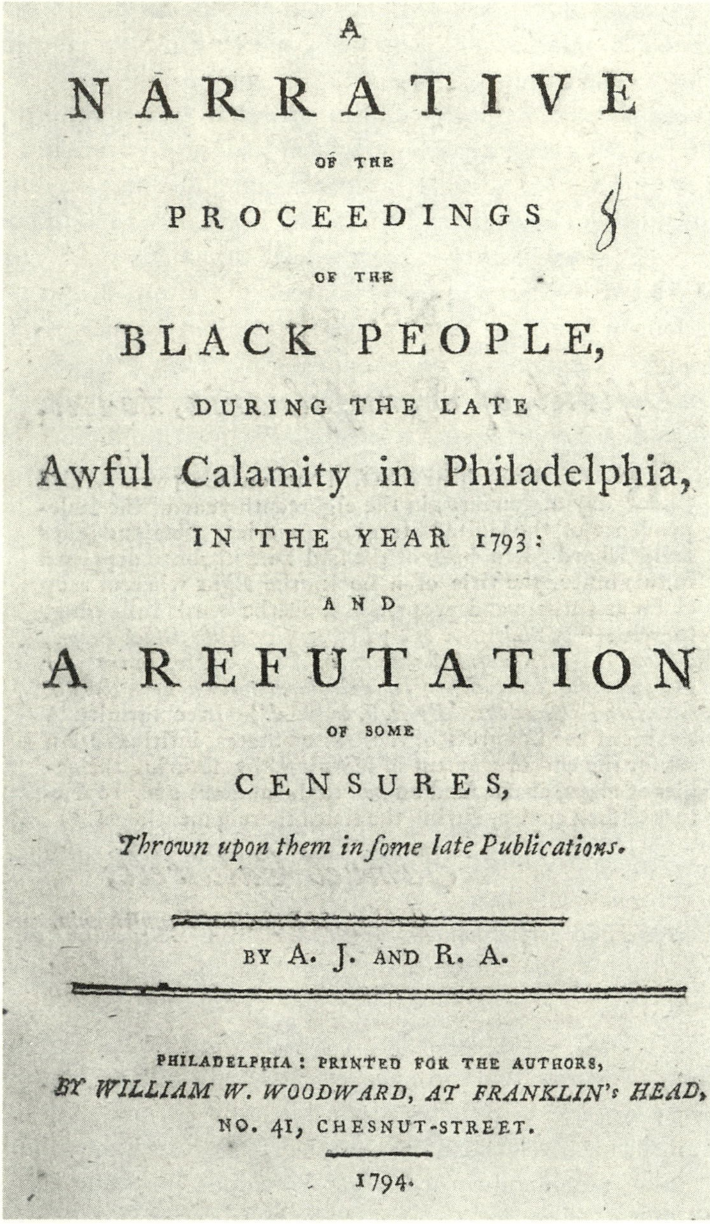

A

NARRATIVE

OF THE

PROCEEDINGS

OF THE

BLACK PEOPLE,

DURING THE LATE

Awful Calamity in Philadelphia,

IN THE YEAR 1793:

AND

A REFUTATION

OF SOME

CENSURES,

Thrown upon them in some late Publications.

BY A. J. AND R. A.

PHILADELPHIA: PRINTED FOR THE AUTHORS,

BY WILLIAM W. WOODWARD, AT FRANKLIN'S HEAD,

NO. 41, CHESNUT-STREET.

1794.

Figure 1. Title page, *Narrative of the Proceedings of the Black People* (1794).

Allen fell victim to the same tensions within sensibility that they set out to critique. Their concern with financial losses undercut their claims to benevolent disinterest.[9] Even as this scholarship illuminates Jones and Allen's challenge to contemporary understanding of sensibility and citizenship, however, it still tends to frame it in terms of appropriation and reaction, not creation.

My point here is not that this scholarship is misreading *Narrative* per se but rather that the emphasis on response and protest can obscure how Jones and Allen leverage the moment to demand a wholesale rethinking of the relationship between citizenship and sensibility in the period.[10] In their initial justification for entering print, Jones and Allen employed stylistic tactics indicative of a black intellectual tradition critiquing those who, as Phillis Wheatley famously observes in "On Being Brought from African to American" (1773), "view our sable race with scornful eye" (5–8) and, as Benjamin Banneker notes in his letter to Thomas Jefferson, "have long . . . looked [on us] with an eye of contempt."[11] For both writers, the stated occasion for entering print provides a vector but not the ultimate target from their arguments.[12] From this perspective, Joanna Brooks argues, the overemphasis on *Narrative*'s status as primarily a response to Carey points to a larger tendency to ignore how the tract "resonates with the impassioned and embittered voices of two men who are themselves only a few years free from chattel slavery, who witness that the slave trade continues with the legal sanction of the U.S. government." These men, she continues, saw "the fragility of fellow-feeling and sympathy revealed during the yellow fever epidemic, and their text demonstrated how insufficient these frameworks were for communicating black grievances."[13] Or, more accurately, how efficient they were at eliding them. *Narrative* may recapitulate the contradictions in contemporary political and racial discourse, but it also strategically reenacts these contradictions to expose rather than reproduce them.

Jones and Allen's emphasis on the white production of virtue throughout *Narrative* suggests that they recognized in 1794 the problem with virtue politics. In that sense, *Narrative* is both descriptive of how black citizens might enter the civic sphere under already operative terms—civic republicanism, benevolence and sensibility, virtue politics, and the like—and prescriptive in the way its account of black activities exceeds these frameworks. While Jeannine DeLombard describes *Narrative* as a "documentary account of black civic virtue," she also notes that if virtue politics failed, Jones and Allen could produce an "altogether different kind of black public presence" by converting impositions of black criminal culpability into "civil 'capacity'" and claims to full citizenship.[14] Converting "culpable legal personhood" was one strategy *Narrative* deployed; at the same time, this chapter argues, *Narrative* produces something quite different, using the ethics articulated in Jesus of Nazareth's discourse on Mosaic law in the Gospel Luke, not contemporaneous constructions of citizenship or personhood, as their guide.

The connection to Banneker in particular might run deeper. Jones and Allen potentially had access to "A Copy of a Letter from Benjamin Banneker to the Secretary of State, with His Answer," printed in Philadelphia in 1792.[15] I will discuss this text in more detail in this chapter's last section, but its path to print is worth rehearsing here as a precursor to *Narrative* and as an illustration of strategies already in play. Banneker claims in the letter, "It was not originally my design" to write a letter critiquing Jefferson's hypocrisy in championing political freedom in the Declaration of Independence while still supporting enslavement. "But," he maintains, "having taken up my pen in order to direct to [Jefferson]" his 1792 *Almanac* "as a present," Banneker was "unexpectedly and unavoidably led" to respond to the racist claims Jefferson makes in *Notes on the State of Virginia* (1785).[16] Banneker sent the *Almanac* in manuscript, noting that he was unsure of bringing it to print. The letter itself excoriated Jefferson through the language of both *Notes* and the Declaration of Independence: "It was" in the early days of the Revolution, Banneker reminds Jefferson, "that your abhorrence thereof was so excited, that you publicly held forth this true and invaluable doctrine, which is worthy to be recorded and remembered in all succeeding ages," before quoting from the Declaration. After Jefferson responded to Banneker, affirming his wish to see a plan for emancipation enacted, Banneker published his initial letter and that response in pamphlet form. He also included the exchange in the *Almanac* he would publish that year. The entire sequence of events shows Banneker manipulating the print public not only to publish an incisive antislavery pamphlet but also to cannily drum up potential interest in his *Almanac.* Jefferson may have been Banneker's addressee, and he was clearly one of Banneker's objects of critique, but it is just as clear that Banneker likely had larger goals in mind from the start. Whether or not Jones and Allen read Banneker's pamphlet or almanac that year, the resemblance in print and rhetoric strategy is striking: Jones and Allen similarly claim to have taken up the pen to refute Carey's *Account* but also capitalize on the opportunity to address other

"*Censures, Thrown upon Them in Some Late Publications*" noted in their pamphlet's title.

To fully understand the theorizing and print strategies Jones and Allen undertake through *Narrative*, we need to first revisit the models of white citizenship proffered contemporaneously in accounts such as Carey's *A Short Account*. While Carey's *Account* was neither the only nor the definitive statement on early U.S. citizenship, it provides—both for Jones and Allen and for my purposes here—a productive point of entry for limning the range of problems and potential solutions at play, along with those possibilities white observers routinely ignored or actively disqualified. Carey's pamphlet provided a distillation of civic republican discourse and a set of formal oppositions (respectable citizens vs. unruly mass, sensibility vs. insensibility, market freedom vs. republican duty) that Jones and Allen could (1) hold up and restage for public assessment, (2) dissect as a reflection of bankrupt citizenship practices, and (3) counterpose to their own model of neighborly citizenship. As I contend throughout this chapter, Jones and Allen's *Narrative*, while addressed to Carey, was not about Carey and his *Account*. Even so, just as black Philadelphians provided Carey and others with a convenient scapegoat for the city's failures, so too do Jones and Allen appropriate Carey as a mascot for how the language of interests, virtue, and management propped up white supremacy and justified abdication of citizenship's more democratic and revolutionary potential.

Carey's Fever: A Crisis in Fellow Citizenship

Yellow fever hit Philadelphia in August of 1793, killing between 4,000 and 5,000 people (10–15 percent of Philadelphia's population), approximately 400 of them free Africans, in a little less than three months. An additional 20,000 fled the city for safety.[17] The federal government was in recess during the epidemic, leaving the recovery efforts to a Relief Committee of voluntary citizens led by Philadelphia's mayor, Matthew Clarkson. As the epidemic dissipated in November 1793, Clarkson charged Matthew Carey, an Irish immigrant, printer, and entrepreneur, with composing the city's official account, including theories about the fever's causes and progression, the activities of the Relief Committee, and the general state of the city during those three horrible months. This account, initially titled *A Short Account of the Malignant Fever, Lately Prevalent in Philadelphia: With a Statement of the Proceedings that Took Place on the Subject in Different Parts of the United States*, ran through five editions published in the United States and Europe and eventually sold "over 10,000 copies." And the publication helped sustain Carey's faltering career.[18] More than a chronicle of the immediate crisis, Carey's *Short Account* presents Philadelphia as a metonym for the nation's civic and economic climate. His and other yellow fever narratives present several problems in the early republic through the fever, among them: (1) the "dissolution" of "natural" bonds, including familial, neighborly, and formal, and (2) a concomitant crisis of commercial regulation, relating to the role of the state in guiding markets and the market's ability to regulate itself.[19]

As he navigates these political and economic problems, Carey employs standard tropes of an early national civic republican style that mixed classical republicanism's emphasis on sacrifice, the common good, and a fear of luxury and corruption with a more favorable attitude toward commerce as an expression of liberty and a path toward and sign of stability and competence, all moderated by a assurance of consequences for intemperance.[20] In this flexible constellation of concepts, Carey links progress to regulation: "Virtue, liberty, and happiness of a nation," he posits, depend on its "temperance and sober manners."[21] Virtuous citizens are not necessarily the yeomen attributed to Jeffersonian mythology but rather the "plain and wholesome" city dwellers whose daily commercial interactions knit them into a community that prized respectability, politeness, sobriety, and industry.[22] City life may provide opportunities for corruption, but sober citizens could resist these temptations with proper self-regulation and institutional oversight, if not on their own merits, because maintaining a public image of self-regulation and politeness could be profitable. Moreover, when otherwise self-regulating individuals fell victim to the temptations of success, strong civic and financial institutions could help rein them in, providing a safety net for the innocent and a bulwark against the market's (or individual's) unpredictability for society as a whole. In such a climate, virtuous citizenship did not require the sacrifice of individual interest for the common good so much as the prudent regulation of an enlightened self-interest—do no harm rather than do good.

On the basis of this civic republicanism, Carey's prefatory remarks in *Account* about prefever Philadelphia strike a tenuous balance between the pursuit of commerce and the regulation of extravagance, individual liberty and culpability, and institutional oversight. For Carey, the stability of the

Federal Constitution brought the new nation from the brink of "anarchy": commerce flourished, and "property of every kind, rose to, and in some instances beyond its real value."[23] The economic boom of the mid-1780s and 1790s, however, undermined this sober ethic and political economic stability: "prospects formed in sanguine hours" replaced the prudent deliberation of less prosperous times, and "luxury, the usual, and perhaps the inevitable concomitant of prosperity, was gaining ground in a manner very alarming."[24] Carey's ambivalence about the relation between economic prosperity and corruption (is luxury "usual" but avoidable, or is it an "inevitable" natural consequence) mirrors fluctuations within early national debates about such correlative or causal relations. But most agreed luxury had consequences: citizens' extravagance and economic intemperance primed the city for "something . . . to humble" their "pride."[25] Even so, the revival of the Bank of Pennsylvania in 1792–1793 and the "liberal conduct of the bank of the United States," a combination of private and public management, looked to have stabilized the market, regulating currency and "saving many a deserving and industrious man from ruin."[26] The consequences of the previous years' glut had apparently taught these "deserving" men a valuable lesson while the banks softened the economic blow. With the federal government managing politics and debt, the banks watching over commerce, and the common citizen sufficiently chastened, the middling sorts and economic elite were looking forward to a prosperous fall quarter in 1793.

The yellow fever tipped the balance of this system, removing the stability and confidence that made common prosperity and individual interest compatible if not complementary. *Account* registers the schism between the two as competing principles of human nature, two orders of natural law at odds. In one of *Account*'s most often quoted passages, Carey observes, "We cannot be astonished at the frightful scenes that were acted, which seemed to indicate a total dissolution of the bonds of society in the nearest and dearest connections. . . . A wife unfeelingly abandoning her husband on his death bed—parents forsaking their only children—children ungratefully flying from their parents, and resigning them to chance . . . masters hurrying off their faithful servants to Bushhill . . . [and] servants abandoning tender and humane masters."[27] The danger the fever presented (real or imagined) overrode the natural familial bonds that had served as a model for good citizenship.[28] Family units disintegrated, and every other form of relation followed suit. Readers should "not be astonished," however, because the consequent flight was equally natural and perhaps stronger than inducements to stay. Carey describes a mass of "people at the lowest ebb of despair" whose actions were dictated by "the great law of self preservation."[29] "Self-preservation," observes Carey, is a "law" stronger than kinship, governing not just human behavior but also the "whole animated world."[30] This law led those with means to flee, while those who could not flee either hid, avoiding their neighbors, or took advantage of the crisis to make a profit. In the latter case, while these people may have risked their lives in the process, the profit motive undermined their claims to goodwill; profit was a seemingly unnatural substitute for other failing bonds.

This general unneighborliness revealed holes in the civic republican matrix outlined in Carey's prefatory remarks and mirrored both federalist and anti-federalist concerns during the constitutional debates in the previous decade.[31] As historian Woody Holton notes, economic growth and stability were preeminent concerns shaping the push for the 1787 constitution. Madison and others were not so much concerned with "replac[ing] selfish demagogues with men of virtue" as they were with reviving a failing economy. From this frame of reference, virtue was important, Holton observers, insofar as it led to economic goods: restoring credit and properly managing specie.[32] Fulfilling one's civic duty translated into fulfilling one's economic debt. These debates asked the same fundamental questions about social and civic relations that Carey's *Account* investigates: what is the role of self-interest in shaping civil and economic society, what are the duties that citizens have to each other and to the community at large, and what is the role of government in directing and/or cultivating these interests and duties?

Carey's *Account* registers these concerns in the social, recording rampant distrust, selfish neglect of duty to family and neighbors, and wholesale abandonment. The disintegration of fellow citizenship in Philadelphia spreads to the national scene as surrounding counties, states, and other "strangers" abandoned those seeking refuge. "The universal consternation," Carey reports, "extinguished in people's breasts the most honourable feelings of human nature . . . suspicion operated as injuriously as the reality."[33] Philadelphians' inhumanity toward each other revealed the weakness of societal bonds between friends and neighbors while the inhumanity of the surrounding communities uncovered a deeper lack of feeling (or substance in that feeling) between citizens within the new republic. If societal bonds could not survive a climate that demanded more of its citizens than politeness and sociability, could the new federal compact? The yellow fever epidemic made suspicious "strangers" out of neighbors and fellow citizens alike.

Despite the dire image of a more general unneighborliness, Carey presents the singular achievements of individuals such as Stephen Girard and members of the Relief Committee, led by Mayor Matthew Clarkson, as models of the virtuous citizenship that could sustain a republic. When "government of every kind was almost wholly vacated," including the caretakers for the poor and orphaned, this "band of brothers" stand in as the stabilizing force, mirroring the influence of the Federal Constitution and Bank of Pennsylvania in the years before the crisis.[34] Girard, a French immigrant and one of the wealthiest merchants in the city, and Peter Helm are representative republican citizens in this instance. "Actuated by . . . benevolent motives," they eschew the safety of retreat to serve the common good.[35] Their sacrifice is twofold: they sacrifice their business interests to oversee matters at Bush Hill without regard for compensation (and they can do so because they are wealthy), and they risk "little less than certain" death.[36] Girard and Helm, Carey continues, "without any possible inducement but the purest motives of humanity . . . came forward, and offered themselves as the forlorn hope of the committee. . . . From the time of undertaking this office to the present, they have attended uninterruptedly, for six, seven, or eight hours a day, renouncing almost every care of private affairs."[37] When focused on this group, Carey's style reflects more the rigidity of early eighteenth-century classical republicanism than the relatively fluid late eighteenth-century model of sobriety and polite sensibility outlined in his description of the prefever commercial and political climate.[38] Girard, Helm, and other "benevolent citizens" comprise a core managerial elite whose affluence and position give them the ability to flee but whose sense of duty compels them to stay. Carey's emphasis on the voluntary nature of their work—sacrificing private interests without the possibility of repayment—enhances their republican credentials as the prototypes of benevolent disinterest. In short, they exemplify the temperance, sobriety, and service that sustain republican virtue as a rationale for elite enterprise.

These few bright spots are just enough to bring the city through the crisis and offer hope for its recovery. Carey's *Account* exudes confidence about the city's speedy return to its prefever form and optimism: "Streets, too long the abode of gloom and despair, have assumed the bustle suitable to the season," and as people return (including President Washington), commerce is picking back up.[39] Even the flight out of the city retroactively symbolizes the success of "the nature of our government" because it "did not allow the arbitrary measures" that a "despotic" government would have initiated in attempting to curtail the epidemic.[40] Overall, then, Carey's *Account* simultaneously excoriates the general inhumanity, naturalizes it as concomitant with crisis itself, and suggests that the nation should not read the episode as indicative of behaviors under normal conditions. This tripartite description was calculated to explain events during the fever in a way that would protect Philadelphia's economic interests in trade and the city's political (and economic) interests in remaining the nation's capital.

More broadly, Carey presents a two-tiered protective civic republicanism, a citizenship practice in which citizens able to maintain the classical republican standard of virtue and duty watch over—either in government or in philanthropy—those citizens for whom the classical model is much too demanding.[41] As a citizenship practice, the two-tiered civic republican model allows citizens to act on their own interests in the comfort that government institutions and benevolent citizens like Girard and Helm would help direct those interests through prudent regulation and could protect citizens from each other. This vertical management made the marketplace less the breeding ground of distrust and corruption of classical republicanism and more a safe place to display and exercise fellow citizenship, which, in turn, opened citizenship practice to a wider range of citizens, identified by their ability to observe protocols of politeness and sociability.[42] At the same time, these citizens become a sign of republican freedom in the sense that the state allows, if not encourages, them to be as self-interested as their morality, material circumstances, and the market permit.[43]

Yet, could the city, let alone the nation, depend on such a division of civic labor? As a January 1, 1794, editorial in the *Philadelphia Gazette and Universal Daily Advertiser* observed, "property" provided a stronger call to patriotism than did love of country, customs, religion, or any number of other ties: "Will not a Turk, or a Spaniard fight as bravely for his Koran or his Crucifix, as any Republican for his property? Let history; let facts decide." How could these citizens reconcile the apparent weakness of fellow citizenship (and their apparent desire for this weakness) in the face of crisis with its ostensible success in more stable times?[44] Without the economic and political stability that turned this defense of property into a public good, this citizenry could not be depended on to work toward a common rather than individual good. In the absence of a robust agential citizenship, the relief effort—at least in Carey's *Account*—became a market, and the benignly self-interested became inhumane deserters or extortionists, their activities too focused on protecting their interests for civic republican discourse to absorb and their work too dependent on wages, their bodily sacrifice too tainted by profit-motive, for his classical virtue to applaud. The problem turns not simply around how persons—strangers and friends alike—ought to relate to one another when the "law" of "self-preservation" and the needs of the community collide but also around who can or cannot be virtuous and how notions of virtue, the common good, and, ultimately, the role of interests in constructing or obstructing the pursuit of this good get framed and toward what ends.

Carey's *Account* does offer possible solutions outside of this tiered structure, even if his narrative perspective tends to obscure them. Carey mentions neighboring cities such as Springfield, New Jersey, and Elkton, Maryland, that offered refuge to their fellow citizens, suggesting that such towns model the "humanity and tenderness" other states ought to show their neighbors if such a crisis should return.[45] While elaborating on scenes of horror, Carey also reveals that people *were* on Philadelphia's streets assisting the suffering, but these others were not included in the "nearest and dearest relations," nor were they "respectable citizens" or members of the Relief Committee. While his narrative calls the audience's attention to the "cries" of a pregnant woman surrounded by her dead family and without a midwife, for instance, he also mentions "one of the carters employed by the committee for the relief of the sick" who helped her deliver her child.[46] Elsewhere, "respectable women" depend on "servant women for assistance."[47] Each instance provides an opportunity for Carey to meditate on the potential virtues of these lesser sorts who also risked their lives during the crisis to help neighbors in the same way that neighboring cities offered assistance to fleeing Philadelphians, yet both of these scenes foreground the abandonment rather than the service, ending with reiterations of the "dreadful spectacle."[48] Moreover, Carey's focus on elite actors implies that only citizens of means and "respectability" could muster the requisite resolution to act and that their force of will carried these common folk with them. From this perspective, Carey's praise for the Relief Committee and recuperation of Philadelphia's citizenry ultimately makes passive citizenship not only desirable but also required for a functional republic.[49]

For this paradigm to hold, those who remained behind but did not fit into either category (virtuous elite or respectable victims) needed to be rendered civically dead or otherwise illegible. Such is the case with Carey's representation of black relief efforts. Even when they make positive contributions, Carey uses the necessity for the presence of *these* people to signal the community's breakdown: without the people representing the "nearest and dearest" connections in society (the "wives, children, friends, clerks, and servants"), Carey explains, "many men of affluent fortunes . . . have been abandoned to the care of a negro."[50] Carey clarifies his distinction between waged service and benevolence as he excepts "Negroes" from the "nearest and dearest" of the community and the expected system of recovery. The civic republicanism that depended on notions of "natural" relationships, like familial bonds, or disinterested benevolence to define social relations had no interpretive frame for valuing their work as legitimate citizenship practice. These scenes instead signal the overall breakdown of white community during the epidemic: white readers see images of an abandoned city, left to black people without having to acknowledge white absence or cowardice.[51]

Blackness becomes Carey's marker for absence, and black Philadelphians come to represent the corruptive elements at work during the crisis. Just after praising Absalom Jones, Richard Allen, and William Gray for organizing free African relief workers, Carey accuses (some) workers of extortion: "The great demand for nurses, afforded an opportunity for imposition, which was eagerly seized by some of the vilest of the blacks. They extorted two, three, four, and even five dollars a night for services that would have been well paid by a single dollar. Some of them were even detected in plundering the houses of the sick."[52] He further undermines their contribution by quoting from John Lining's 1753 observation of black immunity in South Carolina, implying that the risks involved for them were minimal.[53] As Rana Hogarth notes, immunity theories allowed Carey, Rush, and others to minimize the risks and to claim that black Philadelphians in fact had an obligation to stay "because their biology dictated it."[54] Tainted with commercial interest yet incompatible with civic republicanism's regulatory schema, black citizens presented both a visible threat to and a handy release valve for Philadelphia's postfever anxieties.[55] They provided filler for the gaps in Carey's two-tiered civic republicanism, filler that could then be easily excised from the state's civic imaginary. Carey's *Account* reduces Jones, Allen, and Gray's efforts at best to the exceptions that proved the rule of the general dissipation of social bonds, at worst to shady market exchanges and outright theft.[56]

It is not just that Carey's *Account* gives the impression of widespread black theft; rather, by emphasizing the distress of helpless citizens and the general abandonment while, as Jones and Allen suggest in *Narrative*, upholding a select few, he often deemphasizes those who do offer assistance, missing an opportunity to explore citizenship practices that might actually work beyond the managerial elite.[57] Even his account of black citizens enhances the notion that only a community's elite can access civic virtue; all others must, by definition, be operating for selfish, destructive reason. Jones, Allen, and Gray, like Girard and Helm, preside over an otherwise unsung and unruly laboring mass.

Where Carey sought to reassure people that the system worked, that state and financial institutions could properly manage potentially destructive interests in normal conditions, Jones and Allen's *Narrative* suggests that perhaps this management is a crutch, a shell game in which citizens take advantage of the potential individual benefits of civic republicanism's adaptability to commerce while refusing to assume moral and political responsibility for how this commercial ethic could turn fellow citizens into antagonistic strangers.[58] Statesmen such as Alexander Hamilton, who was in the city during the crisis and, like Allen, survived his own bout with the fever, lamented that if fellow citizenship failed in the city during the crisis, then, as Richard Newman aptly summarizes, "the republic could not survive."[59] The rest of this chapter focuses on *Narrative*'s account of the relief effort, contrasting it to Carey's managerial narrative to suggest a neighborly ethics of citizenship that could provide a stronger basis for active citizenship than the "natural" bonds or elite benevolence cited in Carey's *Account*. Whether or not Jones and Allen are explicitly taking on civic republican models of citizenship—they use terms like "sensibility" and "duty" sometimes ironically and at other times in ways that implicate them within civic republican discourse—we might usefully frame what *Narrative* offers as a third way, navigating between the layers of Carey's tiered civic republicanism.

Response and Diagnosis: The Problem with Citizenship as Commerce

Read through *Narrative*'s analysis of the labor market during the epidemic and Jones and Allen's experience as former slaves and free Africans, the civic breakdown during the epidemic was not unexpected. Rather, the stress it put on the white citizenry brought into sharp relief the structural instabilities of a civic republicanism predicated on "more a willingness to get along with others for the sake of peace and prosperity" than on the sense of shared responsibility for the common good or fellow citizenship.[60] While contemporaries like Carey claimed that Federalist regulatory structures could prevent fellow citizenship from collapsing under normal circumstances, *Narrative*'s account of the inability of institutions to regulate the market for relief workers emphasizes the limits of market structures in creating relations between citizens when the underlying ethic governing citizenship practice depends on and encourages atomization and exploitation. Moreover, even as *Narrative* offers a productive critique of civic republicanism's economic valences, its inversion of Carey's style underscores how readily the economic rhetoric of interests can be manipulated to justify anything from benevolent service to the slave trade.

The commercial ethic that remained submerged or managed before the fever comes to a head during the crisis and seems to overpower official regulation. Mayor Clarkson, Jones, and Allen all attempted to regulate the cost of the relief efforts by employing workers through the city and other civic institutions. The presence of these regulations highlights the economic similarities between the moment of crisis and the city under normal conditions. Jones and Allen recount their meeting with Matthew Clarkson about the rising fees: "[Clarkson] sent for us, and requested that we would use our influence, to lessen the wages of the nurses, but informing him of the cause, i.e. that of the people over-bidding one another, it was concluded unnecessary to attempt any thing on that head; therefore it was left to the people concerned."[61] As Clarkson's response suggests, inflation not only overcame the city's ability to influence its workers but also changed the nature of economic exchange itself. Clarkson, Jones, and Allen could "influence" the workers to lower their fees, because the workers were their employees and they provided a flat wage intended to make these services available to all, but the bidding war took the workers out of their direct employ. People offering *these* payments were operating squarely within a market in which their individual means and interests were their own concern. Since the workers were not setting the prices but rather were responding to the effects of supply and demand with individual consumers dictating the price ceiling, neither the mayor nor, perhaps, Jones and Allen saw a need to intervene, and even if they did, they could not.

Jones and Allen's emphasis on the forces of supply, demand, and self-interest reveals that the black workers' response to the market during the epidemic worked by the same logics that governed white activities before, during, and after the epidemic.[62] The "difficulty" of finding "persons . . . to supply the wants of the sick" and the increasing "applications" for services that *Narrative* describes during the fever parallel Carey's earlier description of the "number of applicants for houses" before the fever.[63] The "extravagant prices . . . paid" (the "two, three, four, and even five dollars a night" in Carey's *Account*) mirror the prefever increase of property values to "double, and in some treble what it would have been a year or two before."[64] In both Carey's *Account* and Jones and Allen's *Narrative*, the syntactic focus on environmental forces rather than individual choices—the presence or absence of an agent—absolves the actors of moral responsibility. Rents "had risen" in Carey's *Account*, without mention of the property owners' agency as a factor in driving up prices. The nursing fees, however, increased because "the vilest of the blacks . . . eagerly seized" the "opportunity for imposition."[65] Here, Carey also mentions the increase in demand, but where the demand for housing drove up rents (passively), the demand for nurses provided an opportunity for corruption that black workers actively pursued. Jones and Allen use much the same strategy but inverted, contrasting the bidding war and those who were (passively) paid exorbitant prices to a "white woman" who "demanded" "six pounds" for her services.[66] Their inversion disarms Carey's racialization of economic corruption, using Carey's terms to demonstrate black virtue in the face of white inhumanity.

The facility with which Jones, Allen, and Carey manipulate commercial language reveals the slipperiness of the economic discourse more generally when applied as an ethical tool. The mirroring Jones and Allen enact between *Narrative* and *Account* destabilizes the economic discourse they both use, however tenuous, ironic, or adversarial that use may be. This indeterminacy disrupts any attempt to situate virtue or corruption in any one group.[67] Good citizenship from this perspective depended less on adhering to a set of ethical precepts than on maintaining the authority to set those precepts and to justify one's actions accordingly.

The parallels between commerce before and during the fever and *Narrative*'s vindication of black laborers, then, offer a larger critique of how civic republican logic "protected and facilitated" the economic interests of a white elite, making self-interest, as Joyce Appleby posits, "a functional equivalent to civic virtue" that masks the maintenance of inequality.[68] The "functional" equivalency of self-interest and civic virtue breaks down when citizens are forced to choose between what the rules of commercial exchange allow them to do and what civic duty or fellow citizenship suggests they ought to do. Economic inequalities in place before the fever exacerbate this warlike relation, stripping the polite trappings of the market structure Kloppenberg describes as the "natural harmony of benignly striving individuals," revealing it to be instead a free-for-all.[69] Jones and Allen explain, "When we procured [workers] at six dollars per week, and called upon them to go where they were wanted, we found they were gone elsewhere. . . . Upon enquiring the cause, we found, they had been allured away by others who offered greater wages, until they got from two to four dollars per day. We had no restraint upon the people. It was natural for people in low circumstances to accept a voluntary, bounteous reward."[70] People followed their "natural" inclinations, and individual means would control just how far these inclinations could go. If it was natural for white people in Carey's *Account* to abandon the "nearest and dearest," was it not more natural for black citizens to lay aside questions of fairness to strangers in the name of self-preservation and economic self-interest? This principle holds doubly true for "people in low circumstances," who, unlike Girard and Helm, were not financially secure even before the fever.

Narrative's juxtaposition of pilfering and privateering illustrates how official discourse produces this functional equivalency and its uneven, racialized results: "We know as many whites who were guilty of it [theft and extortion]," Jones and Allen write, "but this is looked over, while the blacks are held up to censure.—Is it a greater crime for a black to pilfer, than for a white to privateer?"[71] The comparison indicts both black and white citizens for taking advantage of the breakdown during the fever to make a profit.[72] Compared to "pilfer," however, "privateer" invokes a more pernicious attitude toward commerce that may be legal, strictly speaking, but also involves an antagonistic ethic that perhaps causes the waning virtue Carey notes in *Account*'s opening lines.[73] Coming directly after a sentence focused not on white theft but rather on people offering accounts that "[look] over" white theft while highlighting black criminality, "privateer" confronts the duplicity of official narratives and structures that essentially legalize white theft.[74] Just as a state's *letter of marque* authorizes the private citizen to approach "foreign" ships in a way that would amount to piracy under other conditions, the collective attitude toward commerce authorizes, if not encourages, citizens to approach each other in ways that would otherwise amount to theft, as if they were not just strangers but also enemies.[75]

Gould has noted rightly that the slipperiness of commercial discourse in both yellow fever narratives points to "the ideological inextricability during this transitional era between sentiment and the capitalist market, between benevolence and supply-and-demand as the regulators of human behavior."[76] In Jones and Allen's pilfer versus privateer figure, Gould finds not a tactical deployment of contemporaneous discourse but rather "*Narrative*'s major flaw": the ironic comparison indicts both black and white citizens for taking advantage of the breakdown during the fever to make a profit; Jones and Allen's insistence on their economic losses during the fever, visually punctuated with an inserted ledger, he argues, destabilizes any claims they might make to disinterested benevolence.[77] We should not, however, take Jones and Allen's reproduction of Carey's narrative as an adoption of the principles subtending that narrative. Focusing so much on the economic discourse misses Jones and Allen's structural critique: economics and market logics of interest, while useful for descriptive purposes, make for poor ethical tools and not all people inhabit the market on the same terms or from the same position.

An expanded reading of *Narrative*'s form suggests that Jones and Allen leveraged this rhetorical slipperiness to proffer an analysis absent in *Account*: citizenship in which state and social convention could turn theft into fair trade depends less on adhering to a set of ethical precepts than on maintaining the power to validate some narratives as impartial and dismiss others as "the insidious arts of whispering slander," Carey's description of Jones and Allen's *Narrative*.[78] These passages do suggest the equivalency and invocation virtue of politics that critics have noted but in terms of the kinds of interestedness the early republic "protected and facilitated."[79] By invoking the institutional distinctions between pilfer and privateer, Jones and Allen signify acerbically on how arbitrarily these concepts can be deployed to suit political ends. They reveal that no matter how enlightened self-interest might be, it still encouraged duplicitous practices contrary to the fellow citizenship Carey attempts to extrapolate from it.[80]

While the fever surfaced this antagonistic tendency, Jones and Allen already had an analogue in an everyday life sanctioned by the state: the slave trade. Both men were former slaves whose family members had been sold when they were relatively young: Jones's mother and siblings in 1762,

Allen's parents and younger siblings in the 1770s to settle his master's debts.[81] Just as Philadelphians attempted to outbid each other for services at the expense of their neighbors' lives, slave owners battled each other for the lives of other human beings. And just as the "purchasers" of slaves, as Anthony Benezet put it, "[encourage] the Trade, [become] partaker in the Guilt of it," so, too, do these bidding citizens bear responsibility for the chaos their bidding engendered.[82] Notwithstanding Carey's view of the Federal Constitution as a stabilizing force, black Americans were still subject to enslavement and the caprice of white interests, with the 1793 Fugitive Slave Law the most recent in a string of setbacks.[83] As Jones explains in a 1799 petition to the "President, Senate, and House of Representatives," the law codified on the federal level the treatment of human beings "like droves of cattle."[84] While *Narrative*'s bidding war and a slave market are not the same, they do operate by similar premises. Neither Jones and Allen nor Mayor Clarkson has (or takes) authority to regulate these exchanges between yellow fever victims, citing the independence of economic exchanges between individuals in a way that parallels the federal government's refusal to "interfere" with individual property rights and the rights of the several states for the sake of preserving the union.

Narrative does not suggest that commerce in itself is corrupt or that state and civic institutions should not have a hand in regulating commerce or providing a framework and direction for civic activity. Jones and Allen cite several black workers who charged for services but always with the caveat that the worker "charged with exemplary moderation" or "enough for what she had done."[85] Recall also that Jones, Allen, and Gray worked with the city's government to coordinate their efforts during the crisis, that the FAS and FAC were both institutions created to coordinate civic activities, and that Allen himself was an especially adept businessman.[86] Rather, depending on a managerial elite (either the federal system, heroes like Girard and Helm, or civic leaders like Clarkson, Jones, and Allen) to ensure that citizens work toward their own general welfare or to simply protect citizens from each other removes the need for citizens to be responsible to and concerned for each other, requiring only that they appear to be so. Even if, as Carey's *Account* claims, citizens' freedom to flee the city during the fever showcases the strength of republican governance, the implication that preventing wholesale abandonment of Philadelphians *by* fellow Philadelphians and those in neighboring states might have required a mandate points to weaknesses in the relation between the citizens themselves. If,

Figure 2. Richard Allen, founder of the African Methodist Episcopal Church. Courtesy, Library of Congress.

under these terms, white Philadelphians could be justified in abandoning the "nearest and dearest" in the interest of self-preservation, then civic republicanism would be inadequate to the task of addressing enslavement, let alone the white supremacy subtending it.

Solution: Neighborly Citizenship

As they restaged the 1793 epidemic's labor market, Jones and Allen both responded to white supremacy through the languages of sentiment and political economy and rethought how those discourses codified structural racism. As is the case with many of the texts I treat in *The Practice of Citizenship*, *Narrative* explicitly frames willful misreadings of black activities as a precondition for articulating white virtue.[87] When *Narrative* moves rhetorically from an economic defense of black workers and Jones and Allen's expenditures to a discussion of citizenship as neighborliness, it also shifts attention away from a politics dependent on the recognition of black worth toward one that holds white citizens responsible for correcting their racism. In this section, I analyze how Jones and Allen theorize neighborliness by exchanging their narrative substrate from Carey's *Account* and late-century models of sensibility for the parable of the Good Samaritan and black citizens' "real sensibility."

Even as *Narrative* inserts black citizens into the civic republican polity of feeling and virtue, its shift in narrative structure and emphasis not only disrupts that discourse's racial-economic valences—that is, whether or not "negroes" and "servants" can be respectable or virtuous citizens—but also undermines respectability and virtue as markers of good citizenship and the individualistic ethos those markers promote. Using Jones and Allen's distinction of a "real sensibility" and the FAS's reference to an "expressive language of conduct" as guides, we can frame what *Narrative* offers in its account of black citizens during the fever as an alternative practice of citizenship based on an ethics of neighborliness.[88] Neighborliness corresponds with the duty to the common good suggested in classical republicanism and embodied in Girard and Helm in Carey's *Account* but with a potentially more democratic ethos of equality and inclusion, demanding that neighbor-citizens serve the common good by serving each other, by being neighborly toward the individuals encountered in everyday life. This openness results in a permeable civic space, resembling more a dynamic web of associations based in mutual aid than a single sphere, a neighborhood rather than a market.

I use the term "neighborliness" to describe *Narrative*'s civic ethics here rather than "piety," "Golden Rule," "mutual aid," "charity," or the like for three reasons: (1) Neighborliness emphasizes that this ethic operates between individuals on terms of moral equality in a way that creates a collective. This emphasis on horizontality, moreover, distinguishes neighborliness from cultures of benevolence, classical virtue, or sensibility. (2) The term connects Jones and Allen's investment in Christian ethics via the parable of the Good Samaritan's narrative formula with their equal investment in developing a strong political structure for emancipation and full citizenship. (3) Consolidating this question under "neighborliness" highlights *Narrative*'s resonances with contemporaneous interpretations of the Samaritan parable as addressing not simply individual morality but also the law's foundations. As Gary Nash conjectures of the black citizens' attitude as they began their efforts, "Philadelphia's black Christians would act as Good Samaritans, reenacting the drama of the despised man who aided a fellow human in desperate need when all the respected men of the community turned their heads."[89] Yet, beyond the allegorical value of this narrative trajectory and its social inversions, the Good Samaritan formula offers a grounding from which we can draw a critique of civic republican logics. That is, rather than read the formula as a suggestion that black Philadelphians were better or more virtuous republican citizens, I want to suggest that the formula and the overall *Narrative* offer an alternative to civic republicanism in much the same way that Jesus of Nazareth uses the parable to offer an alternative to what had become traditional interpretations to Mosaic Law.[90]

Narrative registers neighborliness as a cultural practice in black citizens' "real sensibility": their quest to "be useful" and their "rendering services where extreme necessity called for it."[91] One case, mirroring familiar scenes of abandonment in Carey's *Account*, features the actions of a poor black man set against two others. The comparison between the three upends expected roles and creates space for a more substantive critique and revision of not only how commentators like Carey applied civic republican logic but also of the civic republican logic itself:

> A poor afflicted dying man, stood at his chamber window, praying and beseeching every one that passed by, to help him to a drink of water; a number of white people passed, and instead of being moved by the poor man's distress, they hurried as fast as they could out of the sound of his cries until at length a gentleman, who seemed a foreigner came up, he could not pass by, but had not resolution enough to go into the house, he held eight dollars in his hand, and offered it to several as a reward for giving the poor man a drink of water, but was refused by every one.[92]

The first half of this story follows Carey's narrative pattern: Carey also mentions the plight of "poor" persons "without a human being to hand them a drink of water," "men of affluent fortune . . . abandoned to the care of a negro," and those whose money could not "procure proper attendance."[93] In these instances, Carey's two-tiered model falls apart. With expected neighbors failing and no one willing to risk infection for even a considerable fee of "five dollars," the suffering die alone, die in the presence of a negro (which amounts to the same thing in Carey's *Account*), or, as in the case of a servant girl, die in a cart as the guardians of the poor attempt to find a home willing to take them in.[94] Where Carey's illustrations typically end, however, *Narrative* offers "a poor black man" who "came up" and not only "supplied the poor object with water" but also "rendered him every service he could."[95] When the gentleman offers to pay the black man to help the dying man, the black man responds, "Master . . . I will supply the gentleman with water, but surely I will not take your money for it," punctuating the insufficiency of money as a motivating factor.[96]

The black man's story undoubtedly offers a direct rebuttal to Carey's assertion of black inhumanity, particularly in his refusal of the gentleman's money. Above these evidentiary moves, however, the anecdote provides a more general theory of citizenship missing in Carey's *Account*: an immanent sense of civic responsibility uncoupled from social status or economic motivation. The man's action demonstrates a "real sensibility" that compels him and other black citizens to move forward even as white neighbors hide or stand by because "the dread . . . was so general" as to make friends "afraid of each other."[97] Both groups show a kind of sensibility when confronted with a nearly overwhelming emotional tide—fear, horror, despair, pity, and so on—that suggests a breakdown in sympathy and fellow feeling, but black citizens' sensibility becomes "real" through the "expressive language of conduct," that is, when at sight of "others being so backward," they refuse to let their senses control their actions.[98] *Narrative*'s sensibility becomes "real" or concrete only as it produces measures to alleviate the need that initiated the sensory reaction. (Hence Jones and Allen's position that their "services were the *product* of real sensibility."[99])

The white gentleman in *Narrative*'s vignette offers a useful point of contrast between this productive "real sensibility" manifested through the "expressive language of conduct" and what Markman Ellis usefully describes as the "specular economic voyeurism" of eighteenth-century cultures of sensibility. Despite the appearance of virtue in his attitude, the gentleman's sensibility is no more effective than other citizens' abandonment. He fulfills the expectation that a cosmopolitan gentleman be able to "relate to strangers, to share in the feelings of others, including social inferiors and even animals," and might even occasion admiration.[100] Yet, his concern for the dying man results in inertia: "he could not pass by, but had not resolution enough to go into the house."[101] "Observations on Sensibility, or Felling, as Opposed to Principle," a 1791 article in Carey's *American Museum*, explains the difference: "This [concern] is the work of an *unprincipled man of feeling*, whose nerves with peculiar irritability, can tremble every hour at the touch of joy or woe; whose finely-fibred heart would thrill perhaps with horror at the sufferings of—a fly."[102] The public display of sensibility, "Observations" continues, "supplies the want of religion . . . [,] appears more lovely than all the virtues," and provides a benevolent analogue to the functional equivalency of self-interest.[103] The gentleman *feels* for the stranger very publicly (he was standing on the streets) without a concomitant identification of the stranger as one who, more than an "inferior," requires the gentleman to overcome his irresolution.

In contrast to the poor black man who moves to help the dying man, the gentleman tries to move capital instead, "[holding] eight dollars in his hand," implicitly valuing the man's needs or the value of his own good citizenship at eight dollars in the process.[104] The gentleman is not without virtue. He does call attention to the dying man's need, after all, and in some ways, concern for the dying man supplants class and racial boundaries: the "gentleman" foreigner asks a "poor black man" to help "a poor afflicted dying man."[105] Yet, his recourse to using capital as a proxy, to stand by until the market produced an agent, alienates him from a potential neighbor, resulting in the kind of complacence that created the economic crisis before the fever and a climate of exploitation during the fever. His attempt, like Carey's *Account*, shifts attention away from his inability to help, calling attention instead to those for whom his fee is not a sufficient motivator. Perhaps the gentleman even sees himself as a helpless victim of both the dread the man's wails cause and the manifest inhumanity of passersby.[106] Juxtaposed against the poor black man, the gentleman's inertia becomes less about the gentleman's helplessness in an unwilling market than about the insufficiency of simple sensibility in general as a guide for civic action.

Narrative's analysis of those like the "gentleman," people of status and means looking to pay others for services, suggests that looking upward for models of good citizenship reveals an inadequacy that may be all the more dangerous because it is cloaked in performances of sensibility and class expectations rather than in an active "real sensibility." Where the seemingly "natural" bonds between citizens (family, friends, servants, and neighbors) fail and the gentleman's sensibility and finances prove ineffective (or, as in the previous discussion, counterproductive), the poor black man offers a third way, a neighborly ethics predicated neither on the claims of sociability or kinship nor on performances of sensibility and benevolence. Like the rank-and-file citizens, the man has no claim to respectability—*Narrative* describes him simply as "good natured"—like the gentleman, he cannot simply walk by. Absent any obvious tie to the dying man or social expectation of virtue, the poor black man nevertheless steps forward, his "real sensibility," or piety in the FAS's terms, providing the cosmopolitan link with the stranger even as the gentleman's sensibility fails. This gentleman and passersby dramatize the "'split subject' of citizenship: the individual citizen understood as structured by this central division between private self and public *persona*."[107] *Narrative*'s account of neighborliness suggests this private-public binary is a deceptive one. More perniciously, it enables writers like Carey and the culture more broadly to assign moral credit or blame arbitrarily and strategically in the service of buttressing white citizenship.

Jones and Allen's invoking real sensibility, then, resonates with and intervenes in contemporaneous attempts to distinguish between sensibility as a physiological response to outside stimuli, a performative (and therefore untrustworthy) display of emotion, and an ethical imperative to act informed by reason. These discussions turned to schemes for regulating sensibility through cultivating reason, contrasting sensibility or basic sympathy to teachable principles, such as charity, or suggesting that sensibility was, itself, mediated through reason. Benjamin Rush, for instance, characterized sensibility as the "avenue to the moral faculty," one that needed careful supervision and development because it provided the scaffold upon which society was built.[108] Anthony Benezet claimed the person who "possessed but a small degree of feeling" could still exercise charity because charity "consisteth in the subjection of the mind to known duties."[109] And Jonathan Edwards distinguished between apparent virtue and the "truly virtuous": "some actions and dispositions appear beautiful, if considered partially and superficially," but are revealed to be otherwise when "seen clearly in their whole nature and the extent of their connections in the universality of things."[110] Jones and Allen add to this their experience with how racist accounts could obscure the whole nature of real sensibility. After all, they wrote *Narrative* to correct "partial" accounts of black relief efforts with testimony from those who saw the whole and could "declare facts as they really were."[111] While *Narrative* does not use separate terms to differentiate between "sensibility" as a physiological response and "real sensibility" as a principle, the contrast between the gentleman's inertia and the poor black man's activity, his "language of conduct," suggests that the difference between the two—sensibility and real sensibility—corresponds to these concurrent frameworks, as well as the FAS's invocation of piety. At the same time, reworking sensibility through a narrative about an unsung black man demonstrated that black Philadelphians were not just "ready for freedom"; they were in fact were already doing the work of citizenship.[112]

The parable of the Good Samaritan provides a useful parallel text that offers a vocabulary for articulating the kind of relation between citizens that "real sensibility" should produce and connects events recounted in *Narrative* to the FAS's notion of the pious person as a good citizen of the world.[113] Reading this account through the parable's narrative formula, a formula that would have been familiar to many of Jones and Allen's readers, reveals how their strategy moves beyond setting black virtue against white inhumanity.[114] The conversation between Jesus and a lawyer about law and civic responsibility frames a moment in which Jesus pivots on received understandings of the law to offer a more expansive notion of who is the neighbor or to whom the good citizen should be responsible and responsive. When a lawyer questions Jesus about eternal life, Jesus responds with a question of his own: "What is written in the law?" The lawyer replies, "Thou shalt love the Lord thy God with all thy soul . . . strength, and . . . mind; and thy neighbor as thyself."[115] Jesus tells the lawyer that he has answered correctly, but not to be outdone, the lawyer asks a logical follow-up question: "And who is my neighbor?" Rather than answer the lawyer's question—"who is my neighbor?"—by describing the set of people whom the lawyer should love and thus offering a restricted notion of neighborliness, Jesus offers a parable, a case study, outlining the characteristics of the neighbor as the subject, sensible to another's suffering, in action: "A certain man went down from Jerusalem to Jericho, and fell among thieves, which stripped him of his raiment, and wounded him, and departed, leaving him half dead. And by chance there came down a certain priest that way: and when he saw him, he passed by on the other side. And likewise a Levite, when he was at the place, came and looked on him, and passed by on the other side."[116] As in Jones and Allen's vignette, the parable features an injured man in need of assistance. Respected community leaders and fellow Jews—symbols of the civic and moral good—recognize the man's suffering but go out of their way to avoid helping him. Instead, a Samaritan not only aids the man but also ensures his safety until his recovery. The Samaritan, seeing past the mutual enmity between Jews and Samaritans, "discover[s] the neighbor" in the injured man and becomes the good neighbor, the keeper of the law who will "inherit eternal life," because he acts as the neighbor rather than looking for the neighbor.[117]

This response has deep implications for the construction of community and citizenship as a point of civil law going beyond a simple moral query. In the context of the Mosaic Law, legal scholar Jeremy Waldron explains, love thy neighbor "is emphatically not a moralistic add-on to a legal code"; rather, the maxim "sums up the spirit of the legal code."[118] Using a Samaritan—a people viewed by Jesus' audience as a lower caste or culturally and religiously abject—as the model of neighborliness, Jesus shifts the audience's focus from finding the neighbor among themselves to finding the neighbor-citizen within themselves and, in so doing, expands the boundaries of "my neighbor" beyond respectability ("respectable citizens"), genealogy (whiteness), or political status. The onus falls on the sensible citizen's ability to see the neighbor-citizen in the other person rather than on the other to demonstrate respectability to an already constituted community.[119] The mark of the good neighbor-citizen and the good community, by extension, becomes not simply the ability to extend boundaries over an increasingly diverse set of neighbors but rather the ability to make this extension on terms of equality.

Each case, the parable of the Good Samaritan and Jones and Allen's *Narrative*, inverts audience expectations to reveal an ethics of neighborhood that foregrounds the citizen's choice to be the good neighbor. This interpretation of the parable would not have been lost on those among *Narrative*'s readers familiar with popular biblical commentaries. A similar exegesis of neighborliness, if not necessarily applied to black people, appeared in William Burkitt's *Expository Notes* (1789). For Burkitt, Luke 10:29–37 positions "*real* charity [as] an active operative thing given to the distressed, nor in compassionate beholding of them, nor in a pitiful mourning over them, but in positive acts of kindness towards them. The Samaritan here is an example of a *real* and thorough charity."[120] Burkitt's emphasis on "real" and "positive acts" and his contrast to "compassionate beholding" and "pitiful mourning" reappear throughout *Narrative* in references to black citizens' "real sensibility": "Our services were the production of real sensibility;—we sought not fee nor reward, until the disorder rendered our labour so arduous that we were not adequate to the services we had assumed" they sought to "be useful," and as a result, black citizens demonstrated "more humanity, more real sensibility" than their white counterparts.[121] It suggests a degree of equality lacking in models of disinterested benevolence. This inversion moves beyond setting black virtue against white inhumanity toward redefining what it means to be a citizen or, in the parable's terms, a neighbor.

Narrative answers Carey and the larger culture's implicit query—who is my fellow citizen, who is the good neighbor—by reproducing some of *Account*'s key scenes from the perspective of people of a caste—"servant," "negro," "foreigner"—neglected in Carey's *Account*. Through this staging, *Narrative* suggests that good citizens have a duty "to do all the good" they can toward "suffering fellow mortals,"[122] that is, to approach others as equals not simply out of a desire not to offend but rather out of a position of proactive goodwill. Such contact, "conducted in a mode of good will" across social boundaries (between Samaritans and Jews, free African and white citizens, strangers, etc.), as Samuel R. Delany would later explain, "is the locus of democracy as visible social drama," providing "the lymphatic system of a democratic metropolis."[123] In other words, Jones and Allen realized that this vision of and action toward others as neighbors (*Narrative*'s real sensibility) could create horizontal structures and day-to-day engagements more conducive to egalitarian citizenship than could contemporary notions of tiered civic republicanism.

The neighborly citizen understands that benevolence means more than appearing virtuous; it means mutual aid: collective action against needs that threaten individual competence, in the recognition that a threat to the individual is, ultimately, a threat to all. In the context of the fever, the implication of mutual aid in "suffering fellow mortals" should not be overlooked. Jones and Allen's multiple references to those in need as "fellow mortals," rather than distinguishing between themselves and the people they helped (as in Carey's repeated "respectable" or "benevolent" citizens), suggest a sense of moral equality in the contingency of mortality and the "frailty of human nature," an acknowledgment that circumstance is the only difference between those in present need and those currently able to meet that need.[124] Everyone was susceptible to the fever—Gray dies of the fever and Allen and Alexander Hamilton (who lived just a few houses down from Allen) contract the fever but recover—making death or the threat of death the great equalizer and making the shared vulnerability much more visceral.[125] If the fever itself offers an immediate social equalizer, the notion that no one can "survive on self-interested negotiation alone," as Daniel Vickers posits of the early national backcountry context, suggests a more fundamental codependence and equality.[126] This recognition of fellow mortality, of a shared condition, between individuals presupposes and affirms each individual as having equal moral worth regardless of prior social, political, or economic status. In this sense, Jones and Allen's structure invokes less the Leviticus admonition to offer hospitality to strangers, as strangers, and more an ethos intended to produce ongoing relations of neighborhood.[127]

Neighborly citizenship happens in the day-to-day interactions between individuals, not as commercial agents but rather as members of a community collectively engaged in being "useful" to each other and sharing responsibility for their mutual well-being. *Narrative* illustrates this everydayness through an "elderly black woman" who asks simply for "a dinner master on a cold winter's day" as she "went from place to place rendering every service in her power without an eye to reward."[128] The kind of exchange represented in the woman's movements across the city creates neighborhood rather than a market: a link between neighbors based on a "mutual relation," as Jonathan Edwards explained some fifty years earlier, "equally predicable of both those between whom there is such a relation."[129] If we take seriously *Narrative*'s distinction between the woman's request for dinner and her not having "an eye to reward," the exchange—meeting a present need in return for security against a future need—reworks notions of obligation subtending gradual emancipation and reproduces the framework of societies like the FAS in which members contributed to a general fund against the needs of its collective membership or others. The poor black woman makes an informal contribution to the collective and acknowledges her mutual dependence with those to whom she makes her contribution in the same move. She did not owe white Philadelphians' service but rather offered it freely.[130] In so doing, she made a "master" into a neighbor. And while the woman's example comes from a moment of extreme duress, like the Samaritan's narrative, her actions in the crisis yield lessons for the postfever world.

Such a practice could serve as a bulwark against the atomizing market exchanges dominating the opening pages of Carey's *Account* and the echoes of the slave market that haunt Jones and Allen's *Narrative*. The elderly woman understands that while the "reward" may not be immediate or public, so long as the overall community follows the ethic of neighborliness, everyone benefits. This neighborliness corresponds with Thomas Paine's figure of society as a "great chain of connection" created by "the mutual dependence and reciprocal interest which man has upon man, and all the parts of civilised community upon each other."[131] Such a dynamic form of association suggests a turn from the capitalist citizenship proffered by Carey to something approximating the classical republican notion of civic duty—recognition that being a good neighbor-citizen means sharing responsibility for the community's well-being. Yet, it also builds on a late eighteenth-century sense of democratic voluntarism and equality that shrinks the scope of neighborliness from a distant "common good" and abstract humanity to everyday concrete individual relations.[132] It parallels the openness of late eighteenth-century politeness and sociability but focused less on their middle-class or performative valences and more on the material usefulness of such gestures.

By reading *Narrative* through the parable's familiar formula, then, we see real sensibility as a mode of neighborly citizenship, the good neighbor-citizen producing neighborhood through an immanent impulse not only to identify with the stranger but also to approach the stranger as a neighbor, as a fellow mortal of equal moral worth in a mutually dependent community.[133] This account of black citizens during the fever not only shows the weakness of social status as an indicator of civic virtue but also offers neighborliness as a citizenship practice that creates horizontal relationships between citizens where civic republicanism would suggest hierarchy and allow abandonment. In this framework, the poor black man's labor deserves as much "credit" as Girard's, or rather, their efforts during the fever represent a common, neighborly citizenship that the white Philadelphians in *Narrative*'s vignette do not practice.

Narrative's rhetorical play and shift to neighborliness suggest that Jones and Allen were aware of how unstable appeals to black virtue could be, how easily black virtue could be explained away or transmuted into criminality in the print public. As much as *Narrative* at times works through this politics, the necessity of its existence also speaks to this politics' failures. Yet, it was still a tool that they'd leverage even as they critiqued the capriciousness of their intended audience and virtue's conceptual instability. By characterizing black relief efforts as economic exchange, Carey ensured that readers would interpret their work as private and self-serving instead of political and coming from a concern for the common good. This is why attending to the formal affordances of the parable of the Good Samaritan is crucial.[134] The parable shifted fundamentally the meaning of neighborliness and community. It refuses to function on the terms that the lawyer brought to the conversation—how others can signal to the individual their membership in a preconstituted community. By reframing their efforts as representing the essence of the law and as a process of community building, Jones and Allen also reframe black Philadelphians as political subjects practicing citizenship.

As we have seen in this section, *Narrative* maps a similar trajectory. In *Narrative*'s first act, Jones and Allen described black Philadelphians eschewing the contracts they (Jones and Allen) negotiated on their behalf with Clarkson and the city to make their own contracts. Disagree with the terms, Jones, Allen, and Clarkson (and Carey) might, but they had a right to work on terms closer to fair market value, as did their white counterparts. When *Narrative* shifts registers to acts of neighborliness, it similarly shows black Philadelphians setting their own terms. In these cases, the terms appear as refusals to frame their efforts as purely economic transactions—the poor black man refuses the gentleman's money and the black woman refuses the proffered "reward." At the same time, the black woman also establishes a wider ranging social compact: I do not perform this act as a laborer seeking wages but rather as an equal member of a community in which mutual dependence and responsiveness is the guiding ethic. I render aid to you today recognizing that you will render aid to me later.[135] Here, as elsewhere, *Narrative* does not rely on any single strategy but rather deploys multiple strategies that black theorizers will take up and revise well into the nineteenth century. These two moments offer images of black virtue and critiques of white avarice that ultimately suggest that virtue politics was never sufficient, not just because white Americans would continually misread black public acts but also because a polity based on this kind of performative citizenship would always be insubstantial, not "real."

Experiments in Structural Neighborliness

In the preceding sections, I have contrasted the civic and narrative schematics of Carey's *Account* and Jones and Allen's *Narrative* to outline an ethics of neighborliness, a civic ethos animated by a sensibility made material or "real" through concrete actions. The neighborly focus on being useful to others, on being a good neighbor rather than finding the good neighbor, creates bonds between citizens independent of other forms of association—familial, racial, economic, national, and so on. While, as I have suggested, neighborliness ultimately manifests in concrete actions between individuals, its logics have implications for how civic institutions take shape. Neighborly practices ultimately produce neighborly institutions; the ethos and actions that characterize the neighborly citizen also characterize the neighborly state.

Jones and Allen's *Narrative* contributed to a tradition of writing from Anthony Benezet, Granville Sharpe, Benjamin Banneker, and other antislavery activists drawing on the political resonances of neighborliness via the Samaritan's narrative to articulate a global notion of belonging.[136] In *The Just Limitation of Slavery in the Laws of God* (1776), Sharpe explains, "No nation therefore whatever, can now be lawfully excluded as *strangers*, according to that uncharitable sense of the word *stranger* in which the Jews were apt to distinguish all other nations from themselves . . . *all men* are now to be esteemed '*brethren and neighbours.*' "[137] Banneker uses a similar approach in his 1791 letter to Thomas Jefferson: "It is the indispensible duty of those, who maintain for themselves the rights of human nature, and who possess the obligations of Christianity, to extend their power and influence to the relief of every part of the human race, from whatever burden or oppression they may unjustly labor under."[138] Sharpe and Banneker use neighborliness to combine an appeal to moral equality with a call for social justice. First, they establish the equality of all people—enslaved and free, European and African—as a moral and, in Sharpe's argument, a legal principle extending beyond the confines of a single nation or state, an equality stated in religious precepts yet applicable to a secular state. For Sharpe, the Samaritan parable's articulation of neighborliness suggests that nations can no longer use national differences, however defined, to justify the oppression or exclusion of others: all nations and peoples are to be respected. Second, they argue that acknowledging this moral equality, what Banneker translates into secular terms as "those inestimable laws, which preserved to you the rights of human nature," requires the state and/or the individual to actively work so that not only slaves but also "every individual, of whatever rank or distinction," can "equally enjoy the blessings thereof."[139] For Sharpe, this principle underwrites part of the legal case against enslavement in the British empire. For Banneker, it sets up emancipation and social justice as litmus tests for the "sincerity" of early U.S. republicanism. Banneker's rebuke of Jefferson transforms the self-love and the ability to imagine oneself in another's position (the sympathy in Adam Smith's *Moral Sentiments*) into a more radical neighborly sensibility leading to incorporative, reparative citizenship.

Read through Sharpe and Banneker, the neighborly practices modeled in *Narrative* are not a supplement to republican citizenship. Rather, neighborliness gets to the heart of the kind of society republican governance could produce: one in which citizens "love for yourselves, and for those inestimable laws" of human rights lead them to feel a duty to apply, in Banneker's words, "the most active effusion of [their] exertions" to ensure that all people have equal access to the benefits thereof.[140] Or, to put it in terms familiar to *Narrative*, they have a "duty to do all the good" they can for their "suffering fellow mortals," because it is the best way to secure the good of all.[141] Just as the good neighbor makes neighbors out of strangers, the good citizen or the good state makes citizens out of strangers. *Narrative*'s appendices, including addresses to "Those Who Keep Slaves, and Approve of the Practice," "To the People of Color," and to the "Friends of Him Who Hath No Helper," take up these principles and shift focus from immediate events to "a refutation of some censures" and these structural questions.[142]

Jones and Allen's "*Refutation*"—a term commanding the same typeset in the pamphlet's title as "*Narrative*," suggesting that the two modes of address were coextensive—encompasses answers to developing theories of racial difference implicit in Thomas Jefferson's query: "What further is to be done with them?"[143] Indeed, the expanded cadre of "some late publications" undoubtedly included recent legislation such as the Fugitive Slave Act (February 1793) and the Naturalization Law (1790), as well as the recent exchange between Banneker and Jefferson. *Narrative* proper, then, was of paramount importance but not necessarily the pamphlet's ultimate focus, providing a case study for the kind of citizenship that could take shape after emancipation, a test not only of black freedom but also of the kind of civic space that could result from contact between ostensible strangers. The addresses, in turn, make explicit the paradigms implicit in *Narrative*'s account of neighborliness, applying its example to a broader agenda centered not just on emancipation but also on the full incorporation of black Americans, enslaved and free, as U.S. citizens.

Where yellow fever accounts typically linked blackness with the chaos and "dissolution" the crisis caused, *Narrative* links it with good management and restoration.[144] As the crisis increased, so did the FAS and other black citizens' role in the city's infrastructure.[145] During the fever, the FAS and FAC became increasingly integrated in Philadelphia's government: they paid workers, bled victims, and vetted volunteers, and Clarkson went to Jones and Allen for help regulating rising fees. They provided a bridge between the official committee and city government and those citizens outside this official organization. Prisoners wanting to volunteer, for instance, applied to the elders of the FAC "who met to consider what they could do for the help of the sick," and it was under their supervision that the prisoners "were liberated, on condition of their doing the duty of nurses at the hospital at Bush Hill."[146] The transaction showed the FAC supplementing and, in some cases, replacing the gutted government infrastructure with their own chain of command. Instead of calling on the mayor or the official relief committee, prisoners, many of them black, "applied" to the elders of the African Church. In the absence of a court, the black religious organization filled in the judicial gap.

Tellingly, it is in the context of this work that Rush calls Jones and Allen "two African citizens" in his own *Account*.[147] Similarly, while describing the state of disorder at Bush Hill, *Narrative* reports, "only two black women were at this time in the hospital, and they were retained and the others discharged, when it was reduced to order and good government."[148] Again, their narrative pinpoints an omission in Carey's *Account*, which mentions a "profligate, abandoned set of nurses and attendants . . . hardly any of could character" who "rioted on the provisions and comforts prepared to the sick" without the "smallest appearance of order."[149] These women of "good character" represent the ordinary black folk whose significance has only now reached the light of day.[150] And through them, black presence becomes a central ingredient in the city's return to "good government."[151] Rather than a threat to citizenship and government or a sign of their absence, as in Carey's *Account*, the yellow fever epidemic opens up avenues for citizenship for Jones, Allen, and other black citizens called upon to fill in the gaps in white civic organization.

This confidence and managerial acumen presents a measure of stability within Philadelphia as well as the suggestion that internally, the free African community has its *own* institutions that shadow and, during the fever and the crisis of white government, function *more efficiently than* the white-run government. In this context, *Narrative* not only showcases black benevolence but also, more importantly, demonstrates the strength of black *institutions* with their own "peculiar" brand of republican self-government providing an ethics and structure to guide a black civil society, with Jones and Allen acting as representatives between it and the city.[152] These institutions provided a tactical position, an internal organization and public presence, from which black citizens could not only "make use of the cracks" in established structures of power but also structure their own projects in republican governance.[153] They had limited and uneven involvement with the city's civic sphere before the fever, often petitioning the city for the ability to provide services for black communities that no other institution would. The FAS, for instance, arranged to lease part of Potter's Field (formerly the city's Stranger's Burial Ground) from the city in 1790, conducted marriage ceremonies, and kept records of marriages and births.[154] At times parallel to and intersecting with white publics, this black counterpublic "oscillate[d]" between positions in relation to other publics.[155] The epidemic presented a momentary break that gave free Africans, the institutions they built, and other marginal groups the opportunity to practice citizenship on the public stage in ways heretofore limited by racial logics governing access to the public sphere.

In Jones and Allen's hands, each of these moments come to signify black citizens' civic power, their desire for and implementation of modes of self-government, not just as free people treated as "slaves of the community" but also as citizens who operate as partners in an increasingly dynamic civic arrangement.[156] In each instance, the notion of management suggested in Carey's civic republican model shifts from how institutions and the state could reign in variously interested constituencies to how institutions and the state might best empower and facilitate mutual aid among citizens. That is, the neighborliness animating individual actors in *Narrative* changes the relation between citizens and institutions. Where Carey's respectable citizens show their respectability in terms of their management, *Narrative*'s leaders (Jones, Allen, Rush, Clarkson) enable other citizens to join in the collective recovery effort: Clarkson reaches out to free Africans (even if under false pretenses); Rush trains Jones and Allen to bleed and tend the ill; the FAC, in turn, liberates and superintends prisoners; Jones and Allen train people as nurses; and so on.[157] While *Narrative* does not eliminate all criteria for authority or inclusion—Jones and Allen report that they screened prisoners before releasing them—it does suggest that these criteria should be dynamically based on meeting the community's needs. This ever-widening cast of societies suggests that the successes in Philadelphia's recovery were not based on the strength of a virtuous elite per se but rather on the ability of its various constituencies to recognize the potential partner in each other.

Jones and Allen turn to this broader sense of potential in their appendices as they take on the epistemologies that enabled black exclusion and enslavement and one of their most famous purveyors: Thomas Jefferson. Scholars have tended to read the "Censures Thrown upon them in some late Publications" in the title as an extension of this local discussion and direct reference to yellow fever accounts positing black theft and immunity, Carey's *Account* most prominently among them. The rhetorical resonances with Banneker's pamphlet and signal words throughout the appendices, such as "experience" and "experiment," however, also signal that these "late publications" included Jefferson's *Notes on the State of Virginia*. As Gene Jarrett notes, Jefferson's language and tone "must have been specter" for black intellectuals "as haunting as that of English intellectuals, who looked down on colonial America" and compelled Jefferson to write *Notes* in the first place.[158] And while work on *Narrative* has consistently tied Jones and Allen's arguments to Jefferson implicitly, I think it is important to note that the two men may have had Jefferson in mind very explicitly in much the same way that David Walker and subsequent writers appropriate him as representative (both as a type and as a political voice) of white supremacy.[159]

The "Address to Those Who Keep Slaves, and Approve of the Practice" in particular builds on *Narrative*'s examples of the individual and collective efforts of black citizens during the fever and its model of an incorporative neighborly ethics of citizenship to propose an "experiment." "We believe," they write, "if you would try the experiment of taking a few black children, cultivate their minds with the same care, and let them have the same prospect in view, as to living in the world, as you would with your own children, you would find upon the trial, they were not inferior in mental endowments."[160] The proposal responds to Jefferson's wish in his reply to Banneker "to see a good system commenced, for raising the condition, both of their [slaves'] body and mind, to what it ought to be."[161] "No body wishes more than I do," he proclaims in the opening lines, "to see such proofs as you exhibit, that nature has given to our black brethren talents equal to those of the other colors of men; and that the appearance of the want of them, is owning merely to the degraded condition of their existence, both in Africa and America."[162] Jones and Allen's framing their response to racist logics as an experiment based on observation and experience signifies on late eighteenth-century empiricism and views of character as malleable, open to "cultivation" through proper care.[163]

Ultimately, "Address" harnesses neighborliness as both citizenship practice and empirical method to produce a formula for black citizenship. Read next to Query 14, Banneker's "Letter," and Jefferson's response, "Address" appears to be not only borrowing from (or echoing) Banneker's rhetorical strategy but also refuting Jefferson specifically point by point. The neighborly argument extends to slave owners as a plan for emancipation and to former slaves, on whom Jones and Allen "feel the obligation" to "impress" on their minds the doctrine that "we may all forgive you, as we wish to be forgiven." The passage may seem overly obsequious, but set against Jefferson's use of "natural enmity" as justification for not emancipating slaves or, at best (relatively speaking), the raison d'être for colonization projects, Jones and Allen are clearly and methodically answering specific objections already in circulation in the same way that *Narrative* responds to specific accusations during the recent epidemic.

Where Jefferson posits black inferiority as a given—whether as a natural trait in *Notes* or as a result of "condition" in his reply to Banneker—the "Address to Those Who Own Slaves" sees confirmation bias and faulty data, suggesting that neither inherent inferiority nor racial degradation is the case. To claims that the slaves' "baseness is incurable" or, as Jefferson argues, "the blacks, whether originally a distinct race, or made distinct by time and circumstances, are inferior to the whites in the endowments both of body and mind,"[164] Jones and Allen present their own "degree of experience," the term straddling aesthetic (study of senses) and scientific (study of phenomena) discourse: "a black man, although reduced to the most abject state human nature is capable of, short of real madness, can think, reflect, and feel injuries, although it may not be with the same degree of keen resentment and revenge, that you who have been and are our great oppressors, would manifest if reduced to the pitiable condition of slave."[165] Just as black citizens displayed more real sensibility during the fever, enslaved Africans have maintained a remarkable degree of humanity even in the midst of their enslavement. The passage directly confronts Jefferson's claims that enslaved Africans' "griefs are transient," that "afflictions . . . are less felt, and sooner forgotten," with the suggestion not only that Africans feel as deeply as Europeans but also that Jefferson and others' expectations of "resentment and revenge" bespeak more a white propensity for violence or revenge than the lack of feeling on the part of the enslaved.[166] The "Address" opens with the suggestion that looking for "superior good conduct" from the enslaved would be "unreasonable," and yet "experience" has shown Jones and Allen that enslaved Africans also exceed reasonable expectations. The double move questions standard paradigms measuring the humanity of slaves, challenges the premise that such measurements can and ought to be made, and recalibrates the comparison from one between ancient Greeks and Romans to one between contemporary enslaved Africans and their white masters. Again, the comparison gestures back to *Narrative*'s scenes of black citizens overcoming the dread of the moment—a dread they shared with white citizens—as they went about their work. Both points emphasize black self-regulation over white self-interest; both points build on Jones and Allen's experiential authority and narrative perspective, not necessarily to question the effects of enslavement or standards of civilization but rather to suggest that white observers like Jefferson do not have sufficient experience to report accurate data.

More than an argument that black citizens were more sensible than white citizens or a competition over innate differences between master and slave, *Narrative* and "Address" assume the legitimacy of black observation and testimony, even as they call attention to how white normativity and the violence of enslavement not only fostered an antagonistic sensibility but also blocked white observers' ability to be sensible subjects. This point goes for slaveholders and abolitionists alike. *Narrative* establishes the importance of firsthand observation early on, suggesting that "respectable citizens" could not relate the proceedings of the black people but rather had to solicit Jones and Allen's authority, "[seeing] that from our situation . . . we had it more fully and generally in our power, to know and observe the conduct and behavior of those that were so employed."[167] Their observations of the nuances of bleeding as a cure—they note, for instance, that bleeding at the early onset of symptoms had greater effects than at later stages and that the patient's positive emotional state was correlated with recovery—further establish their empiricist credentials, their ability to analyze evidence and practically apply their conclusions. The "Address," in turn, not only applies this observational "power" as a counter to Jefferson, who appeals to scientific "experience" and his own "observations" in *Notes*, but also advocates including Rush, who eventually admits the fallacy of black immunity to the yellow fever but who also thought black skin a curable condition.[168]

Jones and Allen's request for the experiment of education combines this sensory empiricism with a neighborly civic and social ethos. Education was essential to the production of future citizens, and national debates about education swirled around questions of how best to educate citizens for republican citizenship. Rush, for instance, argues, "Our Schools of learning, by producing one general, and uniform system of education, will render the mass of the people more homogeneous, and thereby fit them more easily for uniform and peaceable government."[169] He saw these institutions as training grounds "to convert men into republican machines."[170] The homogeneity many saw as essential to republican government could be produced through a unified system of education, offsetting other points of difference. The students coming out of this system, joined in the same program of intellectual and physical instruction, will form "such ties to each other, as add greatly to the obligations of mutual benevolence."[171] These ties reproduce the structures of neighborly contact created during the fever, structures that, if temporary, created a society based in mutual aid rather than competition or hierarchy.

The proposal of educating black children "with the same care" and "prospect in view" as white children challenges those who would try this experiment to try it in a neighborly frame and confronts directly gradual emancipation practices in Pennsylvania that, as Erica Armstrong Dunbar catalogues, involved indentures with the proviso that children be taught to read "if capable."[172] The "Address" takes the unspoken assumption of incapacity off the table. Their "care" demands the same degree of rigor and breadth as that for white children, the same training for republican government, creating the same "ties" between them. Training black children with the same "prospect in view" suggests that they be trained for full political and economic participation in the republic as members of what Rush calls a "great, and equally enlightened family" in which benevolence flows horizontally between fellow citizens, rather than vertically between citizens and (their) former slaves or lesser sorts.[173] That is, they should be educated with the expectation of their contribution and with the assurance that access to the full range of liberties will be available to them. And this training should not be framed as some favor for which black citizens will remain in debt but rather as a basic principle of republican governance. Beginning with children in their formative years would produce a new generation fit for participation in a "uniform and peaceable government," because they would have received the same republican training that commentators like Rush prescribed for the general public.

Neighborliness as an approach to emancipation, then, goes beyond momentary benevolence in the face of inequality and oppression, requiring instead structural adjustments and long-term planning.[174] This approach contrasts sharply to the rhetoric of Jefferson or even antislavery groups and activists, such as the Quaker-dominated PAS, Benezet, and Rush, who viewed Africans, free and enslaved, as objects of study or benevolence and a problem to be solved, but rarely as partners or fellow citizens.[175] By suggesting a trial of educating children, rather than the trial of unaided emancipation (gradual or immediate) or a trial of indentureship, the "Address to Those Who Own Slaves" subtly critiques the efficacy of gradual emancipation programs (or at least the logics of pupilage underwriting them), suggesting that emancipation and equal access to central institutions like education were inseparable. Just as the Samaritan of the New Testament or *Narrative*'s poor black man attended to the suffering beyond the immediate, short-term, injuries, so too must any project of emancipation be accompanied by a program of structural adjustment. This experiment requires an approach to policy that rejects conventional wisdom, producing the fellow citizenship that racist logics preempt by encouraging a view of free and enslaved Africans as neighbor-citizens rather than potential threats. Such a program follows the neighborly logic and challenge to white nationalism articulated in both Banneker's letter and *Narrative*: make the good neighbor's incorporative move; do unto black children as you would your own, and they will become as your own children in the process.

Jones and Allen's call for an educational experiment requires less a leap of faith on the part of white citizens and more a larger study building on the data that Jones and Allen's Philadelphia and other like "experiments" already provide.[176] In the short time during the epidemic and under intense duress, Jones, Allen, and others learn bleeding techniques from Rush (or, more accurately, from "copies of the printed direction for curing the fever"); coordinate a corps of nurses, carters, and other relief workers; and manage convict laborers.[177] Individual black Philadelphians and black societies acted out of an ethics of neighborhood that sustained them where the bonds of society appeared to fail almost everywhere else. How much more could black citizens or any other marginalized group contribute to the common weal if their children were given the advantage of formal instruction under conditions in which success was expected? *Narrative* demonstrates that this community of black citizens, finding freedom during the crisis, has proven itself more than ready for the task of republican citizenship.

At the same time, however, *Narrative* and the "Address" speak to a community's disillusionment upon realizing that, despite demonstrating their collective public spirit and responsibility in terms that their erstwhile white judges should have recognized and honored, no amount of "proof" would be sufficient to overcome impediments that had nothing to do with black capacity and everything to do with white power. Again, this offers a distinct contrast to nascent gradual emancipation programs. Benezet's patronage form of gradual emancipation involved registering, supervised labor, and training so that freedpeople "might gradually become useful members of the community" and "become industrious subjects" over time.[178] Jones and Allen's call to educate black children with the same "prospects" as white children directly contradicts Benezet's assumption that newly freed slaves and, more important, their children would require any kind of supervision, patronage, or management beyond those already provided for free white citizens. They reject both the long timeline assumed in Benezet's and similar gradual schemes and the implication that formerly enslaved people owed some form of service to either their former masters or the state. Instead, "Address" suggests that the state, enslavers, and "those who approve of the practice" owe reparations for their sanctioning enslavement.

Seizing the platform that Carey's *Account* provided, Jones and Allen take the opportunity to extend their public liberties into spheres that were otherwise out of reach. They present neighborliness as a citizenship practice animated by a real sensibility that creates the permeable civic space. They then mobilize this political argument in the service of an antislavery appeal and call for structural readjustments that would ease the transition between enslavement and citizenship. *Narrative* reveals the extent to which black print production can reflect the inner workings of black counterpublics, but it also suggests that even in such spaces, black writers sought and found ways to assert authority, not just presence, within civil society. Despite Jones and Allen's efforts, however, the coming decades were characterized more by decline and retrenchment than progress, with even white supporters basing that support on the need for "racial surveillance." This trend would lead both men to reconsider their future in the United States and to give serious consideration to emigration projects.[179]

Still, *Narrative* had an effect. On April 4, 1794, about four months after *Narrative*'s first printing, Carey issued a pamphlet ostensibly in response to a flyer by "Argus" accusing Carey of opportunism, but he also pointedly confronted Jones and Allen's *Narrative*. By then, Carey's fourth edition had replaced his quotes from Lining about black immunity with a paragraph debunking the theory, and in the fifth edition, he had changed the section accusing black workers of extortion from the "vilest of the blacks" to "some of those who acted in that capacity [as nurses], both coloured and white."[180] As Brooks and others have noted, however, Carey re-presents the error of black immunity as a boon for white Philadelphians: "The error that prevailed on this subject," he writes, "had a very salutary effect; for at an early period of the disorder, hardly any white nurses could be procured; and, had the negroes been equally terrified, the sufferings of the sick, great as they actually were, would have been exceedingly aggravated."[181] Even as Carey recants an earlier mistake, he does so in a way that takes away from the merit of black workers.

Jones and Allen's words also continued to resonate with the coming generation of black activists. David Walker builds on their notion of world citizenship and piety in his *Appeal*; Hosea Easton picks up the Samaritan formula in his *A Treatise on the Intellectual Character, and Civil and Political Condition of the Colored People of the U. States* (1837), arguing that only by acting "the part of the good Samaritan" can the nation "open an effectual door through which sympathies can flow, and by which a reciprocity of sentiment and interest can take place"; and Robert Purvis cites events during the fever in his 1837 defense of black suffrage in Pennsylvania, asking, "Does this speak an enmity which would abuse the privileges of civil liberty to the injury of the whites?"[182] Purvis's words seem to echo Jones and Allen's. Each case references 1790s Philadelphia as a touchstone in the theoretical and historical development of black citizenship.

Narrative combines two central threads that subsequent chapters will unfold in more detail: black writer's engagement with the critical political concerns of their day as a function of their own lived experiences and how the texts they produce navigate a web of publics and audiences.[183] Neighborliness does not eliminate interests or disagreement altogether. Indeed, a neighborly approach to citizenship requires a mode of participatory politics that maximizes contact and exchange between citizens to ensure that one citizen's neighborliness does not turn into unilateral oppression. *Narrative* itself signals the importance of deliberation to neighborly institutions through Jones and Allen's constant references to their own deliberations, among themselves and with the mayor, during the crisis. It is to the role of participatory politics in citizenship that *The Practice of Citizenship* now turns. Activists in the coming years become even more focused on formal political participation, but as the black state conventions reveal, the results are also more paradoxical. As the next chapter demonstrates, negotiating the contending imperatives of practical political ends, contemporary political discourse, and the need to persuade an increasingly hostile white public produced performative texts that provide a meta-commentary on the nature of U.S. citizenship.

CHAPTER 2

Circulating Citizenship in the Black State Conventions of the 1840s

We have launched into a new position. Our fathers sought personal freedom—we now contend for political freedom.
—"An Appeal to the Colored Citizens of Pennsylvania" (1848)

The equality of political rights, which is the first mark of American citizenship, was proclaimed in the accepted presence of its absolute denial.
—Judith N. Shklar, *American Citizenship: The Quest for Inclusion* (1991)

Behind the mask of deference lies the authentic demand.
—Samuel Otter, *Philadelphia Stories* (2010)

In the decade after the State of Pennsylvania's 1838 constitution disenfranchised its black citizens, black Pennsylvanians signaled a more aggressive approach to citizenship and activism. While the 1848 Convention of Colored Citizens' distinction between personal freedom and political freedom understates the political nature of the previous generation's work—which included sending petitions to state and federal governments, founding black mutual aid societies and the African Methodist Episcopal Church, and initiating the National Colored Convention Movement—the comparison does signal a change in citizenship practices between the 1790s and the 1840s. By the 1840s, voting had become one of the central citizenship practices and means of policing the civic imaginary: it was a symbol of fellow citizenship among the men who voted and a reminder that those men (variously defined by race and class) and women not allowed to vote were not only inferior but also under the power and protection of those who did.[1] As Judith N. Shklar notes, political rights in the form of voting emerged as "the first mark of American citizenship," and that mark was quickly consolidated with and encoded through whiteness.[2]

This chapter examines the black state conventions of the 1840s as political documents central to an understanding of citizenship practices in the antebellum United States. Recognizing the changing significance of voting in national civic discourse and their own political needs beyond emancipation, black conventioneers interpreted voting and political participation more broadly as *the* defining citizenship practices, the rights and rites that connected citizens in a community, and a citizen's most powerful defense in a republican government. Philip S. Foner and George E. Walker rightly claim, "For keen analyses of the issues outlined and for breadth of research and argument, these addresses are among the outstanding political documents of the period," reflecting "a cross-section of this community" more than any other aggregate of texts outside of the black press itself.[3] And, as work coming out of the Colored Conventions Project at the University of Delaware is beginning to make clear, these conventions represent a host of print and social interactions that we are only just beginning to document, let alone theorize. The black state conventions offer key arguments about participatory politics as a practice of citizenship, and the form itself—a combination of public gatherings and printed proceedings—offers an alternate trajectory for how participatory politics could be enacted. Our tendency to focus on Douglass, Garnet, and other participants individually has obscured how the conventions developed as collective and dialogic institutions in which black political thought emerged not just as an intellectual project but as a set of citizenship practices enacted through print culture. While many scholars quote from these texts for their documentary and evidentiary value, here I foreground the black state conventions as distinct and important political and cultural phenomena, as important as the black press, the slaves' narratives, and the national conventions to our understanding of early black political and print culture.[4]

Delegates envisioned these texts as living documents: simultaneously a manifestation of collective black political life and a means for sustaining that life even as states attempted to cut it off. The conventions provide, in the words of the 1848 "Appeal to the Colored Citizens of Pennsylvania," "a living commentary on the *principle* that governs American legislation, and controls American justice."[5] John Ernest has described the proceedings of the national conventions in similar terms. They are, Ernest writes, "collective performances designed to be a representative embodiment of an imagined African American community."[6] In addition to this historiographic significance, which is the focus of Ernest's study, these conventions, both national and local, not only represent an "imagined African-American community" but also telegraph the terms under which that community was and desired itself to be a part of a larger U.S. national community.

Rather than a single act, exclusive property, or individual decision, the conventions figure political participation as a shared, vital, moving substance and invoke tropes of circulation—blood, power, people, water, and texts—to theorize these practices. The 1840 Convention of the Colored Inhabitants of the State of New York, for instance, describes the franchise as "the life blood of political existence."[7] Taking my lead from the conventions themselves, this chapter uses circulation as a heuristic for analyzing how the conventions functioned as an archive and repertoire of black citizenship—a constellation of texts and gatherings, beginning well in advance of the actual conventions and continuing well past delegates' departure from the physical meeting space. As I outline in this chapter's first section, the emphasis on circulation—in print and otherwise—takes my analysis of the black state conventions well beyond the conventions as singular events or the minutes as self-contained documents. This extended print and public purview also takes us well beyond the view, encouraged in the minutes themselves, of conventions as predominantly male spaces. P. Gabrielle Foreman, Sarah Patterson, and Jim Casey note in their introduction to the Colored Conventions Project that women's work outside the official delegate structure "illustrate[s] the ways in which Black women challenged traditional beliefs about women's place in public society."[8] The male delegates to New York's 1840 convention developed circulation-based theories claiming their right to the franchise as a part of an explicitly rendered manhood citizenship. In so doing, they refused an intersectional critique of citizenship. And yet, just as black men used the convention form to enact participatory politics despite racially ascriptive voting legislation, black women used it and these same theories of circulation to promote gender equality within the convention movement itself and the nation as a whole. I draw on the Ohio conventions in particular as sites where black women placed this gendered and raced production of citizenship in sharp relief.

Reading the black state conventions as a matrix of textual production and physical meetings also invites us to reconsider the printed proceedings as circulating texts that convention organizers envisioned as having the power to change established configurations of citizenship. As I demonstrate through the Pennsylvania conventions, these documents (including minutes, addresses, petitions, and reports) extended and circulated black civic presences via the periodical press and pamphlets, formally modeling and enacting the delegates' vision of republican citizenship as the texts moved among white and black audiences and state institutions. In the state conventions' most radical appeal directly to voters, delegates invoke the people's authority over state institutions and their power to revise or dissolve the civic compact when these institutions fail to be responsive to the people. A new political community materializes not through the formal franchise but rather through audiences' reading, consuming, and acting on these new civic texts. The black state conventions, then, are important not only because of the arguments they make for and about suffrage but also for the work they do *as* texts, as performative speech acts that seek to manufacture the very citizenship practices from which the delegates had been excluded.[9]

Why Voting? Why State Based? Citizenship Practices in the 1840s

In this section, I offer a brief history of the black state convention movement as a distinct counterpart to the more recognized national colored convention movement and how the rise of the black state conventions maps onto a shift in how antebellum Americans linked their political identities to voting as *the* expression of citizenship. Here, I also want to emphasize that localized differences in how white supremacy shaped law necessitated different approaches between states in a way that may have made national conventions more difficult to organize in the 1840s in particular but that created conditions under which state conventions proliferated. This section also offers a general sketch of how convention organizers used print, particularly newspapers, throughout the process to cultivate a sense of urgency and to produce black political presences in states that increasingly refused to recognize black citizenship. Maintaining and circulating a public presence as an explicitly political community was crucial to the black state conventions' overall project.

As states began instituting universal white male suffrage, democratic governance, particularly in the form of voting, became increasingly identified as *the* defining act of full citizenship.[10] As Barbara Welke notes, in the republic's early decades, "the right to vote was not freighted with the political and social significance it would acquire as the century progressed; the rights of citizens were yet in the making." This significance accrued, argues Welke, as gradual emancipation, westward expansion, and waged labor posed the "first major threat" to assumptions about white male citizenship.[11] If, as David Waldstreicher observes, nationalist celebrations during the revolutionary and early national periods revealed an "indeterminacy about who were 'the people' and who were 'the citizens,' or true political actors," the expansion of voting through state constitutional conventions in the 1820s through the 1840s helped reconcile some of this indeterminacy.[12] Voting emerged as the "very practice" of citizenship, a political counterpart to nationalist rituals like parades that consolidated the image of active citizenship and a united white citizenry in the public imaginary.[13] White men could imagine themselves collectively exercising their privileges as sovereigns and see the results of that collective action, particularly after Andrew Jackson's election in 1828.

Even as suffrage served as one of the primary political and cultural points of identification for white male citizenship, it became an even more powerful symbol of dis-identification and political and legal disempowerment for black citizens. The linkage of voting and white manhood resulted in an ascriptive conflation of citizenship practice with race and gender that provided a national standard for citizenship identity in the absence of explicit federal guidelines. Citizens who could not vote or had limited access to other rights, then, were not fully citizens before the law. Instead, as Georgia state courts argued in 1843, such people were in a perpetual "state of pupilage."[14] The restriction of the right to vote contributed to what historian Douglas Bradburn describes as the "denization" of black citizens. States increasingly differentiated black Americans from white as "inhabitants," "denizens," or wards of the state who had some basic rights and obligations (rights to property and public education in some states, tax requirements, etc.) but whose status varied from state to state.[15] Under these terms, black citizens had the burdens of legal culpability associated with personhood without the privileges and protections of full citizenship.[16] By the end of the 1840s, only Maine, Massachusetts, Vermont, and Rhode Island offered unrestricted suffrage to black men.[17] Over the previous two decades, other states had instituted or were in the process of instituting universal white male suffrage but disenfranchised virtually all black men in the process. The loss of the franchise became foundational to further state-sanctioned stripping of black civil rights and symbolized a forcible removal of black citizens from the civic imaginary itself.[18] This logic created a circular argument: black men cannot vote, so they are not full citizens; black men are not full citizens and therefore should not be allowed to vote (without qualification).

This state-based nature of the functional institutions of racial oppression, that is how civic and social exclusion operated in public policy and social custom, created some of the tensions scholars have noted within national movements.[19] Take New York and Pennsylvania, the first states to hold black conventions, for instance. The difference in the two populations' historical experience and the difference in *how* the states enacted their policies—property qualification versus outright denial—affected how each group proceeded.[20] In New York the state's $250 property requirement for voting sanctioned, if in a limited way, black political participation, but this participation was tempered by the economic consequences of enslavement and the state's 1821 gradual emancipation provision, which, at the very least, fostered the perception of dependence on the state's Whig and abolitionist establishment, the fear (manufactured or otherwise) that black New Yorkers were their pawns, and the sense that black New Yorkers needed continued tutelage in the ways of citizenship before joining the polity.[21]

If black activists in New York seemed more willing to emphasize direct involvement with the political process through voting and supporting specific parties, it might also be because they had Pennsylvania as an example of where inactivity on these fronts could lead. Pennsylvania, in contrast, did not constitutionally restrict black suffrage until its 1838 constitution explicitly limited voting to "every white freeman."[22] However, the threat of white violence, coupled with the success of some black communities, particularly in Philadelphia, in creating civic organizations and working through and with white politicians and activists, may have made overt political maneuvers seem less urgent. When Pennsylvania did ratify the constitutional revision restricting the vote to white men, black Pennsylvanians were just as insistent as their New York counterparts in protesting the change and, when that failed, pushing for revision. A constitutionally required ten-year hold on any amendments in Pennsylvania made appeals for legislation less productive than calls for wholesale constitutional change, and this legal wrinkle also complicates easy comparisons of strategy between the two states. Western states like Ohio, Illinois, and Michigan had even stricter rules governing black movement that made convention participants question whether the state and federal government even recognized them as citizens, particularly in the wake of the Compromise of 1850.[23] These complexities prompted James McCune Smith to lament in a May 12, 1854, article for *Frederick Douglass' Paper*, "You cannot pick out of five hundred free colored men in the free States who equally labor under the same species of oppression."

In light of these interstate differences, black activists were continually balancing the benefits of national conventions (particularly for antislavery initiatives, economic uplift, and institution building) and local associations calibrated to deal with the specificity of local politics and variations in racist practices. During an 1840 debate about reviving the national conventions, the *Colored American* typifies many antebellum commentators' vacillation between national and local forms:

> State conventions called for a local and special object, fixed upon by the people, would be likely to be regarded as matters especially their own, matters with the continuance or overthrow of which, depended their own rise or fall, and they would be likely to adopt measures with greater harmony, and carry them out with more efficiency, than in our opinion, would be done by a National Convention, and each State taking into consideration their own local disabilities, would answer all the purposes of a National Convention.[24]

Local specificity was critical, because where the rhetoric of citizenship had nationalist tones, the instrumentalities of citizenship, the institutions that outlined the contours and limits of who could or could not be a citizen, were primarily under state control. It was a matter of scale: focusing on the national, as the *Colored American* suggests, obscured the many more local modes of political organization that were successful, at least for a time, in creating a sustained black political presence. At the same time, the statement warns that focusing too intently on national black organizations and a national "black press" to obtain answers to questions about black political strategy and theory can operate anachronistically, flattening and imposing post–Civil War federal politics on what was essentially a far more locally determined political field. These activists were thinking nationally, but their national political sensibilities were in dialogue with and framed by exigencies and interests.

The black state conventions were a central feature of this political paradigm. As the national convention movement lost steam in the early 1840s and as the rift between black activists and the white antislavery establishment widened, these local meetings provided a forum for discussing issues germane to the particularities of each state. As the *Colored American* posits, success on the state level could more efficiently accomplish change on the national level because organizations at the state level could focus on single issues—education, suffrage, desegregation, and so on—that were of more immediate concern to activists of all stripes, allowing for tighter organization, strategic alliances, and efficient use of limited resources. And, for them, any progress on this political and social front translated to progress in the antislavery cause. "Augustine," writing to the *Colored American* from Pittsburg, Pennsylvania, in 1839 sums up the larger tactic: black citizens should "endeavor to secure their rights, in their own state, before they begin to contend for the rights of citizens of other states," for, as Augustine continues, a good general avoids "engaging too many points at once" or engaging on too wide a front.[25] In either case, the lack of resources would invariably lead to crushing defeat. Augustine, who argued for a national convention just two years earlier (that is, before the ratification of the 1838 Pennsylvania constitution), suggests picking the most important and most achievable battles, and for him, no battle was more important than the suffrage and no tactic more calibrated to win than a state convention.

Beginning and Ending in Print: Black State Conventions and/in Print Culture

Groups organized specifically to address constitutional franchise restrictions date back to at least 1837, when Robert Purvis and a group of black activists meeting in Pittsburgh formally protested the soon-to-be-successful attempt to disenfranchise black men in Pennsylvania.[26] Their "Appeal of Forty Thousand Citizens, Threatened with Disfranchisement, to the People of Pennsylvania" outlines the legal and historical basis for black citizenship in Pennsylvania, with a blistering critique of justifications for black disenfranchisement.[27] Between 1840 and 1861, state conventions occurred in New York, Pennsylvania, Indiana, Iowa, Maine (with New Hampshire), Michigan, Ohio, New Jersey, Connecticut, Maryland, Illinois, Massachusetts, California, and Missouri. The "colored inhabitants" of New York were the first to organize a statewide convention expressly addressing franchise rights in 1840, and the New Yorkers met in three subsequent conventions between 1841 and 1845 for the express purpose of repealing the property requirement for black men.[28] Michigan, Pennsylvania, Indiana, and Ohio all held at least one state convention during the 1840s. After the passage of the Fugitive Slave Act of 1850, black citizens would hold similar conventions in most other free states focused on coping with new threats of reenslavement in addition to local issues.

These conventions constituted more than a single event. They were composed of a constellation of events and texts ranging from debates on the necessity for a convention and initial meetings and advertisements to select delegates to the convention itself and the circulation and public reading of "Proceedings" afterward. Indeed, much of the convention process—issuing calls, passing resolutions, committee reports, debating, and voting—was geared toward generating this publicity. The conventions began in print with calls issued months before the meetings and circulated in black and abolitionist newspapers such as *Colored American*, *Liberator*, *North Star* (in the late 1840s), and *National Anti-Slavery Standard*, as well as more mainstream papers like the *New York Daily Tribune*.[29] These Calls for a Convention usually included a list of grievances, solicited statistical data and reports on the state of the black population, and asked cities and counties to organize locally to elect delegates and raise money.[30] While practical, this highly publicized organizing process—the resulting calls for local public meetings, the local meetings themselves with their voting on resolutions either supporting or condemning the intended convention, and the printing of these resolutions in newspapers—was also a part of the convention's showcasing black civic power and citizenship in practice.

The delegates often convened in a state's capital city (Harrisburg, Pennsylvania; Albany, New York; Columbus, Ohio; etc.) or another major city in a church or public meetinghouse for daily and evening sessions.[31] While some conventions were open to the public or allowed participants to sign in on site, others required delegates to submit credentials, proving their participation in a local nomination process.[32] During the convention, delegates nominated officers, selected committees, and debated and passed resolutions on staple topics such as education, economic development, temperance and other moral reforms, and general resolutions encouraging the community to continue to work toward its own elevation. The conventions commissioned county and city committees to develop the conventions' programs, including petition drives and "other matters in connection with our rights."[33] Other committees might collect statistical data on the number of temperance and literary societies, employment spreads, the availability of education, and so on. During the evening sessions or public meetings, delegates and other activists offered speeches on pertinent issues, such as education, temperance, and economic development.

After the convention, delegates issued the "Proceedings" or "Minutes" of the convention along with at least one, but typically two to three addresses to the public. One often addressed white "voters" or "people of the state," appealing to them for constitutional amendments and general support in the form of petitions. The other, addressed to "colored fellow citizens," requested their continued support of uplift programs and their participation in the statewide petition drive. Most state conventions printed limited copies of their proceedings in pamphlet form, distributing them to states' assemblies and selling them to support the costs of the convention itself and the costs of carrying out its programs. Many conventions also circulated their addresses, if not the entire proceedings, through newspapers.[34] The documents, often much shorter than proceedings issued from the American Anti-Slavery Society or the National Colored Conventions (probably due to the costs of printing), contained the order of business and election of officers, the convention's resolutions, and the convention's addresses to the public.[35] Some conventions strategically delayed reprinting the proceedings in newspapers to maximize the distribution of pamphlets; the convention organizers could then cite this consumption as a sign of public approval.[36] Even so, the conventions cite the periodical press as *the* medium through which its cause would be fought. As the delegates to the 1848 State Convention of the Colored Citizens of Pennsylvania argue, "We must draft on the benevolence and liberality of the *press*; for without its favourable influence, no cause, however pure, may hope to succeed, and with it truth and justice must prove invincible."[37]

After the state convention, delegates returned home to organize county and city auxiliaries to carry out the convention's petition drive and other programs.[38] This proliferation of documents, a veritable cacophony of voices, and constant agitation created a politicized space—different from a periodical, pamphlet, fair, or other form of publicity, yet combining elements of each—that resonated with recognizable events ranging from the Continental Congress and the U.S. Declaration of Independence to contemporaneous states' conventions.[39] These conventions, then, began and ended in print, producing and circulating documents at each juncture in a way that kept their claims to full citizenship constantly in the public eye.

This expanding vision of the conventions beyond the official proceedings also reveals how much the movement depended on women, whose labor official minutes often obscured. While the state conventions, like their national counterparts, rarely recognized women as delegates and in some cases explicitly barred them, women were deeply involved in this larger constellation of events, from commenting on the convention process in newspapers to providing housing and meals and raising funds to printing and circulating convention documents.[40] As Harry Lewis notes, this work, especially operating boarding houses, provided informal venues where women could engage in and continue the conversations happening at the convention halls.[41] But the conversations did not end there. While arguments for suffrage tended to just refer to men, conventions often included black women as they called on black citizens to help carry out their agenda from petition drives to forming auxiliary committees.[42] As I argue in Chapter 5, parlors were also key sites of political conversation and were less restrictive in terms of gendered participation. Indeed, the 1855 National Colored Convention in Pennsylvania called for auxiliary committees "of practical business men" to "hold a series of conversational meetings" in private residences because they would allow them to "get better access to the minds of our females." In parlors, the convention argued, women could "enter freely into the conversations, and correct ideas would finally be inculcated in the sentiments of wives and mothers as to the important part of the great duties which they are to perform in moulding the future character of our youth for improvement."[43] This explicit invocation of parlors points to a broader recognition among male convention goers of ways women might participate within the movement even as they attempted to restrict this participation through the gendering of space. As the Ohio conventions I analyze later in this chapter suggest, women conventioneers saw their own citizenship practices, their "duties," as expanding well beyond these prescribed roles and spaces, and they used the convention to make those claims, whether men wanted them to or not.

The rest of this chapter focuses on three specific cases studies: the Convention of the Colored Inhabitants of the State of New York in 1840, the state and national conventions held in Ohio, and the 1848 State Convention of the Colored Citizens of Pennsylvania. I turn to New York because it was the first statewide convention and provides a model for how black activists used the form. Through a theory of civic circulation and power, the delegates destabilize race or condition-based arguments against black male suffrage by demonstrating how the lack of franchise rights blocks this circulation and creates the very conditions used to justify the restriction of these same rights. Even as they argue on the basis of common manhood, however, the delegates' circulation-based arguments justify a more radical expansion of republican citizenship. The Ohio conventions offer insight into the key roles women played in organizing and sustaining the black state conventions and, more than other state conventions, ways that Jane P. Merritt, Mary Shadd Cary, Frances Harper, and others made use of the convention platform to register women's citizenship practices in ways that official minutes often rendered invisible. Finally, the 1848 Pennsylvania convention suggests a potentially revolutionary practice. In the tradition of David Walker's *Appeal* and sublime appeals to the people more generally, the convention calls for citizens to take responsibility for an electoral system that, they argue, has substituted arbitrary standards for republican principles of self-government. By circulating these ideas in print in the form of petitions, these citizens could harness their collective civic power to reassert their authority over the state. Exploring these three conventions together helps reveal the reciprocity and synergy between staging, print practices, and political participation in offering an alternative mode of citizenship practice even as official channels continued to close.[44]

Power and Circulation: The Making of a Citizen

The 1840 Convention of the Colored Inhabitants of the State of New York convened in Albany, New York, from August 18 to 20 with approximately 140 delegates representing counties across the state.[45] Building on petition drives begun in the 1830s, the convention was organized to create auxiliary committees to facilitate a concerted petition drive.[46] Delegates proposed and voted on resolutions mostly concerned with the significance of suffrage and the most practical means of convincing the state assembly to abolish property requirements. Finally, the convention appointed a committee of six to draft an "Address to the People of the State of New York," outlining the convention's arguments for unqualified suffrage, and a shorter "Address to Their Colored Fellow Citizens," admonishing them to lend their full support to the petition drive.[47] Both addresses were printed and sold in pamphlet form with the convention's proceedings in New York City.[48] In subsequent years, Henry Highland Garnet, McCune Smith, and other convention participants would submit the convention's proceedings and petitions to the state assembly.[49] When delegates carried the convention's 2,093-signature petition to the assembly's Judiciary Committee in 1841, they represented black political interests physically and textually.[50]

The New York delegates recognized the cultural work of voting as the central conduit of civic power, creating the abstract (if not material) equality essential to citizenship practice. The delegates to the New York Convention of Colored Citizens claim that even "the poorest and humblest citizen" has access to public "respect, deference, and consideration" because he is a voter, a member of the civic trust.[51] All voters, the delegates posit, participate in common and have a common share in sovereignty insofar as their votes count equally, regardless of political, cultural, or ethnic differences. Whatever qualified a citizen to vote, by default, made that citizen a part of the sovereign body, a primary citizen responsible for how the government was constructed. Citizens who did not meet these criteria became secondary citizens.[52] Without a share in sovereignty or the ability to give or refuse consent, these secondary citizens were the responsibility of the primary citizens. In a republican sense, they were politically and materially dependent; in the context of gradual emancipation and the black state conventions, they were "slaves to the community."[53] Including such groups (black men, all women, the "invalid," criminals, etc.) in the electorate would taint the political process because these citizens could not be counted on to vote rationally or independently. Like children, they had not reached (and never could reach) the age of majority and so depended on the primary citizens to make decisions for common protection and common weal.[54] In this sense, electoral politics linked manhood and voting as mutually constitutive elements of citizenship.

The convention's "Address to the People of the State" emphasizes delegates' manhood in order to dislodge the conflation of whiteness with manhood: "We base our claim upon the possession of those common and yet exalted faculties of manhood. WE ARE MEN."[55] While some of the delegates could trace their ancestry through several generations of free men, some of whom fought in the Revolution and the War of 1812 and helped build the Erie Canal, for them, manhood supersedes any other qualification (historical or material) or other differences between disenfranchised black men and the unrestricted voting population. "We can find no nation," they write, "that has the temerity to insult the common sense of mankind, by promulgating such sentiment as part of its creed" as skin color. The black delegates are men: patriarchal protectors of home, property owners (or at least those with the potential for it), taxpayers, fathers, husbands, producers, defenders of the state, and so on.

They were men (or not women or children) therefore, not only were they inherently capable of political participation, but also, their nature demanded that they seek it out. "Man is a creature of law," the "Address" posits,

> his nature adapted to government and its various functions. He sympathizes with its modes, and forms, and operations; and this, from the fact that there is not a single shade of revolution in the political aspect of a country, but it is felt to the extreme limits of the body politic; operating upon the individual being of all its subjects.
>
> The deprivation of our people of the elective franchise, and a participation in the various rounds of public duty, shows the evil here spoken of. The powers that should have been thus employed, have not lain dormant. A trait which we possess in common with our common humanity, has been manifested in us.[56]

By combining "common humanity," "nature," and manhood, the delegates were attempting to disassociate citizenship practices—voting in particular—from artificial and arbitrarily applied protocols of recognition and "rank" that were becoming associated with the separation of natural equality from political equality. These invocations of human nature ("common humanity") and manhood suggest an inverse theoretical track to the legal personhood Jeannine DeLombard analyzes in early gallows literature. As DeLombard argues, gallows literature helped produce black personhood:

"passage through the criminal justice system punitively affirmed the black individual's political membership" and could "activate his personhood."[57] Yet, that was precisely the kind of affirmation New Yorkers were attempting to upturn. After all, the delegates observe, they had "no marks of criminality attached to our names, as a class; no spots of immorality staining our characters; no charges of disloyalty dishonoring our birthright."[58] To uncouple blackness from (the perception of) guilt, the 1840 New York convention argues that their personhood—that is the identity that gives them a civic presence and justifies their access to the franchise—is inherent to their identity as men who were not enslaved and who had not committed a crime. Legal status did not make humanity or manhood; instead, the law was subject to an imperative to express the needs of the humans who shaped and were governed by it.

The resulting configuration reverses the temporal logic that a citizen must in some way demonstrate respectability and gain public trust *before* earning political rights. Respectability could not gain citizenship. The practice of citizenship, rather than the citizen's identity, creates the virtue and independence characteristic of the republican citizen. By restricting black access to the franchise, the state has not acted to protect republicanism but rather has "manifestly violated" its "principles." In so arguing, the 1840 New York convention separates the formal structures of consent and deliberative politics from their racially ascriptive underpinnings, instead figuring political participation as the source of respectability and public trust. In place of this racially ascriptive model, the delegates offer a natural law of civic power and circulation: (1) a human being's ("common humanity") innate drive to political participation and self-determination does not disappear in the absence of institutional structures or sanction but rather is manifested through other forms; (2) citizens most productively pursue politics as a collective and in a climate where this civic power can flow freely; and (3) republican governments provide structures through which citizens can exercise this power productively but do not create this power.[59]

Rather than an individual property or privilege (a "franchise" in the literal sense), the delegates frame the franchise as a public resource (*res communes*) like flowing water.[60] Participatory politics, including voting, function as a "channel" connecting citizens in a political community, gathering and directing their collective civic powers. Without access to its "pure and refreshing waters" of free political exchange, the black citizens have been "made aliens and strangers in the country of our birth."[61] This trope of flowing water had potent political and economic ramifications in the age of the Erie Canal. Opened in 1825, the canal connected the Hudson River at Albany, New York (the state's capital), to the western "frontier" of Buffalo (New York), opened new territories to settlement, led to an economic boom, and symbolized the free circulation of ideas and national unity more generally.[62] Preventing access to the canal or other waterways could practically isolate a community, hindering economic expansion and communication with the rest of the nation, and could deprive the nation of that region's resources.

Similarly, the convention suggests, preventing access to franchise rights effectively isolates the disfranchised, cutting the means to accumulating wealth, power, and property, as well as their ability to contribute to the civic good. Ultimately, both the state and the disenfranchised lose. The race-based property qualifications turn the means of citizenship practice, a public property, into private property, an end in itself to be passed down from favored son to favored son in a way that reproduces the "stale primogenital fallacies of the blood-dyed political institutions of the old world."[63] It effectively creates an aristocracy masquerading as republicanism and produces the hierarchies it purports to simply reflect. If republican citizenship is based on equal ownership of and access to political institutions, then the state's racial qualification made its government something other than republican, instead making New York a feudal state.[64]

If the circulation of waterways offers a central trope for how the franchise connects citizens as a functional collective, the trope of circulating blood reveals how this common network promotes material and social prosperity for those with access and material and social degradation for those without it. The franchise is, as the convention's form petition put it, an "instrument of their elevation," not a goad or reward for it.[65] Blocking access to the franchise "is like extracting the living principle from the blood of the system."[66] "Is it any wonder," they ask, "that our energies have been relapsed, that our powers have been crippled, our purposes nerveless, our determinations dead and lifeless?"[67] "From this" outside repression, the convention tells its fellow colored citizens, "proceeded our degradation. This has been the source of our suffering and oppression."[68] The cultural and political advantages of the franchise opened access to political and economic opportunities: "those resources of pecuniary and possessional emolument, which an unshackled citizenship does always ensure"—inaccessible to the disfranchised.[69] Where the framers of New York's 1821 constitution argued that black men needed the property qualification because their blackness signified inferiority (either because of prolonged enslavement, in which case the qualification would serve as a spur, or because of immutable racial differences), the black delegates argued that the state's policy had functioned to create an ontological and teleological signification of black skin that was not empirically evident before.[70]

These circulation tropes provided a language for articulating the inverse causality at the core of racist logic: differences in access produced the material distinctions apparent in 1840 that white citizens then anachronistically read as the basis for the $250 qualification. A generation removed from enslavement, black New Yorkers remained "shackled" to slavery's legacy of political oppression and economic exploitation not because slavery made them unfit for citizenship but because New York's constitution reproduced slavery's subjugation.[71] Prescriptive franchise requirements created material and political conditions of dependence and corruption (or the perception of it). The state and white voters, in turn, read the effects of the voting restriction as justification for their original implementation and continuation. What the delegates analyzed as the effects of unnatural voting restrictions, the white voters read as the manifestation of natural differences. Causes (franchise requirements) become the effects, and effects (dependence and degradation) become the causes.[72] The delegates' model of civic power suggests that condition-based arguments had confused the means of citizenship practice (political participation) with their ends, a sense of community and shared responsibility for the common good.[73]

The delegates' analysis of how civic power circulates and accumulates confronts how white citizens used condition-based arguments to truncate black civic power. They first posit that political participation makes citizens better political agents; the responsibility creates the traits that political participation requires. Political participation "unshackle[s]" citizenship and *makes* citizens functional, providing a structure of identification by dividing civic responsibility (responsibility to and ownership of the civic good) among citizens and making each accountable to the other.[74] Far from requiring inherent virtue or racial and gender homogeneity, political participation fosters the characteristics it requires through communal practice.

In a passage calibrated to demonstrate the importance of franchise rights to the convention's black readers, the convention invokes circulation to illustrate how the suffrage creates commonality within a body politic without requiring homogeneity: "the possession of the franchise right is the life blood of political existence. It runs through all the convolutions of our civil state. It connects itself with our literary immunities, enters into our ecclesiastical associations, and blends with our social and domestic relations."[75] Franchise rights, as formalized and institutionally sanctioned political participation (a "self-protecting instrument"), would secure other political and public spaces from the encroachment of a hostile racial majority or a powerful economic minority.[76] The franchise safeguards public discourse ("literary immunities") and links all the interest-based civic and social institutions that could otherwise atomize a community, creating a common network through which differences can be mediated. Citizens' dedication to republican citizenship, in turn, provides "the connecting chain that runs through the whole mighty mass of humanity . . . the common sympathies and wants of the race." Figured as blood, the franchise displaces the biological bases for fellow citizenship; fellow citizens become "related" through their joining of civic power under the auspices of shared political channels.[77] Citizens do not have to share the same political or cultural views or even particularly like each other so long as they agree that republican government is the medium through which these differences should be worked out.

But there is something more basic to this theory than the belief in a specific mode of participatory politics. Even if franchised and disfranchised citizens do not share the common blood of suffrage, they do still share the basic human need for political self-determination, the need to expend civic energy. Legislation cannot alter this need. As such, the convention further argues, the will to participate in the state may dull due to disuse or appear fragmented due to disorganization, but the power itself never disappears entirely. The power remains, but it lacks the circulation and "natural and legitimate exercise" that directs it into citizenship practice.[78] The convention's "Address . . . to the Voters of the State" explains, "Powers will have exercise, either healthy or unhealthy. The impartial and proscriptive non-suffrage act, has been to us hurtful in the extreme. The powers that should naturally have been thus exercised, were wrested from their legitimate employment."[79] The convention's language echoes Alexander Hamilton's contention for a strong federal government in *Federalist No. 13*: "Civil power, properly organized and exerted, is capable of diffusing its force to a very great extent; and can, in a manner, reproduce itself in every part of a great empire by a judicious arrangement of subordinate institutions."[80] Where Hamilton's arguments focus on creating a federal government strong enough to direct a diverse and wide-ranging civic body, the 1840 New York convention warns that such a government must be able to encompass *all* of its citizens to be productive.

If black citizens' civic "powers" do not appear in evidence, it is not due to their absence. Without a state-sanctioned outlet for the natural inclination toward self-determination, excess civic power might eventually flow into political rebellion, violent revolution, criminality, or movements like the Convention of the Colored Inhabitants of the State of New York. On one hand, the convention argues, black New Yorkers present "the curious and acknowledge creditable spectacle of a people" who have created schools, reading rooms, an educated professional class, and religious institutions to meet these basic needs.[81] That they have succeeded under unequal and unjust conditions is a testament to their ingenuity and determined dedication to republican principles. But, they warn, this development of a state within a state is untenable: "undue and disproportionate development of powers, produces unnatural effects."[82] Unable to pursue happiness by means of political engagement, debate, compromise, or agitation, disenfranchised citizens might eventually seek extra-governmental and eventually extra-legal means. This lack of an outlet could also result in civic atrophy. Like a gangrenous limb, the rot can and will spread to the rest of the community because, despite the social boundaries, the root republican principles that provide the community's foundation and facilitate exchanges between individuals will always be compromised. Moreover, the buildup of unfocused, unused power, like the buildup of water at a dam, could simply explode.

The New York convention's theory of circulation and civic power reveals the relation between conventions and citizenship practice, suggesting that we read the convention itself as a manifestation of black citizens' desire for political participation. Just as Jones and Allen framed their *Narrative* as a response to an encroachment on their liberty, so too do the state conventions situate their claims as a call for restoration and fulfillment rather than dissolution.[83] While the convention's emphasis on manhood limits the scope of its democratic intervention, its emphasis on political participation as essential to republican citizenship and appeal to notions of political desire suggests more radical implications that, as I argue later in this chapter, black women leverage for their own purposes.

Staging Citizenship Through a "Different Medium"

What I have suggested so far is that the conventions mobilize a theory of citizenship in which the circulation of civic power through political participation makes citizenship functional, especially in lieu of a national standard for citizenship. The New York convention leverages this argument to frame its claims to suffrage as a fulfillment of natural law rather than a "foreign issue" or imposition on the rights of white citizens. Yet, presenting these claims through a Convention of the Colored Inhabitants of New York was just as important as their theoretical arguments. The New York conventioneers were keenly aware of the convention as a print cultural form and were equally aware that their own efforts needed to be a carefully staged expression of self-governance in the republican style from start to finish. My argument in this section is not necessarily that the black conventions did anything particularly differently from other conventions but rather that the choice of this form—the convention and circulated proceedings—signifies in recognizable and performative ways that an address or addresses (without the accompanying frame) could not. As "Augustine" put it as Pennsylvanians were organizing their first convention in 1841, "If a majority of the colored people in Pennsylvania desire the right to vote, they must show it in some way." White people, he argues, "must subject themselves to the expense and trouble of holding a great convention" whenever they want to support "any great measure." Black citizens must do the same.[84]

The public and deliberative process of constitution drafting and ratification—whether real or virtual—that occurred across eight states from 1821 to 1849 created a democratic ethos and institutions from the bottom up that netted what we now popularly describe as Jacksonian Republicanism.[85] At the same time, the countless petitions, conventions, meetings, parades, and other nongovernmental forms of citizen participation during the 1830s and 1840s were not, from the antebellum citizen's view, symbolic political demonstrations. Rather, they were a viable, visible, and potentially revolutionary mode of civic engagement in which voting was just becoming accessible to masses of white men.[86] As Nancy Isenberg notes in the context of women's conventions, "Such conventions had a constitutional precedent derived from the right of the people to assemble and petition the government" that offered a recognizable venue and structure for politics despite the participants' legal status.[87] By the 1830s, this direct collective engagement with government produced the sense that citizens "speak in the language of command, and not of prayer, to their Representatives."[88] Each of these instances shares the sense that when established representational structures fail to reflect the views of the consenting people, the people need to take more radically democratic measures. When states were no longer responsive to citizens' needs, these local structures could become agents of revolutionary change—often rhetorically channeling 1776—manifesting in violence as in the Whiskey Rebellion or, as was increasingly the case, in conventions seeking constitutional change.

Though not seeking to supplant state governments as such, the black state conventions worked through the same logic: by serving in the capacity of political representatives who had a share in the state's collective sovereignty and by taking their entitlement to such rights as given even in the absence of official sanction, the delegates to conventions engaged in the political process even if they did not do so in the state house. The problem facing black activists from the outset, however, was that this democratic impulse, as it resulted in an ostensibly more democratic public sphere for white men, often did so through explicitly excising black men and all women from the consenting public, resulting in a majority apathetic, if not outright hostile, to further democratic expansion.[89]

Even as the 1840 New York convention presented its proceedings as a reasoned argument for suffrage rights, its success depended on white approval and allaying white fears.[90] As Charles B. Ray, black activist and *Colored American* editor, observes, the impressions that the convention left on the attending audience—"many of the leading men in Albany of the Whig political party, and of public matters"—and readers of the convention's proceedings were at least as important to the delegates as the outcome of the debates and their theoretical soundness.[91] Ray's comments reveal the measure of aesthetic judgment and persuasion always attendant to deliberative politics, especially in lieu of a civic space fraught with inequity.[92] The Whig onlookers provide a moment of recognition but with an ever-present caveat of difference—"as one of their own class said to us"—that reemphasized the power differential between the convention delegates and the white voters and legislators who made up part of its audience.[93] This need for formal recognition exposed tensions inherent in these conventions as simultaneously practices in and signs of citizenship and at the same time as stagings dependent on voter affirmation for validation.[94]

Integral to this staging was how convention organizers shaped the political community of "colored" citizens the delegates claimed to represent.

The delegates needed to define colored citizens as a group with shared political claims against the state while not reinforcing the sense that they were a separate or somehow "foreign" people. The 1840 New York convention's analysis of how differences in political rights produced material distinctions not peculiar to black citizens was one point of attack, but the battle over black political identity began before the first delegates ever arrived in Albany. The debate about the necessity, efficacy, and purpose of a convention of *colored* inhabitants, before the 1840 New York convention, also reveals the political exigencies that influenced how these conventions shaped their public presences and approached their respective audiences.

White and black activists alike were often ambivalent toward the "complexional" nature of these conventions. William Whipper, James McCune Smith, and other black activists opposed the 1840 convention because of the expense, the possible diffusion of labor, and their sense that the suffrage movement would be better served by an interracial coalition under the umbrella of human rights.[95] After the convention, Whipper famously penned a set of three letters to the *Colored American* critiquing the 1840 convention's emphasis on color as "in direct opposition to the 'rights of humanity.'"[96] White antislavery activists such as Nathaniel Rogers, editor of the *National Anti-Slavery Standard*, went further and accused the organizers of repeating the prejudices of white men in addressing their call to colored citizens. Rogers's editorial on June 18, 1840, addresses itself to the organizers as a "friend" and then argues, "We oppose all exclusive action on the part of the colored people, except where the clearest necessity demands it." Rogers continues, "Time should be taken to discuss the measures to be employed deliberately; and the people should be made distinctly to understand that *our* country is *your* country; our God your God." The language implies that at best, the conventioneers' actions were too hasty, showing a lack of rational deliberation; at worst, Rogers's commentary implies that this deliberation could only occur with their (white) legitimating presence and direction.

Defending the convention against such attacks compelled supporters to articulate the meaning of "color" as an organizing principle, racialization as a political phenomenon, questions of agency vis-à-vis fracturing antislavery organizations, and the tensions between presenting black citizens as autonomous individuals and the public's tendency to read their political actions as the result of white patronage or pawns in the jockeying of political parties.[97] One defender, "Sidney," responded to William Whipper's letters in one of the clearest articulations of a pragmatic political black nationalism in early African America: "Whenever a people are oppressed, peculiarly (not complexionally), distinctive organization or action is required on the part of the oppressed, to destroy that oppression. The colored people of this country are oppressed; therefore the colored people are required to act in accordance with this fundamental principle."[98] In much the same vein, Samuel Ringgold Ward responded to Rogers's *Standard* editorial by pointing out white abolitionists' racial privilege and myopia: their inability "to see a colored man when in the company of other whites necessitates such a convention."[99] Ward upbraids Rogers: "Had you a colored skin from October '17 to June '40, as I have, in this pseudo-republic, you would have seen through a very *different medium*."[100] Sidney and Ward connect being "colored" to a historical experience of antiblackness and to a mode of seeing this oppression as an issue of political power and representation. Being colored in this instance signifies in much the same way as being propertyless might in other circumstances. To have a "colored skin," their analysis suggests, is to be without property in whiteness, a property worth about $250 in New York.[101] This material and historical perspective, Ward and Sidney suggest, gave black citizens a theoretical and experiential understanding of politics different from their would-be white advisors that necessitated naming the racist elements of New York law.

There was more at stake here than political perspective, though. The convention welcomed white attendance—even needed their approbation—but organizers maintained that any political progress would require the kind of publicity that only a gathering arranged by an autonomous black political collective could provide. The political exigencies and the way race framed and suffused these politics superseded the sentimental affiliation Rogers suggests in proclaiming, "Every abolitionist should be a colored person in this case."[102] Every abolitionist, Ray argues, cannot be a colored person because being "colored" is shaped by material and political realities that white citizens, no matter how well intentioned, do not share. Black citizens needed to be *seen* organizing for themselves and in leadership positions in ways that even the antislavery conventions, where, as Ray observed, black participants were often "looked upon as playing second fiddle to" the white organizers, could not produce.[103] Such an event, a "different medium," would demonstrate to the state that, rather than operating as puppets to abolitionist organizations or even the burgeoning Liberty Party, black citizens desired the franchise for their own and the state's benefit, "that as citizens we should possess the privileges and immunities of citizenship: and . . . we are as capable of appreciating and exercising those rights as others."[104] It would position them as political *agents* rather than as objects of legislation or the political wards of white philanthropists. It would allow black citizens to exercise their own civic power more visibly and freely and therefore more productively for themselves and the state as a whole.

The debates preceding the convention positioned the delegates as representatives of a political community of colored citizens. After the convention, the delegates used print to extend the convention's performance, with the circulation of the collected "Proceedings" or "Minutes"—including debates, resolutions, addresses, and petitions—and the conventions' form petitions that articulated the delegates' central position in a shorter form.[105] If, as the convention argued, the suffrage served as the official circuit for civic power, then these documents created an unofficial, alternate route providing a mechanism for black citizens to exercise citizenship by directly engaging the state and their fellow citizens.

The organizers of the 1840 New York convention were keenly aware that the convention's legitimacy—for both white and black onlookers—depended as much on how well it executed its business as a deliberative body (or at least how well it presented this execution to the public) as it did on what the convention actually decided.[106] Ray reiterates again and again that the "Proceedings" (both event and printed record) represent the convention's "respectable and noble" character, revealing the delegates' ability to conduct business without "angry debate," settling differences "amicably and yet without compromise."[107] Indeed, the *form* of these debates and resolutions carried at least as much weight as their content because the text confirms Ray's claim that the convention adhered to a republican style of politics. And, because audiences would read any sign of disorder as confirmation of black difference, the minutes needed to be especially scrupulous on this point.

Rather than including transcriptions or details of debates between delegates—as the national conventions are notorious for doing and as state constitutional conventions did—the minutes mark disagreements as a matter of procedure, in a way that frames them as a democratic process of revision. For example, when some delegates (C. B. Ray, T. S. Wright, E. P. Rogers) supported a resolution encouraging black citizens to buy property to meet the franchise requirements for practical reasons, others (H. H. Garnet, U. Boston, A. Crummell) opposed it because the resolution implied consent to the current requirement. The convention records the debate over the resolution as follows: "A very spirited debate arose on this resolution, owing to the exception taken to that part of it which asserted that the obtainment of a certain amount of property, '*elevates us to the rights of freemen*'. . . . The discussion on the resolution, continued till near the close of the session, when Mr. Ray introduced an amendment, which was strongly opposed, owing to its containing . . . the same objectionable feature as the original resolution." The minutes exclude the back and forth, instead offering procedural commentary: "spirited debate," "discussion," introduction of an amendment, opposition to the amendment, and so on. The delegates adjourn without a resolution and return to the question later but "after some further discussion . . . laid [it] indefinitely upon the table."[108] This presentation offers enough description to give readers a sense of the stakes involved in the resolution's language, the delegates' astute attention to this language (mirroring similar debates about semantics during constitutional conventions), and the deliberative process through which the convention negotiated this impasse. Without the messy details of individual arguments, however, even this clearly divisive issue (it consumes the better part of two sessions after all) reads relatively smoothly.

This formal structure, at once a dialectical progression through compromise and at the same time a dialogic interplay between distinct voices and sections, no less than the resolutions' content, demonstrates the deliberative politics that opponents claimed were beyond black citizens' mental capacities or social conditions. The minutes do not mention the debate again, but later that evening, after several reports, two resolutions appear that resolve the tensions around the original proposal: "Resolved, That we recommend to our people to become possessors of the soil within the limits of this State" and "Resolved, That in recommending our people to possess themselves of the soil, we no less protest against that clause in the Constitution of the State which requires a property qualification of us . . . considering it wrong in principle, sapping the foundation of self government, and contrary to all notions of natural justice."[109] These two resolutions register and synthesize the primary disagreements over the original proposal as dialectical progression. Where the debate account contextualizes the political fault lines, the new resolutions appear as if none of the earlier exchange and deadlock had occurred. In its linear progression, this presentation melds discordant voices into a coherent representative civic voice. But the differences themselves do not disappear. The proceedings produce what Mark

Schoenfield has described in a slightly different context as an "institutionally heteroglossic" document. Internally, the debates offer a range of voices, and the resolutions relate to each other dialogically in a call-and-response sequence mediated, as it were, by the "third party" of the overall corporate author.[110] The individual pieces of the collected proceedings also speak to each other: the preamble with the resolutions, the resolutions with the addresses, the resolutions with each other, and so on. Taken as a whole, the convention proceedings present the delegates doing the work of the republican citizenship through a form that models how republican governments should channel and focus citizens' collective power.

This choreographed civility in presentation does not, however, negate these conventions' radical work. There was instrumental value in orderly proceedings, including the efficient execution of business, the ease of distribution, and the need to instill confidence in the black communities these delegates claimed and hoped to represent. More, as Ward's response to the *National Anti-Slavery Standard* and other detractors' reaction to the conventions suggest, even civilly presented black speech could be insurgent. As the next section suggests, this insurgency was not the exclusive right of black men. Even as the state conventions' largely male delegation made claims about the importance of participatory politics to the circulation of civic power and to republican citizenship, women attendees turned to these tropes to make powerful arguments for their own citizenship claims.

"A Right Granted by a Higher Disposer of Human Events Than Man": Gendered Citizenship and the Black State Conventions

If arguments like those proffered in the New York black state conventions framed participatory politics in gendered terms, the constellation of events associated with the conventions shows how women not only contributed substantively but also leveraged the form as a potential vector into a more fully realized citizenship for themselves. This section takes up some of the arguments and practices of black women during the black state conventions, with particular emphasis on the Ohio conventions and Frances Harper, who participated in the 1858 Convention of the Colored Men of Ohio and critiqued conventions' gender politics more broadly in her fiction. While the chapter (and this section) focuses on the state conventions,

I draw on the national conventions held in Ohio as well because they speak to a larger movement within the state and to a congruence between the way convention participants in Ohio challenged gendered citizenship on state and national levels.

Black women's rights emerged explicitly in the national colored conventions during the 1848 National Colored Convention in Cleveland, Ohio, just two months after the Women's Rights Convention at Seneca Falls. Debate erupted over the "subject of the Rights of Woman," when, on the convention's third day, convention president William Howard Day yielded the floor to a "Mrs. Sanford." Sanford offered a call for women's suffrage, combining previous convention arguments with the Seneca Falls platform: "True, we ask for the Elective Franchise: for right of property in the marriage covenant, whether earned or bequeathed. True, we pray to co-operate in making the laws we obey; but it is not to domineer, to dictate or assume. We ask it, for it is a right granted by a higher disposer of human events than man. We pray for it now, for there are duties around us, and we weep at our inability."[111] In an echo of the New York conventions, Sanford claims political participation (codified in the franchise) as a divinely sanctioned right and as a primary means for facilitating more robust citizenship practices. The "duties" Sanford references are not (just) the duties of the household but rather include the political self-determination central to republican citizenship. For the 1840 New York State Convention, the "elective franchise" was the means to "participation in the various rounds of public duty."[112] Sanford repurposes and expands this earlier convention's articulation of participatory politics to claim the right and duty for women to "co-operate in making the laws we obey" not as secondary citizens covered by fathers or husbands but rather through women's own political energies as rights-bearing citizens.

More radically, Sanford expands the state conventions' focus on voting to include equality in marriage as an essential component for practicing citizenship. She carefully navigates gender norms circumscribing women's political purview by allaying fears that women wish to "domineer" men. This phrasing targets both black men uneasy or hostile to challenges to the current order and a white public already trained to see black women as unsexed or overly aggressive. By extension, Sanford suggests that readings of women as the "lesser sex" hinge not on biological differences or biblical doctrine (she credits Mary with giving Jesus direction and as proof that women were not slaves to "power and passion") but rather on an enforced division that creates structural "inability." Just as black men were arguing that restricting access to the franchise resulted in a degraded "condition" that could threaten the republic as a whole, Sanford argues that excluding women sapped black activism and the republic more broadly of its strength.

After multiple attempts to postpone Sanford's resolution, William Howard Day and Langston (probably Charles H.) argue that an explicit endorsement on women's rights was not needed "on the ground that we had passed one similar, making all colored persons present, delegates to this Convention, and they considered women persons."[113] Day and Langston's solution to the debate infers that the convention's earlier references to personhood implicitly included women attendees. Yet, the difficulty in passing a resolution affirming women's rights suggests that this solution was a retroactive expansion, not a consensus understanding of the term as used. Carla Peterson writes of the solution, "The practical result was in fact an indefinite postponement of any serious discussion of women's rights and of the role that women were to play in future conventions."[114] While conventions continued to invoke notions of common humanity, manhood, and personhood to make claims for manhood suffrage even as they justified holding "colored" conventions because of the specificity of racial oppression, they also demonstrate how the concept could be used to ignore gendered claims. It was one thing to include women as persons; it was quite another to recognize them as equal participants. Even so, while Sanford did not get the resolution that she and those she represented sought, they did force a more explicit statement about gender, personhood, and political equality.

As with the national conventions, the state conventions' official documents often limited or outright rejected women's participation. Here, too, regional differences could be stark. Women remained virtually invisible in the official records of the New York State conventions. In one of the most glaring instances, the minutes from the 1855 convention in Troy offer this account: "The name of Miss Barbary Anna Stewart was stricken out from the roll, several gentlemen objecting to it on the ground that this is not a Woman's Rights Convention."[115] The minutes do not include debate around Stewart's initial inclusion or her excision. This erasure aside, however, the minutes give a trace of Stewart's presence, if only by mentioning her name in the process of rejecting her claims.[116] In this sense, Stewart's attempt to become an official delegate mirrors the fate of the 1837 Pennsylvania "Appeal of Forty Thousand Citizens." As I discuss in the introduction, the Pennsylvania constitutional convention ultimately rejected the

"Appeal's" call to remove the racial qualification from the state's new constitution. Though the attempt failed, the official record bears witness to their insistence on their right to participate. In a similar vein, Stewart's case is suggestive of movements among black women across the decade to have their voices heard on equal terms with men, not just as participants but also as delegates with a share in the vote and official record of deliberations. Stewart's attempt made it into the record, but it also should lead us to wonder how many similar attempts did not.

Male delegates in Ohio, by contrast, recognized women's participation in various capacities from the beginning but not solely because of their magnanimity. Black women of Ohio leveraged their considerable power to force black men's hands, and state convention organizers, including Day and Langston, seemed to support these efforts. Led by Jane P. Merritt, they submitted the following resolution during the 1849 Ohio State Convention: "Whereas we the ladies have been invited to attend the Convention, and have been deprived of a voice, which we the ladies deem wrong and shameful. Therefore, Resolved, That we will attend no more after to-night, unless the privilege is granted."[117] The threat of a boycott resulted in a resolution "inviting the ladies to participate," to "share in the doings of the Convention," with only two delegates recorded in opposition. The next year, Ohio delegates formed a State Society that welcomed men and women members.

We can trace the possible effects of Merritt and others' intervention through the 1849 convention's "Address to the Citizens of Ohio." While most of the convention's documents refer to men and manhood as the basis for participatory politics, the "Address" also frames the convention's arguments in terms of human rights: "We believe also that *every human being* has rights in common, and that the meanest of those rights is legitimately beyond the reach of legislation, and higher than the claims of political expediency."[118] It is tempting to see this language as hewing more closely to the New York convention's slippage between manhood and humanity (and it does to some degree), but the italics and Merritt's confrontation with the convention as a whole suggest a more egalitarian impulse, in language if not in delegate count. The language here ("the meanest of those rights is legitimately beyond the reach of legislation") also echoes Sanford's appeal to the 1848 national convention: political participation "is a right granted by a higher disposer of human events than man."[119] While there is, to my knowledge, no direct evidence of Merritt's or other women's involvement in crafting this "Address," this confluence of interventions in Ohio between 1848 and 1849 is suggestive if not conclusive of their influence. Merritt's husband, T. J. Merritt, was an active delegate at the 1849 state convention as a member of the rules and petition committees. Could Merritt have used T.J. as her proxy during the convention? Did he (and Day, for that matter) see himself as representing her interests where the rules prevented her from doing so herself? The Ohio state conventions invite us to read between the lines of convention-related documents and events for echoes of women's contributions to not only the black state conventions' logistics but also their theoretical content.

While Day and Langston offered procedural support, Merritt and others' threat was effective because of how central women were to making state and national conventions work. Though less visible in the printed proceedings than the official male delegates, women provided part of black conventions' financial, logistical, and, in some cases, publishing backbone. The 1851 Ohio state convention, for instance, recognized "Miss L. A. Stanton, Miss M. J. Hopkins, Mrs. L. M. Jenkins, Mrs. C. Hacley, Mrs. S. Mason, Mrs. S. P. Scurry, Miss L. Harper" for their "pledging themselves to furnish means to publish the proceedings of this Convention." For a movement that was in constant financial straits, this acknowledgment is no small thing. It speaks not only to black women as activist forces but also to their economic power. Reading rooms were another venue where women may have participated in the extended performance of state and national conventions. We know, for instance, that Harriet Jacobs worked for a time in the antislavery reading room above the offices of the *North Star* (Rochester, New York) and that *North Star* reprinted or was responsible for printing minutes and summations of several conventions, including the 1849 Ohio State Convention and the 1850 Cazenovia Fugitive Slave Law Convention. In both cases, convention minutes and coverage would likely have been standard fare for reading room visitors and for women such as Jacobs, who was an avid *North Star* reader.[120]

Women's participation in the conventions as delegates, however, sparked more hostile responses, as Charles L. Remond's motion to recognize Mary Shadd Cary as a delegate from Canada did at the 1855 national convention in Philadelphia. The motion won by a 38 to 23 vote, a solid majority, but also an indication of significant opposition.[121] The minutes list her as the delegate from Canada, one of three women delegates (Rachel Cliff and Elizabeth Armstrong of Pennsylvania were the other two), "which created quite a stir."[122] While the convention minutes do not mention

Shadd Cary further, William J. Wilson's correspondence on the convention for *Frederick Douglass's Paper* (as Ethiop) reveals that she came to James McCune Smith's defense during a debate on a "Resolution on Agriculture." In this context, Shadd Cary delivered what Wilson described as "one of the most convincing and telling speeches in favor of Canadian emigration I ever heard," as she advocated for agricultural pursuits and mechanical education.[123] Moments like Cary's, however, were few and far between.

The division of labor these conventions enforced, wherein women were generally only officially recognized in their capacity as fundraisers, was an ongoing point of contention with black women throughout the state convention movement. Frances Ellen Watkins (Harper), in particular, responded to this tendency in an 1859 installment of her "Fancy Sketches" series for the *Anglo-African Magazine*. While I will introduce the series more fully in a later chapter, this moment is worth noting here. The series protagonist, Jane Rustic, has a dream about a convention for the "Anti-Sunshine Society" (ASS) where delegates pass resolutions to "send out lecturers, and circulate documents and tracts to show the superiority of gaslight over sunshine," to ban women's office holding "unless it be to collect funds" and "petition the man in the moon to weave a curtain of clouds or a shroud of mist to bar the rising of the sun."[124] Harper reimagines the political forum, a reproduction of Ray's emphasis on the conventions' proceduralism, as a space of repressive officiousness and a public whose sense of the common good has gone horribly awry. Jane attempts to object and "make an excellent speech on the utility and beauty of sunshine" to remind the delegates that their resolution would result in famine and desolation. The men, however, shout her down in the language of parliamentary procedure: " 'order!' 'question!' 'Mr. Speaker, Mr. Speaker! The lady is out of order.' " The chair rules in their favor, forcing Jane to yield the floor. In a recapitulation of Stewart's attempts to register her concerns with the 1855 Troy, New York, convention, the ASS convention strikes out Jane's warnings through aggressive parliamentarianism, turning the stagecraft intended to facilitate convention business and render it legible to a judging public into an antidemocratic tool.

The second resolution banning women from holding office outside of fundraising dramatizes Harper's own experience of how convention minutes sequestered women's presence to their financial contributions but muted their intellectual work. A year earlier, the 1858 Convention of the Colored Men of Ohio had invited Harper "to take part in the Convention."[125] The minutes show that she was a top contributor to the convention's funding but otherwise remain silent on how, exactly, she participated. Other women appear as signers of the convention's constitution and as leaders in local committees charged with marshaling support for the Ohio State Anti-Slavery Society. While Jane, Harper's character, wakes to the morning sun and the "satisfaction of knowing that the anti-sunshine convention was only a dream," the resistance Harper allegorized remained very real and in force for decades to come.

"Not Very Courteous Language, Indeed, for Petitioners": Conventions as Sublime Appeal

The 1848 State Convention of the Colored Citizens of Pennsylvania explicitly cites the creation and movement of collective texts (petitions) as a tool for joining politically separate communities. The convention issued "An Appeal to the Colored Citizens" and "An Appeal to the Voters of the Commonwealth of Pennsylvania," printed with the original proceedings and reprinted in Samuel Ringgold Ward's *Impartial Citizen* a year later (Figure 3).[126] Composed by the same committee, the "Appeals" make up most of the proceedings.[127] Aimed at separate audiences but printed side by side, the "Appeals" mirror the dialectic-dialogic model of deliberative politics presented in the debate-to-resolution sequence during the convention itself. While the "Appeals" position each audience dialogically, addressing white voters and black citizens separately, the call for each audience to work toward expanding citizenship rights through drafting petitions operates dialectically, creating a new citizenry. This circulation of petitions from both groups, the convention suggests, could connect civic power through citizenship practices that reaffirm their collective commitment to republican governance. Just as the Erie Canal connected separate segments of the nation, the "Appeals" serve as a conduit connecting citizens' civic power. Just as the lines separating newspaper columns signal that each article belongs to the same institutional structure, the 1848 convention's "Appeals'" structure connects its separate audiences as fellow citizens.

The oscillation in how the "Appeals" deploy the term "appeal" allows us to trace how the 1848 Pennsylvania convention modulated between seeking approval and redress from white voters (supplication) and a radical sense of sublime appeal more in the strain of a jeremiad or manifesto. The *OED*

THE IMPARTIAL CITIZEN.

NEW SERIES— The Wisdom which is from above is without Partiality. VOL. 1—NO. 34

S. R. WARD & CO. SYRACUSE, WEDNESDAY, DECEMBER 5, 1849. PUBLISHER

THE IMPARTIAL CITIZEN,

S. R. WARD, & Co.,

ROBINSON'S ONONDAGA TEMP'RNCE HOUSE

GROTON HOUSE,

BOARDING HOUSE,

WYNKOOP & BROTHER BOOKSELLERS AND STATIONERS

School District Libraries.

More Books!

CITY INTELLIGENCE And General Agency Office.

THE STAFF OF LIFE.

HORACE & CHA'S A. WHEATON

Hard-Ware,

Stoves

Iron and Steel, Paints, Oil, &c.

The Youth's Cabinet.

TRAVELLING AGENTS WANTED.

The Spoiled Heritage.

The Blind Boy's been at Play, Mother.

BY ELIZA COOK.

YOUNG AFRICA.

Extracts from an Appeal to the Voters of Pennsylvania.

WM. WHIPPER,
ABRAM D. SHADD,
J. F. DICKSON,
J. J. G. BIAS,
ROBERT PURVIS,
M. W. GIBBES,
SAMUEL VAN BRAKLE,
Committee.

Harrisburg, Dec. 14, 1848.

Extracts from an Appeal to the Colored Citizens of Pennsylvania.

WM. WHIPPER,
ABRAM D. SHADD,
J. J. DICKSON,
J. J. G. BIAS,
ROBERT PURVIS,
M. W. GIBBES,
SAM'L VAN BRAKLE,
Committee.

Figure 3. "An Appeal to the Colored Citizens" and "An Appeal to the Voters of the Commonwealth of Pennsylvania," reprinted in *Impartial Citizen* on December 5, 1849. Courtesy American Antiquarian Society.

offers several definitions of "appeal" in play during the 1840s: an appeal to authority for vindication or to overturn the ruling of a lower court; an appeal to level a criminal charge before a tribunal or "impeachment of treason or felony"; and an appeal to country, "the people," or a higher principle.[128] Where the first two instances maintain a separation between voters and nonvoters—citizens without civic authority addressing citizens with civic authority—the last instance calls on the collective civic power of Pennsylvania's citizens to revise or draft a new constitution.

The "Appeal to the Colored Citizens" offers court proceedings as the guiding metaphor for both "Appeals": "We intend suing for our rights as *men*; where the Executive and Legislative branches of the government is the Court, and 400,000 legal voters the jury, our own conduct being the witnesses, and true republican principles the law."[129] The "Appeal" defines "true republican principles" through reference to the Declaration of Independence: " 'that all just governments derive their powers from the consent of the governed.' "[130] Regardless of perceived deficiencies in the black population, the fact that black citizens are "governed" by the state of Pennsylvania forms the basis of a contract that entitles them to franchise rights. Pennsylvania's 1837–1838 constitutional convention, by denying black citizens the right to give consent and yet requiring their obedience and loyalty, violates this fundamental republican law. The "Appeal to the Voters," then, applies to the state and voters (addressed as "Sirs") as institutional superiors, "the source of power from which the fundamental Laws of this Commonwealth must derive their origin, power and sustenance," able to overturn the constitutional convention's initial ruling.[131] Yet, by appealing to the voters in this legal context, the "Appeals" present the delegates as equals—advocates rather than supplicants—critiquing institutional errors from a position of moral and legal authority. Just as the act of organizing and addressing the public through a convention enacts citizenship even as it speaks from outside the official sphere, appealing to the voters rather than simply addressing them implies the moral equality of the appealers as recognizable legal agents, despite the imbalance in institutional authority.

Like their New York counterparts, the Pennsylvanians refuse the calculus that black citizens must elevate themselves before enfranchisement, yet they also recognize that the means to enfranchisement require a publicity campaign. Even as the "Appeals" lay black Pennsylvanians' case before the voters, seeking impartial justice based on the laws of republicanism, the "Appeal to the Voters" reveals the inherent danger to minorities when contract-based arguments meet consent-based structures or when republican principles meet racist public opinion.[132] Where Lord Mansfield based the 1772 *Somerset* judgment on the "*language*" of British law, Pennsylvania's voters will judge black citizens based on their actions, even though such "evidence . . . has no foundation in established precedents."[133] Even if the voters were to judge black citizens based on republicanism, the voters are so diverse in "every quality of prejudice" and interpretation of republicanism (which "they are not bound by oaths to support") that their judgment would be capricious.[134] As such, while the delegates appeal to law and principle in the "Appeal to the Voters," the "Appeal to the Colored Citizens" still requests that colored citizens not give white voters an excuse for relying on their prejudices. Colored citizens should "avoid any unjust cause of offence" but instead should work to gather support from a wide a range of citizens.

Scholars have drawn attention to federalist claims about democracy's dark side, a tyranny of the people against property and order, but these state conventions invoke the tyranny of a different sort of majority: black citizens found themselves subject to a racist white majority whose racial animus trumped political principle and law. The Pennsylvania convention further revises this complaint by pointing to elites pulling the levers of this majority, stoking racist resentment in ways that maintained their own power. What early elites framed as a tyranny of the majority, the "Appeal" frames as subterfuge. And it is precisely because the 1837–1838 constitutional convention manipulated white prejudice for political gain that the 1848 convention comes before the public, ten years later, to "sue" for rights already theirs and wrongfully denied rather than simply request them. In this sense of "appeal," the delegates "accuse" voters "of a heinous crime whereby the accuser has received personal injury or wrong, for which he demands reparation."[135]

Despite explicitly positioning the voters as members of the jury and the state government as judge in the "Appeal to Colored Citizens," both the "Appeal to Colored Citizens" and the "Appeal to the Voters" ultimately take on a tone of accusation and judgment, resting on republican law.[136] In rhetoric following David Walker's *Appeal* and prefiguring Douglass's 1852 "Oration," the "Appeal to the Voters" reviews the state's history of republicanism through its own documents:

> We need not search among the antiquated records of the past for a successful vindication of our claims to impartial laws. These

> emblems, of our State's humanity are imperishably recorded in the sublime appeals of her distinguished statesmen.
>
> We do not appear before you as the supplicants for any new form of government which is opposed to the foundation principles of republicanism; we only ask the favor of the application of your own principles to your civil code. . . . You claim that your own Independence Hall is the sacred spot where your republicanism was born, cradled and received a national baptism, and from whence the same vestal fire of freedom is encompassing the globe.[137]

The black population, the delegates write, have watched the white population's "soul stirring appeals in behalf of republicanism, in foreign lands," and cannot help but believe that voters would want the same "progress of free principles" in their "own dearest Pennsylvania."[138] The delegates situate Pennsylvania as the exemplar of republicanism to the world. The proliferation of documents (quotes from the state constitution, the Declaration of Independence), monuments (Independence Hall, etc.), and events within the "Appeal to the Voters" form the basis of a covenant between the state and its citizens.[139] The "you's" throughout the "Appeal to the Voters" punctuate the voters' responsibility for their own laws and how these laws violate the state's self-proclaimed republican principles. As outside witnesses, the "we" of the "Appeal to the Voters" excoriates the "you," the "Appeal's" audience: they should be humiliated by the contemplation of what is written in the law. The invocation of the contractual nature of republicanism in the "Appeal to the Voters" shifts the argumentative burden from the meaning of blackness and ostensible material and ontological differences between types of citizens to the principles of republicanism as applied to *all* citizens.[140]

While the "Appeal to the Voters" engages the voters' responsibility and patriotism, suggesting that the current voters risk forsaking the legacy of their forebears, the "Appeal to Colored Citizens" censures these same voters for breaking their state's republican contract for personal gain. In so doing, the "Appeals" offer an incisive analysis of how electoral politics structured through racial hierarchies worked to limit citizenship even as it appeared to create a more republican government through majority rule. The "Appeal to Colored Citizens" argues that racism functioned as a "*passport* to power" that allowed white citizens to limit potential political opposition as much as they could. They suggest that the state's elite and white citizens more generally have deliberately refused to base their decisions on the very standards they themselves claim to use and have instead used suffrage restrictions not only to disfranchise citizens who could not vote but also to better control those citizens who could. As the "Appeal to the Colored Citizens" argues with chagrin,

> They [Reform Convention] were cunning logicians, and well knew that no argument founded on *condition* would meet the *false prejudices* of *their* constituents. They knew that the period had long since passed when it would be *possible* to *frame* a standard of *condition* that would separate the *white* from the *colored* people.
>
> So they disfranchised us . . . assuming *condition* as their *reason*, and *complexion* as their standard.[141]

The constitutional convention delegates based the franchise requirements on social and economic conditions only to make whiteness the standard for measuring them and in a way that smoothed over differences between white men. Race was never an indicator of civic worth but rather the "*capital*" funding of a shell game in which race emerged as the connective tissue of republican principle, giving the sense that all white citizens were abstractly equal when the delegates were actually trying to make the political field as unequal as possible. As the "Appeal" notes, many of those who supported the suffrage restriction "would not only have *disfranchised us*, but the *poor* of *every nation*, and whole *political* parties, that were opposed to them in the bargain."[142] By focusing voters' attention on protecting their shared interests in whiteness against incursions from easily isolated "others," those in power could more easily mask their maneuvering for more control.[143]

The "Appeal" reaffirms to its black readers that no amount of deference or respectability could have prevented this power grab. Where the 1840 New York convention theorizes and stages citizenship based in part on the prevailing logic of the republican style, and women Ohioans disrupt this staging's gendered logic, the 1848 Pennsylvania convention theoretically dismantles white duplicity. Though the delegates to the constitutional convention are guilty of pandering to racial prejudices, their white constituents are equally guilty for acting on these "false prejudices."[144] The *problem* of racial condition is not in black identity but rather in what Charles Mills has identified as a racial contract "predicated on a politics of the body" that has predetermined "which bodies" are capable of "*forming* or fully *entering into* a body politic."[145] Black Pennsylvanians write from the perspective of those who saw a version of this contract drafted in real time through the state constitutional convention. That process brought into sharp relief the realization that as long as white voters gave ontological, normative, and moral value to skin color, black citizens could never become "elevated" enough. For the black readers of the "Appeals," giving an account of racial oppression that indicts white duplicity and arbitrariness instead of black condition eliminates improvement-then-rights tactics even as it provides reasons for continuing to support moral and material uplift not for the sake of impressing a white public but rather as a good in and of itself.

Last, because the racialization of rights threatens the very fabric of republican government in the state, the "Appeals" appeal to all citizens to revise, if possible, or dissolve, if necessary, the existing contract. The invocation of "the sublime appeals of [Pennsylvania's] distinguished statesmen," particularly the Declaration of Independence, through the structure of a convention that calls its own addresses to the public "appeals" directly links the 1848 convention to a national tradition of government by consent and continuing revolution.[146] This approach shifts voters' attention away from a systems-off citizenship in which the would-be citizen must attain a certain standard before earning full rights to a systems-on citizenship in which, according to the state and nation's founding contracts, all governed citizens receive all the rights of citizenship until they "[forfeit] their rights" by committing a crime.[147]

The "Appeals" reference the "Declaration" in a way that suggests conservation of the current form of government while justifying revolution. The "Appeal to the Voters" reassures the public that the convention is not calling for a radical change in government, citing the Declaration's assertion " 'that governments long established should not be changed for slight and transient causes,' and all experience has proved, that as a people we are disposed to suffer present evils 'rather than fly to others we know not of.' "[148] The "Appeal to the Colored Citizens" likewise justifies its claims through the Declaration's assertion "that all just governments derive their powers from the consent of the governed," again suggesting that the "Appeals" are simply citing the basic premises of the current government.[149] Yet, despite the reassurance that the black citizens are not seeking wholesale change in the quoted passages from the Declaration, the ellipsis between the clause invoking the consent of the governed and the clause invoking the conservation of institutions suggests a more radical edge. Nested between these justifications for working within the current system, the Declaration offers reasons for dissolution: "That whenever any Form of Government becomes destructive of these ends, it is the Right of the People to alter or to abolish it, and to institute new Government, laying its foundation on such principles and organizing its powers in such form, as to them shall seem most likely to effect their Safety and Happiness." The call to revolution in the ellipsis between the two clauses quoted separately in the two "Appeals" mirrors the unspoken yet insistent call for a more radical interpretation of "the people" and their "safety and happiness" between the two "Appeals" more generally, an appeal to directly confront racist state policies as a danger to the legitimacy and stability of the civic compact as a whole.

As recompense for their collective negligence in allowing the state to compromise its republican creed, the state convention appeals to white citizens to join their black fellow citizens in an exercise of collective sovereignty to "institute new Government." More than referencing founding documents, then, the convention asks white voters to join them in producing new texts, a new contract: "Our object in assembling is not only to petition the Legislature *ourselves*, but also to solicit *you to petition* . . . to instruct [legislators] in a course of action."[150] Together, the "Appeals" seek to build an interracial coalition of petitioners, a new interracial majority, around voting rights. The collective action on the part of the whole people could make the state of Pennsylvania stronger, allowing it to join other states that have "succeeded in establishing a republican form of government where men of all complexions enjoy an equality of rights" including Massachusetts, Rhode Island, and Vermont.[151] The act of petitioning—not simply signing a preformulated petition but actively creating and circulating it in conjunction with the convention's work—could realign the terms of community affiliation in a way that matches the boasted efforts to spread republicanism abroad and could establish and demonstrate consensus about a more egalitarian notion of republican government. This sense of appeal, with its framing through a convention of representative citizens and its resonances with the Continental Congress's "Declaration," allows the delegates to "reframe the meaning of popular sovereignty" by invoking a ritual of consensus that supersedes any existing government.[152]

The Pennsylvania convention's more confrontational style reads less like the theoretical treatise on the meaning of the franchise from the 1840 New York addresses and more like a manifesto in the tradition of David

Walker's *Appeal to the Colored Citizens of the World* (reprinted in the same year as the convention by Garnet with his 1843 "Address to the Slaves") and the 1837 "Appeal of Forty Thousand Citizens," respectfully asking the state for redress but maintaining a position of moral and legal judgment. Invoking these contemporaneous documents in their title and tone, the Pennsylvania convention's appeals call for black citizens to work toward their own political liberation with or without the state's sanction even as they argue that the Constitution secures black citizens' rights: "Slaves have but learned to lick the dust, and stifle the voice of free inquiry; but we are not slaves—our right to natural liberty, and qualified citizenship, is guaranteed to us by the Constitution."[153] Like Walker's *Appeal* and the 1837 "Appeal of Forty Thousand," the "Appeal to Colored Citizens" dismantles the racial illogic by which colored citizens had been disfranchised as a part of a larger call to colored citizens to take control of their own political fates. In this way, the "Appeals" may begin with notes of deference, but they have elements of the manifesto at their core: an articulation of a new political position and policy for black Pennsylvanians and an ultimatum directed at the state that these citizens will no longer equivocate about their political rights as citizens.

Even though black citizens need the voters' support to regain the suffrage, they do not depend on these voters for their political identity or sense of political power. Where New York's Charles Ray emphasizes the recognition of Whig onlookers and the presentation of the New York convention, the Pennsylvanians take the white gaze out of the equation: "We shall live and labor in the glorious anticipation of success; but if it should prove otherwise, and you should not consent to repeal the sentence you have passed on Providence, we shall derive the rich consolation that in making this appeal we have discharged a duty we owe to *ourselves*, to freedom, and republicanism—to posterity and to God."[154] If white voters reject the "Appeal," then the voters, not black citizens, have failed, ultimately rendering their constitution invalid via its own republican logic and divine judgment. The declaration echoes the warning that the "Appeal of Forty Thousand Citizens" issued a decade earlier: "no amendments of the present Constitution can compensate for the loss of its foundation principle of equal rights, nor for the conversion into enemies of 40,000 friends."[155] Ultimately, black citizens will be justified in separating from a government that refuses consent from its whole people, and ultimately that government will suffer the consequences of its malfeasance.

Focusing on one meaning of "Appeal" obscures the whole and misses the complexity of the Pennsylvania delegates' position. More than the "Appeal to the Voters," the "Appeal to Colored Citizens" directly confronts the voters' criminal negligence in accepting truncated republicanism, yet because the two appeals were printed side-by-side as a part of the same proceedings, the "Appeal to the Colored Citizens" speaks to the white audience even as it ostensibly addresses black citizens. The result is that while the "Appeal to the Voters" acknowledges white voters and legislators as the governing authority, inheritors of the state's revolutionary heritage and responsible (if not contractually obligated) to continue the progress of republican governance, the "Appeal to the Colored Citizens" accuses the white voters of using this power to corrupt the form of government they claim to protect. This doubling allows the convention to request even as it condemns, to ask for judgment even as it dispenses its own judgment, and to approach the voters from a forbearing (rather than supplicating) posture even as it shapes a unified black political community through a sense of righteous indignation.[156] Each instance represents an algorithm depending on audience reception, a step-by-step protocol leading to either citizenship practices that are more democratic on one end or grounds for disassociation on the other.

The 1840 New York convention frames disfranchisement as the death of citizenship, and black women's agitation in Ohio reveals the degree to which the black state conventions, as a theoretical space and set of print practices, could exceed the limitations its largely male delegates attempted to enforce. Pennsylvanians' invocation of the sublime appeal reveals that the collective struggle to correct institutional wrongs may well be where the practice of citizenship truly begins. It is no coincidence that prominent figures in the conventions of the 1840s—Garnet, Alexander Crummell, and Martin R. Delany—would later argue that, if the nation continued to be unresponsive, the black citizens of the United States should take their civic power elsewhere.[157] If the good citizen in Jones and Allen's *Narrative* makes neighbors out of strangers through empathetic identification, the black state conventions attempt to join citizens through participatory politics, making their fellow citizenship stronger. At the same time, the conventions demonstrate that black (male) citizenship theorizing should not be romanticized as immune from its own exclusions. The black state conventions operated through labor from black women that the conventions themselves often did not recognize as practicing citizenship. As this book's next chapters demonstrate, women, working-class folk, and an assortment of others consistently intrude on these attempts on the part of various black activists to create their own circumscribed versions of citizenship.

By 1850, seventeen recorded state conventions had occurred across eight states, and Garnet began 1849 with a call for another New York convention (this convention never met). Cary took Douglass's invitation for black citizens to submit commentary on Garnet's call to the *North Star* as an occasion to reflect on and critique the movement on the whole. "We have been holding conventions for years—have been assembling together and whining over our difficulties and afflictions, passing resolution on resolutions to any extent," Cary notes in her characteristic bluntness. And yet, she continues, "we have put forth few practical efforts."[158] Among the reasons for this lack of productivity, Cary cites the demagoguery of ministers who have failed to teach practical political lessons in favor of empty religious doctrine and increasing their own wealth. Cary's observations identify problems that would continue plaguing the conventions over the next decades, but she also links political agency to economic agency: "Individual enterprise and self-reliance are not sufficiently insisted upon," she posits.[159] In this way, Cary, whose father, Abraham Shadd, helped prepare the appeals for the 1848 Pennsylvania convention, affirms the conventions' message even as she questions their execution. They were, perhaps, exerting too much energy seeking white approval and not enough cultivating other kinds of power that might prove more effective in realizing full citizenship in practice, if not yet in law. As the next chapter argues, the economic changes of the early nineteenth century were as important to black theorizing as political changes. As white voters in Pennsylvania and New York reaffirmed white citizenship through suffrage restrictions, black activists collectively and individually made the case that economic interest might offer routes to political power that persuasion and electoral politics could not.

CHAPTER 3

Economic Citizenship in Ethiop and Communipaw's New York

By the 1840s and 1850s, black reformers not only began claiming their labor, enslaved and free, as "an integral part of their identities" but also, as historian Leslie M. Harris observes, began seeing "in meaningful labor a path to equality."[1] In doing so, they were drawing on the increased linkage of race and labor in political discourse, the material exigencies of a modern U.S. market economy, and the constraints both placed on black citizenship. Even before the revolution, labor was a hotly contested concept in terms of citizenship practice. By the 1830s, however, citizens had come to understand their economic selves and ideals as coextensive with and, in some cases, the same as their civic selves. This connection between labor and citizenship was even more important for black citizens, whose relation to their own labor and the market was complicated by the economics of enslavement. In the absence of political representation and amid a growing sense that market capital was replacing political capital, black activists searched for economic representatives, men and women who could earn "credit" for their communities in the civic economy, advocating for them in a market that was increasingly figured as the space for, rather than threat to, citizenship practice.

This chapter analyzes developing schematics of economic citizenship—the relation between representations of labor and laborers, the civic credit and political power accrued through such representations, and the rendering of the market as the space for making citizenship—through readings of William J. Wilson and James McCune Smith's pseudonymous correspondences as Ethiop and Communipaw in *Frederick Douglass's Paper* from 1851 to 1854. These correspondences were a part of a larger battle over not only developing capitalist political economics but also the terms for evaluating the representational structures that transform labor to civic value and shifting understandings of representation and citizenship more broadly.

In making its argument through a consideration of the periodical writings of two neglected black intellectuals, this chapter takes up Robert Levine and others' concern with the tendency to put Douglass forward as "*the* representative black male figure of the time." This tendency, Levine suggests, has led literary scholars to "elide some of the most significant dialogues and exchanges of antebellum culture—the very debates out of which Douglass's ideas and writings emerged."[2] While Douglass's thinking has taken center stage in discussions of black economic and political thought, his arguments were not necessarily the most salient for his contemporaries, and they did not develop in a vacuum. Black theorizing around economics emerged from efforts to consolidate a wide-ranging approach to economic citizenship that could simultaneously encourage uplift programs and empower those citizens whose labor was discounted. The focus on single figures flattens this diversity and the productive tension that this chapter and *The Practice of Citizenship* as a whole argues animated black citizenship theorizing. Toward this end, the chapter's first section briefly outlines the economic climate for black citizens in the 1840s and 1850s before turning to the 1848 National Colored Convention, held in Cleveland, Ohio. The 1848 convention's debate, which included Douglass, Martin R. Delany, and a host of other black activists, and the convention's "Address to the Colored People of the United States" highlight two movements that this chapter will analyze in more detail through Smith and Wilson's subsequent correspondences: (1) black activists were refining an economic policy based on mutual dependence that incorporated contemporaneous understandings of economic citizenship with more traditional uplift strategies, and (2) this project required not only a shift in political economic thinking but also new understandings of the relationship between cultural representation, political and economic power, and the structural conditioning of black and white subjectivities commensurate with the demands of economic citizenship.[3]

The chapter's next section turns to *Frederick Douglass's Paper* and the dynamics of the Ethiop-Communipaw debates. I offer separate readings of Wilson and Smith's economic citizenship theories and the contrapuntal dynamic between their theorizing and their narrative strategies. Through his columns as Douglass's Brooklyn Correspondent, Wilson offers a form of economic citizenship in which a "black aristocracy" would "represent" or advocate for its community economically and politically among the nation's "monied class."[4] Wilson develops this tactic out of his understanding of a U.S. political economy resembling more an oligarchy than a republic with economic interest and control of productive resources offering more direct routes to social and political power than public or state channels. Smith's correspondences, in contrast, investigate the black laborer's representativeness, asking several questions: how representative is this figure of the overall type of the laboring classes, how well does this type match a historical sense of species development, and what can we learn about the trajectory of black citizenship and U.S. republicanism from studying these representatives? The representative citizen, for Smith, belongs to the middling classes, the average person of prosperity, if not wealth, in a republican polity rather than an aristocracy.[5]

Like Absalom Jones and Richard Allen before them, Wilson and Smith's critiques develop on the level of form as well as content. Through the framing of their respective pseudonymous personas and the formal and stylistic interplay of their sketches, Smith and Wilson not only explore the subjectivities this kind of urban economic citizenship creates but also suggest the kinds of subjectivities needed to navigate developing economic structures, often attacking each other's "conceptions of truth" through literary criticism.[6] I conclude with an illustration of the aesthetic back-and-forth between the two as an example of what Wilson J. Moses has called "creative conflict," in this case a *staged* call-and-response antagonism between Smith and Wilson, who were close colleagues in life. This print performance ultimately helped them refine each other's (and other correspondents') work and shape public critical discourse in content and in style. Focusing more specifically on Wilson and Smith's negotiation of forms of economic citizenship and black urban life allows us to map the processes by which citizenship was being imagined in the 1850s as neither civic republican, nor democratic, but rather as economic. Their example also highlights the degree to which black conceptions of citizenship unfold not just in speeches, conventions, and pamphlets but also through a highly creative and collaborative community of letters.

Economic Citizenship: "Productive" Labor in Black and White

While white citizens and European immigrants were claiming "productive" labor, variously defined, as a signifier of citizenship and consolidated national identity, the same structures of economic citizenship barred black workers.[7] Indeed, it depended on their exclusion. Black citizens continued wrestling with symbolic and material systems that stigmatized black people through the labor they performed, a hardening racial caste system that saw certain "degraded" occupations as natural for black citizens, and popular imagery that treated black economic aspirations as at once threats and at the same time as empty comedic performances. Employments that earned more money and had greater prospects for upward mobility, like clerking, were closed to black workers even in abolitionist circles, and discriminatory permit practices often prevented black entrepreneurs from taking advantage of more lucrative manual labor opportunities like carting.[8] And because of the continued association of black citizens' menial occupations with notions of dependence, white workers began protesting that working in close proximity to black workers or working at similar tasks lowered their own status.[9] As a result, white laborers enforced racial lines with violence and hostility, and officials who wanted both to cultivate their support and suppress potential interracial labor coalitions used this violence as a pretext for enacting and maintaining restrictive policies.[10] When white and black workers did cooperate in unions and for workers' rights, they often met opposition from white employers and black activists alike.[11]

The trend for most of the free black population in New York and other states was one of either stultifying immobility or steady decline. As European immigration increased in the 1840s, competition stiffened over even the waged jobs black citizens traditionally held. By 1850, Harris notes of New York, "Only 5.44 percent of black men held artisanal jobs," and by 1855, 87 percent occupied so-called unskilled positions, including bootblacking, waiting tables, domestic service, and the like.[12] Not only did white Americans block black citizens' access to economic citizenship, but their own sense of success also depended on a system designed "not to develop, *but to underdevelop Black people*."[13] As black workers continued filling menial positions, they helped ameliorate fears of downward mobility and, at the same time, allowed white workers, who may not have been in any better economic position, to accrue social capital in whiteness.

Gradual emancipation provisions, the 1850 Fugitive Slave Law, colonizationist and racial scientific rhetoric, and black labor statistics all coalesced to support a pervasive sense that black citizens were forming a permanent underclass and could not, nor were ever meant to, become proper U.S. citizens. Horace Greeley, editor of the New York *Daily Tribune*, warned in

1843, "So long as they remain pretty generally bootblacks, tavern-waiters, clothes-scourers, &c., from seeming choice; the right to vote will be of precious little account to them."[14] Greeley's conceit that black "condition" was a matter of "seeming choice," pronounced not two decades removed from gradual emancipation in New York, participates in the inverse causality discourse that used the results of white supremacy to confirm assumptions that black citizens were simply not equipped to operate as economic, let alone as political, agents.[15] The economic order represented by commentators like Greeley and the state constitutional conventions that I analyzed in Chapter 2 saw the representative black citizen as a bootblack or servant, "from seeming choice," who could not profit from the added burden of politics and who had not and could not advance in profession. Moreover, the nation, from this perspective, had nothing to profit by incorporating them as anything more; it had more to profit through suppression. The political framing and economic underdevelopment of black citizens, then, were mutually constitutive.

Just as labor theory offered new ways for defining white citizenship, however, it also provided new ways for framing black activism.[16] Even before the market revolutions of the 1820s and 1830s, black activists had been developing rubrics of economic citizenship and cultures of respectability, partly as a public response to racism but also for the same reasons as white citizens: they believed the habits associated with respectability—thrift, education, self-control, hard work, and so on—would lead to material success and elevation.[17] Yet, if most activists agreed that economic representation was central to black progress, they disagreed about how to resolve the tension between orders of representation, that is, between ideal image and material exigencies or even the language with which to frame their arguments. As one activist asserted in frustration, many were "aiming at the same thing, but . . . had a different way of getting at it."[18] Representations of black labor were "of material of double strength," argued the Committee of Social Relations and Polity at the 1853 Colored National Convention, "having for [their] composition our condition [their lack of economic and political power] and strong prejudicial feelings generated from that condition."[19] Solutions, then, had to confront both the lack of economic power and policies that, paradoxically, maintained the "conditions" used to justify them.

These tensions famously erupted into full debate during the 1848 National Convention of Colored Freemen, revealing not only how activists framed their positions on labor but also how their claims to representative narratives were central to crafting them. John L. Watson (Ohio), fugitive slave and prosperous barber and bathhouse owner, and J. D. Patterson, a waiter, confronted activists including Delany, "who," in their view, "were in the editorial chair and others, not in places of servants" for "cast[ing] slurs upon those, who were in such places from necessity."[20] (These "slurs" reportedly included Delany's claim that he would "rather receive a telegraphic dispatch that his wife and two children had fallen victims to a loathsome disease, than to hear that they had become the servants of any man."[21]) Watson and Patterson were less concerned with the *image* of black labor than with the necessities of a stable income; better a "degraded" servant than a beggar. They suggest that Delany and others' vision was not in line with realities on the ground. Watson agreed that the emphasis on gaining better situations was desirable, but the language of condemnation and individual responsibility coming out of black newspapers and conventions was alienating and misplaced. "We know our position and feel it," he protests; black citizens did not need to be told that their work was not respected in the dominant political economy. They needed, instead, a way to articulate their contributions more positively, to be encouraged even as they worked their way up, and, most important, an economy in which that upward movement was materially feasible to more than a privileged few.

In opposition to Watson and Patterson and in support of the convention's fourth resolution—"the occupation of domestics and servants among our people is degrading to us as a class, and we deem it our bounden duty to discountenance such pursuits"—A. H. Francis (New York) and David Jenkins (Ohio) offered narratives of their individual rise to lucrative self-employment that mapped well onto both popular notions of respectability and the upward trajectory of the classic slave narrative. Francis, for instance, recounts his rise from having "been in nearly all the avocations named in the Resolution" to "owning a mercantile business of $20,000 or $30,000 a year."[22] Though the resolution echoed white commentators, who, just two years before, had used similar language in arguments against black suffrage, it also reflected many of the delegates' sense that their own success served as templates others could follow, proof that the template was successful. Moreover, these delegates were no doubt concerned that readers (both black and white) would take any equivocation from the convention as capitulation: see, even black representatives admit they aren't prepared for economic citizenship. The narratives accompanying these arguments, then, mattered as much as the arguments themselves.

While I will probe this problem more directly in my discussion of Smith and Wilson's sketches, Douglass's mediating practice during this convention offers a practical example of why, for Smith and Wilson, a dialogic approach to representing black economic citizenship offered a powerful complement to their activism: no single person *could* represent or re-present black labor. Douglass's role as convention president demonstrates both the effectiveness and the limitations of these attempts to craft representative narratives of black economic citizenship. To mediate the debate, Douglass rose to "suggest a Resolution so as to suit both parties":

> He thought that as far as speakers intimated that any useful labor was degrading, they were wrong. . . . He had been a chimney-sweep. . . . He had been a wood-sawyer. He wished not that it should stand thus:—White Lawyer—Black Chimney-sweep; but White Lawyer, Black Lawyer, as in Massachusetts; White Domestic, Black Domestic. He said: Let us say what is necessary to be done, is honorable to do; and leave situations in which we are considered degraded, as soon as necessity ceases.[23]

Douglass's testimony apparently broke new ground: he admits to having been a chimney sweep and filling other "degraded" positions. As the recording secretary observes, Douglass "was probably the first that had ever made the announcement from the public stand," a milestone in black public discourse.[24] While Douglass's claim to "firstness" might be tenuous, as Harris suggests, this moment presaged a new generation of black activists who saw "their past as central to their present success" and their identities as laborers "to be central to their sense of self."[25]

What I want to highlight here, however, is that this moment does not happen without the preceding debate and the exigencies of crafting a more inclusive and grounded approach to addressing an economically diverse citizenry. Even as Douglass stands in momentarily as a representative man, some of his amendments were rejected, suggesting the limits of representative man politics, particularly in the standard uplift form, for such a diverse population. The minutes report: Douglass "was followed by several gentlemen, when Messrs. Patterson, Copeland and Douglass, severally proposed amendments, which were on motion rejected. . . . The 4th Resolution was adopted with but one dissenting vote." Douglass's image was a vexed one in this and other moments because even as he (or his image) offered ways to rethink black citizenship in relation to labor, his meteoric rise also reinforced middle-class narratives like Francis and Jenkins's. Still, his efforts did result in an addendum to the original resolution: "except where necessity compels the person to resort thereto as a means of livelihood"—in part because he weaves a narrative in which the republican rhetoric of independent labor could coexist with the reality of black working classes restricted to "degraded" positions. Douglass's compromise, then, met the dual requirements that the resolution encourage black citizens, for whom condition had calcified into caste, and that it also discourage complacency.

While convention delegates would continue debating particulars, with Douglass attempting to mediate with marginal success, a more salient economic model emerged in the convention's "Address to the Colored People." Black communities needed economic power—representatives in trades and industries and proportional ownership of the nation's productive resources—not only to counter prevailing representations of black labor but also, and more important, so "that other members of the community shall be as dependent upon us, as we upon them."[26] "We must not merely make the white man dependent upon us to shave him," the "Address" continues, "but to feed him; not merely dependent upon us to black his boots, but to make them."[27] As Douglass explained during the debate, there was nothing degrading about useful work; rather, "what is necessary to be done, is honorable to do."[28] Even so, the "Address" concludes, the greater the utility citizens could fill, the more power citizens could accrue for themselves and their communities, both black and white. A more equitable distribution of dependence would bring a more equitable distribution of power.

Respect (a materially grounded instrumental politics) replaces respectability (an outwardly focused symbolic politics) as the "Address" focuses less on publicity and more on the power of mutual dependence: "To be dependent, is to be degraded," the convention notes in the republican style; however, complete independence "would be absurd and impossible, in the social state."[29] While "independence" may be "an essential condition of respectability," mutual dependence yields "respect." Black citizens must create systems of mutual dependence for "the necessaries of life."[30] This notion of mutual dependence carries Absalom Jones and Richard Allen's late eighteenth-century neighborly ethics into the mid-nineteenth-century market. To secure equal citizenship, people must not only be willing to be neighborly but also must have the *material capacity* to be good economic citizens: "the equality which we aim to accomplish, can only be achieved by us, when we can do for others, just what others can do for us," to "render [our] share to the common stock of prosperity and happiness."[31] Put differently: make others as dependent on you as you are on them. The state becomes a corporate body as the convention renders the market as a space where equality is produced outside of civil society by means of economic force (figured benignly as dependence) rather than political participation or consent, as such.

Even as the 1848 convention's maxims operate through the rhetoric of respectability, then, its shift to "respect" suggests the delegates' recognition of a more expansive notion of respectability politics that moved well beyond black adherence to bourgeois values for a judging white gaze. Despite the tone of judgment Watson and others noted, the conventioneers were not reducible to a binary between the elite and the "folk." They were, as Gene Jarrett notes of a slightly later generation, "sophisticated agents of social change, not [merely] elitists misguided in their cultural calculus of political power."[32] As Erica Ball has argued, antebellum respectability politics was "simultaneously respectable and subversive," as it called for both moral reform and refused the calculus of white judgment. The shift to respect suggests the delegates' recognition that no interpretation of black public behavior could explain racism's cultural and economic matrices fully or offer a rubric for creating political equality. If black economic power could not persuade white citizens of black equality, at least structures of mutual dependence might mute racism's adverse effects. This shift in emphasis still traded in terms of respectability but with much less emphasis on the moral and public-performative aspects of the discourse and more on its material underpinnings.[33]

Smith and Wilson's debate as Communipaw and Ethiop is particularly useful in this context because they explicitly set out to interrogate and create representational systems specific to urban black labor in New York. New York State offers a productive site for this analysis because the state's $250 property qualification for black male suffrage directly linked political representation to economic and racial representation. Ethiop and Communipaw's debate with each other and other pseudonymous correspondents for *Douglass's Paper* served as a vehicle for circulating a general economic ethos and, as Todd Vogel suggests of the black press more generally, for "reset[ing] the terms of public conversation" to offer a different "quality of representation." And Carla Peterson describes *Douglass's Paper* in particular as "an ideal forum for refuting the niggerolgoists and devising their own definitions and interpretations of race."[34] Wilson's Ethiop column pushes the convention's overall argument further, suggesting a model of economic representation that emphasizes the centrality of the "monied idea" to creating and sustaining the proper position in relation to power. Wilson's ideal representative would apply the vision modeled in his sketches to the problems of black citizenship, standing in a position to understand the overall circulation of economic power with the savvy of a flâneur but with the material capacity and ethical commitment to directing this circulation in the community's interest. Smith's Communipaw, like Watson and Patterson, resists the diminishing attention given to civic virtue, offering a long historical and anthropological point of view in place of their appeals to present exigencies.[35] The subjects of his "'Heads of the Colored People,' Done with a Whitewash Brush" offer insights from which he generalizes about the "average colored person," suggesting that the middling sorts, not an elite, will impel not only black progress but also national renewal.

Developing this ethos as a protracted debate in real time, rather than as a convention record, ensured that their impressions were always fresh and timely. Using the sketch genre gave the two writers the formal flexibility to incorporate speculation, fictionalization, journalism, historiography, and sharp humor. Like their Philadelphia predecessor, Joseph Willson, whose *Sketches of the Higher Classes of Colored Society in Philadelphia* (1841) rendered images of the economic elite of black Philadelphia, Smith and Wilson use the sketched correspondence to render "contours, rather than details; patterns of behavior, rather than individual acts."[36] The sketch genre's conceit of firsthand observation and narrative whim allowed them to enter into a situation in medias res, so to speak, and leave just as quickly for another, not always related, topic, without the expectation of a cohesive narrative structure. It allowed them to take arguments surfaced in the 1848 convention and test them out on the streets, among and from the variegated perspectives of the very folk for whom convention delegates attempted to speak.[37] The correspondences attempt to make visible the often invisible lives of black workers as something more than an undifferentiated mass but rather as a heterogeneous and dynamic community with economic and political potential.

"Position Is Everything": Ethiop's Black Aristocracy as Counter to U.S. Oligarchy

Born in 1818 to a family of Shrewsbury, New Jersey, oyster harvesters, William J. Wilson moved to Brooklyn, New York, in the 1830s, where he opened a boot-making shop. He began teaching in Brooklyn in 1842 and was later named principal of Colored Public School No. 1. In later years, he opened a reading room in the city and acted as editor (if not in name) of several papers, including the *Weekly Anglo-African.* Wilson was active in the New York suffrage movement, a member of the famed Committee of Thirteen, a regular delegate at the national conventions of the 1850s, and he wrote editorials for the *Weekly Anglo-African* in the early 1860s.[38] Of Wilson's physical presence and oratorical skill, William Wells Brown observes, "He is under the middle size; his profile is more striking than his front face; he has a rather pleasing countenance, and is unmixed in race; has fine conversational powers, is genteel in his manners, and is a pleasant speaker upon the platform."[39] He began writing for *Douglass's Paper* as Ethiop, the paper's "Brooklyn Correspondent," on December 11, 1851, and continued writing under that moniker for various publications, including the *Anglo-African Magazine,* into the early 1860s. The "Ethiop" persona, an allusion to both Ethiopia and Phillis Wheatley, signals Wilson's dedication to building black communities and literary histories, a theme I will take up more directly in the next chapter.[40] Brown describes his sketches, which had become a fixture in black periodical writing, as "some of the raciest and most amusing essays to be found in the public journals of this country," arguing, "few men are capable of greater or more successful efforts than William J. Wilson" when it came to that genre.[41] Of all the writers *The Practice of Citizenship* analyzes, with the notable exception of Frances Harper, Wilson demonstrates the most heightened awareness of the newspaper in general, and the sketch in particular, as a field for creative play.

Wilson positions Ethiop as an ideal guide for navigating New York's modern landscape from a black perspective and for black citizens. Ethiop describes himself as "invisible and never out of hearing . . . in the market or the street—the drawing room—the café—or the church," providing a panorama of "'NEW YORK AS NOW,'" that is, "MEN and THINGS in NEW YORK."[42] His style invokes a host of popular theatrical, literary, and historical references playing on the theme, including "New York as It Is," "New York at a Glance," *New-York as It is: Containing a General Description of the City of New-York* (1837), Poe's "The Man of the Crowd" (1840), Dickens's *American Notes for General Circulation* (1842), and Lydia Maria Child's *Letters from New York* (1845). These generic ("New York as now") and formal cues (strolls through the cityscape) give Ethiop's "Brooklyn Correspondent" column an air of documentary journalism as he renders a view of the city with "shades" and "lights . . . bright spots, brighter than [he] can paint them," but it also intervenes in an American (and British) literary scene based in depictions of modern cities as by turns spaces of opportunity and degradation but never as spaces for black citizens. Through Ethiop, Wilson wields his descriptive talents to offer his own assessment of economic citizenship's capitalist core, its "monied idea," taking up and revising other activists' arguments to outline potential paths for black representation among the nation's economic powerbrokers.

From his earliest letters, Ethiop sets out to reveal how racism veils the city's economic doings and how focusing on surfaces leads black folk in particular to mistake an insubstantial respectability for the substance of economic power.[43] Ethiop develops two central metaphors for his analysis: through the metaphor of the stage, he outlines social categories and maps each class's role within the overall economic drama; the figure of the veil, in turn, provides a heuristic for how race obscures the more antagonist and antidemocratic aspects of this structure. He suggests that a change in position in relation to this staging—both economically and narratively—is the only solution to counter a speedily solidifying racial caste system. From such a position, Ethiop's proposed black aristocracy would be able to navigate and manage what Ethiop sees as the functional equivalence of market and civic practices. Viewing this landscape through the subjectivity modeled by Ethiop's column, black aristocrats could remove the city's racial veil, a veneer of collective enterprise and "true republicanism" on the surface of mutual antagonism and oligarchy.[44]

Manhattan is "one vast show," Ethiop explains in one of his earliest letters, a stage where, if they could, the "looker on" would "see, as [he] saw," three rather coherent categories of people distinguished by their racial and class performances: "The *whites* exhibited the two features, wealth and poverty; while the *blacks* exhibited an intermediate one."[45] Rich and poor whites play extreme roles, but they have essentially the same character within the context of the social show, united in the same project of accumulation through a culture of capitalism: "The same white, ghost-like, motionless face, the same hawk-line nose, and thin, livid lip, and restless, wolf-like countenance, indicative of keen scent after what is another's. . . . The propensity for grasping and appropriating, are as indelibly stamped in every face, as the mark of Cain; and though players, all, 'tis all the same, whether priest, prince, or beggar."[46] Ethiop's reading refigures white enterprise as a string of appropriations amounting, in the end, to mutual hostility, a Hobbesian war of all against all; for white characters, upward mobility happens at another's expense. The features contemporaneous white writers associated with whiteness in general and Anglo-Saxons in particular do not signal ingenuity or greatness but rather, like the mark singling Cain's fratricide, serve as a warning that, no matter the trappings, white capitalism is a curse on humanity.[47] In this invocation of *Leviathan* (Hobbes uses Cain as one of his paradigmatic examples) and the Bible's first murderer, Ethiop suggests that the institutions that should have maintained a more republican sense of commonwealth have failed or have become subsumed under the "monied idea."

Capital and interest (not religion, nationalism, participatory politics, or even racial character) govern U.S. citizenship. "Money," Ethiop posits in his December 25, 1851, correspondence, "is the ruling idea."[48] Appeals to racial character are mere window dressing (but no less powerful because of it), an artificial means of ensuring black citizens remain excluded and their labor available. "The *Alpha and Omega* of everything here," he continues, "are dollars and cents; of necessity, therefore, nothing is admissible but what will produce it."[49] Ethiop fills his correspondence with these aphoristic phrases—"It is idle to believe that American prejudice and oppression, have any other than a monied basis," "Interest *Jonathan's* pocket, and you have his confidence," and so on—leading to his penultimate verdict: "*Art, science, philanthropy*, humanity, religion; all the higher qualities and feelings are calculated in dollars and cents, and sacrificed, if necessary, to this same God."[50] Ethiop extends Alexander Hamilton's reasoning in the *Federalist No. 30* ("Money is, with propriety . . . the vital principle of the body politic . . . that which sustains its life and motion") to suggest that making money has *become* the nation's "life and motion," its end and "essential function," not a means to that end.[51] Capital, once seen as a threat to civic virtue, has been raised above it, the standard for measuring all other values. "Whatever does not pay," Ethiop quips, "answers not Jonathan's purpose."[52]

Though he outlines citizenship's economic basis with cynicism, Ethiop does not oppose it. Rather, he opposes how white supremacy limits opportunities for black citizens to take advantage of all the market could offer.

He acknowledges the same antagonistic strain in antebellum capitalist culture that Jones and Allen's *Narrative* outlines in civic republicanism, but he is more concerned with unpacking its racial logic as a pragmatic matter of gaining equal representation. While "the whites have their poor and degraded," they also have "their rich and elevated, whose number is legion."[53] Black communities, in contrast, "present but one phase—a low flat surface" that only reinforces white assumptions and buoys white efforts.[54] The problem is not the existence of classes but rather the relative absence of class diversity within black communities and how the perception and enforcement of uniformity function within the system as a whole.[55]

Through the figure of the veil (or curtain), Ethiop illustrates how this strictly enforced homogeneity structures white cultures of capital. Black performers serve as stable functionaries; they "hold up, as it were, the veil of the *plot*, and perform certain other easy services."[56] Holding up the veil of the plot gestures toward the surplus value that black labor provides—as porters, washerwomen, bootblacks, waiters, and so on—an economic backdrop against which wealthy white citizens have made their fortunes and that allows working white citizens to occupy positions that, if not more productive, gain more credit. Even recent European immigrants fleeing oppression in their homelands and unused to U.S.-style racism, he argues, can "build thereon at the expense of the blood, and sweat, and tears, and groans of the oppressed of this land."[57] At the same time, black figures provide a nationalizing backdrop, an always available empty signifier, "sufficient to swivel up about all the Anglo-Saxon courage and energy there is extant in a sizable nut-shell that may be put and worn in any one of their breeches pockets."[58] Despite the mutual antagonism on rich and poor white faces, the availability of this backdrop of negative blackness, on literal stages as in minstrelsy and on the streets, salves poverty's wounds, empowering its bearers with a sense of belonging through the promise that their Anglo-Saxon character will win out.[59]

As a result, while black citizens "hold up the . . . veil" of the city's economic play, they remain excluded from its principal action. Ethiop sees this material and cultural assault resulting in psychic damage as black communities fall victim to "the *bug-bear* 'CANNOT' . . . [,] a *hideous monster* pursuing us everywhere."[60] Though the "monster" exists in the overt threat of white violence, it manifests more ominously in the seemingly innocuousness of everyday life, the "mundane and the quotidian," as Saidiya Hartman would later term it: "Well may we scoff at black skins and wooly heads,"

Ethiop concludes a year later, "since every model set before us for admiration has pallid face and flaxen head, or emanations thereof."[61] This sense of powerlessness "makes a young woman feel she is a negative being," "drives the trader from the stand, the mechanic from the workshop," and "scares our children in the streets."[62] Black citizens, Ethiop claims, have internalized the current social order as the *only* possibility out of fear and necessity, preventing would-be entrepreneurs from opening shops of their own because of a cocktail of discriminatory policies, hostile whites, and a lack of support at home. Such is the monster's power that Ethiop feels its presence himself: "It even now, impudently steals up behind me, while I write, and seizes my elbow," Ethiop confesses, forcing him to conclude his letter.[63]

Under such conditions, the "respectability" for which some activists called had been reduced to pageantry as a new generation learned to value appearances over substance. Ethiop describes youths who had mastered the signs of respectability—clothing, genteel mannerisms (bordering on "dandyism"), education, and so on—while lacking the economic practices and material power respectability was meant to produce and signify. Chasing after "petty by-paths" in the market, "the drapery and tinsel of education," and believing that "appearing well, would make up for not doing well," they remain "trapped on the wrong side of [the business] curtain, pretending to touch the real in their appearance . . . but never coming close" and, worse still, learning to loath fellow black folk.[64] The public sees "wives and daughters of men, whose occupations are of questionable propriety, promenade our streets, laden with the richest silks of the Indies, and decked with all the gew-gaws of wealthiest whites, often outrivaling them in the splendor of their attire."[65] Such men and women decorate the cover of George Foster's collected sketches, *New York by Gaslight* (1850), overlooking white men at work and business; the black man's cane curls like a monkey's tale, suggesting the comical nature of his façade (Figure 4).[66] These hypervisible black citizens totter between working white citizens, who look every bit as poor as the black youth might actually be; black men and women of "questionable propriety"; and rich white citizens who may not look as fashionable and may not be as educated as their black counterparts but who nevertheless have political power over them.

Even as he recasts contemporaneous arguments faulting black citizens' culture and habits for their political economic position, however, Ethiop reminds his readers that these cultural representations of blackness and the structural conditioning of black and white subjectivity they mask result

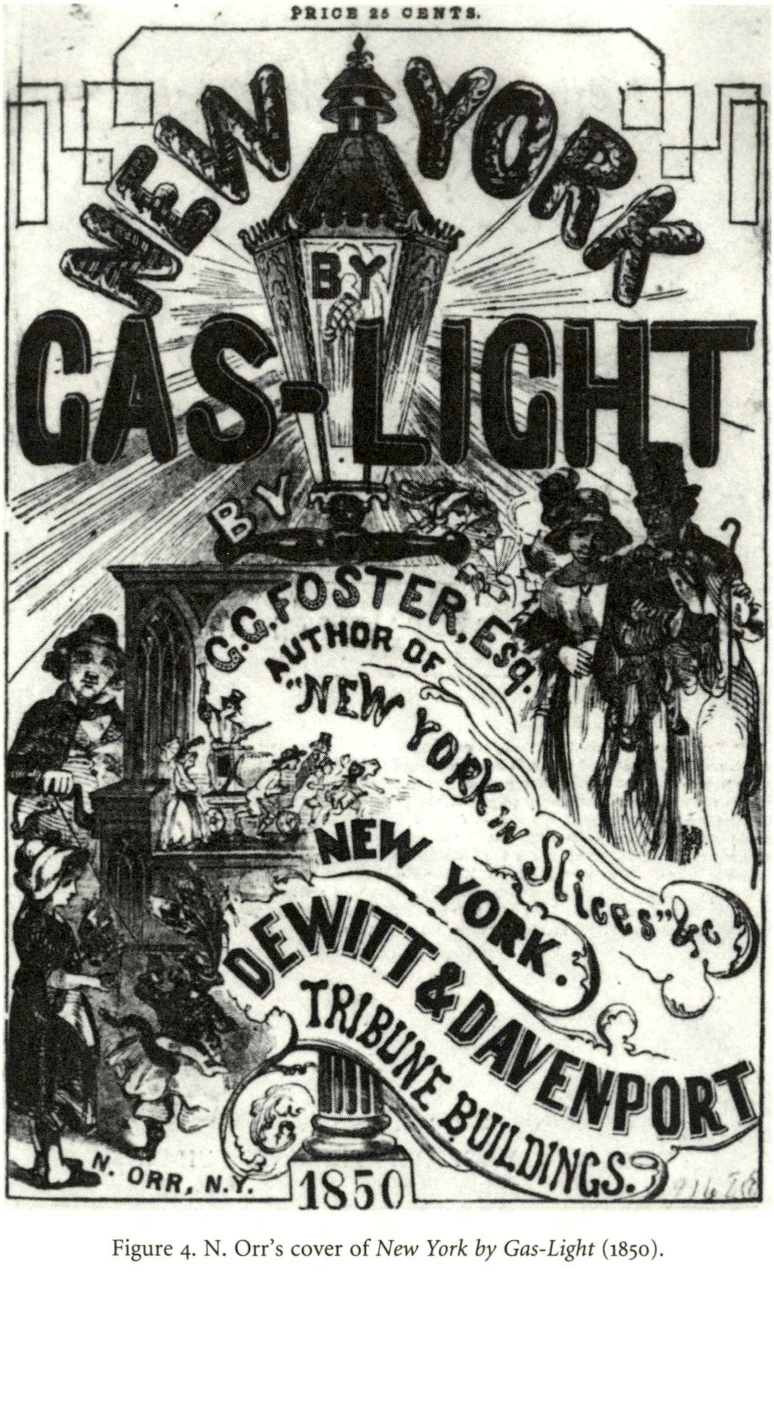

Figure 4. N. Orr's cover of *New York by Gas-Light* (1850).

from a systematic pedagogy of domination. Through the cultural production of racial knowledge, white citizens and "all the world are taught to look at both [white] deeds and men through a magnifying glass of their own construction, which invariably pronounces upon all favorably. You look and behold! it is good!"[67] While national myths coming from contemporaries such as Ralph Waldo Emerson would claim that Anglo-Saxon power resulted from hard work, self-culture, and self-reliance, Ethiop contends, "Their great men . . . owe as much, and often more, to position," to the lens through which they see and are seen, "than to either their own energies or abilities—more to their system of *puff, boast,* and *brag,* than to any real merit in them." Where Emerson claims in *Representative Men* (1850), "Every child of the Saxon race is educated to *wish* to be first," Ethiop suggests that white (or Saxon) children are taught that they *are* first, no matter the quality of their striving or lack thereof.[68] Put differently, white success is as much a result of power (position) and control of representation (*puff, boast,* and *brag*) in the shape of a mythological whiteness, "at the same time both imperfectable and unquestionable," as it is of individual labors (merit).[69]

Ethiop returns to popular culture as a lens conditioning ways of being in the world throughout his sketches, anticipating W. E. B. Du Bois's 1926 claim in "Criteria of Negro Art," "All art is propaganda, and ever must be," as he makes the case for a concerted black political and aesthetic project.[70] It's not (just) that black laborers occupy degraded positions but rather that the culture exalts all things white over all things black, and worse, even black successes are veiled, "[receiving] from the same system an amount of hoots, hisses and pious curses."[71] If white society has in its service a magnifying glass, Ethiop concludes, "Let us have a glass of our own . . . and we, too, may see and teach others to see our own men and deeds as they ought to be seen—as they are."[72] But the black lens must be more than the uplift narratives offered in conventions and papers; it must be coupled with economic leaders to guide "the people" in productive directions and to confront the material conditions framing and codifying the white lens. "Who, then," he asks, "are the guides of the people. . . . Who ought to be? Certainly those whose capacities and energies have led them beyond the pale of mere *speculative theories* to palpable and practical results."[73] Ethiop's answer to this query is not to refigure the centrality of economics to U.S. citizenship practices but rather to reorient black citizens' relation to the nation-state's economic and cultural power structure through black economic representatives, a black aristocracy.

Ethiop introduces the idea of a black aristocracy in one of his earliest correspondences, arguing, "Let those of us who can, (and they are many) turn their attentions to the monied interests in this country; and once fairly in the field, the disabilities complained of, would disappear as an evening cloud."[74] "A black aristocracy must be had," Ethiop concludes, to cultivate the "best means" for not only producing black economic citizens but also reconfiguring the operations of economic citizenship more broadly.[75] Noting that modern industrial capitalism has created untenable inequalities, stripping the city of its humanity, Ethiop nevertheless argues that a black aristocracy can establish balance through proper management and negotiation:

> Alas, it is a sad reflection, that amidst so much *brick and mortar*, amid so much splendor, here is so much of misery and degradation; society is organically diseased here. I venture to say that there is more wretchedness, more misery, more degradation, here in this metropolis amidst the superfluity of philanthropy and religion, than can be found in any whole nation outside of Christendom. . . . Society here needs renovating, *soul* and *body*; and it is the office-work of those to whom I belong to effect it; this is their true mission.[76]

Wilson, like Jones and Allen before him, realized that economic practice and racial structures were integrally connected, dangerous not just to racial minorities but to all citizens. The inverse relation between the signs of modernity ("so much *brick and mortar*") and general prosperity suggests a greater dissonance, a disease affecting both the city's thought life (*soul*) and its material condition (*body*). He observes the same gap between benevolence and praxis in modern New York that Jones and Allen note in yellow fever Philadelphia. The state and established institutions ("the superfluity of philanthropy and religion") have proven ineffective or collusive in creating these conditions, partly because both were governed by the same antagonisms Ethiop notes on the streets in earlier sketches and partly because these conditions profit both sectors. Instead of offering a check on the deleterious effects of industrialization, they have become supportive of it.

Rather than need regulation from civil society or the state, in Ethiop's rendering, the market's logics of interest become the medium through which the disorder might be corrected. "[Engaged] in the various industrial and accumulating enterprises" of the country, the black aristocracy could cure society of this "disease" from inside the market, forging links between society's disintegrated constituencies.[77] Ethiop embraces both interest and the market, if pragmatically, but injects them with a neighborly sensibility. Recognizing that power and representation were already structured hierarchically, most prominently in the "slave oligarchy" but no less so in northern capitalist cities, Ethiop proposes a means of "renovating" this hierarchy so it works toward more just and humane, if not more egalitarian, ends. The black aristocracy's "business," then, involves managing not only capital but also communities, both black working classes and white monied classes, "to the one, offering encouragements and affording substantial aid; to the other, acting as a sort of rectifier of errors—a pruner of excesses; a grand conservator of the whole social machinery."[78] Oscillating between two constituencies, the black aristocracy could understand both, operating at once as visible public guardians and at the same time behind the scenes as the fraternal organization invoked in "grand conservator."[79] They could counter the psychic and material violence of whiteness ("CANNOT"), creating a foundation from which to demand equality for black citizens while focusing the economic elite's attention on constructing a more just society on the whole.[80]

Two factors contribute to the black aristocracy's ability to balance market interest and community responsibility: (1) Ethiop's conception of the market's function as a surrogate for the participatory politics from which many black citizens had been barred and (2) the black aristocrats' ability to move fluidly between multiple spaces and points of view while "feeling" their "position" in relation to black communities. Ethiop sees the monied classes operating by the same mechanisms of circulation that the black state conventions apply to participatory politics. He argues that if black communities focused on cultivating a monied class, "steamboat and railroad stocks would, in the regular course of things, be as much in their [the black aristocracy's] hands as others. Their interests and the *white's* would be in common; and of necessity, an interchange and similarity of feelings would exist between the parties."[81] Ethiop takes this economic growth as a natural process in which the properly managed accumulation of assets will lead inexorably to ownership of central resources. As black entrepreneurs engaged more fully in this growth, increasingly common financial interests among the monied classes would outweigh prejudices, and because "money is the ruling idea," changes in and coming from the monied classes would necessarily (or organically) lead to changes in society as a whole. State-supported discrimination in transportation and other business establishments, for instance, would disappear as black investors became owners of significant stock in them or related operations, and their "influence . . . would forbid the idea of recommending" colonization.[82]

Ethiop realizes that the community's experience with oppression and caste makes the notion of an aristocracy "unpalatable," especially given its contemporaneous usages in reference to the "slave power" and land monopolies, but he argues, "It is as much to the interest of our people to sustain it as to the class sustained."[83] "Happily," he writes in language reflecting Whig notions of the "harmony of interests" and the arguments of contemporaries like Tunis Campbell, "the varieties of our composition make some prefer to arrange, and some to work after arrangements."[84] Because they understand this mutualism, this neighborly ethic, the black aristocrats "naturally discharge" their duties to the community "as do the trees put forth their leaves in summer, or their fruits in due season," so that they resemble less the European variety, "of *mushroom* growth and existence," and more Emerson's "nobles" who "nature provides . . . in every society" to direct the collective "powers . . . by love."[85] These aristocratic trees remain rooted in the community, bearing fruit in an organic sustainable way that contrasts sharply to the gaps in wealth and sensibility Ethiop associates with the city's decline, because the aristocrats' capitalist individualism is balanced with a fellow feeling based on mutual interest and community responsibility. Ethiop follows logic similar to the economics of marginality Peterson describes in *The Garies and Their Friends* (1857), a model that, even as it endorses capitalism, "celebrates not so much individual achievement as the way the characters attend to the collectivity, returning surplus value to the community rather than serving their own special interests."[86] Mapping the civic-market relation in this way reverses the trajectory laid out in the black state conventions in the previous decade—that political equality leads to material equality—suggesting that black citizens can create a more equitable society by force of interest, if not by persuasion or principle. The market would then become a more republican base for broader renovation—more republican because of the more representative sampling of the population constituting it.

Ethiop's black aristocrats are representative, not in the sense of reflecting every citizen's character and potential but rather in a more overtly political sense of representativity, what Nadia Urbinati figures as a relationship of "control (on the part of the represented) and responsibility (on the part of the representatives)."[87] The dollar supplants the ballot as black aristocrats enter the market as representatives among the power-wielding economic elite, "elevated" by "the community who sustain them" to counter white oligarchy.[88] In this dynamic of responsibility and responsiveness, Ethiop's aristocrats differ from Emerson's Representative. For Emerson, the "natural" aristocracy functions as much to assuage class anxiety as it does to "direct" the social landscape. If each citizen did not become independent or otherwise escape waged labor, if all citizens, while created equal, were not equally endowed with property or access to the means of production, the community could at least from the overall climate of progress and productivity or, in Emerson's terms, "the knowledge, that in the city is a man who invented the railroad," which "raises the credit of all citizens."[89] Just as popular participation in electoral politics could valorize a sense of democratic equality despite tending toward less democratic results through the sense or "knowledge" of collective sovereignty, popular participation in the market economy could offer a sense of corporate enterprise and profit with the assurance that, just as elected officials represented a constituency, the economically successful reflected the (potential) vitality of the whole, even if the benefits of that success did not circulate freely.

Ethiop's black aristocracy, by contrast, has an explicit mandate, not as representatives of black potential (abstract and perhaps unattainable) but rather as representatives of black interests (concrete and measurable in terms of economic power). They constitute a specialized professional class growing out of black communities whose job ("office work"), explains Ethiop, is to carry the will of their "people" into the economic seat of power, to "[take] advantage of the infant condition of growing Towns by securing good business localities especially, not only as a source of profit to themselves, but as a great means of inducting Africo-America into the business world."[90] As their economic position short-circuits white supremacy's power, the black aristocrats' ability to feel and share the views of the community that sustains them would keep them responsive to their constituents. Ethiop's black aristocrats' capitalism becomes inseparable from the overall project of community empowerment: they are capitalists in the market, communitarians at home.

Black aristocrats' ability to balance these seemingly contradictory impulses comes from their expansive vision and constant circulation between and within spaces, a subjectivity Ethiop models in his sketches. Harnessing the narrative mobility of the literary sketch, Ethiop oscillates between the "Heights" of Brooklyn, where he can "look down . . . upon that goodly city" clear of obstructions, and the streets where he walks about, sometimes in disguise, close enough to "use [his] own eyes and ears, and arrive at [his] own conclusions."[91] From Brooklyn, the "*bright Eye of the morning* in the back-ground, [guilds] beautifully all before and around," its position of higher ground relative to Manhattan offering an elevated space for observation and the needed distance and time from the center of activity to interpret the disorienting experiences of city life. These experiences nevertheless must be had firsthand for accuracy and to cultivate the proper ethical "feeling."[92] On the ground, Ethiop acts as a participant observer (sometimes disguised), proclaiming in his first correspondence, "And now. Good gentle folks,/Ethiop's again among ye, taking notes."[93] Like a flâneur, Ethiop attempts to make "the rich diversity of modern urban experience accessible to his audience, through the production of images," his columns intended to "paint" day-to-day practices and to provide a geographic, cultural, and economic compass for his readers.[94] Ethiop, then, has a transcendent vision of the whole from above (Ethiop's images of the "*bright Eye of the morning*" invoking the image of Emerson's transparent eyeball) and the personal identification with the community, the confluence enabling Ethiop to draw aside the "dark veil of mystery" to understand the workings of the overall social drama.[95]

The black aristocracy could refigure black representation with similar movements in relation to political economic spaces, managing the city's contending interests on behalf of black citizens through what Urbinati describes as the "*continuing* and *mediated relation* between situated citizens and representatives."[96] Urbinati explains that this kind of "reflective adhesion" between representatives and the people they represent offers the kind of dialogic model of representation essential to democratic politics. Black aristocrats would become emblems of black "corporate capacity," creating a more materially grounded culture in which coming generations understand how the "great business curtain" works and, with this understanding, can distinguish between "actual" and "imaginary" power.[97] "The presence of such a class to urge, assist and otherwise encourage," writes Ethiop, "would cause the really ambitious to step out from among the masses continually and climb up to it."[98] This steady climb would, in turn, create a more representative economic citizenry, disrupting cultures of capital that depend on black surplus labor and a negative blackness and that have resulted in a broader social breakdown. That is, black aristocrats would build the cultural and material structures through which this class of representatives and civic managers could be reproduced, creating a population that increasingly resembled, at least in part, the productive economic habits of its representatives. No longer holding the veil of the play, no longer functioning as expendable support, black citizens could transform the stage itself, or they would build their own.

Here, then, is the crux of Ethiop's economic citizenship and the source of the black aristocracy's sense of identity and responsibility: communities will produce economic representatives who understand their relationship to the community as one of responsibility and responsiveness. Their collective work will eventually net a new generation of economic citizens, whose investments will give them the power needed to make themselves competent participants in the structures of economic representation. Just as the proper narrative and visual position allows Ethiop to see through the veils separating black citizens from real power, the proper economic position would allow them to break through to economic power, creating unofficial modes of representation and advocacy in lieu of official political oligarchy.

Communipaw's Polity of the "Best Average Colored" Citizens

Where Ethiop's model of economic citizenship depends on the ascendancy of a representative aristocracy to counter U.S. oligarchy, Smith's Communipaw questions notions of economic citizenship altogether. His sketches, particularly the "Heads of the Colored People, Done with a Whitewash Brush" series, pull citizenship practices out of the market, or more precisely, they subordinate market interests to a narrative of republican ideals, highlighting the average citizen's life worlds, the little republics they create out of their homes and communities. Against Ethiop's calls for an aristocracy to renovate U.S. oligarchy, Communipaw invokes an ethos of commonwealth republicanism, a polity based on the middling sorts and focused on cultivating a "public spirit" that cherishes liberty and freedom as its highest end.[99]

Early in his responses to Ethiop, Communipaw deduces that Ethiop's focus on economic exigency has led him to succumb to the veil figured in his own analysis, throwing money at what is essentially not a question of capital or management but rather of ideals. Communipaw responds directly to Ethiop's "monied solution" on February 12, 1852, associating Ethiop with a refrain from Sir Walter Scott's popular *Heart of Midlothian or Tales of My Landlord* (1818, reprinted in Philadelphia in 1852): "'Jean! will siller do't?'" (will silver do it?). Through the allusion, Communipaw implies that Ethiop's "dollar remedy" intensifies the decay his black aristocracy is supposed to renovate.[100] By assuming that, as one of *Heart*'s characters famously puts it, "siller [silver] will certainly do it in the Parliament House, if ony [any] thing *can* do it," Ethiop and others who suggest an economic solution to racial caste capitulate to structural inequalities, cynicism, and moral ignominy as normative facets of economic citizenship.[101] Moreover, just as "everyone" knew that Scott, not "Jedediah Cleishbotham," authored *Heart* (and that Wilson was Ethiop!), everyone would recognize that Ethiop's aristocracy would simply be a pseudonymous repackaging of U.S. oligarchy.

Communipaw agrees with Ethiop's assessment of money's centrality to U.S. culture and politics—in Communipaw's terms, "gold" has become the "Key Stone of American morals and religion"—but he comes to very different conclusions about solutions for black communities and the nation more generally.[102] Smith recasts eighteenth-century fears of commercial corruption as antebellum anxieties about capitalism. The pursuit of gold, Communipaw observes, "builds houses, 'nets the land with railroads,' tills the soil—in short, hastens the day of less physical and greater mental labor." But it also "contract[s] the soul," making one unfit or unable to take advantage of the new capacity for mental development. "Hence," argues Communipaw, "American society is a poor, dumb, blind dog to whom the sun in the heavens and the sweet harmonies of nature, and the deeper harmonies of humanity are as a closed book."[103] Material accumulation has outstripped citizens' capacity to act humanely toward each other or to deal ethically with the demands of the economic citizenship Ethiop himself describes.

Ethiop's aristocracy, because of its very position in relation to wealth, would not be able to resist cooptation by the overall marketization of morality and would be unable or even unwilling to cultivate the "feeling" or neighborly sensibility central to Ethiop's model.[104] For Communipaw, this lack of feeling is not a fault of the people so much as the logical concomitant of wealth itself. In passages suggestive of late eighteenth-century debates, Communipaw argues that bonds of economic interest are neither substitutes for nor generative of "bonds of sympathy."[105]

"Gold," rather than enabling renovation, "freezes up the humanities and all their surroundings," because "the beginning of such association was money; the middle progress of it, money; the aid of it money."[106] Communipaw's maxims trump Ethiop's faith that his aristocrats would remain responsive to the communities that nurtured them. "The wealthy," Communipaw continues, "are never a progressive class; they are by necessity conservatives. Cotton would become king. Hundred thousand dollar black men would be no better than hundred thousand dollar white men."[107] Communipaw invokes the wealthy northern black businessmen and the "rulers of the five-points," who either cater to a white-only clientele or whose money comes from businesses of ill-repute, suggesting that the black aristocrats would not only conserve intraracial class barriers but also conserve and perhaps perpetuate racial caste and the slave power in the name of wealth.[108] Frances Harper put the point more emphatically in 1859: "The respect that is only bought by gold is not worth much. It is no honor to shake hands politically with men who whip women and steal babies."[109] If money is the ruling idea, and Communipaw and Ethiop agree that it is and that it has been bad for society, then producing an aristocracy would only perpetuate its faulty premises, further exposing black citizens to its atomizing properties.

Communipaw's critique of Ethiop and the nation's "monied idea" reflects not only McCune Smith's observation of U.S. culture but also his research in natural history, specifically his understanding of how class worked and his belief that caste systems caused civilizations to stagnate and regress.[110] "If we look at the sources whence nations advanced in civilization draw their intellectual power," Smith argues in "Civilization; Its Dependence on Physical Circumstance" (1859), "these sources will be found to spring from the common people—the physically vigorous."[111] Essays such as "Lecture on the Haytien Revolution" (1841) and "On the Fourteenth Query of Thomas Jefferson's *Notes on Virginia*" (1859) further outline his understanding of the relation between labor and progress: laboring classes are the source of a nation's progress, the "stirrer[s]-up of true civilization," and wherever caste is "established . . . civilization is arrested, and either remains stationary . . . or sinks back into barbarism."[112] Black Americans, free and enslaved, represent the nation's progressive class, those "whose 'common destiny' is 'labor,'" and they will be the guardians of its republican promise and the source of its progress in the arts and in political thought.[113]

Where Ethiop sees characters in a social drama, Communipaw, like Smith, sees varieties of the human species contributing to an epochal process in which liberty and "human brotherhood," not money, are the ruling ideas. Through Communipaw, Smith merges the scientific, the spiritual, and the political as he outlines an evolutionary millennialism that applies evolutionary theory to human development and enshrines "Liberty" as humanity's ultimate end. The current fervor for gold is an "intermediate" epoch, Communipaw explains, the "ichthyosauri and plegiosauri," linking the past to a future era of more perfect human brotherhood. Just as the prehistoric amphibious reptiles that seemed to Georges Cuvier "best to deserve the name of monster" were understood as links in the development of contemporary species, "wealth and caste," like the "only half lunged" creatures, link two civilizational moments but do not represent the more beautiful "systems" to come.[114]

Looking forward to this system, Communipaw sees the reign of "*Liberty.*" Taking on a prophetic tone, Communipaw calls on readers to "seek *Liberty* with the full and entire energies of our soul, and," he predicts, "the smaller matters of personal comforts will be added to us."[115] For Communipaw, liberty aligns with full participation in political life and the free mingling of peoples and ideas represented in concepts such as the republic of letters (to which I will return in a moment). His source text, Matthew 6:33 ("But seek ye first the kingdom of God, and his righteousness; and all these things shall be added unto you"), appears near the end of a chapter in which Jesus of Nazareth admonishes his audience to be wary of outward displays of piety (respectability) and not to worry about attaining worldly possessions. This same scripture contains other cautions concerning wealth and the dignity of humble service and would have been familiar to many. For Jesus, seeking the kingdom of God would not necessarily make one materially wealthy. Rather, seeking the kingdom of God would change one's perceptions of the world and the terms by which wealth would be evaluated. Similarly, Communipaw suggests that "personal comforts" pale in comparison to the collective benefits of seeking liberty and what that does for how one judges and attains prosperity.

Contemporaneous economic citizenship may be part of the process, but like the prehistoric reptiles, it is a very crude one. "Our present weal," Communipaw concludes, "can only be made better by a nobler idea," a return to first principles, rather than an adaptation to current errors. In a model with Aristotelian undertones, Communipaw suggests that the "middle tens . . . the rising and progressive class," not a wealthy elite, will continue evolving and perfecting the nation's civic ideals because "they seek the upper tendon—not for its wealth, but for its position" through "thrift, punctuality, enterprise and persistent energy, such as the pursuit of mere wealth never stirred up in the human soul."[116] Only through the efforts of these middling folk, who, in Aristotelian terms, "possess the gifts of fortune in moderation," their souls made vibrant through their labor, will the relation between economics and ethics be brought into balance.[117] If the majority of free black people occupy so-called degraded positions at the moment, Communipaw offers the compensatory narrative that black laborers possess the collective experience and the rough moral stuff out of which this class can most productively be formed.

Communipaw is not after simple inclusion. Rather, through Communipaw, Smith offers a "counter-statement of [a] political subject," as Nikhil Pal Singh would later posit of black politics more generally, primed "to widen the circle of common humanity."[118] Communipaw's common folk, even the single mother working as a washerwoman, are the last hope for republican citizenship. "We must work this out *here*," that is, liberty and human brotherhood, "or for ages the chance may not come again."[119] That "work," not waged labor, constitutes the core of black citizens' civic practice.

Communipaw's "Heads of the Colored People" concretizes this salvific process through ten sketches detailing the lives of black citizens identified by trade: news vender, bootblack, washerwoman, sexton, steward, editor, inventor, and schoolmaster.[120] Two focus on single women, a washerwoman and a schoolmaster, making a living on their own, while the others follow men (single and married) starting lives and families after New York's 1827 emancipation. Through these installments, often appearing next to Ethiop's column on page 3, Communipaw rethinks the relation of these people to the civic community, repositioning some of Ethiop and black conventions' most vilified laborers as representative citizens based on their ideals, not their finances, and resituating citizenship practice in the home and social institutions, as personal fulfillment displaces money as the ruling idea.

This strategy is particularly evident in "The Boot-Black," the series' second installment. The sketch models how one could and ought to strive toward moral and material success and, at the same time, celebrates those whose lives began in slavery, plodded upward through gradual emancipation, and ended established in the middle class. Appearing on April 15, 1852,

"The Boot-Black" begins as Communipaw's reminiscence of a formative figure from his childhood, a man who provided an image of responsible manhood: "Man and boy I have known that stride and that smile as long, if not longer, than my earliest recollections of—cake."[121] More than personal reflection, however, "The Boot-Black" suggests how the virtues associated with labor, regardless of its status, could "stir anew the current of life" and cultivate in postemancipation New York the same kind of civic ethos associated with agrarianism and the artisan republicanisms of the earlier decades.[122]

Situating stories of black labor, family, and civic identity in a postslavery, prefreedom world was central to Communipaw's project.[123] The bootblack had been enslaved, "part of the livestock," at the Livingston manor until he, like many black New Yorkers in 1827, "finding himself in possession of himself . . . took sloop and came down to the city."[124] Communipaw's reconstruction of Emancipation Day resists the "constructed amnesia" around northern slavery that buttressed (white) labor discourse and black disenfranchisement.[125] Similarly, the news vender, another of Communipaw's characters, spends the better part of his young-adult life evading slavecatchers after his escape from a Virginia plantation (that Communipaw strongly suspects to have been Thomas Jefferson's), until a shipwreck leaves him with both legs amputated at the knee. Both narratives suggest that the insistence on a liberal market contributes to this amnesia, because it ignores how the economics of enslavement and its concomitant racism complicated black citizens' relation to the market and property and continued to frame not only the associations between black labor and "degradation" but also the world economy. Ignoring these historical realities by asking black workers to prove their civic worth in the same market that valued and continued to value them as "livestock," as if they were suddenly disembodied and washed free of the entailments of white supremacy, not only alienated black citizens from their newly acquired (and threatened) freedom to work but also elided the material effects of the Fugitive Slave Act, unequal franchise and labor laws, and the legacies of abolitionist paternalism, specters that continued to haunt black politics in New York.[126] Even as newly free people like the bootblack and news vender took possession of themselves, the economy and public policy shifted to limit and take advantage of the limits of that putative self-possession. More ominously, as I will discuss later, this sense of self-possession contributed to the economic and political world that had enslaved them previously.

Communipaw's historicized reading allows him to use the bootblack and others to sketch what he sees as the progressive ideals and habits gained from labor "*made with a will*," ideals and habits important not only for black citizens but also for the state's future.[127] Bootblacks, Communipaw reflects, "as a class are thrifty, energetic, progressive. Free muscles, steadily exercised, produce free thought, energy, progress."[128] The passage plays on "free," signaling the importance of both the physical exertion involved in the work and how the bootblack's freedom to labor (his emancipated muscles) and to choose a profession produces the progressive energy Smith attributes to laboring classes more generally in "Civilization."[129] Emphasizing physical exertion, moreover, mitigates the image of luxury that bootblacking existed to support and strengthens its connection to the kinds of manual labor more often promoted as productive of mental character, such as blacksmithing or farming. If, as Thomas Jefferson posited in *Notes on the State of Virginia*, "it is the manners and spirit of a people which preserve a republic in vigour," then Communipaw's bootblack would show how this spirit could thrive in the city in the least likely of homes and among those whom Jefferson rejected.[130]

Indeed, the sketch emphasizes the bootblack's home as the central location for his civic and economic identity, valorizing its function as a site of resistance even as the sketch recovers the important work of women in the urban economy.[131] The bootblack's wife is central to the family's overall success. As Communipaw explains, "At first, business was slow with him, and both were dependent on the labors of the laundress," with her services advertised on "a modest piece of tin announc[ing] '*Washing and Ironing done by Mrs.*,'" hung outside their rented basement apartment next to his own sign.[132] Their economic and domestic life reflected the typical economic arrangement of urban New Yorkers. The jobs black men could find were often not enough to support a family, and women were the primary earners.[133] The passage, however, lacks the negative moral judgments often found in contemporaneous accounts of black women working. In contrast to contemporaries such as Martin Delany, who would read her work as a sign that "we are all a degraded, miserable people, inferior to any other people as a whole, on the face of the globe," Communipaw weaves it into a narrative of a family's economic and social emergence after emancipation.[134] In this context, Communipaw's lack of commentary asks important questions: Why would the bootblack's wife not work to help support their striving? Why would we not recognize them as equal partners in a collective endeavor?

Though "Boot-Black" reinforces some gender conventions, particularly concerning marriage, the nuclear family, and the patriarchal role of the father, it also suggests that such conventions should not be used to obscure material fact or become grounds for condemning people whose honest labor underwrites the very civic virtues the conventions were intended to foster. The bootblack and his wife work so that their children might have an education and a safe economic and domestic environment: "His boy should have as much learning as money could buy. . . . These hopes and resolutions gave renewed force and longer reach to his studies . . . lent new vigor to his right arm."[135] Conforming to the gender values of his day, the bootblack hopes for a son who could take full advantage of everything education and his growing funds could offer, but they have daughters instead. The children, however, "only added to the energies of our hero," and with these energies, his business and property grow: "now a separate apartment from his kitchen parlor and above ground, yet at a most economical rent."[136] On the way to seeking liberty, the bootblack becomes "our hero," and the girls grow up to be independent women, one "teaching in a private school of her own, assisted by her only surviving sister, and pupil."[137] The two women, though unmarried, symbolize the bootblack and his wife's success, even as the bootblack realizes a personal dream he thought would have to wait for the next generation: he opens his own shop.

Working through this trajectory with a bootblack makes "elevation" accessible to a larger group than Ethiop's black aristocracy allows. And, in contrast to Ethiop's reliance on representative and exceptional leaders, "Boot-Black" presents an immanent model, a reconfigured example of a middling type, an example of what the common laborer and his family might achieve: "One former bootblack," Communipaw notes, "is now a merchant tailor in Newark; another a self-relying farmer in Essex County."[138] It is no accident that Communipaw's other examples go on to be "self-reliant," on one hand, and a businessman, on the other. The two echo the 1848 convention's revised resolution; they worked at so-called degraded labor "where necessity [compelled them] to resort thereto as a means of livelihood," and as Douglass suggested, they left these "situations" once they could.[139] Moreover, Smith had real-life, well-known referents for his sketch. One of the great (intentional) ironies of "The Boot-Black" is that Wilson himself owned a boot-making shop before becoming an educator and rising to prominence within Brooklyn's black community.

Still, this sketch's main character prospers *as* a bootblack; he does not leave the "degraded situation," despite knowing "that his calling was looked down upon."[140] Rather than "raising" the bootblack to the middle class through a shift in position, Communipaw alters the means for evaluating respect; the laborer determines the character of the labor and its effects, not the labor itself: "Wiser than dandy opinion, he found it and has proved it—Ethiop and Horace Greeley to the contrary notwithstanding—well fitted for him to exercise by means of it, all the faculties which make a man useful to his family and a credit to the State: he was willing . . . *to stoop to conquer, and he has conquered*: and he laughs to scorn the capering *principle martyrs* who would rather starve . . . than handle a shoe-brush."[141] Communipaw links Ethiop to Greeley, accusing both of the same "dandy opinion" Ethiop condemns young men for, namely of mistaking money and status for actual wealth and progress and of refusing to "stoop to conquer," that is, censuring labor that could be instrumentally productive and fulfilling (a "calling") in the name of symbolic dignity. Communipaw's bootblack creates his own status. Because of the bootblack's attitude toward his work, bootblacking becomes, for him, a craft akin to tailoring or writing (Communipaw compares "boot polishing" to "word polishing"), making him less a casual worker and more an artisan who develops his business as he hones his craft and builds his family.[142] Rather than aspire to jobs associated with the middle class—a developing white middle class—Communipaw finds a black middle class traveling down a different, divergent path. This path may not enjoy the current growth of wealth or social approbation, but it will survive the current stage of economic development "at a less expense of moral excellence."[143]

By presenting his representative citizen as average, even in his distinctiveness, Communipaw critiques the tendency to focus on the exceptional man's individuality and difference from the group, a tendency that leads to statistically skewed results.[144] Bootblacking, Communipaw concludes, "is *the* calling which has produced the best average colored men, and has made men of *character*, not of *wealth*."[145] The sketch seems to bear this progression out, providing a concrete example of Communipaw's theory of economic citizenship: the bootblack and his wife sought liberty and uplift for themselves and their family first; the business success was added in the process. Indeed, by the time Communipaw offers his narrative, the bootblack has one of the "most distinguished boots our city boasts of," regularly supports youth at the Free African School, was "elected church-warden" at

St. Philip's, and "owns a fine property in sight of the Manor on which he was 'raised,' and on which . . . he and his children might have remained in brutal ignorance."[146] The bootblack's home has become a model republic in its own right, and Communipaw's framing of him as a type suggests that his model can and is being reproduced across the city. One bootblack could never generate the kind of change Ethiop and Communipaw both seek, but as a representative (average rather than exceptional) of a much larger class, his success presages the greater revolution to come. "Heads," then, intervenes in an economic debate that relied too much on assumptions that a more elevated job, measured against a flawed white standard, was a more (civically) productive one. The bootblack shows the movement from slavery to freedom to citizenship, not through aristocratic management but through hardworking, critical and self-critical, self-government.

Even as individual installments in the "Heads" series contest Ethiop's aristocracy, Communipaw's narration models a subjectivity calibrated to negotiate competing demands of civic and market spaces. Where Ethiop's aristocrats "feel" their position through an oscillating perspective on a vertically oriented physical and political economic plane, Communipaw's representative citizen inhabits an interstitial space on a horizontal axis. Smith situates Communipaw at "the poste of door keeper, not to the Senate . . . but to the outermost enclosure leading to the Republic of Letters."[147] The Republic of Letters invokes a space where, Communipaw explains, "if they be but true" to their ideals, citizens can live "free from *caste*, and Cass and Filmores."[148] Moreover, contrasting the Republic of Letters to the Senate, Communipaw also implicitly taps into the antiaristocratic impulses of the French Enlightenment and the revolutions of the 1840s, echoing Paine's use of the republic of letters as a model for egalitarian polity: "As the republic of letters brings forward the best literary productions, by giving to genius a fair and universal chance; so the representative system of Government is calculated to produce the wisest laws, by collecting wisdom from where it can be found."[149] The young Smith invokes this structure in his 1837 travel journal for the *Colored American*: "The genius of the institutions of America," he explains, is their "gathering around them and fostering mechanical genius and enterprize from every portion of the Globe."[150] The yet-unrealized "genius" of U.S. republicanism is its inclusivity, the promise of a form of government and national culture that could incorporate new peoples and ideas based only on the principles of hard work, ingenuity, and liberty, not race or class.

"The Whitewasher," Communipaw's eighth "Heads" sketch, explores this doorkeeper position in practice, pointing to a governing polity of ordinary people, whose silent work belies their deep understanding of how power circulates and their ability (yet untapped) to direct this circulation. Whitewashers, Communipaw explains, exert an "invisible but irresistible power, before which parlor doors, chamber doors, and all other fastenings and hindrances at once give way."[151] Whitewashers developed this power as a part of their skill at their craft, a perfect combination of physical work and intellectual acumen ("Our whitewasher," for instance, "is a chemist . . . in his way").[152] Smith returns to this point in 1855, when he explains in his 1855 introduction to *My Bondage and My Freedom* that the "secret of [Douglass's] power" is his history as a laborer. Douglass is "a Representative American man—a type of his countrymen," not despite having been enslaved and having worked as a "degraded" laborer in freedom but *precisely because* he has "passed through every gradation of rank comprised in our national make-up, and bears upon his person and upon his soul every thing that is American."[153] Labor, in this model, is one of several activities that not only creates material security but also develops the habits and subjectivity for the work of collective governance.

Communipaw, then, links the intellectual and civic project of the Republic of Letters to the citizens whose physical work and social position would disqualify them from a more restrictive notion of a bourgeois public sphere by identifying this project with laborers, such as bootblacks and whitewashers ("Heads . . . Done with a Whitewash Brush"). As the subtle allusion to Psalm 84:10 suggests, the post of doorkeeper to the Republic of Letters is preferable to a leading position, perhaps as an aristocrat or politician, in "the tents of wickedness" or, in this case, a corrupt state built on economics of enslavement.[154] But while the scripture speaks to a humble posture, Communipaw's rendering the position as a "poste," a job or office, suggests a position of power: the doorkeeper who safeguards republic and, in the spirit of the whitewasher's ethos of free circulation, ensures the door remains open to all comers. (As we will see in the next chapter, Wilson will pick up on the doorkeeper trope as *the* optimal position for critical citizenship.) Figured as a doorkeeper, Communipaw's ideal representative would ensure that this free circulation remained robust, providing a transformative bridge between the "heads," or genius, of the average "colored citizens," a condemnatory black elite, and a republic that has heretofore rejected them.

Romantic Projects, Real Limitations

So far, I have outlined how Wilson and Smith map competing logics of economic citizenship and representation through their correspondences as Ethiop and Communipaw, the one suggesting that a model of black aristocracy could counter white oligarchy, the other suggesting that the nation's civic life must be reoriented away from the market toward a middling laboring polity. Even as Ethiop and Communipaw debate the implications of economic citizenship as a national phenomenon, they ground their sketches in New York life and culture. The two are constantly adjusting to each other as well as to the city's volatile political, economic, and racial milieu. And it is this engagement with concurrent events that provides the criteria by which they evaluated each other and through which each writer framed his response to the other.[155]

Where Communipaw's sketches suggest Ethiop's reading of economic citizenship contributes to historical and political amnesia, Ethiop accuses Communipaw of forwarding a dangerous romanticism, too concerned with an idealized past and future and not focused enough on present economic and political dilemmas. In a May 13, 1852, response to "Boot-Black," Ethiop situates Communipaw's "Heads" in a romanticized past lacking "faithfulness" to the harsher realities of a "monstrous" present. True, Ethiop admits, "a determined man, no matter how low his condition, or what his color, despite all opposition, may, if he persevere, raise himself up to the highest *niche* in the profession he marks out for himself; and, at the same time, have not only a name and a praise among men, but something more substantial for himself and children."[156] Yet, such men are, by and large, exceptions to a general rule of racial oppression and economic mediocrity—they do well on their own but cannot do much for their communities on the whole.

By way of illustration, Ethiop describes a recent trip to St. Philip's Episcopal Church—the church Smith regularly attended and where Communipaw's bootblack meets his wife. Ethiop reminisces about his own arrival at "Old St. Philip's!!!" where he heard his "first sermon" after arriving in the city and where he, like Communipaw's bootblack, "first saw one whose shadow ever walketh by" his side. Yet, in direct contrast to the nostalgic "Boot-Black," Ethiop leaves the past to describe a disappointing present.[157] When he arrives expecting to see the lasting effects of the bootblack's presence, he encounters instead an "atmosphere" that "seemed cold and strange":

> I listened—but heard not, as once, the short quick-step of the little old man, as his goose-quilled shoes squeakingly glided up the *aisle*, announcing, by their presence, to everybody, that "meeting was now in." He was not, there!!!
>
> And as I bowed my head in silence, I heard a voice; but oh! it was not the meek and heavenly voice of the *Rev. Peter Williams*; it was another's. . . . I looked, and lo!! it was a *white* man!!! a *dictator* sent to dictate to his flock, and he did dictate: and they, I fear, alas! have learned too well how to submissively obey.[158]

Neither the bootblack's familiar step nor Rev. Peter Williams, first rector of St. Philips, is present. The fact would not have surprised Ethiop's readers, since Rev. Williams died in 1840. The observation does, however, date Communipaw's account and suggests that the bootblack and his type are dated as well, symbols, like the church's "old hanging chandeliers," of a bygone era.[159] The "relief of the past" eludes Ethiop as he struggles to come to terms with the present, the irony of current events at St. Philip's increasing the sense that Communipaw's sketches describe a historical moment that, perhaps, never was.[160]

Ethiop's disappointment was not a fictional stretch but rather a riff on a controversy at the church over the Fugitive Slave Law that *Douglass's Paper* had been chronicling over the past weeks. And the sketch was all the more cutting to parishioners like Smith because of it. In "St. Philip's Church and the Fugitive Slave Law" (April 29, 1852), George T. Downing recounts how this historically black church came to officially support the Fugitive Slave Law.[161] As Downing explains, Smith submitted an announcement from the Committee of Thirteen "inviting the congregation to a meeting to take measures against kidnapping" in the wake of the capture of Horace Preston, who had been living in Williamsburg, a black enclave in Brooklyn.[162] Instead, the church's white pastor, "his satanic majesty," pledged his all-black congregation's support of the law.[163] The congregation agreed, Downing surmises caustically, not because they supported the law but rather because "blacks will submit to *whites*, and bear nothing from one of themselves, even though it be proper."[164] The rejection was all the more galling because Preston's capture was "highly irregular," even for a fugitive slave rendition. He was initially charged falsely with "petty theft" so he could be held for his supposed master, and among several of the weak arguments offered as "evidence" of his previous enslavement, the supposed owner's lawyer claimed that Preston was more likely a fugitive than not because he was black.[165]

For Ethiop, this flashpoint suggests that the bootblack and others may have found a measure of personal success and independence but without the power to change institutions in a way that would last longer than a generation (a white episcopacy appointed the white rectors, after all); this success dies with them. As many of Ethiop's New York readers knew, the church's rejection of Smith's invitation was no new development. All of the men filling pastoral duties at St. Philips after Williams's death through 1860 "were white," because the Episcopal Church's General Theological Seminary refused to admit the black students such as Alexander Crummell who might have succeeded Williams. And while they were "dedicated to St. Philip's and enormously helpful to the parish both as pastors and as allies in the effort to gain admission to the [Episcopal] convention," they were only part-timers, and the parish continually petitioned for a full-time black rector.[166] Ethiop, knowing this history, offered his moral: the large Episcopal congregation and black communities by extension will continue to "submissively obey" white authority, simply because it is white, as long as men like the bootblack remain isolated in their success rather than rising to the occasion like an "[Oliver] Cromwell" and expanding their power beyond their homes.[167]

Just as Communipaw's romantic vision of the past and projected future has very little connection to reality, Ethiop suggests, so too do Communipaw's economic insights. They go too far afield of the mechanics of the "real" economic world and they reproduce the same economic veiling that glosses material inequality in white cultures of capital, "deaden[ing] susceptibilities it should have quickened," as black citizens become satisfied with individual success and mediocrity.[168] Ethiop also reveals that Communipaw isn't exactly his virtuous, nonmaterialist adversary. All of his protagonists are deeply imbedded in the market—identified only by trade—and he validates the "Boot-Black" with examples of other bootblacks who left the profession for more lucrative ventures, but Communipaw obscures this fundamental material underpinning in his narration. Communipaw's call for patience and his long historical telos could be read as disingenuous at best and a surrendering of black agency to the regimes of racial power he is supposed to be opposing at worst. Neglecting the "real" of capital in favor of a salvific evolutionary process, Communipaw's well-intentioned depictions—a

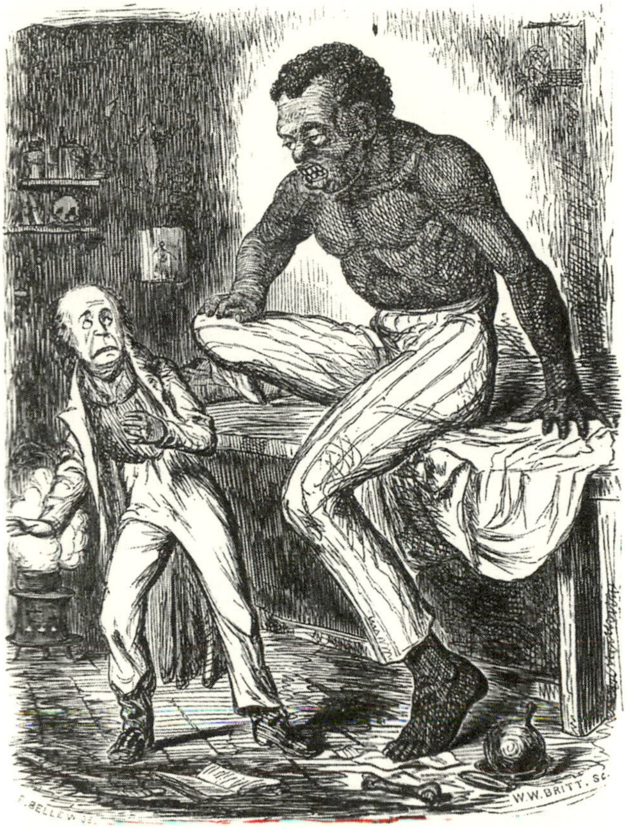

Figure 5. Frank Bellew, "The Modern Frankenstein," *Lantern*, January 31, 1852. Notice the stick-like drawing on the wall in the background.

perversion of "natural" economic processes—could come back to crush the community he's working to bolster, "and he," Ethiop quips in an April 8, 1852, correspondence, "like poor *Frankenstein*, may well exclaim, 'Oh! horrid monster, was it for this that I created you?' "[169] The reference links Communipaw (and Dr. Smith) to both Mary Shelley's novel and contemporaneous political caricatures. "The Modern Frankenstein" appeared in the January 1852 issue of *Lantern*, featuring a shocked Horace Greeley, who, thinking he was creating black humanity from a prefigured template, finds himself facing a nightmarish monster (Figure 5).[170]

Ethiop's analogy replaces Greeley with a cringing Communipaw, whose ideals, though fascinating in theory, suggest a grotesque, unnatural caricature of citizenship in practice. Perhaps, as Ethiop's visit to St. Philip's illustrates, Communipaw's classical model would create a more docile but no less destructive monster, one too strong for even Dr. James McCune Smith to subdue. Trapped materially by a changing economic landscape on one side and philosophically by a romanticized past on the other, Communipaw's "conceptions of truth" remain in "shackles."[171]

By concluding this chapter with Ethiop's critique of Communipaw, I do not mean to suggest that Ethiop's vision was either more accurate in his historical moment or that it offers a better vision of economic citizenship. One of Communipaw's central critiques of Ethiop's economic agenda was his sense that "to the mass of us, such pursuit would be vain, as a reality, for the reason we could not" obtain that much wealth under an economic and political regime skewed toward antidemocratic white, not simply self, interest.[172] The following year bore Communipaw's argument out as the real estate opportunities and the already available foundations for an aristocracy in Manhattan disappeared. In 1853, the city condemned Seneca Village and bought out its black residents to make space for Central Park. This land grab not only displaced a well-established black community but also eroded that community's political power, because the state's payment was not enough to allow them to reestablish themselves in the city. Without the $250 in property the state required for voting, they were effectively disenfranchised.[173] At the same time, the white economic elite Ethiop suggested would yield to the force of black economic power supported the Fugitive Slave Law, and the private owners of the city's public transit system continued requiring black patrons to ride in segregated cars, despite an 1854 court ruling against such practices. The court, in turn, reversed its course two years later, with a jury ruling in favor of the Sixth Avenue Railway Company against James W. C. Pennington, whom a conductor unceremoniously ejected from his seat in 1855. The judge's standard for ruling in the Railway Company's favor: would the "admitting of colored persons into the cars [injure] the business of the company in any way."[174]

Even so, Ethiop's analysis turns out to be the more accurate of the two as an assessment of the century's economic and political trajectory as the corporation replaced the "self-employed household" as the primary unit of economic production.[175] Ethiop's black aristocracy model combined corporate organization and its concomitant shift in notions of individual autonomy with a guiding ethic of communal solidarity and democratic logics of participation, prefiguring, in a way, twentieth-century experiments: the economic philosophy of Booker T. Washington's Negro Business League, the civic philosophy of W. E. B. Du Bois's call for a "talented tenth," and the rise of black cooperatives. And, as labor historians point out, Communipaw's vision of a polity of the middling folk, while accurate in its articulation of the increasing significance of "middle class values," if not power, misses the mark in its hope that these common folk, black or white, could maintain a sense of artisan republicanism in the face of industrialization.[176] Economic development would become an even more critical point of attack for Wilson, Douglass, and others as they began shaping policy and institutions for freedmen and women after the Civil War.[177]

Still, Communipaw's emphasis on a polity of middling laborers and on participatory politics poses a productive critique not only of Ethiop's aristocracy but also of this trajectory: what costs must the "community" pay for ceding the vision of an egalitarian polity Ethiop himself invokes to these structures of economic citizenship? Communipaw's warning against relying on self-interest to counter racism without a concomitant change to the nation's investments in white supremacy and capitalism's rewarding atomization over communalism proved prophetic as state and national institutions continued to articulate, in increasingly explicit and violent terms, the ways that black interests did not matter. Where black aspirations became more insistent, so did white resistance, culminating in the violence of "Bleeding Kansas" in the middle of the decade and, in New York City, the 1863 Draft Riots. As the decade wore on, the effects of the Fugitive Slave Law, the inconsistencies of state actions and federal decisions favoring and then retracting black rights, increasing competition and hostility from working-class whites combined with recalcitrance from white employers and the dearth of masters willing to take on black apprentices, and the constant threat of violence led many black city dwellers to move to Canada and to more rural areas in the state. On a smaller scale, black Manhattanites were making similar moves to Harlem and Queens in response to white violence and the hope of more opportunity.[178] Even as their newspaper personae attempted to recuperate urban spaces, Wilson and Smith encouraged this in-state movement, outlining with other reformers the city's deleterious effects in conventions and addresses.[179]

While it is tempting to read Communipaw and Ethiop's debate as a binaristic conflict between intellectuals—what Singh usefully frames as the conflict between liberal and civic-republican tendencies paradigmatically outlined in the Washington–Du Bois debate—Smith and Wilson were more often than not collaborators in public fora like the state and national conventions and in institutions like the Committee of Thirteen.[180] That they stage this debate in *Douglass's Paper* even as they cooperated in practice suggests the importance of open and incisive critique not only to their activist community but also to citizenship practices more broadly. The next chapter analyzes the role of critique as a practice of citizenship, returning to Ethiop and the questions of access and the national imaginary raised in Communipaw's "Whitewasher" as black writers grapple with the meaning of citizenship and participatory politics following the violent closures of the Kansas-Nebraska crisis and *Dred Scott v. Sanford.*

CHAPTER 4

Critical Citizenship in the *Anglo-African Magazine*, 1859–1860

In a February 1860 essay for the *Anglo-African Magazine* (1859–1860), William J. Wilson, writing as Ethiop, asks, "*What for the best good of all shall we do with the White people?*"[1] Turning the tables on the usual racist formulation, Ethiop's essay invites readers to rethink U.S. history as a narrative of white duplicity and avarice that ultimately threatens republican citizenship at home and abroad:

> Twice have they quarreled with, stripped off, and fought the mother who gave them origin and nursed them till they were grown; and once have they most unmercifully beaten their weaker and more pacific neighbor; and then despoiled him of a large portion of his lands, and are now tormented with longing after the balance.
>
> If we go back to an earlier page in their history, we find them stealing and appropriating what? Why, men, women and children from abroad and consigning them to a perpetual bondage.[2]

Viewing the sordid history of familial violence (the American Revolution and War of 1812), imperial unneighborliness (the U.S.-Mexican War), and theft in property (American Indian land) and persons (enslaved Africans), Ethiop concludes that white Americans are "no nearer the solution of the problem" of self-government "than they were at the commencement of their career."[3] Instead of the republican form of government outlined in the Declaration of Independence and Constitution, Ethiop finds "*a long continued, extensive, and almost complete system of wrong-doing.*"[4] Following *Dred Scott v. Sandford* (1857), even the Judicial Branch seems to have "reverse[d] the very principle of law," giving "wrong, injustice and inhumanity the benefit of the doubt" over "right . . . justice . . . [and] humanity."[5] Something has gone similarly awry with the public judgment that should have been a guide to and check on the state. The "recent death struggle" in Kansas suggests "those honest and frank differences of opinion that beget and strengthen sound opinion," the critical debate essential to participatory politics, have been replaced by "low petty captiousness and cowardly vindictiveness."[6] As a result, the land of "*E Pluribus Unum*," a land that might have cultivated equality among difference and diversity, had become instead a land of "prejudices, bitter hates, fierce strifes, dissensions, oppressions, and frauds."[7] Events in the 1850s had given Ethiop little faith that white Americans could acquire the critical sensibilities needed to achieve the republican ideals articulated in the nation's founding documents. Instead, for the sake of humanity, "white" people must either physically withdraw from the United States—an idea that strikes him as equally "wrong in conception" as black removal—or they must "lose their own peculiar and objectionable characteristics" and stop being "white" altogether.

Ethiop's sarcasm calls into question the mythological underpinnings of white citizenship, while his insistence on doing something with "white people" reasserts collective and collaborative agency over citizenship's framing and gestures toward critical practices that call on us to imagine and enact other possibilities.[8] Ethiop's question, at once facetious and at the same time deadly serious, opens space for a more pressing project: what to do about an avaricious attitude and set of framing narratives that close off U.S. citizenship to "whites only" and that authors whiteness as a natural and universal position. Using Wilson's critiques of public consciousness, Frederick Douglass's responses to the events of 1854, and writing in the *Anglo-African Magazine* as guides, this chapter examines practices of critical citizenship: a process of disruption, meant to disquiet and discomfort, that draws on counterhistory to produce new visions of what citizenship might have been, could be in the present, and might become in the future.

As social geographer Anna Secor has noted, "The discourses and practices of citizenship can be seen as founding a . . . proprietary, circumscribed space of rationalization" that separates the citizen from the stranger.[9] The resulting enclosures do not negate critique as such (Ethiop, for instance, describes a public that is contentious to the point of dissolution); rather, in Ethiop's terms, it permits "honesty and truth" only "of a certain character" through a regime that polices "truth" such that "no man can" dare express it "without risk of life."[10] This way of doing citizenship functions as a vicious feedback loop that reinforces white citizenship: visions of white citizens simultaneously under threat and at the same time inherently superior, a fear of insurgent nonwhite "others," and the assumption that citizenship and the access it provides constitute a zero-sum game. Its policing ensures that citizenship remains static and calibrated to protect white citizens from "the disruption, contestation, and unresolved agitation of politics" and that these disruptions, when they do occur, can be ascribed to faults within racialized and gendered others, rather than the white republic itself.[11] No matter how articulated (through science, history, philosophy, aesthetics, or sophistry), however, at its core, white citizenship relies on violent enforcement, the threat of death and isolation, to maintain its borders, and it ensures that those in political power can always rely on appeals to white supremacy—explicit or veiled—to quell any emergent clamoring for more radical citizenship practices. This power draws on and, in turn, helps construct a historical narrative and national mythology (whether organized under white supremacy, nationalism, imperialism, heteronormativity, or some other unilaterally identified schema) that flattens difference in the name of "unity," order, or the preservation of a revolution already won. White citizenship thus encourages elision, misdirection, enforced silence, and the disavowal of material and qualitative differences in lived experiences that would require redress.

As this chapter outlines, black writers theorized acts of critical citizenship that, by contrast, require intrusiveness: its practices demand not just crossing boundaries but also disturbing the commonsense assumptions and distributions of power that shape and maintain them. It confronts white citizenship by constantly probing how power "impose[s] order" on this space, time, and experience, even within movements (such as abolitionism) that challenge established political orders.[12] These citizens insist on historical complexity and interpretation, not as authoritatively explaining the present but rather as a means for interrogating and revising the assumptions that make current social and political arrangements seem natural, timeless, and desirable.[13] These moments often occur most forcefully through the exertions of those whose presence, voice, or existence has been put in question, those whose approach to the prevailing common sense of citizenship is insurgent, not conciliatory. Critical citizenship, then, is untimely and uncomfortable; from the perspective of those with investments in maintaining borders, its insistence and openness can seem distasteful and insurrectionary. The critical citizen operates as an agent of consciousness raising, in constant circulation, expanding the realm of possibility of the civic imaginary in a way that shifts focus from creating an acceptable or respectable blackness to contesting citizenship frameworks and public tastes that authorize such distinctions.

The rest of this chapter proceeds by first examining how Wilson's contemporaries, including Frederick Douglass and writers for the *Anglo-African Magazine*, assessed the state of national taste and the desires for white citizenship it cultivated. Using Douglass's commentary on the Kansas-Nebraska Act and Anthony Burns's rendition as focal points, I sketch a national discourse that evinced broad agreement that, regardless of legal interpretation, the United States was "not made especially for" black citizens.[14] Even those admitting the legality of black citizenship, as did Supreme Court Justice John McLean in his dissent to *Dred Scott v. Sandford* (1857), appealed to notions of taste to forestall calls for unconditional black citizenship. Following this line of criticism, the chapter's next section analyzes what *Anglo-African* contributor S.S.N. theorized as "fugue" citizenship: a national predilection to allow debate on content—interpretations of the Constitution, slavery's boundaries, and maintaining unity with the white republic—but to freeze and punish attempts to critique the structure itself. I then turn to the *Anglo-African Magazine* (1859–1860), edited by Thomas Hamilton, as an example of a different approach to citizenship and political community, one hinging less on cultivating a shared identity and more on shared critical methods and reading practices. Exemplary of this approach is Wilson's "Afric-American Picture Gallery" series, appearing in the *Anglo-African* from February to October 1859, which takes as its setting an imagined picture gallery as a challenge to modes of collective memory and institutional framing and a site for cultivating critical citizenship.

Matters of Taste and Law: A Critique of National Judgment

Black theorists read events spanning the 1850s—from the Compromise of 1850, the Kansas-Nebraska Act (1854), and Anthony Burns's rendition (1854) to *Dred Scott v. Sandford* (1857) and the Lincoln-Douglas debates (1858)—as flashpoints demonstrating how whiteness and white supremacy shaped and delimited the parameters of citizenship, not simply in terms of rights but also in terms of the range of citizenships that could be imagined and practiced. Douglass registered this simultaneous policing of boundaries and cultivation of national taste in 1854 while speaking on the Kansas-Nebraska Act in Chicago, Illinois. Passed as a compromise bill in May 1854, the act functionally repealed the Missouri Compromise (1820) by allowing Kansas and Nebraska's white inhabitants to vote on whether each state would allow or ban enslavement upon entering the Union. From the outset, Douglass links the political climate that created the act to the multiform ways that whiteness was promulgated as the highest order of humanity and the sole qualifier for citizenship in fact, if not necessarily in law. "The word white," Douglass contends, "is a modern term in the legislation of this country," a symptom of "our national degeneracy" that installs a "limitation of humanity and human rights" not present at the drafting of the 1787 Constitution.[15] Douglass's argument historicizes this new emphasis on whiteness, pointing out how it shifted citizenship's meaning away from the proactive communal work of self-governance between and among citizens and toward a protective posture that defined citizenship through and for whiteness.

While Douglass's observation overlooks earlier federal legislation such as the Naturalization Act of 1790 that explicitly restricted naturalization to white men and the history of state-level disenfranchisement I cover in Chapter 2, his claim points to a larger trend within U.S. politics during the 1840s and 1850s. Speaking specifically to Black Codes, which penalized or outright barred black citizens who attempted to move into states including Illinois, Douglass notes, "Every inch of ground occupied by the colored man in this country" was "sternly disputed" from the "ballot box" to the "altar."[16] The result is a version of white citizenship that rendered Douglass and those he represented "intruders" in spaces where they ought to be welcome by right. Public discourse more broadly accepted black exclusion from citizenship (or white power to exclude them) as a tacit foundational principle and, conversely, black inclusion, to the extent it was allowed, as a boon of white sufferance.[17] The "crisis" in Kansas, then, was a crisis in maintaining a putatively white union and the rights of white people, whether as free-soilers or as property holders, within that union.[18]

Douglass's comments, however, go well beyond the Kansas-Nebraska Act. On scales large and small, white citizens responded to black citizenship and black self-assertion as intrusions on and as threats to a way of life protected by white supremacy and a fragile sense of national unity defined through white nationalism, whether framed as free labor, proslavery, or protests against the Fugitive Slave Act on the grounds of state sovereignty. Days after Congress passed the Act, Anthony Burns, who had been living and working in Boston for the past year, was apprehended as a fugitive slave.[19] As per the 1850 Fugitive Slave Act, a federal commissioner tried Burns without a jury or the ability to testify on his own behalf. Despite fiery vigilance committee meetings, an unsuccessful rescue attempt, and Rev. Leonard Grimes's efforts to raise the $1,200 needed to purchase Burns's freedom from his willing master, Burns was escorted to Boston Harbor on June 2, 1854, by "America's largest show of military force in peacetime."[20] "Thousand upon thousands of people," one observer noted, crowded buildings lining their route to "gaze upon [the] *strange spectacle*."[21] Boston Mayor Jerome V. C. Smith and others hailed the event as a triumph of law and order and a necessary measure for the preservation of the Union, while most white abolitionists seemed long on fiery rhetoric but short on action. All in all, Burns's return to slavery offered a microcosm of northern sentiment. The nation was not heading inexorably toward civil war. Instead, many northerners were attempting to maintain a delicate balance: they bemoaned the spread of slavery suggested in the Kansas-Nebraska Act, repudiated enslavement and the Fugitive Slave Act as infringements on their *own* rights, labor, and state sovereignty, but shied away from open conflict on behalf of actual fugitives and black citizens, especially when such actions could be seen as disturbing a fragile peace.[22]

Contemporaneous antislavery observers coded the legal and moral implications of events from 1854 in aesthetic terms: the nation seemed to have either lost its ability to recognize justice as beautiful or had developed tastes of a different sort altogether. Henry David Thoreau, for instance, condemned the public's shallow "taste" and how its concern with the beauty of past revolutions allowed and encouraged them to ignore "the braver and more disinterestedly heroic attack on the Boston Court-House, simply because it was unsuccessful!"[23] The problem, for Thoreau was in the public's inability to recognize beauty. Where Thoreau blamed faulty tastes, however, Douglass challenged the processes through which beauty was legislated. In an editorial for *Frederick Douglass's Paper*, Douglass outlined a taste regime that cultivated a desire for white union and a concomitant aversion to discourse and people who might disrupt, disturb, or otherwise intrude on that union. The "true American" hears the "discord" of injustice represented in moments like Burns's rendition not as discord at all but rather as sweet music:

> How sweet to the ear and heart of every true American are the shrieks of Anthony Burns, as the American eagle sends his remorseless beak and bloody talons into him!! How grateful to the taste and pleasant to the eye, is the warm blood of the sable fugitive. He is now getting his desert. How dare he walk on the legs given him by the Almighty? He thought to take possession of his own body! to go at large among men, but he forgot that this is a civilized and Christian nation, and that no such unnatural and monstrous conduct could be allowed.[24]

This image of Burns invokes Prometheus, the Titan of Greek myth who stole fire from the gods for humanity. As punishment, the Olympians chained Prometheus to a rock for eternity and tasked an eagle to devour his liver daily as he writhed in pain only to have the liver regenerate overnight. The allusion, suggestive of both gothic horror and a worthy price for human freedom, symbolizes national beauty but not as a call to defend humanity. Instead of cheering the collective as a would-be Hercules attempting to free Burns, the public celebrated the punishment of one who would steal (himself) from them and hailed this punishment as a fitting sacrifice "on the altar of Union."[25]

Douglass grounds his argument in an understanding of "beauty" as less a transcendent ideal and more an institutionally and collectively shaped sensibility, a representation of and way to enforce consensus. The public did not fail to discern the gross injustice of Burns's rendition; rather, they found beauty in the system that saw him returned to slavery, and this system, in turn, catered to them. As Patrick H. Reason's frontispiece for *The Anti-Slavery Harp* (1848) suggests, the eagle performed its work—attacking a black woman as she attempts to protect a child in the foreground—under the sanction of the U.S. Capitol and the flag (Figure 6). The image becomes more macabre in Douglass's hands as he lingers on the flavors—"how grateful to the taste and pleasant to the eye"—of Burns's blood in the eagle's beak as a much anticipated "des[s]ert." Burns's rendition and the spectacle surrounding represent the national "taste" for black blood such that the sacrifice isn't a sacrifice at all for participants but rather a sweet delicacy worth savoring.

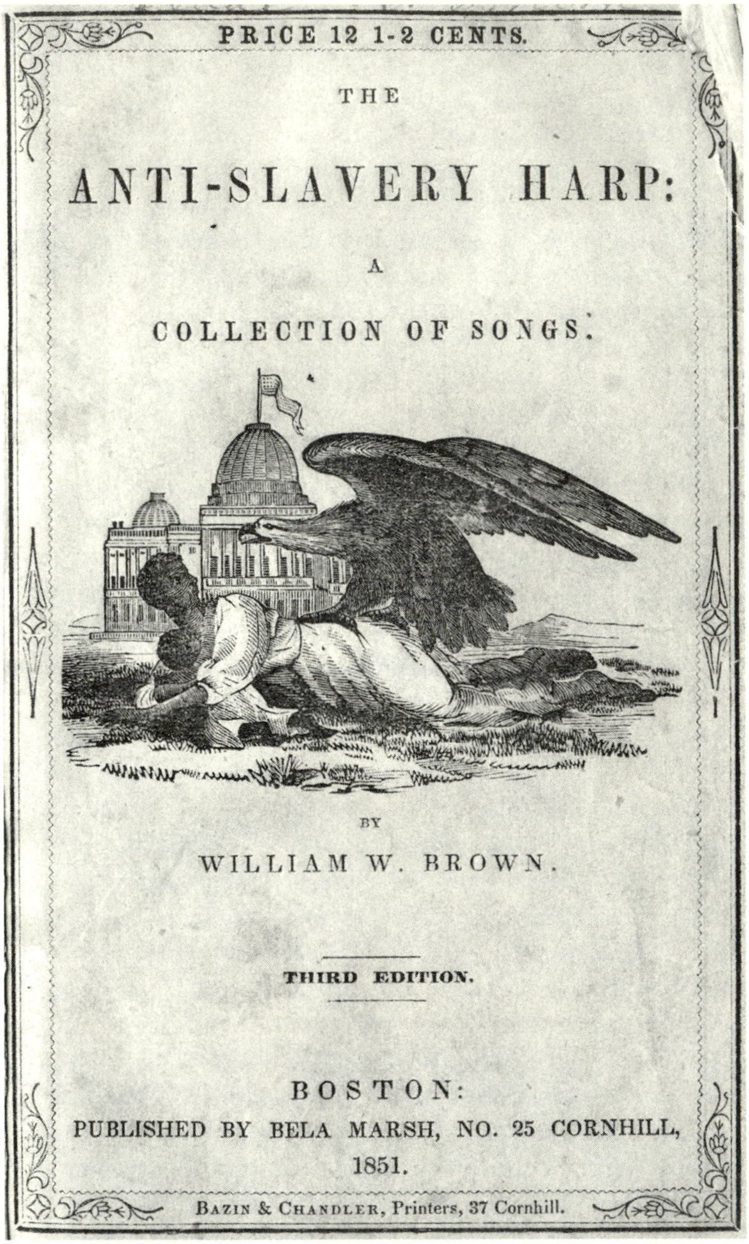

PRICE 12 1-2 CENTS.

THE

ANTI-SLAVERY HARP:

A

COLLECTION OF SONGS.

BY

WILLIAM W. BROWN.

THIRD EDITION.

BOSTON:
PUBLISHED BY BELA MARSH, NO. 25 CORNHILL,
1851.

BAZIN & CHANDLER, Printers, 37 Cornhill.

Figure 6. Frontispiece by Henry Patrick Reason, *The Anti-Slavery Harp: A Collection of Songs for Anti-Slavery Meetings*, comp. William W. Brown, 3rd ed. (Boston: B. Marsh, 1851). Courtesy Library of Congress.

The rise of an explicitly antislavery Republican Party in the mid-to-late 1850s and denunciations of *Dred Scott v. Sandford* (1857) would seem to attenuate Douglass's critique of national taste, at least in relation to states such as Massachusetts that had legal traditions of defending black citizens against kidnapping and capture. Yet these same responses suggest that this taste regime provided a powerful vehicle for racist logic such that even arguments defending black rights could reinforce white citizenship's boundaries. Benjamin R. Curtis's and John McLean's dissenting opinions in *Dred Scott*, as well as newspaper editorials, were quick to point out the license Justice Roger B. Taney's opinion took with the history of black citizenship and the dangerous diversion the lower and higher court rulings took from prior legal and historical precedence.[26] Taney famously ignored black political and military involvement to argue that, when the Constitution was framed, people of African descent "had for more than a century before been regarded as beings of an inferior order, and altogether unfit to associate with the white race, either in social or political relations; and so far inferior, that they had no rights which the white man was bound to respect."[27] In dissent, McLean noted that several states had granted "persons of color" voting rights and, by logical extension and tradition, had "recognized them as citizens . . . in the slave as well as the free States."[28] Further, the making of "citizens of all grades, combinations, and colors" through the "late treaty with Mexico" at the conclusion of the U.S.-Mexico War suggested that even subsequent color-based restrictions passed by the states did not negate the *potential* for any "freemen" to be federal citizens.[29]

While McLean challenged Taney's historical facts and his interpretation of federal law, however, he did not challenge the white supremacist assumptions underwriting Taney's opinion. Even as he affirmed the legal basis for black citizenship, McLean also admitted that the government was "not made especially for the colored race" (an echo of Stephen A. Douglas's 1858 claim that "this Government was established on the white basis").[30] Like Douglass in 1854, McLean argued that black political participation and traditions of birthright citizenship guaranteed recognition of black citizenship in law, but unlike Douglass, he argued that this recognition and its broader social implications were unintended consequences.[31] Whether a "colored citizen" would necessarily be an "agreeable member of society," McLean hedges, "is more a matter of taste than of law."[32] McLean falls back on the notions of taste that Douglass condemned in 1854. Rather than challenge theories of racial difference or that portions of the citizenry could be disagreeable, McLean concludes that given the history of U.S. citizenship, "it must be admitted that we have not been very fastidious."[33] Racism might guide social practice, but it cannot affect the law as written.

If, as Hoang Gia Phan has chronicled, Douglass and other political abolitionists distinguished between a strict construction of the Constitution and "legislative intention" in practice to suggest that the Constitution did not, if read on its own terms, support enslavement, McLean uses a similar method as a framework for black citizenship.[34] The founders' lack of "fastidious[ness]" in not encoding the Constitution with racial restrictions implies that while citizenship was clearly "intended" for white Americans alone, the actual documents codifying citizenship do not bear those intentions out. As Phan's analysis of midcentury strict constructionism suggests, separating "the authority of the Constitution" as a text from the "aura of the Founders" could provide a powerful (and powerfully historicist) hermeneutic for reading the Constitution in favor of black citizenship. Yet, as McClean's dissent reveals, this hermeneutic could coexist with and even supplement a broader (if implicit) endorsement of white citizenship as writers distinguished between legal requirements and social practice.

How McLean deployed the separation between the legal and the social, the letter of the law from intent, elided how public taste, especially given new instantiations of popular sovereignty and the responses to Burns's rendition, created law and affected citizenship in practice. By suggesting the potential distastefulness of "colored citizens," McLean tells a story that allows for a distinction between them and white citizens, a difference that, if it didn't touch citizenship in terms of federal law (which it did), nevertheless tacitly situated black citizens as somehow outside the consent-giving or sovereign "we" who judged such matters. The implicit laws of taste underwrite the explicit laws of the land. As Hartman notes in the context of Reconstruction, such constructions of "private" taste and its "privileging of sentiment and natural affinity facilitate subjugation as well as the violation of rights and liberties."[35] Indeed, McLean's appeal to taste fits well within the ways the racial contract has, as Charles Mills notes, "underwritten the social contract, so that duties, rights, and liberties have routinely been assigned on a racially differentiated basis."[36] McLean draws a fine line between the letter of the law and that law's intended (or, in this case, unintended) consequences. In so doing, McLean produces the sense of black intrusion Douglass outlines in 1854, a sense that did not need to be codified in law (or explicitly articulated in the social contract) to have an effect. At the same time, his appeal to taste absolved white citizens of their racism: neither the fact that black citizenship was distasteful nor white citizens' aversion to black citizens could be helped. The result is a construction of white citizens as powerless to do anything about either this legal openness or their distaste for it. Black citizenship was simply a burden that white citizens must bear and should be applauded for bearing.

Fugue Citizenship and Intrusive Politics

As I have suggested through Douglass's 1854 writing and the *Dred Scott* opinions, the Kansas-Nebraska Act, Anthony Burns's return to enslavement, and McLean's dissent all point to a way of framing white citizenship that renders other visions of citizenship and other citizens unpalatable. Yet, as I argue in this section, it's not just that McClean and others framed groups of citizens as unpalatable but rather that this cultivated taste for a whole white union contributed to the evacuation of critical practices more generally. This way of doing citizenship, to borrow from Russ Castronovo, relies on and encourages "cultural, emotional, and psychological investments that legitimate and even idealize acquiescence and impassivity" as patriotism to the detriment of more active and potentially disruptive citizenship practices.[37] History becomes a terrain for the retroactive and repetitive naturalizing of white supremacy, and this recursive narrative, in turn, encourages citizens to see citizenship as a thing already achieved and in need of protection rather than as a practice always in process that requires (rather than forestalls) disruption and intrusion.

Anglo-African contributor "S.S.N." theorizes this system and the political and popular culture supporting it as "fugue" citizenship in an August 1859 essay titled, "Anglo-Saxons and Anglo-Africans." Fugue citizenship characterizes the smoothing out and erasure of difference in and through formal politics, judicial decisions, historiography, and, most prominently, the ecstatic performance of public speech through "poetic license used with the facts of history." "Almost every American writer, speaker or politician, who would gain applause for himself, or a good hearing from his audience," S.S.N. explains, "is sure, Paganini-like, to play upon this one string. . . . Now the Thema [*sic*] is 'Anglo-Saxon Energy,'—(invading Mexico, perhaps), now, 'Anglo-Saxon Enterprize,'—(re-opening the Slave trade!), then 'Anglo-Saxon Piety,' (with holding bibles from Slaves, and hating negroes generally!) . . . variations on the martial, religious, mechanical and general superiority of the great Yankee nation." The collective performance ultimately frames citizenship as a utopian promise of white unity: individual citizens are not only distilled from historical subjectivity but also use history selectively and distortedly to create a new collective "Anglo-Saxon" identity. Orators and artists travel across the country (physically and in print) giving virtuoso performances on themes following romantic theories of racial destiny: the notion that each "race" or people had a unique character and historical trajectory and that "Anglo-Saxon" destiny was superior to all others. This "romance" of " 'The Great Anglo-Saxon Race' " sutures "the wounds they themselves inflict on the 'Apostate American People,' " wounds Ethiop notes as a history of violence and theft in "What Shall We Do with the White People?" The audience, in turn, enables and authorizes artists to operate within a fixed thematic range, lending themselves as "stops to an organ, to be played upon, as the performers conclude with a grand Fugue movement, on 'Anglo-Saxon blood.' "[38]

While, as S.S.N. notes, this structure occurs in multiple forms—speeches, treatises, visual arts, and so on—the fugue metaphor gets to the heart of the managed polyphony that creates compliant citizens and polices critical discourse. The formal structure of the fugue—a contrapuntal repetition on a single theme—ensures that each voice, no matter how "tonally" different, and each subject, no matter how ostensibly divisive, repeat the central dogma: the superiority and defense of "Anglo-Saxon blood."[39] Constructed through "a fantasia on some national melody," this "romance" appealed to white desires and anxieties about the loss of political power, which I chronicle in this book's first three chapters: the loss of political power to economic interests (Chapter 3), the loss of more direct forms of self-governance through electoral politics (Chapter 2), and the bait-and-switch of a supposed more free-market liberalism in exchange for ceding collective responsibility for the common good (Chapter 1).

Abraham Lincoln's speeches during his 1858 debates with Stephen A. Douglas for the U.S. Senate provide a useful case study of fugue citizenship at work. Indeed, Lincoln's responses to questions of black citizenship and the recorded audience response follow S.S.N.'s fugue schematic to the note. Lincoln opened the crucial fourth debate playing the question of racial equality for humor: "While I was at the hotel today," he begins, "an elderly gentleman called upon me to know whether I was really in favor of producing a perfect equality between negroes and white people."[40] Perfect equality here invokes three pillars of white fear: "making voters or jurors of negroes . . . qualifying them to hold office," and allowing them to "intermarry with white people."[41] After audience laughter at the absurdity of the question (how could any reasonable white man want such things?), Lincoln articulates the position he held throughout the debates to continued applause: "I have no purpose to introduce political and social equality between the white and black races." "Not want[ing] a negro woman for a slave," Lincoln quips to "cheers and laughter," did not mean he "want[ed] her for a wife."[42] Lincoln explicitly links "political and social equality" to desire and taste, not law or rights, so that the purported distastefulness of black subjects becomes paramount to how the state partitions citizenship. Throughout, Lincoln consistently critiques Stephen Douglas's popular sovereignty arguments and Justice Taney's *Dred Scott* opinion as they related to the potential expansion of slavery. Yet, in an echo of McLean, he recapitulated the taste regime that underwrote them.

Whether or not Lincoln's comments reflected his personal philosophy is less important here than how he deployed the fugue structure to elicit the audience's response, a response that he had included in the reprints of the debates and circulated during his 1860 presidential campaign.[43] Both suggest that this rhetoric reflected what Lincoln and his fellow Republicans believed audiences wanted to hear, and the recorded audience responses both confirmed that point and gave subsequent readers cues for when Lincoln was being facetious rather than earnest. Even when Lincoln defends black citizens' rights "to life, liberty and, the pursuit of happiness" and "to eat the bread, without the leave of anybody else, which his own hand earns," he does so in a way that reaffirms Ethiop's image of a populace capable of speaking truth only "of a certain character" and only as it reinforced a circumscribed notion of citizenship.[44]

Lincoln's arguments in support of free labor and black rights received applause but only as he observed three rules defining white citizenship: (1) racial differences existed (passively), and such differences must necessarily require separation and hierarchy; (2) white superiority within this hierarchy must be asserted and defended continually; and (3) one can advocate for black rights so long as such advocacy does not disturb the first two assumptions.[45] The question of social equality is literally laughable, and the collective laughter at the expense of black citizenship, like the taste of Burns's blood, provided compensation for white "anxiety about both civil capacity and civic participation."[46] Drawing on racial science reminiscent of Thomas

Jefferson's *Notes on the State of Virginia*, Lincoln concludes, "There is a physical difference between the white and black races which I believe will forever forbid the two races living together on terms of social and political equality. And inasmuch as they cannot so live, while they do remain together there must be the position of superior and inferior, and I as much as any other man am in favor of having the superior position assigned to the white race."[47] Under this threat, white citizens are simultaneously powerful and helpless. The invocation of racial competition for "position" masks how state and social power created and enforced these very inequalities and played working whites and European immigrants against black citizens (and each other). Rather than the agents of racial oppression, white citizens become potential victims in constant need of protection. Political, social, and economic differences among white citizens become subordinate under not only the sense of racial accomplishment, as I have suggested in my analyses of voting and economic citizenship, but of collective fear and self-defense. The sense of citizenship (as property or position) under threat ensures that civic cohesion can always be achieved as long as the state and those who would exercise political power can conjure the specter of incursion.

The point of fugue citizenship, then, is not to empower the citizenry but rather to manage it through a manufactured consensus tethered to white identity politics, policed speech, and fear. Fugue citizenship enacts a contract between citizens and the state that demands citizens not disrupt this performance's recursivity. In exchange, the state and public performers use violence (physical, cultural, and psychic) to shield these citizens from the potentially disruptive demands of raced, gendered, and classed others.[48] It provides an escape from politics and difference, what early twentieth-century psychological definitions of "fugue" would describe as "travel to some unconsciously desired locality," often caused by confronting some "intolerable reality of everyday existence."[49] In the case of white citizenship, the "intolerable reality" included histories, citizens (black men and women, enslaved and free, white women, American Indians, and others), and ways of doing citizenship that would not go away. This agreement, as S.S.N. reveals, ensures that Europeans, whether Anglo, Saxon, French, or German (and later others), could be "washed and become regenerated" as white Americans. The collective citizen-subject instead inhabits a newly created utopian realm of fellow citizens made abstractly equal through rituals of national identification.

S.S.N.'s essay and Douglass's writing point to the larger cultural patterns and structures of white citizenship subtending Lincoln's speeches and the political and judicial debates over the Fugitive Slave Law and *Dred Scott*. As I have suggested throughout the preceding sections, these patterns don't necessarily police citizenship's legal frameworks only but rather the boundaries of public speech and thought so that nonwhite subjects and citizenship practices that do not reaffirm white supremacy become unthinkable or at least unspeakable. These patterns and structures offer a sense of empowerment to those whose identities they manage (e.g., those who applauded Douglass's Promethean Burns or those who could laugh at Lincoln's quips) but expels as dangerous and unpalatable those whose identities it cannot manage, refuses to acknowledge, or exorcises in the framing process.

Critical citizenship, however, also reminds us that those excised from the national imaginary, those rendered absent from the body politic, do not go away; they never will. The excluded, silenced, flattened, or forgotten haunt the spaces that attempt to exclude them. Such haunting, Judith Butler notes, "become[s] politically effective precisely in so far as the return of the excluded forces an expansion and rearticulating of the basic premises of democracy itself."[50] Indeed, Douglass is "not ashamed of being called an intruder" because he claims "a right to be here and a duty to perform."[51] If, as Phan has argued, Douglass used the "man from another country" trope to read justifications for enslavement out of the U.S. Constitution, he uses the "intruder" trope to read black citizens and disruptive citizenship practices in.[52] From the perspective of those viewing Douglass's practices as intrusive, the status suggests a refusal to see him as belonging, as having a place, as producing knowledge about citizenship. From the perspective of the intruder, intrusion becomes a position of power, an insistence on being present and the productive disruptions that insistent presence can create.

In this chapter's remaining sections, I theorize this perspective in more detail through the *Anglo-African* and William J. Wilson's "Afric-American Picture Gallery." Thomas Hamilton and the contributors to the *Anglo-African* were dedicated to just such a disruptive rearticulation of citizenship's boundaries, to reopening its structure through critical practices that cultivated a "taste" for participatory plurality and the intrusive politics central to critical citizenship. The *Anglo-African*, in form and content, suggests a model of critical citizenship as a self-reflexive, dialectical process of becoming, while Wilson's series provides a case study of the critical citizen on the ground. While from the position of Douglass's "true Americans," these intrusive voices haunt the promise of national unity, from the perspective of critical citizenship, this promise itself and its veneer of "impenetrable whiteness" become the objects of horror and sites in need of rupture.[53]

Reading Anglo-African Wise: The *Anglo-African Magazine*'s Critical Project

A lifelong newspaperman, Thomas Hamilton founded the *Anglo-African* with his brother Robert in 1859 as an outlet for "the twelve millions of blacks in the United States . . . to assert and maintain their rank as men among men . . . [to] speak for themselves" (Figure 7).[54] "No outside tongue," proclaims Hamilton's "Apology," "however gifted with eloquence, can tell their story; no outside eye, however penetrating, can see their wants."[55] Hamilton's mission statement echoes similar proclamations in black periodicals from the first edition of *Freedom's Journal* (1827), which opened with "We wish to plead our own cause. Too long have others spoken for us."[56] And Hamilton would have been well versed in this tradition and the art of publishing from his work on black and antislavery papers like the *Colored American*, the *Mirror of Liberty*, and the *Peoples Press* (which he edited in 1843).[57] Where his predecessors published weekly papers that gave the most space to topical essays, reports on current events, and antislavery articles, Hamilton published the *Anglo-African* in a monthly magazine format that gave the most space to scholarship and literature aimed at "uphold[ing] and encourag[ing] the now depressed hopes of the thinking black men, in the United States."[58] The magazine ran for sixteen issues from January 1859 to April 1860 with a subscription base of about 500.[59]

The *Anglo-African* didn't simply challenge historical fact or present counterhistories that privileged one group over another (e.g., replacing a redeemer white race with a redeemer black race); rather, it challenged the terms on which history coheres and exerts force in the material world.[60] The magazine, Ernest notes, was a venue in which writers could "speak Anglo-African wise," where they could "address the eternal by speaking historically—to give voice to principles sounded throughout history by people of various backgrounds" with an "understanding of race as a systemic construction" based on "successive and layered violations."[61] This stance toward race makes the text "Anglo-African." Yet the contributors to

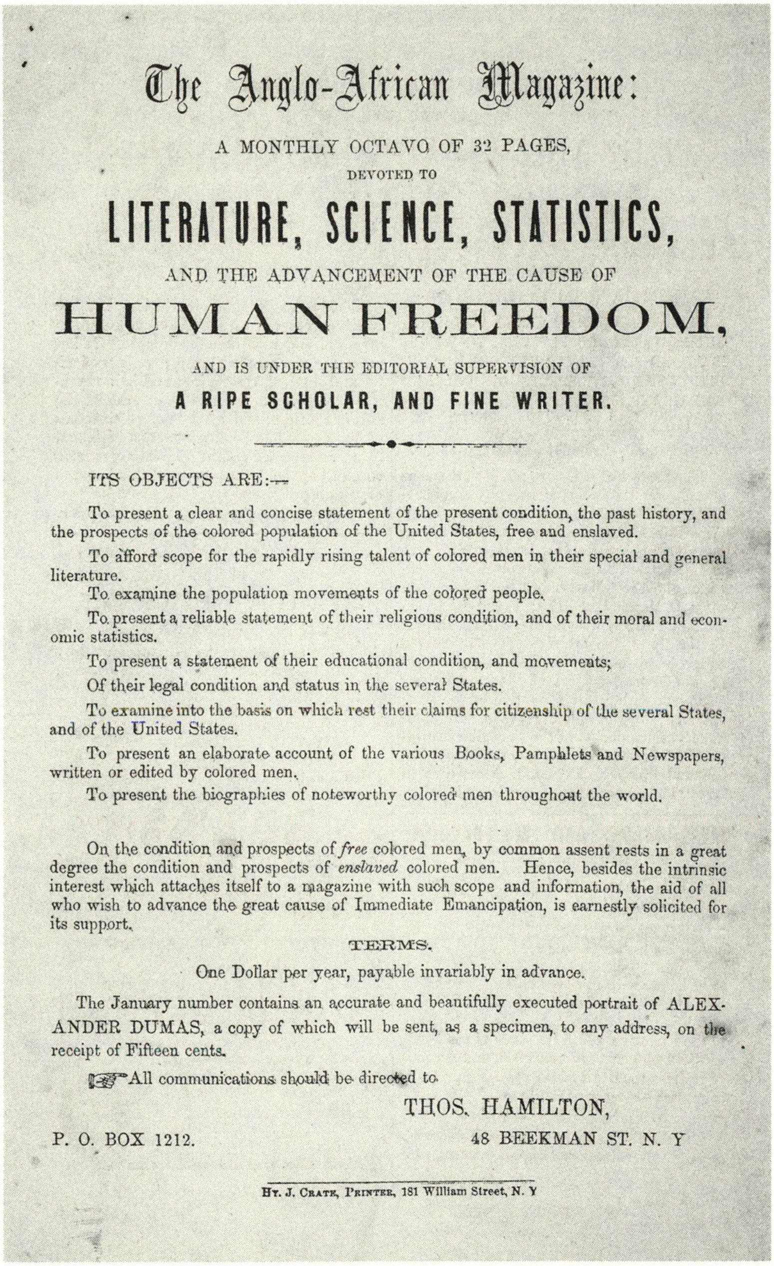

The Anglo-African Magazine:

A MONTHLY OCTAVO OF 32 PAGES,

DEVOTED TO

LITERATURE, SCIENCE, STATISTICS,

AND THE ADVANCEMENT OF THE CAUSE OF

HUMAN FREEDOM,

AND IS UNDER THE EDITORIAL SUPERVISION OF

A RIPE SCHOLAR, AND FINE WRITER.

ITS OBJECTS ARE:—

To present a clear and concise statement of the present condition, the past history, and the prospects of the colored population of the United States, free and enslaved.

To afford scope for the rapidly rising talent of colored men in their special and general literature.

To examine the population movements of the colored people.

To present a reliable statement of their religious condition, and of their moral and economic statistics.

To present a statement of their educational condition, and movements;

Of their legal condition and status in the several States.

To examine into the basis on which rest their claims for citizenship of the several States, and of the United States.

To present an elaborate account of the various Books, Pamphlets and Newspapers, written or edited by colored men.

To present the biographies of noteworthy colored men throughout the world.

On the condition and prospects of *free* colored men, by common assent rests in a great degree the condition and prospects of *enslaved* colored men. Hence, besides the intrinsic interest which attaches itself to a magazine with such scope and information, the aid of all who wish to advance the great cause of Immediate Emancipation, is earnestly solicited for its support.

TERMS.

One Dollar per year, payable invariably in advance.

The January number contains an accurate and beautifully executed portrait of ALEXANDER DUMAS, a copy of which will be sent, as a specimen, to any address, on the receipt of Fifteen cents.

☞All communications should be directed to

THOS. HAMILTON,

P. O. BOX 1212. 48 BEEKMAN ST. N. Y

HY. J. CRATE, PRINTER, 181 William Street, N. Y

Figure 7. Prospectus, *Anglo-African Magazine*, February 1859. Courtesy American Antiquarian Society.

the *Anglo-African Magazine* were also invested in cultivating citizens who could read "Anglo-African wise," that is, readers with the critical judgment by which to see around the corners of systems that maintained white supremacy, who were familiar with not just the literary and historical world the *Anglo-African* drew on but also the underlying political principles subtending Hamilton's editorial practices. Reading Anglo-African-wise draws attention to the kinds of citizens who produce critical texts and to the tastes and sensibilities this work might cultivate among the broader citizenry, a sensibility that welcomes intrusions, citizenship's messy work, and the discomfort both produce.

The magazine cultivates this reading practice in part through its sheer diversity, its openness to arguments that intrude on and interrupt each other: the monthly bursts at the seams with contending discourses, philosophies, and political sensibilities. The magazine's first issue opens with an image and biography of Alexander Dumas, and subsequent issues reproduce sheet music and lyrics for A. J. R. Connor's "My Cherished Hope, My Fondest Dream" (a song "written, composed and arranged for the piano-forte, and most respectfully dedicated to miss Sarah Matilda Cornish"), offer scholarly essays like the four-part "Statistical View of the Colored Population of the United States" and William C. Nell's "Colored American Patriots," and publish serialized fiction like Martin R. Delany's *Blake*. Katy Chiles's argument about *Blake*'s serialization in the *Anglo-African* might be applied to the magazine as a whole. Each individual piece, she argues, "simultaneously constitutes its own entity and contributes to a larger whole," not "seamlessly," but rather "the friction, overlay, and conversations among these 'texts within a text' can be best explored as the production of intratextuality."[62] These articles are unified not by their conformity to a single construction of blackness or black destiny but rather in their attitude toward historical memory and commitment to political self-determination and imagining a wide range of black futures. Hamilton, for instance, explicitly opposes black emigration.[63] Yet the *Anglo-African* also published J. Holland Townsend's "Our Duty in the Conflict," which promoted fighting for "political equality of the races in this country"; James T. Holly's six-part "Thoughts on Hayti," which calls on the "colored people of the" United States to help develop Haiti as "the most advanced negro nationality"; and Frances Ellen Watkins Harper's "Fancy Sketches," which, as I will discuss in the next chapter, uses a "mischievous" protagonist to challenge the ease with which critical discourse around all of these issues could become reduced to polite "chit chat."[64]

In contrast to the fugue "romance" S.S.N. outlines, with its management of national identity and conflicting points of view, the *Anglo-African* offers a more democratic mode of reading that invites readers to take part in constructing the "meaning" of the "text." "*Anglo-African*," as term and publication, initiated a collective and participatory project of building different, if not entirely new, idioms of citizenship and peoplehood, a direct assault on "Anglo-Saxon" romances that attempted to codify a single white national subject. When Hamilton argues in his "Apology," "The negro is something more than mere endurance; he is a force," he *is* relying on a construction of racial destiny similar to the "Anglo-Saxon" romance S.S.N. critiques. His larger project, however, invokes "the negro" as a "force" of ideas and methods demonstrated in subsequent articles, both singly and collectively.[65] The articles might constellate around the theme of "Anglo-African" life, but contributors don't even agree on what an "Anglo-African" might be or if such a thing exists (outside of or without the magazine). S.S.N., for instance, wonders at how "we have become by some mysterious process—'Anglo-Africans,'" but he must admit with some chagrin that "the fact must be patent for are we not writing for an Anglo-African magazine?"[66] The "fact" of "Anglo-African-ness" is "patent" not because "Anglo-African" is any more accurate an identity than any other. Just as state conventions' "Proceedings" collected the differentiated voices and interests of delegates under its corporate authorship, the institutionally heteroglossic space of the *Anglo-African* creates an imagined community of Anglo-Africans, fleshed out, so to speak, through the collective efforts of its contributors. Writers, including Hamilton, continue using different designations: colored, black, Afric-American, American, African, Negro, and so on. In this context, "Anglo-African," like citizenship, is a "process," not an identity. The magazine and those contributing to and reading it create "Anglo-African" practices, an intellectual project that disturbs the narrative of white citizenship.

The Critic and His Discontents: Washington's Bones and the Corpus of U.S. Citizenship

William J. Wilson's "Afric-American Picture Gallery" series provides a useful case study of reading Anglo-African-wise as a critical citizenship practice that exposes and revises white citizenship's aesthetic, historiographic, and physical landscapes. I am concerned in this section with the critical attunement that Wilson models in his sketches and how Wilson uses Ethiop's intellectual development to model the critical citizen at work, both individually and as part of variously constructed collectives. The series ran in the *Anglo-African* in seven installments, from February 1859 through October 1859, in which Ethiop writes sketched descriptions of at least twenty-seven "pictures."[67] The series blends Afrofuturist meditations, cultural criticism, and the wit that readers of *Douglass's Paper* had come to expect from Ethiop. The series, as is often the case for the sketch genre, is difficult to pin down in terms of "plot." Unlike Wilson's city sketches for *Frederick Douglass's Paper*, where "Ethiop's" ideas seem directly connected to Wilson's, Ethiop in the *Anglo-African* functions increasingly as a dynamic character distinct from the author. For most of the series, Ethiop claims the gallery as a space of solitary contemplation; however, as the series progresses, Wilson introduces a cast of characters who visit the gallery, often intruding on Ethiop. These figures include a fugitive slave, black and white professionals, a white reader questioning the need for an "Anglo-African" magazine or "Afric-American" picture gallery, and "Thomas Onward," the gallery's attendant. Tom, who I will discuss in more detail below, consistently refuses to allow the gallery to become a site accessible only to a privileged few or to allow its visitors to use history and debate to retreat from the material world. In addition to these interlocutors, Ethiop leaves the gallery in a two-installment narrative arc that takes him to the Black Forest, home to "Bernice," an artistic genius, who has captured and imprisoned his former master for murdering Bernice's son.

The series moves readers and its narrator through spaces of alternate ordering, from an imagined picture gallery to sites of marronage, that disrupt utopian projections of a beautiful white republic and the closures of citizenship such projections enable. This movement has led Ernest to identify the series with an "aesthetics of liberation" capable of "accounting for the dynamic relations among artistry, history, and community." The sketches, he notes, "seem both testaments to and examples of" this aesthetic.[68] The installments mix Wilson's previous project of guiding readers through Brooklyn's cultural geographies with the conventions of catalogues from galleries such as New York's Düsseldorf Gallery, the moralism of John Ruskin's *Modern Painter*, and articles about the state of "American Art" and art audiences in *The Illustrated Magazine of Art* and *The Gentleman's Magazine*. Installments typically featured Ethiop's descriptions or "sketches" of several images, though at times his thoughts about writing the sketches leave little room for the actual sketching. The task of writing these descriptions for his *Anglo-African* readers instead often serves as an inciting incident for Ethiop's thinking about history and politics.

Most of the gallery's objects focus on a temporally and thematically varied transnational Afric-American history and are organized in a way that demands movement and viewer participation in the meaning-making process. Like the articles and images that make up the *Anglo-African*, the images populating Wilson's imagined gallery range in theme and form from Phillis Wheatley and Toussaint L'Ouverture to the Underground Railroad and "Sunset in Abbeokuta" to George Washington and "The First and Last Colored Editor." As far as I can tell, neither the gallery nor its images have direct material referents. Though images of Wheatley, Washington, and others were in circulation, they do not exist in the ways Ethiop describes them. Instead, Ethiop writes about images that are themselves (Wilson's) sketches or rough outlines of what might or ought to populate a space and public imaginary that ought to exist. While some of the images depict geographically specific locales, the gallery does not necessarily arrange artifacts by geography or historical timeline, leading Ethiop to observe on several occasions that the gallery should be better organized. He suggests, for instance, that Pictures 5 and 6, *The Underground Railroad*, should be split. Rather than situating the paintings side by side on the gallery's southern wall, Ethiop argues that the depiction of the South (before) in Picture 5 should be placed on the south side and Picture 6, a depiction of the North (after), placed on the north side.[69] At the same time, Ethiop numbers his written entries, suggesting an ongoing negotiation between the gallery's ostensible disorder and his own desires as a critic to make sense of and draw lessons from it in a way his readers can consume.[70]

Wilson's series, then, is not so much about physical space, though Wilson remains committed to creating actual picture galleries and reading rooms, but rather a fictional rendering of critical citizenship as a historical, a cultural, and an intellectual project. Surrounding Ethiop with landscape and history paintings in particular taps into the role exhibition halls, art unions, and galleries served in antebellum culture as popular entertainment and as pedagogical conduits for shaping ideas about citizenship.[71] Picture galleries were ideal spaces for developing this critical positioning because, as Michel Foucault notes of exhibitions more generally, they allow patrons to encounter multiple seemingly discordant sites in "a single real place."[72]

Ethiop himself reflects on this principle in the series' second installment: "Pictures are teachings by example," he posits, "From them we often derive our best lessons."[73] "A picture of a great man," Ethiop continues, acts as a storehouse of collective memory that "calls up the whole history of his times," recalling past events but also leading the spectator to "the philosophy of them."[74] These distilled memories become "reimpressed" on the spectator's mind. They overlay the particularities of individual experience and subjectivity with collective and participatory remembrance and can promulgate a consensus about how citizens ought to look and act and the "philosophies" that should inform citizenship practices.[75] By anchoring Ethiop's sketches in a seemingly disordered array of images—imaginary or otherwise—Wilson develops Ethiop's (and his readers') taste for a conception of collective memory as a web of associations—some contradictory, some incriminating, some inspiring—suggesting that the proper attitude of a citizen to the national symbolic is the attitude of the critic to the work of art.

From the first installment, the gallery signals its concern with art's production of historical understandings and how this understanding in turn shapes our experience. Ethiop's first sketches take up Pictures 1 and 2, *The Slave Ship* and *The First and the Last Colored Editor*. While the two paintings are not hung next to each other in the gallery (*Slave Ship* is on the gallery's south side, *The First and the Last Colored Editor* on the north), the narrative shift from *Slave Ship* to *The First and the Last Colored Editor* places before visitors the past, present, and future of "Afric-America" in a way that suggests a conversation between them, juxtaposing ostensibly incompatible sites of enslavement with sites of freedom, scenes from the distant past with scenes of a distant future. The two images create an open-ended frame narrative for the series as a whole.

As the gallery's first image and the series' first sketch, *The Slave Ship* sets an agenda of turning the American mythos on its head through some of British North America's founding sites. Visitors encounter a large landscape painting "near the entrance, on the south side of the gallery, and in rather an unfavorable light" offering a "faithful" image, "even to every shrub, crag and nook," of seventeenth-century Jamestown harbor. Featured prominently in the image are "the *slave ship*," "Dutch-modeled and ugly, even hideous to look upon, as a slave-ship ought to be," and "a group of emaciated *Africans*, heavily manacled, the first slaves that ever trod the American continent."[76] The Europeans themselves bring with them the wild savagery of gothic America, symbolized not by the racialized, dark wilderness or its indigenous inhabitants but by a "small boat" carrying slaves from ship to shore: "The small boat struck by, and contending with a huge breaker, is so near the shore that you can behold, and startle as you behold, the emaciated and death-like faces of the unfortunate victims, and the hideous countenances of their captors' and high and above all, perched upon the stern, with foot, tail and horns, and the chief insignias of his office, is his Satanic Majesty, gloating over the whole scene."[77] While the superimposed image of Satan diverges from a more mimetic representation of the slave ship, Ethiop suggests that the painter hews closer to "purest truth" because of it, for "What is more truthful than that the devil is ever the firm friend and companion of the slave ship?" The entire scene recalls the sublime picturesque of J. M. W. Turner's *The Slave Ship* (1840) and John Ruskin's description of it in *Modern Painter*.[78] In a revision of Turner and Ruskin's reading of Turner, Ruskin's "fiery path and valley, the tossing waves by which the swell of the sea is restlessly divided" and "fantastic forms, each casting a faint and ghastly shadow behind it along the illumined foam"[79] become Ethiop's "fierce and angry waters of the bay, which seem to meet the black and dismal and storm-clad sky."[80] Ethiop maintains Ruskin's view of the "guilty ship" "girded with condemnation," but where Ruskin's description blends the ship and flailing bodies from the *Zong* massacre (1781) into his admiration of Turner's picturesque seascape, in Wilson's gallery, the "small ship," its human capital, and the moment of arrival remain the "crowning point."[81] In other words, Wilson has Ethiop take up not only the memory of Jamestown but also art criticism around depictions of the middle passage.

With this introduction, the gallery and Wilson's series call upon patrons to see slavery as central to the nation's political and aesthetic history and Europeans as its gothic villains, not its victims or intrepid heroes. The sublime struggle depicted here is less against an immense nature than against the "hideous countenances" of the slavers and their little boat. Where the tragedy in Turner's *Slave Ship* involves mass murder of 133 enslaved Africans in the name of profit, the tragedy in Wilson's *Slave Ship* involves a mundane scene in the slave trade that would be repeated along the U.S. coast for the next 250 years.

The First and the Last Colored Editor, Ethiop's second sketch (but not the gallery's second painting), positions black print culture as a countervailing center of gravity, a scene within the larger narrative of "a positive and purposeful self-identified African America."[82] In contrast to the dark looming image of *Slave Ship*, *The First and the Last Colored Editor* is a "small, but neat picture" hanging "on the north side of the gallery."[83] In the painting, "quite a young man" sits at a desk piled with copies of previous black newspapers from *Freedom's Journal* to *Frederick Douglass's Paper*, reading the first editorial of the First Editor, who, "unperceived by the Last Editor, is looking intently over his shoulder."[84] As Benjamin Fagan has noted, this image might be a representation of Thomas Hamilton, the *Anglo-African*'s editor.[85] The image might also reflect Wilson himself, who, James McCune Smith reveals in a letter to Gerrit Smith, was "sub rosa editor of this weekly [*Weekly Anglo-African*], that is, he writes the Editorials."[86] Either way, the painting visualizes the responsibility a new "colored editor" takes on as part of a black editorial tradition, a responsibility Hamilton and Wilson perhaps shared as they prepared to launch the *Weekly Anglo-African Magazine* in July 1859.

Whether a reflection on a specific contemporaneous black editor or a meditation on black editorship's historical role and future, *The First and the Last Colored Editor* positions black editors as masters of the craft accessible through the papers they edited. It is an intellectual tradition through which critical practices have been honed over the decades, complemented by archival practices (the papers have, after all, been preserved) ensuring future "colored editors" will not only be in a position to learn from and find inspiration in this tradition but also will be judged by those who came before. This genealogy of black editorship recalls classic aesthetic treatises advising study of past masters to "lift up our souls to the standard of their own genius." Longinus, for instance, asked readers, "What would *Homer* or *Demosthenes* have thought of *this piece?*" Imagine, he continues, if "such celebrated heroes must preside as our judges, and be at the same time our evidence?"[87] The painting, though small, and the continuity it represents stand in contradistinction to the scenes from the Middle Passage and frames print as the bridge "linking together of our once scarcely hopeful past with the now brightest present."[88] If Atlantic slavery as depicted in *Slave Ship* was a site of cultural and historical rupture, *The First and the Last* also suggests that future generations can find and participate in creating new roots out of the "cultural grounding" previous generations' textual production provided.[89]

As these first two paintings reveal, the "Afric-American Picture Gallery" series as a whole probes again and again the implications of which figures, images, and narratives are chosen to represent citizenship. They also foreground how disrupting these patterns can help produce different citizenship practices. Ethiop articulates this principle explicitly for his *Anglo-African* readers, as he contemplates a portrait of Toussaint L'Ouverture. While a picture of George Washington "recalls to mind the American Revolution," a portrait of Thomas Jefferson "brings before the mind in all its scope and strength . . . the Declaration of Independence." The L'Ouverture portrait, however, completes the thought and "carries us forward to the times, when its [the Declaration of Independence] broad and eternal principles, will be fully recognized by, and applied to the entire American people."[90] The portrait "force[s] upon" Ethiop's mind the whole history of the Haitian people, a history that invokes for him a future in which the Declaration of Independence might be fully realized, not as a product of a specifically white U.S. revolution but rather as a constitutive element of an ongoing hemispheric revolutionary process in which the successful slave revolution offers the key to "the sublime idea of freedom."[91] The positioning of the three revolutionaries creates a triptych, inviting visitors to provide the narrative between paintings—to fill in the empty spaces on the wall in a way that unsettles and demands continued work. For the critical citizen, the revolution remains unfinished.

As an overall work of fiction, the series represents a creative enterprise focused not just on exposure or suspicion—that is, uncovering hidden ideological content—but also creating new, potentially more satisfying objects. Even as Ethiop attempts to impose order on the gallery's arrangement, Wilson, as series author, curates Ethiop's experience and the journey for his readers in a way that models critical inquiry. The gallery space and art objects it conjures enable (or force, as Ethiop suggests of portraiture) viewers to see what had been occluded or rendered unseeable and unhearable (black print archives) or to see common images (*Slave Ship*) from a different angle. These objects interrupt the recursive fugue citizenship S.S.N. theorized in their insistence on facing contradictions and ruptures and their refusal to offer consolation.

Ethiop's criticism and commentary on his method of criticism provides a complementary practice through which critique emerges as an expected and necessary concomitant of reading history, acting in the present, and imagining the future. Whether or not *The First and the Last Colored Editor* or *Slave Ship* had a physical referent, Ethiop's translation of the images Wilson sets before him constructs an almost novelistic double-voiced discourse between Ethiop-the-critic-observer and the painting-object-of-critique, both characters in Wilson's fictional series. Ethiop is constantly in creative tension with the gallery itself and, the narrative's structure suggests, he should be. Through images such as *The Slave Ship* and *The First and the Last Colored Editor* and their juxtaposition to others, including *The Underground Railroad*, a bust of Ira Aldridge, and a portrait of Phillis Wheatley, the gallery compels Ethiop's ostensibly moody eye to comment on the connections between images and, more important, the mental processes counterintuitive juxtapositions might provoke.

Even if readers were aware of the inspiration for some of these sketches—portraits of Wheatley, Washington, and Jefferson were in circulation enough—Ethiop's movement through the gallery and his method of analysis provide models for how they could approach objects—those monuments, songs, and orations—meant to consolidate citizenship as an escape from politics, anxiety, and difference. His meditation on the pedagogical uses of art and his critique of public taste make each sketch a primer on how to read events in time—past, present, and future. This ethos applies to citizenship more broadly: critical citizenship in practice often does not gratify "the popular American feeling," especially when that feeling hews toward closure, but instead attempts to be more "faithful" to citizenship as a collective, open-ended process.[92] Taken together, Wilson and Ethiop present critical citizenship as a set of practices linking cultural production, consumption, and criticism.

Ethiop's engagement with *Mount Vernon*, a painting depicting a scene where slavery's past and present haunt grounds sacred to the national mythology, shows this connection between creative and critical work. The sketch follows Ethiop's meditation on Haitian revolutionaries, and it opens with Ethiop's commentary on Mount Vernon and George Washington in the national imaginary. The two, Ethiop muses, have "something to do with every spring of the machinery of American society; social, political, and religious": "Mount Vernon exclaims the breast-laden patriot; Mount Vernon echoes the good old ladies, Mount Vernon is piped, Mount Vernon is harped; Mount Vernon is danced; Mount Vernon is sung." "How careful ought we to be," he concludes, "in word or deed about Mount Vernon."[93] The nation walks by a mythos propped up by Washington's fading legacy and objects such as the ubiquitous Mount Vernon canes "manufactured from some of its decaying relics."[94] Touching the venerable landscape is metonymically linked to touching the nation's core.

Wilson's *Mount Vernon* features "Decay . . . written by the Artist's pencil more legibly than in letters."[95] Paralleling the decaying Washington canes,

Ethiop shows Washington's bones weakened by time and in the care of slaves—perhaps relatives of those he posthumously emancipated. As he scans the painting, Ethiop comes across Washington's tomb: "The first thing that here arrests the eye is the recently dug up coffin of Washington; just behind which stands the ghost of his faithful old slave and body servant; while in front, a living slave of to-day stands, with the *bones* of Washington gathered up in his arms, and labeled 'For Sale' 'Price $200,000; this negro included.' 'Money wanted.'"[96] The scene uses the same techniques as *The First and the Last Colored Editor*, ancestors from the past presiding over the events of the present. As Ivy Wilson observes, "Ethiop's description of Washington disallows the body from emerging, dissolving the corpus and reducing it to a set of bones."[97] *Mount Vernon* literally frames the "corpus" of Washington, the abstracted ideal citizen, in the arms of the discorporated black slave, the sale of the two amounting to a bargain for a national icon.[98] But while Wilson refuses Washington an embodied afterlife, Washington's "servant," potentially a reference to William "Billy" Lee, who features prominently in John Trumbull's *George Washington* (1780), returns to bear witness and stand in judgment. Lee was Washington's longtime "manservant," who rode with him during the Revolutionary War. He was the only of Washington's slaves freed immediately upon Washington's death, per Washington's will. As Douglas Jones notes, Lee's gradual disappearance as a distinct figure in Washington portraiture maps a corresponding erasure of black people as politically or aesthetically viable subjects.[99] In Ethiop's analysis, however, it is Washington who is fading from memory so that he wonders "how we shall preserve even the name of Washington many years long."[100]

Mount Vernon, then, intervenes directly in the contemporaneous production of Washington iconography and both its embeddedness within proslavery discourse and the erasure of enslavement from commentaries that would reclaim Washington and his generation for antislavery purposes. Junius Brutus Stearns's *Washington as a Farmer at Mount Vernon* (1851), for instance, featured George Washington presiding over a prosperous plantation with slaves at work, children at play, and the first president benevolently conversing with what might be his overseer. As Maurie D. McInnis notes, the "painting emphatically reminds viewers of the enforced agricultural labor of Washington's slaves, but it does so in a way that suggests slavery was a benevolent and natural institution."[101] The whole image communicates the continuity between the ideal (and ideally dead) Washington and the vision of a nation of virtuous overseers ruling under his singular authority. Presented just a year after the Compromise of 1850, the painting shows the proslavery ideal of the benevolent master, but through George Washington, this ideal and the economic system it represents become inextricably linked with the nation as a whole.

If the Mount Vernon and Washington of the past could still be invoked for utopic purposes, the Mount Vernon of the 1850s confirms Wilson's reframing and Ethiop's impressions. Throughout the 1850s, Mount Vernon was in dire disrepair. The Mount Vernon Ladies' Association (MVLA) set to raising the estimated $200,000 (not coincidentally the price of Washington's bones plus slave in Ethiop's sketch) needed to purchase the property from John Augustine Washington, who himself owned or employed slaves.[102] But Congress and other would-be supporters, even members of the MVLA, were hesitant if not hostile to the idea of monumentalizing *that* Mount Vernon, precisely because of its *present* condition. "Mount Vernon had for decades," McInnis reminds us, "served as the symbolic embodiment of Washington and the virtues he represented. Now the dilapidated buildings referred instead to the unhealthiness of the institution."[103] Discussions about Washington's home inevitably circled back to debates over slavery as either a national institution or a national sin. "Here we have Mount Vernon transmogrified into a regular slave shamble," Horace Greeley editorialized in his *New York Tribune* in 1858, "where human beings are sold out to the highest bidder—the proprietor living on their wages—until they are returned on his hands."[104] In Greeley's analysis, Washington's heirs have defiled the idyllic Mount Vernon of old, "transmogrifying" the utopian ideal into a dystopic nightmare, the once beautiful inspiration now a gothic horror.

And yet even assessments like Greeley's slip back into mythology, exculpating Washington and the founding generation of responsibility for the present. While Greeley's commentary appears critical in the sense that it condemns Mount Vernon's current state, it nevertheless relies on an idealized version of the plantation's history: the source of the decline is not the presence of enslavement (Washington owned slaves) but rather the visual degradation (emphasis on "shamble," not "slave") and clear evidence of the current owner's economic reliance on this labor without the sheen of gentry benevolence. Greeley's interpretation renders the antebellum Mount Vernon as a gothic deviation from an otherwise heroic legacy.

In place of this decline narrative, Wilson's *Mount Vernon* negates the binary by overlaying the dilapidated Mount Vernon with reminders of its more visually pleasing but no less morally bankrupt past. The principle recalls Frederick Douglass's excoriation of white Americans for relying on the virtues of their ancestors to "excuse some folly or wickedness of their own."[105] The image Wilson sets before Ethiop and his readers, however, suggests that the past had its own "wickedness" in need of covering and that small-scale acts of benevolence such as Washington's posthumously freeing his slaves do very little to counter a lifetime of slaveholding and a system that defends the practice. The Mount Vernon of the 1850s *is* Washington and the nation's legacy, perhaps a more enduring one than either Washington's name or political career. If Washington's image had been excised from the present scenes of Mount Vernon slavery, either in attempts to reappropriate the space as national monument or in efforts to maintain Washington's iconic status, his bones remained wrapped in the bargain—or his slaves remain wrapped in the bargain with his bones—and both Washington and his former slaves, like the First Colored Editor, continue to hover and demand an accounting.

"Wild Sublimity": The Black Forest's Critical Stance and the Slave Sublime

Even as Wilson uses Ethiop to outline critical citizenship as a reading practice, the "Afric-American Picture Gallery" series also suggests that critics (amateur or professional) must be wary, lest they begin to "speak too metaphorically" and lose touch with an ethical responsibility to engage actively in the material world. *The Black Forest* narrative arc, nested within the series' April and June installments, combines gothic science fiction, marronage, and slave narrative. It reminds us that critical citizenship requires self-reflection and its own openness to intrusions so that it doesn't risk reinscribing a different version of the closed structure it was supposed to open. Wilson takes Ethiop through a series of inversions calibrated to force him to think about not only the contradictions within U.S. legal code and practice but also his own position within that system. The intergenerational tension the sequence develops between Bernice, Ethiop, and Tom stresses tensions inhering to the citizenship, print, and institutional practices I outline throughout *The Practice of Citizenship* and an unresolvable conflict within critical citizenship: how to negotiate citizenship's entailments of exclusivity and the unruliness of critique. Wilson's narrative solution to this problem centers less on conclusive answers or reconciliation and more on a vision of the critic who must consistently face ongoing interrogation and the limits of his own criticism. If citizenship based in white supremacy is predicated on "matters of taste" and beauty that police citizenship, the Black Forest's sublimity and each character's response to it model the subjectivity of a critical citizen who resists arrest.

Because this narrative has only recently received critical attention and wider access, it is worth reconstructing in some detail. Three installments into the main series, Wilson's style changes, as the "gallery Boy," "Thomas Onward," presents Ethiop with a portrait of himself (Tom, the gallery boy) to hang in the gallery. A couple of days after viewing Tom's portrait, Ethiop attempts to sketch Picture No. XI, "marked 'The Black Forest' ": a "landscape painting" of "grand and beautiful scenery, dark back ground shadows and the air of profound mystery . . . pervade[ing] it."[106] Ethiop is "attracted" to painting, but Tom's portrait and its artist's identity continue to demand his attention.[107] Tom then presents Ethiop with an invitation from Bernice: "Come over to the Black Forest and examine some of the pictures and other curiosities there. Two days journey by stage and by foot for a man, and none others are asked!"[108] Description then gives way to more dialogue and character development as Ethiop's role shifts from authoritative chronicler to limited narrator and inexperienced sojourner.

By bringing Ethiop from the contemplation of a beautiful image safe inside the gallery to an encounter with its sublime referent and the artist who produced it, Wilson takes Ethiop through a process that attunes him to possibilities exceeding even those presented in the gallery's framed images. Set in the midst of a post–*Dred Scott* landscape, the Black Forest intrudes on the surrounding spatial and narrative order: "a huge mountain forest, whose crest loomed up blacker and blacker as the clouds of coming evening rolled up from bellow the horizon. Here in all its grandeur and wild sublimity was the native landscape spread out before me, the same that I saw in beautiful miniature but a day before hanging on the walls of our Afric-American Gallery."[109] Ethiop describes the *physical* Black Forest in terms of the sublime set against the gallery painting's beauty, signaling not just its physically intimidating presence but also its challenge to established ways of seeing the world. The sublime, following Kevin Hetherington, "make[s] use of the limits of our imagination, our desires, our fears and our sense of power/powerlessness." It taps into that part of us that allows us to think about that which we cannot know/comprehend through established channels of understanding, ultimately opening new imaginative vistas, new senses of power, and objects of desire.[110]

The distinction signals the Black Forest's disruption of the surrounding aesthetic regime, including Ethiop's own attempts to render a beautiful, redemptive narrative of Afric-America through his sketches in the gallery. If citizenship has often been premised on its boundaries (those it admits and excludes, those it makes visible and those it renders invisible, and those to whom it gives place and those whom it displaces), then Wilson's depiction of the Black Forest in terms of the sublime presses against those boundaries and the imaginaries that support them.[111] Where the art in the gallery recalls a past purposefully forgotten, the sublimity of the physical Black Forest not only invokes an orientation to the present—against the national structures that, despite their critique, Ethiop's images work within—but also *actively* disrupts that present's stability.

Wilson enhances the link between the Black Forest's sublimity and disruptive politics by encoding the space in terms of marronage. Ethiop refuses "to disclose the precise locality of the Black Forest, nor fully the manner of people dwelling there." As Peterson argues, marronage paradoxically highlights the "fundamental homelessness," or perhaps placelessness in Ethiop's rendering, "of blacks in the new world" and provides respite from slave society's ravages.[112] We know that at least one of the forest's residents is a fugitive slave and that the forest's other residents are, if nothing else, actively opposing state power. Whether or not these other residents are fugitive slaves, however, the Black Forest represents Neil Roberts's more recent theorization of marronage as "a multidimensional, constant act of flight."[113] Flight, Roberts notes, "can be both real and imagined," enacted as one moves—physically and intellectually—away from enslavement and toward a future state.[114] In this sense, the Black Forest is not just a space where fugitives might live but also a physical manifestation of a way of life: space does not make marronage; practices make marronage.[115]

In Wilson's Black Forest arc, these practices begin with a fugitive who decided to "do something" with the white people, or at least one white person. Wilson pairs Ethiop with Bernice, whom Ethiop describes as "a glory to look upon." The older man becomes Ethiop's mentor, a "*Gamaliel*" to Ethiop's Paul.[116] While in his "hut" (perhaps an intratextual reference to *Blake*, which was appearing concurrently), Bernice shows Ethiop his workroom, filled with "busts, statues, statuettes; landscapes, portraits, fancy pieces; paints, pallets, mallets, chisels; half finished sketches, studies in plaster," and duplicates of Tom's portrait and *The Black Forest*.[117] The "profusion" of work leads Ethiop to realize that Bernice is "the executor" of the paintings he's spent so much time admiring. This recognition of Bernice's artistic "genius" allays any qualms Ethiop feels about his own vulnerability and suggests a contrapuntal relation between the gallery's art—some historical, some not—and the material world.[118]

The Black Forest disrupts not only Ethiop's (and readers') received spatial sense but also assumptions about temporality, the timelessness of white citizenship, and the potential futures of Afric-America. Wilson embeds within the narrative a future-past narrative foretelling or retelling the end of white America. Ethiop spends the day watching Bernice work, until he comes across a tablet, purportedly from the "year 4000," engraved in "words . . . curiously spelt by the aid of 41 singular, new and beautiful characters."[119] Unable to determine the tablet's origins, aside from Bernice's claims that it "was dug out of the mountain peak of the *Black Forest*," Ethiop wonders, "Is it fiction, is it history, is it prophecy? Who can tell?"[120] Ethiop fills the rest of the day translating the text "by dint of hard study," eventually producing a twenty-five-verse narrative detailing the history and demise of "The Amecans, or Milk White Race," who destroy themselves "and their works" through their own "evil deeds."[121] While the Amecans were technologically advanced (the Amecans developed a "path of iron" [railroad tracks] with "swift running vehicles" powered by steam [trains]), they were also avaricious and relied on enslaved labor, much like the white Americans Ethiop describes in "What Shall We Do with the White People?" The Amecans don't disappear in the race war Lincoln envisions (and Jefferson before him). While the "forefathers" of the tablet's black author "increased much in substance and in numbers; and much in strength and in wisdom also," the Amecans fade away into obscurity, rendered feeble by their own technology and avarice: "yea as a cloud did they vanish from off the face of the whole land."[122] Neither noble savage nor redeemable master race, Wilson consigns the Amecans to ancient history in an inversion of the settler-colonial narrative of the disappearing native.

This text from the future enters the present as an ancient artifact, placing Ethiop in a position not unlike the Last Colored Editor, reading a text that projects into a potential future even as it connects him to the past.[123] The tablet's generic indeterminacy would seem to discredit its contents or, at the very least, any reader's ability to properly frame and interpret its text. However, this generic question, posed just after referring to the tablet as a challenge to the professional discourses of history, ethnology, and literary history (or the history of the book), highlights the interconnectedness of the three discourses, suggesting their mutual indeterminacy as equal parts fiction, history, and prophesy. Antebellum racial science and popular opinion proposed a historical and biological telos in which African-descended peoples were inherently inferior and suited for enslavement. This tablet, however, potentially authored by a future people of African descent and found in a space of marronage, reads the historical arc of the nineteenth century as indicative of white degeneration.

As Ethiop finishes his translation, Bernice interrupts his reverie and invites him deeper into his lair, where he shows Ethiop a scene that makes him fear for "[his] own safety."[124] The intrusion forces Ethiop to confront in real life the kind of narrative viewed only at a remove in the gallery and serves as a potent play on the image of fading whiteness presented in the Amecan tablet. Bernice has his former master chained to the wall of a small cell. Ethiop encodes the transition in gothic terms: "From the artistic, the beautiful and the curious, we had just quitted, an object of the most appalling my eyes ever beheld stood before us. Was it a man, was it even human?"[125] Felix "lunge[s] for" Ethiop; "he raved, he shirked, he tore his hair," yelling "imprecations," but only the word "*Bernice*" was intelligible. "A stout heart only saved" Ethiop "from petrification on the spot," and he begins to lose confidence in his host.[126] As Bernice explains, the man, who Ethiop describes as "this white trembling *Felix*," had held Bernice and Bernice's wife and children "as property" until he sold them.[127] Sometime later, Bernice continues, "the wretch blew" his remaining son's "brains out without provocation and without warning."[128] Bernice eventually escaped, coming to the Black Forest, where he "acquired" the man through secret means and where the man will remain until his death.[129]

The scene works initially through conventions of gothic doubling: the slaveholder has become the captive and the slave has become the dispenser of justice, reversing the narrative of law and order and national wholeness subtending Anthony Burns's rendition. Yet Bernice's inversion ultimately leads Ethiop to question the nature of law altogether. "Felix" and Bernice "conversed much and freely. He spoke of the wrong done him; I spoke of mine. He spoke of his wife and children left behind. I reminded him of the sale and separation of mine. . . . He plead earnestly for his rights. I told him he had no rights that I was bound to respect. . . . I was now the master and he the slave."[130] If, as Toni Morrison points out, white writers attached the gothic of slavery to "bound and violently silenced" black bodies, this moment of the unbound black subject conversing "much and freely" revenges this violence on the former master.[131] Bernice's invocation of justice, in the language of Justice Taney's majority opinion, silences Felix's pleas and Ethiop's qualms alike. Much like the fugitive slave, whose testimony counted little in court, Bernice's master can only beg "for liberty" or death's release. This engenders contempt, not pity—contempt for the former master, contempt for the system of laws that supported him, and, most of all, contempt for northern complicity in maintaining these laws.

The "common sense" of Bernice, the black speaker, challenges the constraints of what the putative wholeness of white citizenship codifies as visible, audible, and thinkable, and in doing so, he undercuts the basis for Felix's language and unmoors Ethiop's sense of the relation between law and morality. Faced with the injustice of Bernice's former master's actions and the horror of what Bernice has done to him in retribution, Ethiop appeals to "law, redress, justice &c." Bernice, however, forestalls Ethiop's recourse to law for consolation. "'*Laws*!'" Bernice "exclaim[s] almost frantic" in response, "'*Law!!*' What laws, what justice is there for the oppressed of our *class*? What laws except to oppress them harder? What laws except to pursue and rob them from cradle to the grave, yea even beyond both."[132] The "law," Bernice reminds Ethiop, is on Felix's side: it allowed him to dispose of Bernice's family, and that same law would free Felix and authorize him to reenslave Bernice and to enslave Ethiop.

In this signal moment of critical citizenship, the narrative reveals that the system cannot be "fixed" because it is not broken; it's designed to work this way. Rather, the system must be broken first.[133] As Teresa Goddu argues about a similar scene of enslavement and punishment in *Letters from an American Farmer*, the "idealized fable" of law and order and beautiful union "cracks under the weight of history."[134] Wilson's narrative (now a former slave binding his white former master as a black spectator looks on) keeps the crack in view, despite even Ethiop's attempts to reconcile it through familiar means. The moment in the cave is a litmus test: Ethiop could remain in the gothic mode, afraid of Bernice and the implications of his actions because Ethiop's judgment, his sense of possibility, cannot expand beyond the closures of the state and its laws. Or, realizing he has nothing to fear in Bernice, Ethiop could "discover within" himself "a capacity for resistance of quite another kind," as Kant usefully frames the sublime response, and leave with an expanded consciousness.[135] The Black Forest disrupts chains of communication that would condemn Bernice (or Nat Turner and Denmark Vesey) as a threat to national stability and calls on critics like Ethiop not only to point to such breaks but also to recognize his embeddedness within those chains.[136] The sublimity of the sequence emanates from Ethiop's reaction to the deeper political, economic, and social implications of Bernice's arguments and actions, not from the sight of Felix. At the scene's end, Ethiop reflects that he "too now regarded" Felix as a "wretched fiend."[137]

Despite Ethiop's new understanding, the sequence and Ethiop's gothic-coded response present several cautions for the would-be critical citizen. It's not that Bernice's actions are too fantastic for Ethiop to grasp but rather that Ethiop can too easily distance himself from their implications by aestheticizing them as framed pictures. The space and Bernice's exceptional status also make them easily compartmentalized, especially since Ethiop emphasizes their physical distance from the gallery and the strangeness of the events he witnessed there. Hence, the Black Forest is a "*Picture* Outside of the Gallery," and Ethiop can joke about an encounter with slave catchers on a stagecoach on the way to the Black Forest, characterizing them as "two portraits that ought to be hung up."[138] Ethiop glibly fantasizes about the prospect of capture: "I prepared myself . . . and should have summary work with them, had a hand to hand encounter taken place, just such as fugitives should make in a like case."[139] While showing his approval for violent resistance to slave catchers, Ethiop also separates himself from the imminent danger a fugitive or any black person traveling after 1850 would have faced. Ethiop's adventure allows him to observe and describe in detail two specimens of "genuine American stock," and their intellectual "rout" at his hands disabuses the men of "the assumed or imagined mental superiority of white men."[140] Despite moments of danger when "fingers began to twitch and pistols move from their places," the scene demonstrates the potential power of Ethiop's critical perspective, the voice of "a common sense black" subject causing the white men to shrink in chagrin, their superior arms notwithstanding. The three part ways at the depot, the slaveholder and the slave catcher continuing their hunt without Ethiop taking actions to actually "hang" them or impede their progress.

Yet, as Bernice notes in his discourse on the law, Ethiop was never that safe. He may have routed the men rhetorically, but Bernice's story about his son's murder, accounts such as Solomon Northup's *12 Years a Slave* (1853) of free black men taken as slaves, and Wilson's own vigilance work in Brooklyn tell of the physical threat Ethiop faced and the legal and political power that could have been marshaled against him. Rhetorical power Ethiop may have had, but the Fugitive Slave Act ensured that he would not have been able to use it in his own defense should the two men have been determined to kidnap him. Ethiop's weak appeals to the law during his encounter with Bernice and Felix place in sharper relief his previous conversation with the slaveholder and slave catcher and his musings about who *ought* to be hung up.

Ethiop's state of mind upon returning to the gallery in the July installment suggests that even as the space and images in the gallery give him critical purchase for challenging grounding fictions of white citizenship, they also allow him to become too comfortable in an aestheticized world of memory. The space and its art can foster a critical sense; they cannot do the work of critical citizenship. Caught between the horror of what Felix had done to Bernice and the sublimity of Bernice's retribution, Ethiop's narration stops. Faced with Bernice and Felix, the series and Ethiop, mimicking Crevecoeur's Farmer James or Douglass's Listwell in "Heroic Slave," abruptly leave the Black Forest for the gallery's more comfortable and safer setting. The Fourth Paper, the last installment of the Black Forest arc, ends with "To be continued." The Fifth Paper begins with Ethiop back in the gallery. While his last sketch was numbered 14, his next sketch is numbered 19, suggesting that either something should be there, but Ethiop has not or cannot write it down, or that the scenes in Bernice's hut were supposed to be numbered, but they exceeded Ethiop's ability to organize them. Either way, Ethiop reaches an impasse that Wilson does not force him to navigate, leaving readers to fill in the space between installments, just as visitors to the gallery fill in the interpretive space between paintings.

In lieu of a resolution, readers find Ethiop sitting in his "big armchair" to "take in the beauties and excellences of Pictures No. XIX and XX, 'Preaching and After Preaching,' and No. XXI, 'A Head of Phillis Wheatley.' " The paintings lead Ethiop to think about other instances of the slave sublime, including praise for "the Margaret Garners who rather than their babes even shall clank a chain, prefer to send them up to their God who gave them."[141] When Ethiop's mind returns to Bernice, he experiences "such a storm of choloric feeling as will serve for all of life to come."[142] For consolation, Ethiop reminisces about "the days when Banneker lived and told of the stars and of the rising suns, and Wheatley sung their praise to listening worlds."[143] As Ivy Wilson and John Ernest have argued differently, these images crystalize the connection between art and radical resistance outlined in Bernice's narrative.[144] Ethiop's reflections provide a useful instance of liberation historiography—informing his readers, readers of the *Anglo-African*, about a history of resistance, artistic and violent, and reminding them of their own revolutionary potential—but it also stops him from returning to Bernice's imprecations against present-day law or the implications his brand of justice might present. Ethiop instead describes these scenes—even Margaret Garner—in terms of wistful reminiscence on a more radical black past and uses this reminiscence to distance himself from his present world. They allow him to create the kind of escape he critiqued in previous sketches and that characterize more passive models of citizenship.

This installment reveals that perhaps Ethiop learned the wrong lessons from the Black Forest: he attempts to turn the gallery into his personal enclave, mirroring a central problem with the Black Forest: it risks reproducing the systems of power it could potentially upend. Only those invited can enter, and Bernice, or maybe the forest itself, only invites men. Ethiop displays a similar attitude toward the gallery, despite his advertising its contents through his sketches. Even before the Black Forest sequence, Ethiop had begun thinking about the "Afric-American Picture Gallery" as *his* space, speaking in a conspiratorial "we" of "our *secret.*—Our pleasant hiding-place, where we have so often and so long shut ourselves from the blast and chill of the world," and mourning the loss of "the luxury of solitude."[145] Once, after repeated interruptions, Ethiop even asks Tom "to bar it against all further intruders"—perversely reproducing the way Douglass argued law and custom had made black citizens "intruders" in 1854.[146]

More ominously, as scholarship on maroon societies and in geographical studies reveals, spaces like Bernice's Black Forrest and Ethiop's gallery offer tactics that can fit within the spatial strategy of white citizenship without disrupting its overall structure—sometimes strengthening that structure instead. In the context of practices examined in this book, spaces like the state conventions constantly risk serving the very strategies they mean to disrupt as they become static locations of officiousness and the *accepted* location for black agency. Black citizenship can thrive as long as it remains within this space without appreciably affecting the surrounding civil society; indeed, that society could often turn acts of resistance into comedic performance. These narrative moments and spaces allow readers to elide their counterhegemonic implications in their representation of figures not embraced in the national imaginary (American Indians, African Americans, women, Catholics, etc.), because the overall narrative gives them an "authorized placement."[147]

Ethiop's sketching within the gallery allows him to propose an alternative framework for mapping a critical civic imaginary with a taste for understandings of citizenship outside of what white supremacy makes sensible. At the same time, his trip to the Black Forest exposes the dangers of critical projects becoming disconnected from lived reality and the operations of power. In both instances, Ethiop neglects two principles of citizenship I've outlined in previous chapters, neighborly contact—the meetings between strangers that foster horizontal civic exchanges outlined in Jones and Allen's *Narrative*—and circulation—the free movement of civic power among a diverse citizenry. By neglecting these principles, Ethiop short-circuits the power his critique and Bernice's lessons could offer, reproducing the proprietary enclosures that he means his work to prevent. Wilson's series provides a third figure, a doorkeeper, who, as I argue in the next section, completes a composite sketch of the critical citizen and installs intrusiveness as an institutional and collaborative practice.

Young Tom: The Critical Citizen as Doorkeeper and Trickster, or Beating the Intellectual Bounds

Critical citizenship requires mundane, everyday interruptions and collaboration as much or perhaps more than extraordinary encounters such as those described in the Black Forest arc. The way Wilson produces these intrusions and Ethiop's inability to manage them suggests the importance of a degree of intrusiveness, of mischievous contact, to the project of critical citizenship and public discourse through both institutional and noninstitutional means. Young Tom, the third image in Wilson's Ethiop-Bernice-Tom triptych, embodies the critical citizen-subject, the "Anglo-African" in circulation, who refuses to be pinned down and refuses Ethiop's (and perhaps Bernice's) debilitating isolation. We might think of this Tom as the picture gallery's version of Esu, the "god of the crossing" or "gateway god."[148] As Heather Russell explains, Esu is a tricky shape shifter not necessarily because his form changes but rather because "he shifts the *shape* of received knowledge" in a way that represents the epistemological challenge of the "African Atlantic subject."[149] Rather than utopian consolation, Tom suggests instability, restlessness, and a willfulness that keeps the spatial and temporal location of citizenship fluid—ordered but not static or circumscribed.

Ethiop introduces Tom in the third installment with near-mythological terms. Tom is a "brown-faced boy," a "shrewd little rogue," not an "*Old Tom* . . . nor an *Uncle Tom*, nor a *Saintly Tom*," but rather "a real live *Young Tom*, up to all conceivable mischief and equal to all emergencies."[150] Of Tom's origins, Ethiop writes, "Though he has seen all of life . . . one would scarcely conclude that this boy has come down to us through nearly three hundred years of hard trial. . . . He was almost whipped into existence, whipped into childhood, whipped up to boyhood. He has been whipped up to manhood, whipped down to old age, whipped out of existence."[151] In contrast to the stability of Harriet Beecher Stowe's Uncle Tom, Wilson's Tom calls to mind trickster-like narrators such as Henry Bibb, "who was whipped up," and Harriet Jacobs, who creatively uses space and language to gain freedom. Yet Tom is not "able to remember a tithe of the hard things done to" him. He instead represents constant renewal: a youth who has come "out of . . . mountains of dust and ashes without one bit of sackcloth upon [him] . . . fresh, smiling and free."[152] This is not to suggest that the "nearly three hundred years" have disappeared. Though his body does not show the marks of his past, the lifetimes of experience have made Tom "a shrewd little rogue."[153] In short, Tom's life encompasses the history of Afric-America as a palimpsest, generation overlaying generation as in the image of *The First and the Last Colored Editor*.

Tom's youth signals that this history can be transformed from scenes of death to scenes of creative and regenerative possibility, the "agency within potentiality" Roberts associates with marronage.[154] Roberts, building on Steven Hahn, draws our attention to marronage's "poeticist political imaginary" in the "total refusal of the enslaved condition."[155] From this perspective, Roberts argues, "Freedom is not a place; it is a state of being." For Tom, this analysis might be extended to suggest that freedom and marronage are tethered to those practices of intrusion, disruption, and critique associated with critical citizenship. Because Tom exercises marronage as a state of motion, being, and practice, he has avoided Ethiop's preoccupation with and retreat to history and Bernice's self-imposed isolation. Instead, he seems to have distilled the lessons of the past without becoming trapped by their traumas. His movement within and outside the gallery and his placement at its door, the interstices, reminds us that marronage does not equal isolation and can be most radical as maroons circulate in and intrude upon unfree territory.

Indeed, Tom often intrudes at crucial junctures throughout the series, bringing Ethiop "to a sense of the present moment," forcing him to move. Earlier in the series, "our little brown-faced boy in attendance" brought in two patrons, who leave Ethiop "bothered and puzzled."[156] The encounters compel Ethiop to articulate the *Anglo-African*'s and the gallery's overall mission to larger issues of print culture, reception, and racialization, thus anchoring his historical sketches to present concerns and the continued building of political communities. "These pictures, as a whole," he tells a "colored lady," who visits the gallery on a faultfinding mission, "serve as simple reminders of what the people of color were, now are, and will yet be. What they have gone through, are going through, and have yet to go through."[157] Elsewhere, Tom brings in a man who Ethiop describes as "not Anglo-African, but Anglo-Saxon, or Anglo-American or something of that sort." The man's contention that writers for the *Anglo-African* ought to write for "ably conducted magazines in the country, such as *Harpers'* or the *Atlantic Monthly*" because "it would be more creditable" leads Ethiop to deliver a "sharp" discourse on how racism "colors" judgments of merit, aesthetic and otherwise.[158] By bringing Ethiop in contact with contentious visitors "without paying heed to" his "embarrassment" (by agitating him into outlining the gallery's critical mission), Tom forces Ethiop to confront competing interpretations, to think about his work in the gallery as a public process, and to engage with that public as a critic even when he would rather brood.[159]

That Wilson makes this mischievous character the gallery's doorkeeper suggests that critical citizenship can also function as an institutional ethos. Critical citizens are not necessarily against structures and institutions; rather, they work to ensure that these structures and institutions remain accessible and self-reflexive. Tom, then, represents the free play at the heart of the gallery that makes Ethiop's sketches possible and the principles of contact and debate that activate its critical project. For instance, after "three weeks' barricading the doors" of the gallery following his trip to the Black Forest, Ethiop finds solace in the "justness" of his sketches and memories of the past. But, "a loud rap at the door [brings him] to a sense of the present moment and to [his] feet. Wondering who the intruder might be that dared to thus disturb [him], [Ethiop] bade him enter. It was *Tom*—yes, Tom, with a package of letters in his hand. . . . Somehow or other, there was a wicked twinkle playing about the corners of his usually wicked little eyes."[160] Tom's eyes twinkle, we discover, because "the little rogue had been operating on his own hook" in Ethiop's absence, "pointing out the Gallery to the various magnates around for his own special amusement," including a "doctor . . . and the Professor . . . , and the Philosopher with him; and a little lady in black, and a tall lady, and a fat lady, and a strange nice lady from abroad," the litany continuing with others, "some queer ones . . . a crusty old gentleman, (white) . . . and two colored gentlemen."[161] Like Douglass, Tom's intrusion marks a duty fulfilled, not a deviation. He agitates Ethiop, bringing him out of his reverie and post–Black Forest malaise. Tom has mischievously orchestrated a site of contact where strangers moving about the gallery engage in "free, characteristic, and remarkable" conversation, covering a range of issues from the condition debate and economic citizenship to "The First Colored Convention." His work demonstrates that even the most determinedly isolated space can become the site of collective critical citizenship if one is "wicked" enough to make it happen.

Members of the "strange" assemblage, a microcosm of activist and professional circles, challenge each other and Ethiop to think beyond disciplinary confines or social backgrounds. Picture No. 26, *Condition*, is a painting of a "*colored youth*" who has a "face marked with ignorance and the indifference of stolid content." He is "surrounded by abject wretchedness" and sparks a debate among the visitors about if or how "such a subject" could "be improved."[162] It's a familiar debate by 1859, and the term itself came weighted with the implication that racial inequalities could be solved through uplift and moral reform programs meant to raise black individuals and communities to meet an amorphous standard of excellence. The Doctor describes the problem in terms of "nature," an abstraction that "meant nothing," Ethiop notes, but carried weight because it was delivered from "so high an authority, and so deliberately." The Philosopher, in turn, "entered upon a learned dissertation, upon the nature of the world in general, and our *poor little 'Condition' in particular*," but ends even further away from concrete answers than the learned doctor.[163] Ethiop interjects, hoping to bring the debate to a close and perhaps to get the group out of "his" space: "the youth's condition, not his nature . . . demands change." Ethiop's "impetuosity" in responding, however, results in further debate, now about solutions for changing "condition": "Will our Gallery-friend inform us then, how he would effect that change," one of the visitors prods.

As the conversation turns to material means, the "lady from abroad" chimes in suggesting reform programs: "let the light of culture beam upon him" to change his "moral and religious state" followed by "*wealth*" to change his material condition, and she posits, "You place beneath him a power, and put in his hands a force, that will be felt throughout the entire ramifications of human society."[164] The lady "had such a neat way of putting her propositions, that it was not an easy task to disturb them without risk." That is, between protocols of politeness and the rhetorical force of her articulation, the lady would seem to have settled the debate but again without articulating exactly *how* such a change could occur.

Where these observers reproduced arguments that had been circulating in black circles from as far back as the mutual aid societies of the late eighteenth century, one of the visitors, described as an "old lady," begins questioning the question itself and so initiates a moment of critical citizenship. She breaks them out of the framing dictated in one picture with its emphasis on degradation and the black subject as an object of reform and introduces another vocabulary entirely. The woman, "who had hitherto been a quiet spectator," warns against the group falling victim to "metaphorical veils." "You are not understood," she chides the assembly, pointing out that they have abstracted the image and its problematic to the point of incomprehensibility and immobility.[165] Here, the arrangement of the gallery works in tandem with the chaos of contact as the woman calls the group's attention, somewhat inadvertently, from *Condition* to *Farm Life in Western America*, a landscape painting covering the wall and showing an active community living out, not coincidentally, the project of economic citizenship Wilson outlined in *Douglass's Paper* earlier in the decade (discussed in Chapter 3). Through discussing the image, the old lady dismantles the doctor's argument about biology and gives material purchase to the lady's similarly abstract appeal to reform: "Colored folks farming!!" the old woman exclaims, "Now here are colored folks farming for themselves; and don't their grain grow as well as if they were white; and don't it sell as well. . . . Here is a colored man tending his own mill; and is not the flour as white as any other? and are not all the town, white and colored, running to procure it?" "Away with your metaphorical, metaphysical nonsense," she admonishes the group, "and give them plenty of wherewith to do with, and they may wear their color without let or hindrance."[166] Wilson seems to play at least part of the old lady's discourse for entertainment—she speaks in vernacular, and her critique comes from her mistakenly thinking that the group was talking about "Farm Life," not "Condition." But she also echoes reprints of Sojourner Truth's "Aren't I/Ain't I a Woman Speech," and her ostensibly plain language disturbs the group's disciplinary siloes and ideological commitments in a way similar to Tom's disturbance of Ethiop's solitude.

The woman's interjection in the conversation and the conversation more broadly demonstrate the kind of horizontal, dialogic critical citizenship Ethiop finds lacking in U.S. civic discourse. With Tom's assistance, the gallery shifts shape from Ethiop's enclave to an intellectual commons in which Tom and the other "intruders" engage in tearing down Ethiop's physical and intellectual encroachments.[167] It's a social process of tearing down barriers to common use, specifically those not authorized by the commoners. Imagining the picture gallery as a commons does not eliminate criteria for use, entrance, or organization; rather, it suggests that they are collectively decided and that the process of deciding can be messy, contextual, and improvisational. Ethiop violates that collective right in his attempt to bar entry and in his staking private ownership over his position in the gallery as authoritative interpreter, symbolized physically by "his chair," which the "old lady" usurps, and intellectually in his attempts to make definitive interpretive claims, which the group's constant questioning won't allow. In this sense, critique functions as a perpetual process of beating the intellectual bounds of citizenship, the collective vigilance against and breaking down of encroachments and unilateral policing.[168]

The point of this critical practice isn't a predetermined sense of what the outcome ought to be or a return to some original or ideal state. The group that intrudes on Ethiop's solitude does so in a physically and verbally perambulating way. As they move through the gallery, they take up issues as they come. Just as the gallery's arrangement leads Ethiop's historical critique to make disruptive connections between figures and events, so too does this group's perambulations lead them to connect land, labor, economics, and self-esteem in ways that surprise everyone involved (except perhaps the "old lady," who surprises herself by shifting to a different painting). Significantly, the most critically efficient voice comes from a woman who views the question from the perspective of those most affected by it and from a position that views them as fellow citizens—as neighbors—rather than objects for social experimentation. Regardless of intent, the woman, now sitting in Ethiop's "good old Gallery arm-chair," changes the nature of the conversation and gets the group moving in a direction that eventually ends at Picture No. 27, *The First Convention*, an image of the 1830 Convention of People of Color held in Philadelphia. Their movement through the gallery tracks one path for black political agency from the "abject wretchedness" of *Condition* to the economic citizenship in *Farm Life* to the politics of the state and national convention movements, suffused throughout with critique: interruptions, intrusions, and agitation across social, economic, gender, and racial lines.

By introducing into the gallery elements of neighborly contact and circulation, of beating the bounds, Tom changes the way Ethiop and his readers encounter the images it contains, now as a public conversation rather than as a solitary writing or reading exercise, and how knowledge is produced from them. Tom (representing critical citizenship) doesn't necessarily oppose boundaries as such; he is, after all, the doorkeeper. Rather, the young trickster, like Communipaw's Whitewasher, works to keep those boundaries permeable and dynamic, to ensure passage between space and subject positions. In contrast to Bernice's narrative of genius and revenge, Tom offers a fugitive story, constantly on the move in a way that, following Rancière, lives "in the interstices" rather than the margins of the very language and structures he disrupts.[169] Instead of producing a countersite, Tom's movements and critical sensibilities—his willful disobedience and insistence on creating *contact* and on his own free circulation—call into question the management or attempted framing of all the sites he touches. Tom activates the methodology of critical citizenship, living in a constant state of revolutionary becoming and connecting histories, institutions, and peoples from a stance that takes such disruptive connections as a normative political practice necessary for democratic citizenship. We can see Tom's ethic at work in the Free African Society's negotiation between official and unofficial civic spaces, the black state conventions' leveraging of print circulation to change the constitution of the sovereign people, and Smith and Wilson's sketched debates in *Douglass's Paper*.

Tom provides the link between Ethiop, Bernice, and the world their work seeks to engage; however, like Wilson's triptych of Jefferson, Washington, and L'Ouverture or the *Anglo-African* itself, no single character gives the whole image of critical citizenship. The three—Bernice, Tom, and Ethiop—form a collective subject, a collective sense of who the critical citizen is and what the critical citizen does. Like the articles in the *Anglo-African*, they are at odds with each other—Ethiop's unease with Bernice's revenge set against Tom's intrusions in the gallery and Bernice's challenge to Ethiop's critical judgment—even as they work together, one keeping the impulses of the others in check, one provoking the others to action. The critical citizenship they practice has no room for the white people of Ethiop's "What Shall We Do with the White People," those described in the Amecan tablet, or those spoken into being in the Douglas-Lincoln debates. Outside of Bernice's captive, they do not *do* anything with the white *people* physically. Instead, they challenge the tendency to freeze structures of citizenship, to suture its fissures with consensus myths, such that critique becomes relegated to its content rather than its framing. They forecast the end of white citizenship. In so doing, the *Anglo-African Magazine* and the "Afric-American Picture Gallery" model the tensions within both the single critical citizen and, as importantly, a state that cultivates critical citizenship not in order to resolve such tensions but rather to maintain them. Critical citizenship's reward is not the comfort of celebratory nostalgia but rather agitated forward motion.

CHAPTER 5

Pedagogies of Revolutionary Citizenship

Where the *Anglo-African Magazine*'s first volume opened with a portrait and biography of Alexander Dumas—an avatar for the magazine's emphasis on art and history—the 1860 volume presents Ira Aldridge's Aaron from *Titus Andronicus*, William Shakespeare's earliest tragedy (Figure 8). The image signals a more overtly militant orientation for 1860 but also maintains the magazine's insistence that art and scholarship constitute a form of insurgency. Originally, *Titus Andronicus*'s Aaron was neither noble Othello nor redeemable hero. Rather, he is a captive of the Roman Empire, master manipulator, and an ostensibly unrepentant villain. While Shakespeare's original provides little room for reading Aaron as anything but aggressive, Aldridge collaborated with playwright C. A. Somerset to reenvision the tragedy for Victorian England audiences. Most notably, according to contemporaneous reviews, Aldridge's version omits "the deflowerment of Lavinia, cutting out her tongue, chopping off her hands, and the numerous decapitations and gross language which occur in the original . . . and a play not only presentable but actually attractive is the result."[1] Aldridge elevates Aaron to the status of a tragic hero whose relationship with Tamora "appears to be of a legitimate description" and whose actions stem from potential jealousy at Tamora's marriage and the noble defense of his son. The Shakespearean villain becomes Aldridge and the *Anglo-African*'s champion, mirroring black print culture embracing figures like Nat Turner, Joseph Cinque, Madison Washington, and other leaders of slave rebellions to constitute a "constellation of freedom."[2]

The *Anglo-African* capitalizes on Aldridge's harried yet determined look, the child at his feet mirroring the sense among the magazine's writers that they were battling for their children's futures and for the futures of enslaved children. The engraving's caption, "He dies upon my scimitar's sharp

Figure 8. Ira Aldridge as Aaron in Shakespeare's *Titus Andronicus*. Daguerreotype by William Paine. Printed by the London Printing and Publishing Company, 1852; reprinted in *Anglo-African Magazine*, January 1860. Courtesy Library of Congress.

point, / That touches this my first-born son and heir" (4.2.91–92), enhances this determined stance. At least some of the magazine's well-read audience would likely have been familiar with the caption's context, a monologue in which Aaron not only pledges to defend his son, a result of an interracial relationship with Tamora, Queen of Scythia, but also defends his and his son's blackness:

> I tell you, younglings, not Enceladus,
> With all his threatening band of Typhon's brood,
> Nor great Alcides, nor the god of war,
> Shall seize this prey out of his father's hands.
> What, what, ye sanguine, shallow-hearted boys!
> Ye white-limed walls! ye alehouse painted signs!
> Coal-black is better than another hue,
> In that it scorns to bear another hue;
> For all the water in the ocean
> Can never turn the swan's black legs to white,
> Although she lave them hourly in the flood. (4.2.93–103)

Aaron's references to the child as "a slave" and his own status as a captive resonates with standard antislavery tropes in which parents, usually a mother, lament the loss of a child. This image, however, recalls less the fleeing Eliza Harris than the defiant Margaret Garner, who killed her daughter rather than see her returned to slavery. Yet, it is unclear whether or not Hamilton and his editors chose this image in direct response to recent events, including John Brown's failed raid on Harper's Ferry and subsequent execution at the end of 1859. The December 1859 issue announced that the January 1860 issue would be "embellished with a splendid steel engraving (London) of IRA ALDRIDGE, with a sketch of his life," and several articles in the magazine mention him in the 1859 volume.[3] Whether in direct response to recent events or part of the magazine's broader interests in black arts, the widely disseminated engraving, placed at the head of a magazine dedicated explicitly to encouraging a beleaguered black intelligentsia, speaks to a sense of siege and defiance among the magazine's editors. Aaron's speech, especially when read through the *Anglo-African*, turns a phrase associated with purity (white-limed) into an insult associated with vacuousness, while blackness becomes the color of stability, temperament, and conviction. If Anthony Burns's rendition epitomized this downward trend in the possibilities for black citizenship, the *Anglo-African*'s appropriation of Aaron set alongside intensifying slave rebellions, fugitive rescues, and vigilance committee work throughout the 1850s suggests that black citizens refused to go down without a fight and that this fight would become identified with rather than counter to their citizenship.[4]

This chapter returns to the intersection of material acts—antislavery violence in particular—and literary representation: how black writers thought about slave uprisings, communal defense against kidnapping and capture, and the founding of maroon communities as models for revolutionary citizenship; how they represented them in literature; and how they theorized literary representation as part of a revolutionary process, "a form of political insurgency" that Franz Fanon describes in *The Wretched of the Earth* as "awakening the mind" but which Frances Ellen Watkins Harper figures in terms of conversion through encounters with the slave sublime.[5] Harper's writing, speaking, and activism in particular explored the cultural work necessary for sustaining a prolonged battle for emancipation, even if, or perhaps especially when, violent conflict seemed not only imminent but also necessary.[6] She and others draw on local revolutionaries—Margaret Garner, the "Tennessee Hero," and John Brown—along with a broader hemispheric and biblical archive—Zumbi dos Palmares, Moses, and Naomi—as resources for instilling a revolutionary ethos and as a multimodal response to the complicated, chaotic, and dour outlook at the start of the 1860s.

This chapter, then, is not about violence as such but rather about invocations and representations of violence such as Aldridge's appropriation of Aaron as one strategy through which black writers crafted disruptive, counterfactual narratives that cut against the grain of the "facts" of white supremacy, its political and cultural superstructure, and an abolitionist sentimentalism that rendered enslaved people—and black people more broadly—as voiceless objects of sympathy. These narratives produce more than counterhistory. Writing about David Walker's calls for white Americans to repent for their enslavement of others, Robert S. Levine has noted that counterfactual narration represents "an attempt to imagine or create a different history from what he suspects will be the social reality" of contemporaneous conditions, a "narrative moment of 'undoing' that seeks to encourage change by insisting on" new possibilities.[7] Just as Aldridge's revisions to *Titus* create a new play that deconstructs the previous model to construct a more satisfying alternative, the narratives of black revolution I discuss here inaugurate a different reality altogether. They represent slave rebellion, Underground Railroad work, communal self-defense, and affirmations of black life more broadly as fundamentally political acts—as citizenship practices that speak new potentialities into existence. "For Harper," Frances Smith Foster notes, "literature was one of the many tools necessary to create a better world."[8] Carla Peterson amplifies this conjunction between speech and action, noting that for Harper and others "speaking and writing constituted a form of doing, of social action continuous with their social, political, and cultural work."[9] Black theorists saw the representation and dissemination of these narratives as performatively reproducing and enacting the revolutionary practices they describe.[10]

In this book's larger trajectory, revolution represents the creative, world-making aspect of critique. As I note in the previous chapter, critical citizenship is largely (but not exclusively) backward looking. It seeks to identify and interrogate the frames—historical, political, economic, and aesthetic—shaping and binding (thinkable) citizenship practices. It is disruptive in the sense that these consciousness-raising acts require not just crossing borders but also disturbing the commonsense assumptions and distributions of power that shape and maintain them. Revolutionary citizenship is largely (but not exclusively) forward looking, though I would not call it utopian. In this sense, while slave rebellions are certainly moments of critique, characterizing them as revolution emphasizes not just their physicality but also, as important, the way they created new worlds and, even in failure, reaffirmed a sense of potentiality. Revolutionary citizenship's project entails disseminating and triggering these radical political moments of reordering—of breaking down in the name of making new.

Using Harper's growing understanding of revolutionary citizenship as a guide, this chapter's first section begins with her "conversion" to a more radical aesthetic, which she links to her response to Solomon Northup's *12 Years a Slave* (1854). Her 1857 edition of *Poems* marks this shift as her poetic focus moves from the supplicating slave to the black mother in rebellion. This change in tone also indicates a broader development in black political discourse. The next section theorizes this turn as part of and contributing to the "Spirit of '56": an explosion of rhetoric in black writing that embraced slave rebellions as *the* site of revolutionary citizenship not simply in deed but, more important, as sites of citizenship theorizing. I conclude with Harper's understudied *Anglo-African Magazine* fiction, "Fancy

Sketches" and "Triumph of Freedom—A Dream." While "Two Offers" has gained critical attention for its position as an early African American short story, it is through these other works that Harper more fully explores pedagogies of revolutionary citizenship. Through poetry and short fiction, Harper organizes and reboots the theories and practices of citizenship I outlined in previous chapters—the urgency of critical citizenship, the black state conventions' emphasis on participatory politics, and the street-level protocols of responsibility and responsiveness outlined in Absalom Jones and Richard Allen's yellow fever *Narrative* and the Communipaw-Ethiop debates—around a collective project of wholesale structural revolution, from "home culture" to the Constitution.

The intractability of white supremacy and avaricious self-interest, combined with narratives of loss outlined throughout this project, points to the difficulty of keeping faith in a political system and culture that, as Harper's fiction graphically details, was founded on and materially supported by the heart and blood of enslaved men, women, and children. Revolutionary citizenship is about calling on black citizens to keep faith not in divine intervention or even in white citizens' capacity to think beyond whiteness but in black citizens' and their allies' determination to make democratic citizenship work despite these facts.

Conversion and a Slave Mother's Critique of Sentimentalism

Born in Baltimore, Maryland, in 1825, Harper had become a fixture on the antislavery and reform lecture circuit by the 1850s (Figure 9). Her first book, *Forest Leaves*, recently recovered by Johanna Ortner at the American Antiquarian Society, appeared around 1846. She is perhaps still best known for her two editions of *Poems on Miscellaneous Subjects* (1854, 1857); her short story, "The Two Offers" (1859); and her post–Civil War novel, *Iola Leroy or, Shadows Uplifted* (1892). Popularly known as the "bronze muse," by the late 1850s, Harper gained recognition from her peers as a leading figure in antislavery, vigilance, moral reform, political activism, and literary production—categories that were pieces of the same project.[11] The *Anglo-African Magazine* illustrates her significance among the literary and activist pantheon. An ad for Harper's *Poems on Miscellaneous Subjects* (1857) appears in the midst of more overtly radical texts, including William C. Nell's *Colored Patriots of the American Revolution*, Frederick Douglass's *My*

Figure 9. Frances Ellen Watkins Harper, in *Poems* (Philadelphia: George S. Ferguson Co., 1898). Courtesy Library of Congress.

Bondage, and My Freedom!, and accounts of the "Nat Turner Insurrection" and *The Life of Capt. John Brown* (Figure 10). Overall, the ad echoes this sense of myth making, of a need to tell and find stories about black radical action, patriotism, and revolutionary energy. The context reaffirms Harper's position at the forefront of a black radical democratic movement,

PUBLICATIONS FOR SALE

AT THE OFFICE OF

THE ANGLO-AFRICAN MAGAZINE,

48 BEEKMAN STREET.

COLORED PATRIOTS

OF THE

AMERICAN REVOLUTION:

WITH SKETCHES OF SEVERAL DISTINGUISHED COLORED PERSONS: TO WHICH IS ADDED A BRIEF SURVEY OF THE CONDITION AND PROSPECTS OF COLORED AMERICANS.

BY WILLIAM C. NELL.

396 Pages. Price $1. Postage 18 cts.

This work has been compiled as a means of enlightening public sentiment on an interesting, but much neglected department of American History; and is graced with an introduction, by Mrs. Harriet Beecher Stowe and illustrated by engravings of Crispus Attucks, the First Martyr in the Boston Massacre of March 5th, 1770; Peter Salem, on Bunker Hill; and a *fac-simile* Autographic Certificate of General Washington, tendered to a colored soldier. The increasing interest on the general subject of Slavery, invests this book with a rare attraction at the present time; for throughout its pages are exhibited various phases of the "peculiar institution," interwoven with incidents of patriotism and bravery of colored Americans in "The days that tried men's souls"

MY BONDAGE, AND MY FREEDOM!

BY FREDERICK DOUGLASS.

One Vol., 12*mo.* 464 *pp.*, *Illustrated.*
Price $1 00, *Postage paid.*

—"It cannot fail to be read with avidity, as one of the most striking illustrations of American Slavery, which either fact or fiction has presented to the public."
New York Tribune.

"The book is written with the happiest descriptive power, with nerve and vigor of expression, and with richness of style. It has an ample resource in phrase, great perspicuity, and musical, resonating, and half rhythmic style, which reminds the reader of the author's origin, and of the native melodies of his race. The book manifests a high, and to us, unexpected polish. The interest aroused and kept up by a perusal of this book, of a high order, and rarely degenerates."
Detroit Daily Advertiser.

A VINDICATION

OF THE

CAPACITY OF THE NEGRO RACE,

FOR SELF-GOVERNMENT,

And civilized progress; as demonstrated by Historical events of the Haytien Revolution; and the subsequent acts of that people since their National independence.

WITH A FINE LIKENESS OF

FAUSTIAN I. EMPEROR OF HAYTI.

A Lecture by Rev. J. Theodore Holly.

Price 25 cts. Postage paid.

POEMS,

ON MISCELLANEOUS SUBJECTS,

By Frances Ellen Watkins.

Price 12 cents. Postage 2 cents.

THE NAT. TURNER INSURRECTION.

A FULL AND RELIABLE ACCOUNT.

Copies sent to any address, postage paid, on receipt of Five Cents. address,
Box 1212, THOS. HAMILTON, N. Y.

THE BOOK FOR THE TIMES!!!

THE LIFE OF

CAPT. JOHN BROWN,

THE LIBERATOR OF KANZAS,

AND THE

HERO OF HARPER'S FERRY:

BY JAMES REDPATH.

An elegant 12mo. volume of 400 pages, Illustrated and embellished with a superb

STEEL PORTRAIT

OF THE

GLORIOUS OLD MAN.

This book is now ready, and is a work of thrilling and fascinating interest. Price One Dollar.

☞ A liberal per centage of the Profits resulting from this publication, will be given to the family of BROWN.

Single copies sent to any address, post paid, on receipt of price. address, THOS HAMILTON,
P. O. Box, 1212.] 48 Beekman Street, N. Y.

Figure 10. Advertisement, *Anglo-African Magazine*, January 1860. Courtesy American Antiquarian Society.

Table 1. Comparison: "The Slave Mother" (*Poems* 1854) and "The Slave Mother (A Tale of the Ohio) (*Poems* 1857)

"The Slave Mother" *(Poems* 1854)	"The Slave Mother (A Tale of the Ohio)" (*Poems* 1857)
Heard you that shriek? It rose So wildly on the air, It seemed as if a burden'd heart Was breaking in despair.	I have but four, the treasures of my soul, They lay like doves around my heart; I tremble lest some cruel hand Should tear my household wreaths apart.
No marvel, then, these bitter shrieks Disturb the listening air; She is a mother, and her heart Is breaking in despair.	Oh! if there is any honor, Truth or justice in the land, Will ye not, as men and Christians, On the side of freedom stand?

Thomas Hamilton's sense that there was demand for her writing, and her centrality to a well-stocked library.

Harper's appearance on this list of texts focused on insurrection and revolution was no accident. Her 1857 edition of *Poems* takes rebellion and the lessons it offers as one of its key themes. Among other additions to the 1854 collection (some of which I will discuss later in this chapter), it includes "The Slave Mother (A Tale of Ohio)."[12] The poem reenacts Margaret Garner's killing her infant daughter in 1856, voiced in part through a Garner-inspired maternal voice. Garner and her family escaped across a frozen Ohio River into Cincinnati, Ohio, in January 1856. When slavecatchers tracked them down and surrounded their refuge, Garner refused to hand over her daughter as a new asset, presenting instead a bloody knife and a corpse. The poem is remarkable for the way it simultaneously works through and resists the call for sentimental identification common in antislavery poetry. The differences between this poem about a slave mother and those appearing in the 1854 edition on the same subject offer a useful starting point for thinking about Harper and others' approach to violence.

Compare 1857's "The Slave Mother (A Tale of the Ohio)" to 1854's "The Slave Mother," a more generic poem (relatively speaking) recounting a familiar scene of a mother's despair as she is separated from her children during a slave auction (see Table 1). The 1854 "Slave Mother's" speaker reconstructs the sounds, sights, and emotions as a mother watches as her son is sold away: "Heard you that shriek? / . . . Saw you those hands so sadly clasped" (1, 5)—calling on readers to pay attention to the sights and sounds they might hear every day but to which they have given little heed. The poem plays on a common sentimental trope of a mother losing a child—typically to death or other tragedy. Antislavery poets used this trope of loss as an affective bridge through which readers, by the end of the poem, might identify with the slave mother's humanity: do not marvel at "these bitter shrieks" (37); any mother would react similarly. "She is a mother" (39); she is human.

"The Slave Mother," "Eliza Harris" (*Poems* 1854), and the 1854 edition of *Poems* more generally follow this classic sentimental pattern, asking readers to see the horrors of enslavement and feel sympathy with enslaved subjects. "Eliza Harris," based on Harriet Beecher Stowe's character from *Uncle Tom's Cabin* (1852) who famously hops across a semi-frozen Ohio River to protect her child from enslavement, uses this strategic bridge even more explicitly: "Did a fever e'er burning through bosom and brain, / Send a lava-like flood through every vein, / Till suddenly cooled 'neath a healing spell, / And you knew, oh! the joy! you knew you were well?" (41–44). Ultimately, the poems construct enslaved bodies as "flesh"—Hortense Spillers's term for the captive body evacuated of "any hint or suggestion of a dimension of ethics, of relatedness between human personality and its anatomical features, between one human personality and another, between human personality and cultural institutions"—in need of sentimental reconstitution to be made legible as human.[13] The metaphor closes the gap between readers who have not experienced enslavement and Eliza's feelings of freedom, substituting their memories of a fever for her escape from enslavement in the process. In this sense, these early poems render their subjects as objects for their readers' consumption.

Harper's reconstruction of both the 1854 "Slave Mother" and "Eliza Harris" through Garner in 1857 rethinks what constitutes political speech, who can produce it, and how that speech might be made legible when coming from fugitive subjects. "The Slave Mother (A Tale of the Ohio)" shifts focus from the readers' experience of the heartbreak of a sale to Garner's judging voice and her contemplation of her soon-to-be-dead daughter's innocence. It refuses the enslaved body as object in favor of a black woman's voice and actions. The 1854 poem's "bowed and feeble head—/ The shuddering of that fragile form" (6–7) gives place to an accusing "I"—"I have but four, the treasures of my soul" (1)—and active hands that "do a deed for freedom" (43). The poem does not simply show a woman reacting, seemingly out of instinct; it allows her room to narrate her calculated decision with authority and out of full knowledge of her child's potential future in slavery. Mae G. Henderson, Cheryl Wall, and bell hooks, among others, have figured this act of self-inscription as "talking back," "no mere gesture of empty words" but rather an "expression of our movement from object to subject—the liberated voice."[14] Speech here entails more than the making of sounds (or "voice" in the Aristotelian sense); rather, it allows members of a community to "indicate what is useful and what is harmful, and so also what is just and what is unjust."[15] The difference between voice and speech inheres less in the utterance itself and more in the regimes of power (aesthetics) organizing language.[16] Where the speakers of Harper's 1854 poems passively ask readers to hear and feel, Harper's 1857 slave mother herself theorizes her position as a fugitive between enslavement and freedom.

When a narrative voice does take over in "The Slave Mother (A Tale of the Ohio)," it does so less to explain than to amplify, challenge, chastise:

> Sends this deed of fearful daring
> Through my country's heart no thrill,
> Do the icy hands of slavery
> Every pure emotion chill? (57–60)

The lines dare readers to contemplate the mother's logic and its implications. Yet, because Harper titles both poems "The Slave Mother," read together, they suggest that both women might be the same (type of) person, that the wordless sounds issuing from the suffering mother-made-flesh in "The Slave Mother" (1854), if approached from a different angle, might be delivering a similar message. In this vein, "The Slave Mother (A Tale of the Ohio)" shows Harper moving beyond dominant antislavery sentimentalism even as she works through its familiar terrains. Harper saw the word, literary and spoken, as capable of disrupting the distribution of the sensible *and* of suggesting new configurations. Invoking Garner's voice rather than her body and privileging her call to justice rather than appealing to readers' judgments, Harper uses sentimentalism not to bridge an experiential gap but rather to expose it: the gap between freedom and slavery, love and loss, superstructure and base, theory and practice, word and deed. And by drawing attention to sympathy's limits, she affirms her readers' capacity for right feeling even as she challenges them to recognize that this feeling is insufficient or even beside the point.[17]

To be clear, the 1854 poems were radical in their own right. As Michael Stancliff has noted, "The ethical disposition" and, I would add, aesthetic and political challenge of the slave women for whom Harper advocated would remain the guiding political touch point of her pedagogy into the twentieth century."[18] "The Slave Auction" (*Poems* 1854), for instance, similarly refuses the sentimental moment of substitution, instead informing readers, "Ye who have laid your love to rest, / And wept above their lifeless clay, / Know not the anguish of that breast, / Whose lov'd are rudely torn way" (17–20). The common sentimental trope of a lost loved one might bridge the gap between readers and speakers with similar experiences of death and loss and bring them closer to the poem's subject. But death, with its concomitant implication of a permanent end to suffering, is a poor metaphor for the kind of separation initiated in an auction, which entails prolonged, embodied suffering: "Ye may not know how desolate / Are bosoms rudely forced to part, / And how a dull and heavy weight / Will press the life-drops from the heart" (21–24). Admitting—or being confronted with—what one "may not know" becomes just as important as and a key concomitant to moments of identification. The combination produces an unresolvable tension, energy that cannot be dissipated in the catharsis of "right feeling" but must be released in different ways.[19] Part of what I want to point out here, however, is how focusing on the slave in rebellion—even if that rebellion entails the refusal of identification—rather than the slave in suffering opened new intellectual possibilities and that we can look at the mid-1850s as moment of shifting from one register to the other.

Harper theorizes this disruptive potential and the changes it could initiate through her own experience with literatures of enslavement. In an October 20, 1854, letter to William Still from Temple, Maine, Harper declares her "conversion" to the Free Produce movement after reading *12 Years a Slave* (1853), Solomon Northup's narrative of kidnapping, enslavement, and return. "I spoke on Free Produce," Harper tells Still, before confessing almost conspiratorially,

> And now by the way I believe in that kind of Abolition. Oh, it does seem to strike at one of the principal roots of the matter. I have commenced since I read Solomon Northrup. Oh, if Mrs. Stowe has

> clothed American slavery in the graceful garb of fiction, Solomon Northrup comes up from the dark habitation of Southern cruelty where slavery fattens and feasts on human blood with such mournful revelations that one might almost wish for the sake of humanity that the tales of horror which he reveals were not so.[20]

Faced with Northup's "tales of horror," Harper delivers a critique of Harriet Beecher Stowe's sentimentalism that scholars would refine over the next 150 years. Harper does not, like some of her black contemporaries, criticize Stowe's emigration conclusion or her sentimental politics as such. Rather, she is more interested in how sentimentalism, particularly its emphasis on vulnerable black bodies or individual virtues over capitalist flows, mutes the effectiveness of telling or retelling black stories. Stowe's "graceful garb" remains linked too closely to "luxuries drawn from reluctant fingers." It obscures, giving a glimpse of slave society but veiling the "unmentionables," the implicating private parts, in a way that, as Salamisha Tillet's critique of feeling politics suggests, "privilege[ed] the affect of white [and other readers'] sympathy over structural and symbolic justice for her African American characters."[21] Graceful garb—Eva's piety in death, Tom's forgiveness, and even the reunion of formerly enslaved characters abroad—clothes American slavery in the illusion of an affective economy based on cruelty and individual avarice, hiding its underpinnings in an Atlantic world economy and the middle-class consumer culture that made the success of *Uncle Tom's Cabin* possible, one in which the book, gracefully garbed and gilded on the shelf, could be a sign of the proper response without any material concomitant.

As Harper frames it in her letter to Still, *12 Years a Slave* by contrast closes the distance between her daily practices and the material and moral economy supporting them and, through this revelation, replaces sentimentalism's emotional transfer with a materialist project. Scholars have long critiqued sentimentalism and sentimental antislavery in particular for erasing enslaved subjects as, writes Lloyd Pratt, "the reader narcissistically substitutes him- or herself for the enslaved."[22] Harper's aesthetics, however—both explicit and modeled in poetry—suggest that while sentimentalism can lead to erasure and the "consolation of tears," it can also make "subjects restless, unwilling to accept customary and stultifying social patterns as either pleasurable or desirable," particularly in works that bring readers to the brink and leave them there.[23] Just as Harper begins to sympathize with Northup, the book implicates her not as a fellow sufferer who might identify with Northup's loss of family but as the cruel master or, at the very least, one of his customers: "Oh, how can we pamper our appetites upon luxuries drawn from reluctant fingers? Oh, could slavery exist long if it did not sit on a commercial throne?"[24] Now understanding her economic ties to slave labor, Harper cannot see commodities without also seeing the traces of their modes of production—she sees blood on cloth and whips in her sugar.

More than an implicit critique of Stowe's brand of sentimentalism, at least as presented in *Uncle Tom's Cabin*, this moment allows Harper to develop potential reading and writing practices conducive to reproducing and disseminating this conversation, what Paulo Friere calls "a profound rebirth," "a new form of existence" so "so radical" that the convert comes to "understand their characteristic ways of living and behaving" as continuous with and contributing to "the structure of domination."[25] This conversion invokes the "godly sorrow" articulated in Paul's second letter to the Corinthians: "For godly sorrow worketh repentance to salvation not to be repented of: but the sorrow of the world worketh death. For behold this selfsame thing, that ye sorrowed after a godly sort, what carefulness it wrought in you, yea, what clearing of yourselves, yea, what indignation, yea, what fear, yea, what vehement desire, yea, what zeal, yea, what revenge!"[26] Where "the sorrow of the world" leads one to regret, godly sorrow, Paul explains, leads to repentance, and repentance means a change within the self and change within the community. Similarly, *Uncle Tom's Cabin* created the right feeling of sorrow in Harper, but *12 Years a Slave* led to repentance, zeal, and (economic) revenge and reparation. Whether or not Harper was a new "convert" to Free Produce—her uncle, William Watkins, Sr., had been active in Free Produce in the 1830s—her letter's framing of her public advocacy as a conversion narrative based on a singular reading experience signals her recognition of art as a vehicle for destabilizing established practices and that this kind of art was most effective in its capacity to reveal but not completely bridge (indeed, in its refusal to bridge) the distance between the reader and the narrated subject.[27]

What Harper describes in 1854 as a distinction between "graceful garb" and "mournful truths," a difference between sentimental erasure and affective tension, she reconfigures by 1856 in terms of agitation. "Be Active," which appeared in *Frederick Douglass's Paper* on January 11, 1856, for instance, chastises the "idle pity / Gazing on [slavery's] mighty wrong" and removes the emphasis on feeling altogether. As if directly rebuking the speaker from "The Slave Mother," the speaker in "Be Active" commands, "Stop not now to ask the question / Who shall roll the stone away?" Rather than the view-feel pattern in "The Slave Mother," the speaker in "Be Active" follows couplets describing slavery with couplets commanding movement: "See that sad despairing mother / Clasp her burning brow in pain" leads to "Lay your hands upon her fetters / Rend, oh! rend, her galling chain!" (13–19), and "Yearly lay a hundred thousand / Newborn babes on Moloch's shrine, / Crush these gory reeking altars; / Christian, let this work be thine" (21–24). These poems are not narratives of triumph and consolation but rather, like "A Tale of the Ohio," are discomfiting and tragic. They refuse to offer the slave's body or experience up for erasure. Instead, they suggest a new pattern: see, act.

The Expressive Language of Slave Rebellion and the Spirit of 1856

The shifting discourse of the 1850s indexed by Harper's changing aesthetic sensibilities would suggest that the stories most important to black writers in theorizing a more radical citizenship practice were less those about cataloging white depravity or cultivating white sympathy and more about Margaret Garner's defiance and a proactive blackness. The additions to *Poems* (1857) and Harper's broader aesthetics of conversion outline what I examine in this section as a broader development in black citizenship theorizing: "Spirit of 1856," a reworking of the tropes commonly associated with the 1776 American Revolution through scenes of antislavery violence. These sentiments surfaced not just in Harper's work, convention documents, and newspaper articles but also in journals and poetry. It suggests that black writers felt themselves approaching a tipping point and were looking to histories of antislavery violence—both distant and recent—for epistemological purchase.

The Spirit of '56 resonates with the Spirit of '76 that historians like Benjamin Quarles describe in black writing, with its references to the Declaration of Independence, Patrick Henry, and rhetorical linking of violent antislavery as part of a republican defense of liberty and citizenship. Samuel Ringgold Ward's April 10, 1850, editorial for his *Impartial Citizen* in response to the 1850 Fugitive Slave Law epitomizes this discourse: "The thing, the only thing for a Blackman to do, in these circumstances [facing slave catchers], is, *just what a white man would do in like circumstances.*

Make the business of slave catching so perilous that no man will dare engage in it. Make it the last act in the drama of ta slave-catcher's life. Make him understand what was the import of Patrick Henry's immortal motto, 'LIBERTY OR DEATH.'" The reference to Henry makes legible and authorizes Ward's appeal to violent resistance as quintessentially American in nature. In contrast to the Spirit of '76, signaled in Ward's rhetorical invocation of Patrick Henry, the Spirit of '56 draws its inspiration and validation from and foregrounds narratives of fugitive escapes, communal self-defense, and slave insurrections in a way that reconfigures how black writers were able to think about antislavery violence as a citizenship practice and, in particular, black resistance as producing its own theory.

To be clear, the Spirit of '56 is not locked to the year 1856, though 1856 does mark a distinct shift in black rhetoric. By the passage of the Fugitive Slave Law of 1850, black public discourse had become more amenable, if not outright embracing, of violent self-defense as a right and sign of citizenship and community. The increase in white attempts to recapture and kidnap nominally free black people, local efforts to protect fugitive slaves (some successful, some not), and the continuing threat of white riots all suggested that the more moderate tones of the previous decades were ineffective as either persuasive politics or placating deterrent. The fate of Henry Highland Garnet's "Address to the Slaves of the United States" marks this movement. In 1843, the National Convention of Colored Citizens held at Buffalo narrowly rejected the address in part out of fear of violent retaliation toward free black communities if they endorsed, implicitly or explicitly, slave insurrections. By 1849, the Ohio State Convention would resolve to purchase and distribute 500 copies of the 1848 edition, which Garnet printed with the second edition of David Walker's *Appeal.*[28] While the version of the speech printed in 1848 explicitly discouraged violent rebellion as "inexpedient," both this printing and reviews from 1843 explicitly called for slaves to leave their masters if they refuse to offer wages. If their masters attempt to force them to remain, Garnet admonishes enslaved men, "then commence the work of death" with a clear conscience because "they, and not you, will be responsible for the consequences. You had far better all die—*die immediately*, than live slaves, and entail your wretchedness upon your posterity."[29] It's not just that Garnet justified antislavery violence (if in limited cases) but rather that he framed these acts by slaves as acts of citizenship by citizens: "Forget not that you are native-born American citizens," Garnet tells them, "and as such, you are justly entitled to all the rights that are granted to the freest."[30] Garnet makes these arguments not simply as a matter of divine mandate or natural right but also because, as citizens, slaves had a right to liberty and a right to defend that liberty.

This increase in language about violence and death paralleled writers' thinking about black politics as inflicting violence on the slave state. In 1851, Charles H. Langston told an Ohio state convention, "I would vote under the United States Constitution on the same principle . . . that I would call on every slave, from Maryland to Texas, to arise and assert their *liberties*, and cut their masters' throats if they attempt again to reduce them to slavery."[31] Langston argued for Ohio's black citizens to petition and agitate for franchise rights because he understood disfranchisement as itself a form of state-sanctioned violence and black politics as an insurgency as dangerous and structurally violent to white power as armed slaves. The metonymic link between voting and insurrection points to not only how black citizens were embracing overt references to physical violence but also how they were coming to understand and talk about violent antislavery, especially on the part of enslaved people, as practices with key lessons for citizenship more broadly.

And yet, there *was* something singular about 1856 as an apex year sandwiched between the more familiar 1854 and 1857. Several of the poems Harper added to *Poems* (1857) were written in response to events from 1856—most notably, "The Slave Mother" and "The Tennessee Hero." The year began with Margaret Garner's harrowing escape and return to slavery, but 1856 also saw "Bleeding Kansas" demonstrating the willingness and ability of the proslavery regime to mobilize violence and John Brown and others' willingness to meet that violence with equal force on the frontiers. Slave states experienced an "outbreak" of unrest, including a failed slaveholder attack on a North Carolina maroon community, a conspiracy "involving over two hundred slaves" supposedly uncovered and foiled in Texas, another "involving some three hundred slaves and a few whites" on the Arkansas-Louisiana border, and multiple other reports of conspiracies and actual violence coming out of Tennessee, Kentucky, Missouri, Maryland, Alabama, Virginia, and South Carolina.[32] The "Tennessee Conspiracy" punctuated the year: Tennessee's Cumberland River Valley erupted in December 1856 with reports of a potential slave insurrection conspiracy around Cumberland Iron Works. Whether or not the conspiracy was real, the slaveholders' response was swift and violent. It resulted in a mass hysteria that slaveholders used to justify the torture, beating, and killing of enslaved and free people of color and (accused) white allies.[33] Southern papers attempted to downplay these events as isolated even as other reports, letters, and legislation suggest that, at least in the slave power's mind, it was only a matter of time before "the big one" erupted. Harper and others, then, were not simply producing romanticized images of slave rebellion or engaging in hyperbole; they, in many ways, were preying on slaveholders' fears of a coming revolution. The point was not so much translating antislavery violence as it was framing, interpreting, and transmitting subjugated knowledge and the world-making potential it created.

Grounding the rhetoric of citizenship in actions by enslaved people and antislavery activists operationalized the language of revolutionary violence for black citizens in ways that allusions to Patrick Henry's "give me liberty or give me death" could not. It suggests that such legacy platitudes inadequately articulate what Charlotte Forten (Grimke) revises as a determination to have "liberty and death" in the face of Anthony Burns's return to slavery in 1854 with the support of the U.S. military. If, for white contemporaries growing nostalgic about the revolutionary generation, slavery represented that political death against and through which they defined life and liberty, then the maxim had to be redefined for those living in and touched by chattel slavery—those looking to theorize the living principles articulated by the putatively dead.

Forten registers this difference in her journal. Writing of a dinner at William Lloyd Garrison's home on May 31, 1854, during the Anthony Burns trial, Forten recalls, "At the table, I watched earnestly the expression of that noble face, as he [William Lloyd Garrison] spoke beautifully in support of the non-resistant principles to which he has kept firm; his is indeed the very highest Christian spirit, to which I cannot hope to reach, however, for I believe in resistance to tyrants, and would fight for liberty until death."[34] Forten, like many others including Garnet and Ward, couched her convictions in Henry's famous words. The change from "liberty or death" to "liberty until death," whether conscious or not, however, underscores a sense of desperation, betrayal, and resolution among writers in the late 1850s, activists who, in the face of the U.S. National Guard's escorting Anthony Burns back into slavery, did not see liberty and death as necessarily opposite destinations or mutually exclusive choices. Death might be the inevitable concomitant of doing a "deed for freedom," to return to Harper's language in her poetic rendering of Garner. Indeed, Garner's defense lawyers attempted to prevent her return to slavery by claiming that Ohio's right to try—and potentially execute—her for the murder of her daughter superseded federal law or her master's property rights.[35] In this case, the choice in the moment was not one between liberty and death but rather between enslavement and relative liberty until execution.[36] In neither Forten nor Garner's case is enslavement equivalent to death (else why would Garner have killed her daughter in mercy?); rather, Forten's reflection suggests that so long as white citizenship (tyranny) was the order of the day, Garrison's faith in moral suasion could not be an option for her. At the same time, her alteration of Henry's aphorism suggests that received revolutionary models were likewise insufficient. As Harper's poetry was already showing, however, Patrick Henry's was not the only generation of revolutionaries available as models of a transformative citizenship practice.

In Chapter 1, I examined how Richard Allen and Absalom Jones develop the notion of an "expressive language of conduct" as a means for cutting through the civic republican and liberal discourses of the late eighteenth century. Put simply, they read actions as texts through which one might extrapolate larger principles and political realities. James McCune Smith and Frederick Douglass extend this concept in 1856 and 1857 to argue that slave rebellions and fugitive defense actions over the past century point to the underlying philosophy of white supremacy and the mode through which enslaved people have made their demands known. Writing about British West India emancipation in 1856, Smith suggests that violence presents a language more suitable to convincing white Americans than moral arguments: "Our white brethren cannot understand us unless we speak to them in their own language; they recognize only the philosophy of force. They will never recognize our manhood until we knock them down a time or two; they will then hug us as men and brethren. That holy love of human brotherhood which fills our hearts and fires our imagination, cannot get through the—in this respect—thick skulls of the Caucasians, unless beaten into them."[37] Black citizens and abolitionists more broadly had been celebrating the August 1, 1834, inauguration of emancipation in British territories as a de facto Independence Day for over two decades, partly as a protest of July 4 and partly in the hopes that the United States would eventually follow the British example. Smith suggests that the time had come to stop revering emancipation in the British Empire, a weak freedom "conferred" in a foreign land through a foreign government. Black citizens in particular needed to find other days, examples of freedom as a "right seized upon and held" in the United States, days like "when Denmark Vesey suffered gloriously in Charleston, as the head of an insurrection [in Charleston, South Carolina, in 1822], or when Nat Turner turned all Virginia pale with fright [in Southampton, Virginia, in 1831], or when those brave men fought at Christiana" to protect supposed fugitive slaves from kidnapping in 1851]."[38]

Ultimately, Smith's critique is less about British West Indian emancipation and more about the uses of that history in a post–Fugitive Slave Law and post–Kansas-Nebraska Act United States. This reality—one where retrenchment, not emancipation, seemed most likely and where even "free" land folds under slavery—requires disruptive, even tragic, narratives that make the "blood [stir], as it ought to stir."[39] What began as an implicit indictment of passive emancipation and a seeming call for violence becomes an explicit celebration and refinement of insurrection and fugitivity as already articulating and enacting an emancipatory project in the United States. *These* men and women are earning their freedom and expounding on the "philosophy of force," the only language and philosophy "our white brethren" can understand.[40]

Though Douglass explicitly disagrees with Smith's call to disavow British West Indian emancipation or his argument that it was a freedom given rather than earned, he nevertheless supports Smith's underlying premise of self-assertion, agitation, and celebrating Atlantic world insurrections. Forwarding this argument in an 1857 speech on British West Indian emancipation, Douglass frames rebelliousness among British slaves as a key contributing factor to eventual emancipation: "What Wilberforce was endeavoring to win from the British Senate by his magic eloquence, the Slaves themselves were endeavoring to gain by outbreaks and violence. The combined action of one and the other wrought out the final result. While one showed that slavery was wrong, the other showed that it was dangerous as well as wrong."[41] Slave insurrections, large or small, did not lead directly to emancipation, but they did communicate in the indisputable language of conduct the "fact of their discontent" in a way that Wilberforce's words could not. In that sense, enslaved people helped create the conditions for emancipation—they created the counterfactual narrative possibilities that made Wilberforce's arguments possible. Douglass finds ready material for rethinking rebellions as an expressive language, as producing a form of knowledge, in more recent black activities in the United States: "Hence, my friends, every mother who, like Margaret Garner, plunges a knife into the bosom of her infant to save it from the hell of our Christian Slavery, should be held and honored as a benefactress."[42] The problem in the United States, from Douglass and Smith's perspective, was not the absence of assertive statements from enslaved folk—Douglass and Smith cite several recent examples. The problem, as they frame it, was an absence of those willing to learn from these acts and to frame them as acts of revolutionary citizenship rather than isolated events, pleas for sympathy, or counterproductive.

"As if Gas-Light Were an Improvement on Sunshine," or Fancy Sketches of Truth Telling

Harper's writings in the *Anglo-African Magazine* represent a concentrated effort to theorize this history of revolutionary citizenship as pedagogy and everyday practice. Her prose, "Fancy Sketches" and "The Triumph of Freedom—A Dream" in particular, not only theorizes the ideological shifts necessary to meet the violence of white citizenship and racism but also thinks through how literature can enact this shift. The *Anglo-African* was an ideal venue for this thinking, not necessarily because of its actual readership but rather because of the mission Hamilton set for it—to address/write/speak to Anglo-Africans. This mode of address set the conditions for Harper to call on readers in "Our Greatest Want" to lay the "foundations of an historic character" through the work of "a few earnest thinkers, and workers," who could cultivate a "noble devotion to the cause of emancipation" and a "healthy public opinion."[43] Harper follows through on this call with sketches that telegraph how *parrhesia*—fearless truthtelling to those in power and against popular opinion—and storytelling to a receptive audience can animate listeners to shift from idle spectatorship to active work through encounters with the agitational force of the slave sublime.[44]

The "Fancy Sketches" first appeared in the November 1859 issue of the *Anglo-African Magazine* and appeared regularly until the *Magazine*'s final issue in March 1860. There were five installments in all, the first set just before a wedding reception in "the city." The rest set in Jane's Aunt Melissa's country home, which also functions as a boarding house and introduces readers to an array of characters, including Jane, Melissa (Jane's aunt), Miranda (Jane's cousin), Mr. Ballard (a potential suitor for Miranda), and a rotating set of boarders and extended family. This setting provides a backdrop for observing a cross section of free black life, while

Harper uses the conceit of parlor conversation to overlay Atlantic world history as characters read the history of *Quilombo dos Palmares* (a seventeenth-century Brazilian maroon republic), with the sectional crisis and revolt.

While the *Anglo-African* never attributes "Fancy Sketches" to Harper directly—it appears under "Anonymous" in the table of contents and by "Jane Rustic" in each issue—Harper is almost certainly the author. The series takes up themes and character types from "The Two Offers," which appeared in two parts over the *Anglo-African*'s September and October 1859 issues.[45] The concept of "home influences" appears across both "The Two Offers," which situates the home as "the best school for the affections" and "the birthplace of high resolves," and the title of Fancy Sketches No. III, "Home Influences, and Negro Courage, or Fancy Sketches," which similarly takes on the problems arising out of mistaking "impulsive affection" for "intelligent love." Both texts also examine the destruction that can be wrought by marriages based in economic calculations rather than, as Janette puts it in "The Two Offers," "an affinity of souls or a union of hearts."[46] Jane Rustic levels an even more explicit critique of marriage as an asymetrical legally binding agreement: "It is a fact that I do love to have my own way; and I have never seen the man I would like to pledge myself all through life to obey; I shouldn't prefer promising to-day, what I should do twenty or thirty years hereafter. I have quite an objection to that clause in the marriage-ceremony."[47] "Fancy Sketches" also take up the education theme from "Our Greatest Want," with one character describing it in precisely those words: "I think our great want . . . is a proper education."[48]

These thematic and phrase recurrences further support Peterson's original claim that Harper authored "Fancy Sketches" and suggest that the narratives within Harper's short stories and sketches form a literary universe, if not a unitary whole. That is, while the two narratives feature different characters, these characters are homologous; they inhabit the same neighborhood. Harper later published "Fancy Etchings" (alternately titled "Fancy Sketches"), another sketch series appearing in the *Christian Recorder* from 1871 to 1874, under her own name and revisits similar thematic and structural elements.[49] She repeats character types and names across series: Jane Rustic of "Fancy Sketches" resembles "Aunt Jane" in the postbellum "Fancy Etchings," and Janette Alston from "The Two Offers" bears a striking resemblance to both Jane Rustic and a female antislavery lecturer in "Fancy Sketches" No. V.

Through each installment, Harper models not only gendered schemas of governance between "the domestic household" and "national affairs" but also how each arena feeds into (bleeds into) the other. Even as Jane and her relatives consistently hold up women's roles in child rearing and proper domestic governance, Ballard speaks of his own desire to read to his children and take part in their moral and activist rearing. Conversations between Aunt Melissa, Jane, and Miranda reveal their desire to be independent political agents in public. Indeed, "Fancy Sketches" is rife with the tensions between Jane's unmet aspirations and unrealized hopes for herself and the limitations of her social, economic, and gendered world. At the end of "Fancy Sketches" No. II, she consoles herself, "Oh well, it may be that in the spirit world all my aspirations will be met, my yearnings satisfied, my wishes realized and my hopes fulfilled." But, she asks herself in the sketch's concluding line, "Am I patient enough to wait?"[50] While this moment resonates with the sentimental trope of reuniting with long-lost loved ones in the "spirit world," in a sketch that began with Jane's dream about being shouted down at a male-dominated Anti-Sunshine Convention (discussed in Chapter 2) and her uncle meeting Miranda's talk of "new ideas of woman's rights and woman's missions" with the conviction that a woman's mission "was to keep the house clean and stay home and take care of her husband and children," this moment also registers Jane's impatience with the political world, her need to find intellectual fulfillment at home *and* abroad.[51]

Because Harper did publish work in the *Anglo-African* under her own name and because she was already a famous lecturer and literary figure, her use of a pseudonym for "Fancy Sketches" does not necessarily indicate a need to mask her gender or some other aspect of her identity; rather, we can read Harper's pseudonym as her explicitly situating "Fancy Sketches" within multiple literary traditions. On the level of character, "Jane Rustic" communicates the "plain-speaking" wisdom of a "country girl," not unlike Ethiop's "old woman" and Thomas Onward. Peterson draws attention to links between "Fancy Sketches'" country setting and Wordsworth's sense that "the rustic or common life is best suited for poetic representation, but the poet must use common language, enhanced with 'colouring' of the 'fancy imagination.'"[52] In addition to the Romantic tradition that Peterson outlines, the sketches resonate with what was by 1859 an established black tradition of pseudonymous sketch writing that included Sarah Forten, who wrote as "Magawisca" in the *Liberator*, as well as James McCune Smith

(Communipaw) and William J. Wilson (Ethiop), whom I discuss in Chapters 3 and 4, T. Joiner White (Observer), Philip A. Bell (Cosmopolite), and others writing for *Frederick Douglass's Paper* and the *Anglo-African*.[53] Rather than conceal, these pseudonyms were open secrets. For those in the know, Harper's donning the Jane Rustic moniker signaled a mode of address and set of key terms—black aristocracy, education, wealth, and moral uplift—signifying on previous pseudonymous writers and their ideas.

In this vein "Fancy Sketches" differs from Wilson and Smith's work in several important ways: (1) Harper situates Jane Rustic among a black middle class, and most of the action happens in parlor spaces rather than a public gallery or on urban streets. (2) Harper develops Jane more fully as a character, not just a pseudonymous persona, from the start. (3) As a young unmarried black woman, Jane does not inhabit the same privileged position—male professional—from which to speak and be heard. While Smith and Wilson's figures could be assured freedom of movement and space to speak within black circles at least, Jane was often dismissed or misinterpreted, even among her peers. She is nevertheless confident within herself, speaking her mind despite the ease with which her male and married female counterparts attempt to dismiss her. (4) If Wilson's Ethiop critiqued a utopian promise of white citizenship, Harper's Jane deconstructs the "metaphorical veils" of those citizens whose class, race, gender, and/or geographical privilege allows them to discuss antislavery and reform activism as idle "chit-chat," those who have convinced themselves that the immediate threat of racial violence (both physical and structural) is too remote to require anything more than abstract speculation. The series argues for the cultivation of a "home culture" that could help prepare black citizens for what Harper sees as a siege on "Freedom" in the present and a greater conflict in the future.

The first installment, "Chit Chat, or Fancy Sketches," opens with Jane at a wedding where attendees rehearse the kind of tactical debates I discuss in previous chapters. All angles are represented—black aristocracy, violent revolution, emigration, education and moral reform, and so on—but sapped of a sense of urgency. The first speaker echoes accords in conventions, periodicals, pamphlets, and speeches: "'Give us wealth,' said he, 'and that will give us position; white men will court our society, and gold, though yellow will be the most potent whitewash we can find.'"[54] Other speakers include an "emigration friend," "a dark-browed and enthusiastic speaker" who argues that he "would have our race live out their own individuality, and build up their own character"; a man "whose fair complexion scarcely showed his identity with the negro race" arguing for "staying and fighting it out"; and "an impetuous youth who was a good soldier when there was no battle to fight."[55] The whole exchange reads like a well-rehearsed play or a twice-told tale. The youth pledges to support the slave "if he will only throw down his sugar knife, cast away his cotton hook, and strike for liberty."[56] This last comment makes Jane "mischievous enough to say I thought his life might vie with the wandering Jew's if he never lost it till he laid it down in a negro insurrection."[57] The young man's "speech had a very exciting effect," and no one in the group denied slavery's heinous nature or the necessity of immediate abolition, but his speech and the feelings they conjured were a long way away from concrete action.[58]

Jane intrudes, knowingly breaking gendered social conventions of silence and deferral. The man, as well as the crowd, dismisses her, but the damage is done. Jane's humor disarms him as "others smiled, and some of the women tittered."[59] Jane's *parrhesia* exposes both the patriarchal attitudes of a man whose only recourse is to claim he does "not think it worth while to combat" a woman's critique and how such men use talk of rebellion as a scapegoat for their lack of activity, shifting attention from their own complacency to assumptions about enslaved people's cowardice. This man's own incompetence undercuts his argument: he calls for slaves to throw down the very objects—"knife" and "cotton hook"—that would help them in their "strike for liberty" (an echo of Garnet's "Address"). As Jane observes further, "Several fugitives had been taken from [their] State, and I had never heard of his arming in their defense."[60] The conversation, in Jane's words, amounts to "so much buncombe," not because of the arguments themselves but because the group has manufactured a stance of helpless detachment.[61]

This conversation could have been lifted out of convention proceedings, newspapers, Ethiop's gallery, or country parlors, and these were precisely the arguments filling the pages of Thomas Hamilton's *Weekly Anglo-African*, the *Anglo-African Magazine*'s weekly counterpart. Jane's thoughts about the young man ironically echo an exchange during the 1858 Convention of Colored Citizens in Massachusetts between Charles Remond and Josiah Hensen, in which Henson responds to Remond's fiery rhetoric with ridicule: "Remond might talk, and then run away, but what would become of the poor fellows that must stand?"[62] Many prominent black activists—Mary Ann Shadd Cary, Martin R. Delany, Douglass, Garnet, McCune

Smith, and Harper herself, among others—were taking part in feverish debates about the future of black citizenship and activism. Was emigration (selective or en masse) the answer to full citizenship and emancipation and, if so, to where? Did the crisis over the election of Abraham Lincoln signal an impending resolution, whether political or violent, and what role should black citizens have in bringing about this resolution? This was especially the case in the *Weekly Anglo-African* from roughly December 1860 through February 1861, when McCune Smith, Garnet, and others engaged in heated arguments that devolved into ad hominem attacks, leading one commenter, "Lizzie" (Elizabeth Hart), to admonish, "It is painful to me in the extreme and more especially so, that it should occur just at this time of all others, when all should be peace, love, and union among our people and all should cling together as one man."[63] Just as pressing for Harper, however, was a more immediate issue: how could black citizens best support the efforts of escaped and escaping slaves? To Lizzie's call for cooperation, Jane might have added her own suggestion that the discussion had long strayed from practical debate to idle "chit chat."

"Fancy Sketches" mirrors this debate but frames it as the chatter used to fill the time and show off rather than the kind of discussion characteristic of critical debate.[64] These were people who, Jane observes, preferred lamplight to sunlight "as if gas-light were an improvement on sunshine."[65] They observe the forms of past practices but stop short of their disruptive possibilities. And yet, the ease with which they produce this debate and its very ubiquity offer a warning that current activists, if they are not careful, risk becoming—in one observer's words, a "disgrace," too focused on their own "wrangling and bitterness" to attend to the needs of the communities they purport to represent.[66] They risked observing the form of critical citizenship or the form of early debates in the 1850s or through the first conventions—just as a lamp gives the form of light—without realizing its substance.

Jane's critique of the company's empty rhetoric recalls neighborly citizenship's challenge to those trading in the rhetoric of respectability and reform to "do all the good" they can, in *Narrative*'s terms, for their "fellow suffering mortals." Peterson makes this connection in her own analysis of sympathy in "Fancy Sketches," arguing, "The feeling subject identifies with the suffering object in order to understand his (or her) plight and come to his (or her) aid" in a spirit of "'congeniality'" that acknowledges "relationships of interdependence and mutuality."[67] The people making up Harper's wedding party, by contrast, do not recognize slaves or "the colored people" more generally as moral equals, nor do they think about their concerns as proximately related to their own. Talking about the impediments to improving the "condition of our people" is sufficient to prove their credentials, and it enhances their (false) sense of distance and independence from the objects of their shallow sympathies.[68] Worse, these "impediments" have taken on an abstract, timeless quality.

Harper's sketch amplifies this warning, as she refashions Plato's allegorical cave into a drawing room and his shadowy pantomime into expensive clothing—"golden chains"—and specious debate.[69] Unlike Plato's cave dwellers, Harper's partygoers ought to see, ought to *feel*, the contradictions and their own moral inconsistency: "Fingers used to the wash-tub were glittering with jewels, women were vying with each other in rich laces and elegant brocades; hands hardened by labor were encased in fine and delicate gloves; necks that had sweated in getting up excellent dinners for 'white folks,' were adorned with golden chains, and arms that had been weary in carrying heavy burdens were gleaming with golden bracelets."[70] This critique, though in line with other arguments about economic prudence and the lures of performative respectability, would have struck a materialist nerve closer to Harper's endorsement of Free Produce and would have been an unwelcome reminder "of the back regions that alone made the performance possible," a violation of what Karen Halttunen calls "polite social geography."[71] However, this same set of social protocols allows the gathering to reframe Jane's words as stemming from her country backwardness and as an attempt to gain a young man's affection. They pity her, and her friend reminds her that he "thought people ought not to argue in society."[72] People ought not to draw back the curtain to reveal the "unmentionables" holding the parlor play together.

While the characters are apparent caricatures, the whole scene nevertheless offers a potent warning that contemporary activists risk replicating this vacuity if their focus becomes too insular and disconnected to actual events. As my discussion of Bernice and the Black Forrest suggests, one of the risks for any insurgent politics is that it can serve the hegemonic strategies such practices were meant to disrupt, especially as spaces like conventions, parades, and the like become static, codified as *the* accepted site of oppositional agency. Such a counterpublic could thrive—to a degree—as long as it remained within this space without appreciably affecting the surrounding society, like lymph nodes in the overall system.

Harper's point here is not which tactic—wealth, education, rebellion, emigration, and so on—is more viable; Jane never quite takes a side, though she seems least satisfied with the emigration option. The point is the spirit—or lack of conviction—behind each argument. Harper's sketches offer histories of the present—not the congratulatory remembrance of past successes like the account of the first Colored Convention that appears in the *Anglo-African*'s inaugural issue or the catalogue of great representative black men that Delany, Garnet, Wells Brown, and Nell produced but rather a sober assessment of contemporary politics. In other words, "Fancy Sketches" does not deal in hypotheticals. Just as Wilson and Smith's sketches distill lessons from New York and Brooklyn streets for Douglass's readers, Harper, writing for a black audience for whom the names "Tennessee hero," "Aunt Sally," and "Margaret Garner" had the power to conjure a host of other recent events, aimed on one hand to invoke and circulate their sense of urgency and on the other to fulfill Hamilton's mission statement for the magazine: to "uphold and encourage the now depressed hopes of thinking black men, in the United States."[73] For "Fancy Sketches," this mission expanded to center explicitly "thinking" black women like Jane (and Harper herself) and ostensibly genteel spaces like parlors as sites where revolutionary citizenship might be taught and (em)plotted.[74]

Stories to Be Passed On, or "Zombi"

If Harper was so active on the lecture circuit and in vigilance communities, why did she place Jane in a country parlor? Why stage this conversation here rather than in a speech or set the main action at a convention? As Foster suggests, appreciating Harper means understanding how she "played her audience, used her poetry [and prose] to strike chord of sentiment," on one hand, and attending to the synergistic political aesthetic at work across her prose and poetry, on the other.[75] This synergy, to continue Foster's metaphor, suggests that Harper played form and genre the way Ella Fitzgerald worked the Great American Songbook: "She took advantage of the sentiments introduced or encouraged by other popular writers. . . . Within these stereotyped outlines, however, Harper paints more subtle shades" (31). Trying to rescue nineteenth-century black writing from sentimental readings by emphasizing the plot's political engagements misses the claims that writing makes about the imbrication of the domestic and the political.

Rather, as Robert Reid-Pharr posits, reorienting our critical sensibilities to think about the "domestic sphere as the center of black political life, the place at which community is formed and resistance is mounted," invokes an ethos of marronage. It draws on circulatory senses of citizenship developed in the colored conventions, which themselves recognized and relied on parlors and other gendered spaces as crucial to citizenship practices.[76] Indeed, Harper's sketches reveal that parlor spaces can generate and reproduce models of engagement that might operate more effectively and more freely than those imagined through more explicitly political (and masculinist) fora such as conventions. Despite the potential for stagnation, then, Harper found value in the parlor and the kinds of conversations it could host: a space where theories and practices of citizenship could be discussed and disseminated in an active and evolving intellectual tradition.[77]

"Fancy Sketches" draws this practice out most explicitly over two installments centering on the narrative of *Quilombo dos Palmares*, the seventeenth-century Brazilian *quilombo* (marron society) and its leader, Zumbi (alternatively spelled here and in nineteenth-century accounts as Zombi).[78] Harper introduces the narrative in "Zombi, or Fancy Sketches" (February 1860) as a part of a conversation about "negro courage" and education between Jane, Jane's cousin Miranda, and Mr. Ballard, a student who is presumably courting Miranda. Zumbi was not a new figure for Harper. It is a well-known story in Brazil and was often cited in eighteenth- and nineteenth-century histories and, later, antislavery tracts. And, as Monique-Adelle Callahan's work demonstrates, Harper's poetic rendering of Zumbi in "Death of Zombi" (1857) shows Harper developing a "mythology of black resistance" and transnational literary vision in response to a range of local and global events in a turbulent 1856.[79] In "Fancy Sketches," Ballard offers to read a prose version of "Zombi" as an example of stories to be told to children in preparation for what is to come, and his telling follows the standard nineteenth-century pattern: After helping the Portuguese defeat the Dutch, explains Ballard, the former slaves refused to "[lay] aside the implements of war for the badges of slavery" and "constituted a nation under the name of the Palmerese [*sic*]."[80] The society prospered for almost one hundred years, growing to over 20,000. When Portuguese armies finally attacked them, Zombi and his compatriots held them off until their ammunition and provisions ran out and Portuguese reinforcements arrived. While many of Palmares's citizens were captured and enslaved, the nation's leaders "resolved not to be taken alive" and instead leapt to their deaths.[81]

Similar to Wilson's "Black Forrest" sequence, "Zombi" points to the "thrillingly sublime" courage of those who fought against enslavement as models not only for "negro courage" but also for citizenship (Palmares was a republic, after all).[82] The examples Jane and Ballard produce (including "that Tennessee hero" who "received 750 lashes, and died" because he would not betray an escape plan and "stories of Margaret Garner, of Aunt Sally, of Toussaint L'Ouverture, of Denmark Veazy [*sic*], of Nathaniel Turner . . . and others") provide the ethical center of Harper's narrative landscape, constitutive stories that could give purpose to the "intellectual acquirements" and wealth Jane finds among her friends and family and the apathy Harper senses among her readers but without the debilitating isolation found in Wilson's sketches. Jane makes an argument for "Zombi" as a constitutive narrative for the whole of African America and those fighting for greater freedom—a community that is sieged by an ostensibly overwhelming force and from which, in Jane and Ballard's view, sacrifices on multiple fronts will be required: liberty until death.

"Zombi" links the development of Atlantic world *quilombo* to free black communities in the United States, as Ballard and Jane juxtapose Palmares's governance and defense to cultivating a "well-directed home education" and broader "home culture" to black America, a project that, Jane observes, "may need more true courage and fortitude than the battle-field calls for."[83] The connections are stronger than they appear on first reading. As Steven Hahn has noted, free black communities, North and South, could themselves be viewed as "historically specific variants of the broad phenomenon of maroons"[84] And, as Peterson has argued, these spaces provided a "foundation of black nationalist thought" throughout the century, and it intensified during the 1850s and early 1860s.[85] In this context, Ballard's description of how the Palmares "formed a government" and "placed stockades[,] not knowing how long they would be permitted to live unmolested it was necessary to provide for the common defense," speaks to a sense of being under siege that Jane registers in her contempt for black men who "can put on pretty little aprons with showy rosettes, and march amid the darkness of the Dred Scott Decision, over the very streets where the trembling fugitive is dragged back to bondage."[86] It's not that Jane condemns the parades as such. For nominally free black citizens to parade in the streets would be laudable as a spatial practice, a display of community solidarity, and even an act of intrusiveness in certain contexts given the history of white violence against them. But, like the conversation at the wedding party, they seem a misplaced use of resources for the political exigencies of the post–*Dred Scott* era, especially if an equal measure of support cannot be found for vigilance committees and uplift more generally.

Jane's frustration leads to a call for black citizens to rethink the efficacy of traditions like parades and everyday politics more broadly in the context of a more dangerous political terrain. "Peace has its tests of valor as well as war; and," Jane concludes: "if I hear a colored man boast of what he would do in the event of an insurrection, and yet not brave enough to identify himself with the colored people, but shrinking from social contact with them on account of their ignorance, poverty and social disadvantages . . . [if such a person] is not brave enough to battle with them in freedom . . . then I am not sure that he will be courageous enough to risk his life for me in slavery."[87] Practices in freedom—the infrastructure that neighborly, economic, and critical civic practices can foster and the kind of engaged citizenship the wedding party lacks—create the bonds and material support through which the collective could make larger scale changes.

The choice of Palmares over Haiti is significant in the context of emigration and the history of republican governance in the hemisphere. Peterson observes that focusing on Palmares signals not only Harper's opposition to emigration but also an uneasiness with Haiti's "tragic history of degeneration," an uneasiness shared by her contemporaries in the United States, including James T. Holly's conclusion that the nation showed none of the necessary "elements of morality and industrial progress."[88] Moreover, as one of the earliest models of republican governance in the hemisphere—older than Brazil, the United States, and Haiti—Palmares represents a key founding moment for the tradition of citizenship theorizing I have been examining throughout *The Practice of Citizenship*—one based in "equal laws" and "equal rights" with "no hideous slave-code" to compromise its institutions.[89] Finally, Palmares and Zumbi might have been attractive to Harper because of its past-ness: it provided grounds for historical mythmaking that suggested a tragic yet resilient continuity between ancient Carthage, black Diaspora marronage, and the antebellum United States without the entanglements of contemporaneous politics in Haiti or the United States.

This tradition is not meant to catalog triumphal victories or occasion celebrations of revolutions fought and won; rather, it offers the sobering forecast of uncertainty and hard work recapitulated across Harper's letters and fiction for the *Anglo-African*. They all reveal a preoccupation with the power of sacrifice and making meaning out of losses that seem to be piling up, both in the short term and over a longue durée. Carthage provides an apt point of comparison for Jane as she ties enslavement to European imperialism and wonders if her contemporaries "would be willing, like the women of Carthage, to sacrifice" their jewels "for the good of their race" against, again, a destructive European force.[90] Though Carthage and Palmares faced spectacular and highly visible sieges, Harper's analogies suggest that the need for vigilance among black citizens is no less urgent. Harper echoes these sentiments in "An Appeal for the Philadelphia Rescuers," a call to support those who attempted (and failed) to rescue Moses Horner in June 1860: "Let the hands of toil release their hold upon their hard-won earnings, feeling that there is no poverty like the poverty of meanness, no bankruptcy like that of a heart bankrupt in just, kind, and generous feelings."[91] Free black communities were in a protracted struggle in which everyday social life could create a false sense of comfort. The recapture of many of Palmares's citizens in "Zombi" should serve as warning for free black citizens about the precariousness of their own position, the ease with which allies can become enemies, and the destructive potential of white supremacy and imperial avarice more generally. The differences between Carthage, Palmares, and Jane's parlor matter in this analogy as much as the similarities.[92] Just as Rome provided an ideological model for the early U.S. republic, so too might Palmares and Carthage and the African-centered power they represent provide ideological grounding for black citizens.

Harper renders this principle poetically through an example closer to home in "The Tennessee Hero" (1857), another story Ballard and Jane suggest should be told frequently and to which Ballard accords a "degree of grandeur and sublimity."[93] The poem's titular hero, based on accounts from the 1856 "Tennessee Conspiracy," similarly resolves to die as an act of freedom and in a way that protects the continuing revolution. Before he dies, however, the hero proclaims, "I know the men who would be free; / They are the heroes of your land" (21–22); they themselves proclaim, "They must and will be free!' " (16) through the expressive language of conduct. The speaker draws our attention to the nameless collective of whom the hero is a representative, not in an exceptional way but in a synecdochal way. If, as Callahan argues of Harper's "Death of Zombi," "Zombi emerges as a type of resolution, synthesizing freedom and death in a single act of heroic self-sacrifice," Harper's "Tennessee Hero" and her retelling "Zombi" in the parlor suggest that this synthesis was at work in more than these highly visible men.[94] Rather than memorialize past actions or the martyrs of the recent, the hero praises the living revolutionaries and, from his white listeners' perspective, the ongoing threat they pose. He knows the "men who would be free": those who not only desire freedom, but, in this context, are executing their plan for freedom and who are already free based in that determination. Both Palmares's leaders and the Tennessee hero have the courage to be free and act on it, and Harper distills their courage into lessons applicable in everyday practice. By reshaping this narrative and setting it in ballad stanzas reminiscent of drum taps, Harper renders it at once a rallying cry and at the same time a rhyme clear enough for children to recite.

This work suggests that Harper's invocation of the sublime throughout "Fancy Sketches" and elsewhere functions as more than superlative; rather, it provides a key to her political aesthetic. Importantly, Ballard *reads* "Zombi" (and suggests that people read "The Tennessee Hero") as a narrative circulating through print and, in a reflection of the black state conventions, intended for collective consumption and primed to incite reenactment or, to use Harper's phrasing, "agitation" and conversion. As if to model this process, Ballard's reading "Zombi" initiates a sublime response for Miranda, but in contrast to Ethiop's encounter with Bernice, her response affirms action and retelling rather than isolation and (generic and physical) containment. The narrative "stir[s]" Miranda's "soul" so that she vows "to be an active worker, and not an idle spectator." "And we like to call these objects sublime," writes Kant, "because they raise the soul's fortitude above its usual middle range and allow us to discover in ourselves an ability to resist which is of a quite different kind, and which gives us the courage [to believe] that we could be a match for nature's seeming omnipotence."[95] Agitation leads to overcoming and an expanded capacity to resist and act in the world against what once appeared to be an insurmountable power. While neither the narrative nor this analysis equates Miranda's newly discovered resolve to physical resistance, the narratives do place before her monumental moments that, as with Harper's account of her response to *12 Years a Slave*, lead Miranda to expand her imagination of the possible in the face of the ostensibly unassailable force of whiteness. This is necessary preparatory work.

Both Jane and Ballard suggest that the circulation of such narratives in conversations and in print could contribute not toward an immediate uprising but rather toward "the gradual uprising and improvement of the masses." It is important, then, that Jane does not respond to Miranda's desire to "do something" with a call to march on the South, and she resists the urge to replay the bombastic conversations she critiqued in previous installments. She instead draws our attention to something more mundane and, at least on the face of it, far removed from Palmares or even U.S. fugitives:

> Now, I tell you, Miranda, one thing we can do, we can do it ourselves and try and enlist others in the same work, and that is to try to sustain the "Anglo-African." It is one of the most welcome papers that reaches me, and I want it to live. . . . I want the Anglo-African to live at least as one of our monuments. I have the first volume, it was presented to me nicely bound, and it forms one of the valued books of my small library. I would like to see that book bound in the houses of our people, and kept in existence as something to stimulate our young people to an interest in their improvement and progress.[96]

While Miranda's inspiration might come from this distant narrative, her work must start with the local. Aside from the explicit plug for the struggling magazine (Harper sprinkles several throughout "Fancy Sketches"), the passage configures the parlor as a space for cultivating a revolutionary consciousness: receiving the *Anglo-African* as a gift book (advertised in multiple weeklies and in the December 1859 issue) adds to her "small library," which contains or perhaps binds the word to a project of people-building, as a monument to and living agent in the creation of an Anglo-African (America), starting with childhood education.[97] We can read Jane's "small library," then, as a generative node of revolutionary citizenship that maintains the force of the slave sublime through print and oral traditions. Having the *Anglo-African* on display, having conversations about what it is and means, is as important as its content.

The project of monumentalizing the Anglo-African for which Jane calls is less about the object itself and more about the set of practices required to create such a monument: the active binding, keeping, and transmission of the text as part of a larger project involving the demolition of slavery and its infrastructure. Indeed, the second, unquoted, Anglo-African suggests a slippage between the preservation of the printed word ("Anglo-African") and the perpetuation of the Anglo-African as collective constituted through their shared citizenship practices. Jane's parlor, then, resonates with the conditions of marronage that Wilson explores in the "Afric-American Picture Gallery" but is infused with practices of contact and circulation that not only connect intellectually sites of marronage that are temporally and geographically distant but also focuses this work outward, between generations and into the broader body politic. For Peterson "these seemingly trivial sketches . . . raise fundamental questions about social value, political strategy, and literary composition of vital interest to free blacks in the antebellum North."[98] At the same time, the sketches demonstrate how black citizens can engage these questions collectively. The entire scene works to foster the mode of reading and responding characteristic of critical citizenship rather than "idle spectatorship" as a part of the fabric of everyday life in the parlor conversations among friends and potential lovers, stories passed on as precious gifts, and the foundation that would support all other pursuits.[99]

Harper and others were not being overly romantic when they imagined potential revolution out of these conditions—exaggerated timetable, perhaps, but not the will of the slaves to revolt, the untapped potential of coalitions set against the slave power, or work already under way in and through black parlors. The long history and ubiquity of formal and informal actions supporting fugitives has led historian Carol Wilson to note, "Self-defense actions represent one of the most significant yet neglected examples of black initiative in U.S. history."[100] Such was the case in the 1850 spiriting away of William and Ellen Craft by Boston's free black community. Accounts note that no one could come near their shop "'without being seen by a hundred eyes, and a signal would call a powerful body at a moment's notice.'" The most harrowing accounts place Lewis Hayden in his basement "before the slave hunters and above [barrels of] gunpowder, lit match in hand."[101] "Black communities did more than simply declare their intention to fight," Wilson notes, "they did fight."[102] The defense and rescues of fugitives like William and Ellen Craft and Shadrach Minkins demonstrated the degree of community organization necessary for successful vigilance work, organization that required many unnamed and non-overtly-activist black citizens to mobilize at a moment's notice. Zumbi's defense of Palmares might initially seem distant from the sites of vigilance and rescue work in Boston, Philadelphia, Christiana, or myriad other northern cities, but vigilance narratives reveal that these people similarly saw themselves as communities under siege, and they similarly armed and organized themselves for common defense.

Visions of Citizenship Ascendant

If "Fancy Sketches" models pedagogies of revolutionary citizenship as an everyday parlor and print practice, Harper's other work takes a more metaphysical approach that maps how the sublime encounter catalyzes the movement toward structural change. "The Triumph of Freedom—A Dream," Harper's other short story in the 1860 volume of the *Anglo-African*, illustrates the agitational process Jane and Ballard witness in Miranda, connecting their conversation to contemporary events—including attempted fugitive rescues and John Brown's raid on the federal arsenal at Harper's Ferry—and, at the same time, providing context for the ethical deployment of violence. "Triumph" appeared in the January issue of the *AAM* (the same issue as "Home Influences") and is perhaps better known than "Fancy Sketches" because it appears in Foster's *A Brighter Coming Day*. The story draws heavily on Harper's correspondences during the months preceding Brown's execution, and it reflects her encounters with fugitive slave rescue attempts, both successful and unsuccessful. Through this material, she builds a new mythology for the movement, translating Walker, Garrison, Brown, and others into the prophets who lay the foundation for a new dispensation, a "new baptism."

In brief, the first-person narrator falls asleep and has a vision in which she is guided to the altar of a goddess in a "robe of flowing white" that upon further inspection "was not pure white" but had "great spots of blood" all over it. As the narrator and her guide watch priests attesting to the goddess's righteousness and attempting to cover these spots with passages from sacred texts, a young man, "his face pale with emotion and horror," calls out, "'It is false.'" Guided by this young man, we discover that the altar's foundation is composed of "piles of hearts laid layer upon layer," including "the hearts of a hundred thousand new-born babes," "the hearts of desolate slave mothers, robbed of their little ones," of crushed manhood, of "young girls, sold from the warm clasp of their mothers' arms," and of "hearts in which the manhood has never been developed."[103] Slavery's effects on the soul aren't incidental in this image; they are the foundational elements of its moral and economic structure.

As Stancliff notes, this narrative can operate as "a republican allegory of the abolitionist moment" that "serves as a brief history of abolitionist rhetoric, a figuration of its providential import and its place in the progress of the republic."[104] At the same time, the narrative offers lessons for social movements and citizenship more broadly. The description of the young man is just suggestive enough to invite savvy readers to think of Walker, Garrison (especially for those familiar with Nell's *Colored Patriots*), or Elijah P. Lovejoy. Walker's *Appeal* lit a fire among antislavery and proslavery advocates alike; proslavery southerners placed a bounty on his life and passed laws limiting black literacy and mobility in its wake. Antislavery activists and free speech advocates more broadly regarded Lovejoy, who was gunned down in front of his newspaper office in 1837, as the first white martyr of the cause and later described him as a John the Baptist to John Brown's Messiah.[105] The reference to the "young man," however, is also general enough to fit the profile of many radical abolitionists or passionately critical citizens. And like evangelical narratives of the Spirit of God inhabiting and changing the converted, their words create and inhabit new creatures ready to change the world.

Harper again turns to the sublime as the aesthetic anchor for this revolutionary citizenship. The narrator describes the man's initial word as "sublime in its brevity" and the subsequent demonstration as so powerful that it unleashes "the spirit of Agitation," the mental processes associated with critical citizenship. Even as the goddess calls for her priests to hide her "beneath [their] constitutions and laws" and "beneath the shadow of [their] pulpits," Agitation pierces "into the recesses of her guilty soul," and she "tremble[s] before its searching glance."[106] The sublime figure and Agitation pursue their audiences, exercising the politics of disruption and circulation that, as with the telling of "Zombi," provide a direct call to action, this time on the mass scale for which both Jane and Ballard advocate.[107] A second, "aged" man then appears with "gray hair float[ing] in the air," leading a group of men attempting to overthrow the goddess. "A blood-stained ruffian, named General Government," however, arrives to defend her, and the man and his companions are imprisoned and hanged. The goddess's "minions" then "[drain] the blood from his veins," but the blood, "like the terrible teeth sown by Cadmus . . . woke up armed men to smite the terror-stricken power." The story ends with this army unseating the goddess and enthroning Freedom in her place.[108] After the conflict, the bodies of the man and his followers become "stepping-stones of Freedom to power," figured as both a monument to their heroism and support for the next phase in the revolution.

"Triumph" takes on a tone of prophesy that connects the old man to John Brown and echoes accounts of his failed raid and subsequent trial that consumed periodicals, including the *Anglo-African Magazine*. Indeed, Harper's description of the aged man reproduces language from her letters to Brown and others that appeared in the *Weekly Anglo-African* and the *National Anti-Slavery Standard*.[109] Harper praises Brown and his company for having "rocked the bloody Bastille" and suggests that their "bodies may be only her [freedom's] first stepping stones to dominion." Harper uses similar language in a December 9, 1859, letter published in the *National Anti-Slavery Standard*: "Virginia has sacrificed that dear old man who laid his hands upon the bloody citadel of American slavery and shook the guilty fabric to its base; shall not, my dear friend, his blood be a fresh baptism of freedom, his grave a new altar where men may record more earnest vows against slavery?"[110] Brown becomes a Christ figure whose execution creates a "new altar," a new civic ethos upon which men and women like Miranda might construct more active or "earnest" citizenship practices. Like Jones and Allen's "real sensibility," Harper's "more earnest vows" call on citizens to dedicate themselves to freedom not simply as an ideal or article of faith but rather as a "common cause" that compels them to action. For Harper, the raid on Harper's Ferry shook the nation's constitutive documents—the "fabric" (paper) upon which citizens had written its narratives—in a way that might create the impetus for a greater moment of revision. Where citizens "so fresh, from the baptism of the Revolution" could frame a Constitution that would "permit the African slave trade," "the dark intent of the fugitive clause," and white supremacy's codification in law, citizens receiving the "baptism of freedom" would author a new compact.[111]

In the context of "Fancy Sketches" and Jane and Ballard's call for a mass movement with enduring monuments, this imagery contributes to the larger narrative of common defense and sacrifice Harper outlines in "Zombi" and other installments. Importantly, though the old man is perhaps the story's central figure, "Triumph" develops in several stages—critique to agitation to action to critique and so on—that recall Miranda's response to "Zombi." Freedom's final enthronement depends on the "freemen," reminiscent of "those who would be free" in "Tennessee Hero," who go into battle against "hoary forms of gigantic Error and colossal Theory" with "fresh vigor" *even as* enslaved men "burst their chains."[112] "Triumph" sketches the kind of collective ethos needed for radical change. Though the actual overthrow happens almost spontaneously from both ends—free and enslaved people rising up simultaneously—it is the result of an accretive process of consciousness raising and contingency. Where "Zombi" provides historical grounding for Harper's calls for greater vigilance, and "Fancy Sketches" more broadly offers frameworks for applying and disseminating this model in everyday practice, "Triumph" looks forward to what might happen as a result of these cumulative efforts in the hopes that the penultimate resolution might be close at hand.

The baptism metaphor is apt, then, not because Brown, Harper's old man, or any single person delivers the people but rather because he is a part of a chain of citizens and texts that inspire the people to deliver themselves to practice citizenship as an expression of neighborhood without the limitations on human rights that Douglass notes in 1854. Even as Harper invokes physical violence—a clash between humans and Titans (Error and Theory), former slaves and a colonial power (Palmares and Portugal), John Brown and the government—she also uses a Christian typology (the narrator recalls John of Patmos) that frames the penultimate war as "not against flesh and blood, but against principalities, against powers, against the rulers of the darkness of this world, against spiritual wickedness in high places."[113] Put somewhat differently, by using narrative formulas from classical mythology, historical slave rebellions, and Christian tradition across a series of texts, Harper produces a pragmatic ethos of vigilance and a multimodal response to the complicated, chaotic, and dour outlook at the start of the 1860s.

If slavery has been described as a "multi-headed hydra," Harper imagines her own multiheaded hydra or, in the case of "Triumph," a Cadmus-like hero whose death and blood only multiply the members of his cause. The progression of events in "Triumph" and its publication in the same issue as "Fancy Sketches" suggest that Harper understood what the contributors to *Antislavery Violence* note in 1999, that "the roots of antislavery violence lay deep in American history and culture" and that "antislavery violence served as a means of uniting slavery's black and white enemies."[114] This futurist perspective, constantly on the verge, searched out footholds for hope, despite evidence that would encourage hopelessness. It cultivated faith, despite evidence that would encourage doubt. These narratives, then, were as much about encouraging the already converted—preaching to a beleaguered choir—as they were about converting the apathetic mass. More, as "Triumph" suggests, this revolution might not be reducible to a slave insurrection; rather, free black life was another front in the same war.

While "Zombi" and "Triumph" evoke a sense of grandeur, "Fancy Sketches" grounds their ideals in everyday practice. "This is a common cause," Harper writes to William Still in 1859, "The humblest and feeblest of us can do something," and as "Fancy Sketches" suggests, this work of everyday, active citizenship requires its own degree of courage.[115] As Jacqueline Bacon usefully notes in a slightly different context, the claims to being humble channel the "dual tendencies within Christ's teachings, which refer to both submission and liberation" and which authorize a more radical approach to politics generated from those who occupy the humblest positions. The humblest of all was also the liberator of all—through the word.

Through these stories, Harper organizes the theories and practices of citizenship I've outlined in previous chapters—the urgency of critical citizenship, the black state conventions' emphasis on structural change and participatory politics, and the street-level protocols of responsibility and responsiveness outlined in *Narrative* and the Communipaw-Ethiop debates—around a collective project of wholesale structural change, from "home culture" to the Constitution. Her insistence on maintaining the link between theory and practice, between form and substance, gets to the heart of the story that *The Practice of Citizenship* set out to tell, a story about how black writers in the early United States imagined citizenship as an expansive set of actions calibrated not only to distribute power evenly among a diverse citizenry in freedom but also to use this power to liberate those in slavery.

And yet, the seeming intractability of white supremacy and avaricious self-interest combined with narratives of loss outlined throughout this project points to the difficulty of making citizenship work along these lines and of keeping faith in a political system that, as "Triumph" graphically details, enshrined a goddess founded on and materially supported by the heart and blood of others. With no way of knowing that South Carolina would secede from the Union in December 1860, that the states would be at war the following year, or that birthright citizenship would eventually become the federal standard, Harper and others nevertheless offer a vision of what citizenship might have been and what it has yet to become. That their challenge was not consistently reflected in U.S. institutions and civic practices does not diminish its power; rather, black theories of citizenship persist in their urgent call for citizens to engage actively within others in a spirit of common humanity and mutual aid, and they reveal the degree to which citizenship on these terms can be a radically imaginative process.

CONCLUSION

"To Praise Our Bridges"

The preceding chapters have unfolded a narrative of black citizenship practices and print culture before the Civil War. The point has been less the what—whether and when black Americans were legal citizens—and more the how—how did black citizens theorize and enact citizenship through print culture and how, in turn, did this work shape early black print. Each chapter has taken up a citizenship practice—neighborliness, circulation, economics, critique, and revolution—alongside the multiple spaces—pamphlets, conventions, sketches, periodical literature, and poetry—where black theorizing and practice happened. Black citizenship theorizing and practices constituted black citizens as political subjects, framed and reframed their condition and actions as articulating core principles of republican citizenship, and predicated the work of citizenship not on building comfortable or beautiful consensus but rather on confronting and embracing a disruptive and revolutinary sublime. The blackness of black theorizing emerges from its approach and perspective, what Samuel Ringgold Ward, writing in 1840, would call seeing through a "different medium."[1] The sites, purposes, and styles of theorizing changed over time, but this medium makes this work recognizable as a set of cultural patterns designed to deal with a fundamentally unjust society. The story of black theorizing, then, is less in the individual theories themselves and more the processes through which black writers generated citizenship in a nation whose definition of "citizen" was often deferred, improvised, and increasingly premised on turning assumptions about black exclusion into legal fact. By way of conclusion, I want to reflect on the relation between black theorizing, form, modern practices, and how the people who have shaped the field of early African American print culture have informed my approach across this book.

Aesthetically and formally, black theorizing and citizenship practices surfaced in black writers' experimentation with implicitly ephemeral forms such as the sketch, with popular forms such as the convention, pamphlet, or ballad, and with collaborative venues such as newspapers. They invoked concepts such as the sublime (or the beautiful or sensibility) to articulate citizenship's disruptive, revolutionary properties or to develop models of representation and affiliation. And they grounded these abstractions in embodied practices, including antislavery violence and mutual aid. Margaret Garner, Zumbi, and events including the Christiana resistance (1851) and the Tennessee conspiracy of 1856 became more than indexical examples of black self-assertion, the horrors of enslavement, or moments invoking sympathy. Black collectives and individuals framed antislavery violence as producing knowledge about citizenship and read the lessons from spectacular events such as the 1793 yellow fever epidemic through and into the more mundane encounters in the "everyday life-spaces" of the street, shop, and home.[2] Speaking and writing these narratives was not just about historical awareness or emotional appeals; rather, it was about learning from, circulating, and extending their political energies.

Black theorizers distilled these lessons through forms such as the ballad for easy distribution and consumption and used forms of public address and petitions to expand accounts of black citizenship and invite reenactment. The form was part of the argument, to invoke Hayden White's germinal formulation. But these forms were not static. As Caroline Levine has argued, form, as well as politics when considered as a form, "involves activities of ordering, patterning, and shaping" that carry with them "affordances" or "particular constraints and possibilities."[3] The message of black convention addresses, for instance, depended on their leveraging the affordances of the convention form *and* of their emergence from a "state convention of colored citizens." The fact that a convention of citizens produced these events and documents confronted the policing of political speech that often happened (and continues to happen) through overt moments of antiblackness as well as under the veil of universalism, white identity politics, and liberal goodwill. In a different but no less important vein, Frances Ellen Watkins Harper staged her parlor conversations in sketches, a form that carried expectations of intellectual exploration but that was also dominated by male voices. In so doing, she intervened simultaneously in a political and literary field and reframed gendered spaces (parlors) and practices (child rearing) as foundational to preparing for radical politics and for doing the work of revolutionary citizenship. She and black women conventioneers pushed to make their labor visible, supporting conventions and other institutions that excluded them even as they worked against that exclusion. In both cases, writers were developing and contesting practices of blackness even as they reimagined citizenship's contours.

In practice black theorizing was messy, always entangled with its contemporary moment and its own internal conflicts. Men reflected the misogyny of the day, as was the case in the convention movement, and writers could misjudge the trajectory of events, as might have been the case in both James McCune Smith and William J. Wilson's economic theorizing. Harper's parlors depend on a particular kind of literate education and domesticity that risks sliding into the elitism she condemns. That messiness makes black theorizing an indexical style of "shadow politics" that could reify political norms and at the same time radically utopian, as black theorizing became increasingly antithetical to those norms and constantly pushed toward a world otherwise. This archive calls on us to question our critical practices with an eye toward black writing as a site through which, as Gene Andrew Jarrett reminds us, "race, nature, slavery, politics, emancipation, liberty, and citizenship are defined in their contemporary terms, not retrofitted from our own."[4] Doing so requires reading black print as a site of theoretical production and our own roles as theorizing with and alongside it, rather than bringing "theory" to black writing. This tension informs Absalom Jones and Richard Allen's simultaneous citations of black virtue, the Free African Society's emphasis on public morality, and their critiques of how power underwrote the virtue discourse their white contemporaries mobilized. It is also symptomatic of black theorizers' position as people who understood features of citizenship such as voting and labor as essential practical modes of political representation but who were also aware of the myriad other ways electoral politics and capitalism could and did function as technologies of white supremacy.

Black writers interrogated the rhetorical production of white citizenship: how language, form, and performance produced senses of rationality, virtue, and worth. I have generally avoided including terms "ration," "civil," "respectable," and the like in my articulations of black theorizing (outside of its performative value) because, as I discuss throughout the book, they were often applied after the fact as a way of buttressing a predetermined sense of whose speech deserved recognition. Black theorizing places these terms in question. Its modes of engagement are fundamentally different from the "conversations" about "x" that public commentators and politicians often call for or stage after yet another racist, sexist, homophobic, transphobic, ableist, and/or xenophobic infraction. Where such conversations often end with one side or another declaring the conversation itself as progress or both sides retreating back to their silos, the practices I have outlined here are invested in reshaping structures, not individual acts, and conversations based in deep understandings of history and white supremacy and the need for reparative justice.

The "before the Civil War" of this study does not mean that these practices and black theorizing disappeared after 1861, after the Fourteenth Amendment (1868), or after the election of Barack Obama as president of the United States in 2008. The number of state and national conventions skyrocketed (approximately eighty conventions held between 1865 and 1877) as black citizens—many of them newly emancipated—set about the work of by turns organizing their new political reality and confronting ongoing productions of white citizenship. The Fourteenth Amendment may have set birthright citizenship as a national standard (that did not include American Indians, Chinese immigrants, or others at the time), but the Supreme Court and Congress had eroded much of its protections for black citizenship and U.S. republicanism by the 1883 *Civil Rights Cases*, an erosion that culminated in *Plessy v. Ferguson*'s "separate but equal" doctrine in 1896 and that reverberates to this day. Black Lives Matter, "a Black-centered political will and movement building project" organized by Alicia Garza, Patrisse Cullors, and Opal Tometi in 2013 in the wake of the murder of Trayvon Martin and through a combination of national social media networks and local chapter organizing, is an of echo nineteenth-century vigilance committees and their use of print to witness and intervene in violence against black citizens.[5] These two flashpoints (#blacklivesmatter and vigilance committees) are not the same. Though separated by roughly 150 years, however, their forms bear a striking resemblance to each other, suggesting the ongoing work of black citizenship practices through circulation, neighborliness, and critique.

Almost one hundred years after the Fourteenth Amendment's passage, the Mississippi Freedom Democratic Party (MFDP), led by Fannie Lou Hamer, continued the critical and intrusive politics earlier black theorists articulated. During the Democratic National Convention of 1964, Hamer and the MFDP delegates insisted on being heard and breaking the frame of Mississippi's white-dominated Democratic Party. The MFDP had spent the year holding meetings and precinct elections and establishing itself as an official part of the National Democratic Part. As it vied for credentials to be seated among the state's delegation, Hamer testified to the violence she and others faced as they attempted to register to vote the previous year. (Hamer herself was severely beaten to unconsciousness by black inmates who were themselves under threat of violence.) She ended her testimony with this warning: "And if the Freedom Democratic Party is not seated now, I question America. Is this America, the land of the free and the home of the brave, where we have to sleep with our telephones off the hooks because our lives be threatened daily, because we want to live as decent human beings, in America?"[6] Hamer's *parrhesia* speaks to the authority she has assumed for herself and those she represents. She questions an America that never was but one that she believed (had to believe) could be, despite itself. Could America be the "America" of myth at all, she seems to ask. She was not testifying to be judged by her audience, but rather, as with the 1848 Pennsylvania "Appeals" I discuss in Chapter 2, their response to her would be the basis upon which she would judge them. In the end, the convention offered the MFDP the compromise of seating two delegates, which they roundly refused, despite pressure from national leaders, including Dr. Martin Luther King Jr. and Bayard Rustin. Hamer famously responded, "We didn't come all this way for no two seats." They sought full representation as their due as citizens of the state who did the work.[7] Hamer and others returned to Mississippi disappointed but not cowed. While formal recognition on the national stage was refused them, for the moment, they redoubled their local efforts.

Hamer's sentiments recall the climatic stanza from Langston Hughes's "Let America Be America Again" (1936):

> O, yes,
> I say it plain,
> America never was America to me,
> And yet I swear this oath—
> America will be! (75–79)

As the poem's constant refrain, "America never was America to me," suggests, this work is not about returning to some original moment of equality or even fulfilling promises laid out in founding documents. Hughes's speaker ends the poem with a call to "make America again!" (86). The speaker's call, like Hamer's judging question, is not for a return to some ideal but rather an imperative to remake the country in the image Hamer conjures in her testimony and that early black theorizers articulated—"The land that never has been yet" (63). To be "America," in other words, America must constitute itself in such a way as to be worthy of the very citizens it so often seeks to deny and through the practices its structures so often attempt to manage and suffocate. This, then, is the premise of black theorizing: claiming citizenship is not an end point but rather the initiation of a transformative process.

I want to close with a reflection on my own journey in the field and its connections to the theorizing processes *The Practice of Citizenship* has outlined. During the "Early African American Print Culture in Theory and Practice" conference (2010) at the McNeil Center and the Library Company of Philadelphia, Frances Smith Foster expressed concern to my panelists and me that our use of European theoretical models to frame early African American texts might be obscuring the work these texts were doing. At the time, I was interested in how the black state conventions "fit" into conversations around Jürgen Habermas's *Structural Transformation of the Public Sphere* (1962) and Michael Warner's then dismissal of black participation in early American print in *Letters of the Republic* (1990). As African Americanists (and later Warner) were quick to note, Warner's characterization of Wheatley and Jupiter Hammon as "the exceptions that prove the rule" of black absence was only tenable if we took white characterizations of print and the public at face value and if we ignored the print archives that would suggest otherwise.[8] I wanted to join the fray. Were the state conventions an example of a "counterpublic" in action, a print counterculture as Joanna Brooks had defined it, or were they in a more liminal space, what I called at the time a "meso-public"? I was deeply engaged with the 2005 *William and Mary Quarterly* forum, "Alternative Histories of the Public Sphere," alongside a 2008 forum on "Democratic Style" in *Rhetoric and Public Affairs*, and trying to find language for articulating the relationship I saw emerging between black print, black intellectual traditions, and an American landscape that seemed determined to silence both.

While I do not want to disavow how formative that forum and my reading of and around Habermas were to my reading of early African American print, Smith Foster's question revealed some very real limitations to this approach. Her probing helped me realize that I was looking for terminology and theory to talk about an expressive culture that was producing its own theories and terminologies. This was, in fact, the principle that drew me to early black writing in the first place and a core principle of African American literary studies from Mae G. Henerson's "talking back" and Peterson's "doers of the word" to Houston Baker's "blues," Hortense Spiller's "mama's baby," and Henry Louis Gates Jr.'s "signifyin(g)."[9] The turn, for me, was applying this principle to citizenship, a concept that we had not traditionally thought of as "belonging" to black writers or black print culture. In this framework, black invocations of citizenship are less an appropriation of a discourse and more claiming ownership of one. Ward had already supplied the phrase, seeing "through a different medium," that aptly got to what the state conventions and black print culture, more broadly, were about. Jones and Richard similarly offered "expressive language of conduct" and "real sensibility" as sophisticated concepts for theorizing fellow feeling from the perspective of black writers in ways that models drawing on Benjamin Franklin, the early republic's political elite, or even early slave narratives could not provide.

The field has changed much since that conference, both in terms of access (for some) to digital archives and in terms of the critical apparatus around early African American print culture, an apparatus that Smith Foster, the conference's subsequent volume, and numerous anthologies and special issues have helped shape.[10] Nazera Wright, Benjamin Fagan, Britt Rusert, and others are theorizing black print practices using the terms—"girlhood," "chosen," "fugitivity"—emerging from black print and black studies and doing so in ways that, as Fagan posits, "insists not only that we remember the people along with the print but also that our own approaches be shaped by the theories and practices developed by the black men and women who lived with the print we study."[11] This focus demands not just an attunement to the ethics underlying black print practices (or the competing ethics underlying them) but also, as Wright observes, a dedication to reading "through and under the lines" for "what is *not* being said as much as for what *is* being said."[12] Doing so requires what Rusert describes as a "reading method that attempts to run alongside and keep up with the frenzied and dynamic experiments of early black writing and performance" and that resists replicating the production of black objecthood by focusing on black practices.[13] Their work involves not simply questioning what and who we study but also where—those "unexpected places" of Eric Gardner's work that include ephemera, convention minutes, scientific papers, and nonbook objects of all sorts.

In so doing, we have come to a deeper understanding of African American literary histories that are plural and that are not teleologically oriented to an eventual "renaissance" in Harlem.[14]

I tell this story and bring Wright's, Fagan's, and Rusert's books together here not just because of their proximity to my own—each book was published between 2016 and 2017—but because each of their formulations builds on and explicitly acknowledges work from Smith Foster, Joycelyn Moody, Carla Peterson, John Ernest, P. Gabrielle Foreman, Eric Gardner, and others, senior scholars who have helped create a generative, collaborative field. It is in that spirit of collaboration that I quote from them at length here. I recognize that the convention of a conclusion is to end with an articulation of the book's arguments in a way that foregrounds my own words. And yet, part of what I see as this book's intervention is that there's power in acknowledging these roots and networks of polyphonic, collective engagements. These books register a flashpoint, if you will. Their work constitutes moments of (literary) critical citizenship, a dialogic and dialectical process on the order of Ballard's reading "Zombi" that should prompt us to respond with Miranda's enthusiasm to "do something" and Jane's insistence that this something begins by reading the *Anglo-African*—acknowledging and learning from the practices that have come before and forging ahead toward something new.

NOTES

Abbreviations

AAPG	*"Afric-American Picture Gallery"*
AAM	*Anglo-African Magazine*
AAS	American Antiquarian Society
BAP	*Black Abolitionist Papers*
C	Communipaw
CA	*Colored American*
CCP	Colored Conventions Project
E	Ethiop
FDP	*Frederick Douglass's Papers*
FJ	*Freedom's Journal*
LCP	Library Company of Philadelphia
NASS	*National Anti-Slavery Standard*
PF	*Provincial Freeman*
WAA	*Weekly Anglo-African*

Introduction

1. See, for instance, Williams, "Oration," in Porter, *Early Negro Writings*, 343; Sidney, "Oration," in Porter, *Early Negro Writings*, 355; "Constitution and By-Laws of the Brotherly Union Society," in Porter, *Early Negro Writings*, 51; Whipper, "Address," in Porter, *Early Negro Writings*, 105.

2. Delany, *Condition*; Douglass, "The Meaning of July Fourth for the Negro," in *Selected Speeches and Writings*, 188. Whenever appropriate, I use the term "black citizens" to describe black people in the United States to reflect how free people of color referred to themselves and to reinforce the principle that, in lieu of explicit federal policy (which the nation didn't have until the Fourteenth Amendment), black citizens staked their claims to citizenship when they engaged the state, the nation, and each other *as* citizens.

3. "Proceedings of the National Emigration," 33. The claim of "fellow citizen" had such a strong resonance that the 1854 convention drew attention to its refusal to use the term "citizen" to signal its departure from a U.S.-based politics: "We have not addressed you as citizens—a term desired and ever cherished by us—because such you have never been. We have not addressed you as freemen,—because such privileges have never been enjoyed by any colored man in the United States" (33). The break with what had by then become a standard convention of black political address spoke as loudly as the convection's agenda in favor of emigration.

4. Notable recent exceptions to this trend include Fagan, *Black Newspaper*; Wright, *Black Girlhood*; and Rusert, *Fugitive Science*.

5. See, for instance, DeLombard, *Shadow*; Phan, *Bonds of Citizenship*; and Crane, *Race, Citizenship, and Law*. DeLombard, for instance, tacks the production of black personhood in terms of legal culpability. This construction comes largely from the perspective of white print—even when the texts forward a black civic presence—and definitions of personhood and citizenship set forth by the state itself. DeLombard then traces how this black civic presence—both black authored and not—interfaces with these definitions of personhood. But, and here's an important difference, the parameters of personhood are already set by the state or white writers. *The Practice of Citizenship* does not take the state's definition of citizenship at a given moment as the only possible definition. Rather, even as the United States restricted the parameters of "citizen," other schematics were not only possible but also being articulated and (if sometimes in a limited way) enacted. Martha S. Jones's *Birthright Citizens* is a welcome corrective to this trend.

6. Scholarship seeking theoretical models and critiques of U.S. citizenship often turns to Douglass, placing him alongside Ralph Waldo Emerson, Henry David Thoreau, and others as representatives of early national political thought. This work has been enlightening in its depth of research and thought, and yet, we cannot stop with Douglass.

7. Rancière, *Dissensus*, 35–36. I also draw on Judith Shklar's breakdown of citizenship into four categories: standing, nationality, active participation, and "ideal republican citizenship" (*American Citizenship*, 3–13). While citizenship as practice would seem to fall squarely into the participation category, as this book demonstrates, black writers saw citizenship practices as shaping and shaped by notions of respect and responsiveness (standing), civic virtue, and narratives of belonging (nationality).

8. I am grateful to Bascom for his commentary on a talk delivered at the 2016 Unit for Criticism and Interpretive Theory's Faculty Fellow's symposium. See "Citizens as Verbs."

9. See Certeau, *Practice*, 9; Somers, *Genealogies of Citizenship*, 25; and Secor, "Citizenship," 353.

10. Certeau, *Practice*, 9.

11. Phan, for instance, has argued that legal divisions between enslavement and freedom facilitated the linkage of legal personhood to a citizenship codified through the nation-state. *The Practice of Citizenship* suggests black writers were imagining a different vision of citizenship in which the nation-state and the entailments and privileges associated with legal personhood might by turns facilitate and contain citizenship practices, but these practices, not the frameworks, constitute citizenship itself. See Phan, *Bonds of Citizenship*, 16–20.

12. Nelson, *Commons Democracy*, 7.

13. Hartman, *Scenes*, 50–51.

14. Jones, "Petition," in Porter, *Early Negro Writings*, 331.

15. Ibid., 330.

16. Secor, "Citizenship," 353.

17. Garnet, "Address to the Slaves," 94.

18. See Porter, *Early Negro Writing*, 3. Both Porter and Stepto call our attention to the deep connection between the movement toward freedom and the search for aesthetic form. See Stepto, "Teaching Afro-American Literature," 8–24.

19. Frances Smith Foster, "A Narrative" and *Written by Herself*; Moody, *Sentimental Confessions*; Ernest, *Liberation Historiography* and *Chaotic Justice*; Peterson, "Capitalism," 558–559,

and *Doers*; Eric Gardner, *Unexpected Places* and *Black Print Unbound*; and McHenry, *Forgotten Readers*.

20. Frances Smith Foster, "A Narrative," 715. Another way to think about Foster's framework is that early African Americans were crafting their own "constitutive stories," narratives that, following Rogers Smith, structure and link all other "institutional practices and customs, demographics, socialization systems, psychological drives, and other such structural features of political life." See Rogers Smith, "Politics of People-Building," 73.

21. This literary historical work has borne fruit over the past two decades, and we might well look back on these years as a renaissance (one in a long series of energizing rebirths) of early African American literary studies. McHenry's work on literary societies, Ernest's analyses of "liberation historiography" and the chaotic contingency of racial formations, and Jeanine DeLombard's recovery of early American gallows literature all reinforce Foster's invitation to tell different and multiple "interesting narratives" about early African America. Among these interesting narratives, recent work from Benjamin Fagan offers a history of the early black press through the paradigm of "black chosenness" (*The Black Newspaper and the Chosen Nation*); Nazera Wright recasts our understanding of gender, age, and black literary history through her examination of black girlhood (*Black Girlhood in the Nineteenth Century*); and Britt Rusert outlines the interventions and possibilities of black science writing as fugitive practice in *Fugitive Science*. Digital projects, including the Black Press Research Collective, led by Kim Gallon, and the Colored Conventions Project at the University of Delaware, are breaking new scholarly and pedagogical ground in expanding our understanding of and access to a range of black texts that have often been used more for historical context than as living political, cultural, or literary documents.

22. See, for instance, the essays in Stein and Cohen, *Early African American Print Culture*; Ivy Wilson, *Specters of Democracy*; Levine and Wilson, Introduction to *The Works of James M. Whitfield*; and Brooks, "Early."

23. See Clytus, "Visualizing," 29–66; Ivy Wilson, *Specters of Democracy*, 145–168; Eckstrom and Rusert's "Introduction" to and exhibit on the "Afric-American Picture Gallery" ("Just Teach One") are indispensable for teaching and contextualizing Wilson's series.

24. In this sense, black theorizing untangles Rouseau's paradox. Concluding her argument that liberal arts education has long promised the "knowledge, discernment, and orientation" necessary for democratic citizenship, Wendy Brown notes that if it continues to be dismantled, we will be faced with the paradox Rousseau posits in *The Social Contract*: "in order to support good institutions, the people must antecedently be what only good institutions can make them into" ("The Humanities," 36). In context, Rousseau was articulating what he saw as a central dilemma for the legislator: to create democratic institutions, the legislator needs the kind of people that, paradoxically, can only be produced through democratic institutions. Black theorists often refused this temporality. Instead, they note that the process of creating democratic government creates the kinds of people who can do the work of democratic citizenship.

25. Ernest, *Liberation Historiography*, 279; Fagan, *Black Newspaper*, 7–8.

26. See Vogel, "Introduction"; see also Wilson, "Periodicals."

27. "A Note on Leaders," *WAA*, May 4, 1861.

28. Fagan, *Black Newspaper*, 8.

29. Thankfully, the Colored Conventions Project's massive recovery and transcription project is changing both the range of conventions we study and how we study them. See

Colored Conventions: Bringing Nineteenth-Century Black Organizing to Life, colored conventions.org.

30. Taylor, *Archive and Repertoire*, 3.

31. Ibid., 3. Taylor differentiates between embodied expressive culture and written culture, in part, to contest how writing became the privileged site of knowledge production and the backbone of Western colonialism..

32. Here, I invoke form as a way to think about aesthetic, social, and political structure, that is, a broadened sense of form that includes "patterns of sociopolitical experience" (1) signaled in Levine, *Forms*.

33. Smith, *Works*, 13.

34. Sedgwick, *Touching Feeling*, 128. I thank Trish Loughran for drawing this connection between my line of thinking and Sedgwick early in the writing process.

35. Spillers, *Black, White, and in Color*, 203.

36. Sedgwick, *Touching Feeling*, 146.

37. DeLombard, *Shadows*, 29. Wong's *Neither Fugitive nor Free* is important on this front, too, in its recovery of black freedom suits.

38. Weheliye, *Habeas Viscus*, 8.

39. Pratt, *Strangers Book*, 3.

40. See, for instance, Frances Smith Foster, *Written*; Peterson, *Doers*; Zafar, *We Wear the Mask*; Brooks, *American Lazarus*; Goddu, *Gothic America*; Reid-Pharr, *Conjugal*.

41. Johnson, "On Agency," 118. See also Brooks, "Early," and Jarrett, *Representing*, 15–17.

42. For a slightly different genealogy of U.S. citizenship that traces a similar instability, see Carrie Hyde's *Civic Longing*, which was published as this book was going into production.

43. *Castronovo, Necro-Citizenship*, 8. See also, Hartman, *Scenes*; Berlant, *The Queen of America* and "Citizenship"; and Tillet, *Sites of Slavery*. On the relation between enlightenment philosophy and white supremacy, see Mills, *Racial Contract*.

44. Hartman, *Scenes*, 118.

45. I thank the participants in the Unit for Criticism manuscript workshop for helping me draw out this connection. Berlant theorizes cruel optimism as relation in which "something you desire is actually an obstacle to your flourishing" (*Cruel Optimism*, 1).

46. Shachar, *Birthright Lottery*, 2.

47. Castronovo, *Necro-Citizenship*, 23 and 3.

48. Ibid., 6.

49. Ezekiel 37:3–10 King James Version (KJV).

50. Peterson, *Doers*, 3.

51. See Rancière, *Dissensus*, 44–51, and Bentley, "Warped Conjunctions," 292.

52. Rancière, *The Politics of Aesthetics*, 39.

53. Bentley, "Warped Conjunctions," 292.

54. Easton, *Treatise*, 49. As subsequent chapters will suggest, writers throughout the nineteenth century will return to this theme of the unnaturalness of racial discrimination.

55. Nelson, *Commons Democracy*, 6.

56. DeLombard and Phan, for instance, trace how constructions of black personhood were central to conceptions of legal personhood and citizenship more broadly. See DeLombard, *Shadow*, and Phan, *Bonds of Citizenship*.

57. The notion that the denial of citizenship or, in other contexts, personhood amounts to state-sanctioned violence appears in multiple contexts and under multiple names. See, for

instance, Mbembe's discussion of necropolitics in "Necropolitics," Patterson's social death thesis in *Social Death*, or Galtung's discussion of "structural violence" in *True Worlds*, 68–71. Justice Earl Warren echoes Easton in his 1958 dissent in *Perez v. Brownell*, describing citizenship as "man's basic right," without which one becomes a "stateless person" without the ability to assert or defend any rights at all. Just over one hundred years after Easton, Arendt theorizes citizenship as the "right to have rights": the right "to live in a framework where one is judged by one's actions and opinions . . . and a right to belong to some kind of organized community." See *Perez v. Brownell* (1958); Arendt, *Origins*, 376–377; and Somers, *Genealogies*, 1–29.

58. Castronovo, *Necro-Citizenship*, 3, and Brooks, *American Lazarus*, 8.

59. Vincent Brown, *Reaper's*, 127.

60. On shadow politics as a parallel to official political activities such as voting, see Anderson, "Black Shadow Politics"; Newman, *Freedom's Prophet*, 209–237; and Ivy Wilson, *Specters*, 5–6.

61. For a similar discussion, see DeLombard, *Shadow*; Phan, *Bonds of Citizenship*; Rogers Smith, *Civic Ideals*; Crane, *Race*; and Bradburn, *Citizenship Revolution*.

62. While noncitizens, such as foreign nationals, could do some of these activities, my point here is that citizenship was always defined in terms of participation and against categories of exclusion rather than through any positive articulation.

63. As Rogers Smith's account suggests, however, this patchwork was porous at best in terms of allowing the federal court and Congress to give "national content to the rights" of citizens, especially given opposition from the advocates of state-centered interpretations, largely from slave-holding states, who were in control of the government in the early nineteenth century. See Rogers Smith, *Civic Ideals*, 149–152, 173–180, and 187–189. Pryor (*Colored Travelers*) and Wong (*Neither Fugitive nor Free*) trace the intersections of black travel (within and between states), freedom, and black citizenship.

64. Article IV, Section 2, Clause i. Robert Purvis and the signers of the "Appeal of Forty Thousand" cite this clause as one of the first proofs of black citizenship as the Pennsylvania Constitutional Convention debated restricting franchise rights to white men in 1837.

65. U.S. Constitution, Article IV, Section 2.

66. See DeLombard, *Shadow*, 51; Phan, *Bonds of Citizenship*; Kettner, *Development*; and Bradburn, *Citizenship Revolution*. Phan offers insightful readings of the relation between the figure of the bondsman and the Constitution's constructions of citizenship and personhood through the Privileges and Immunities Clause, Article I (Section 2), Article IV (Section 2), and the "migration and importation" clause (11–16).

67. See Bradburn, *Citizenship Revolution*, 260, and Nash, *Forging*, 119. Before the Naturalization Act of 1790, individual states developed their own naturalization policies, all requiring a basic oath of allegiance to that individual state and some minimum residency requirement with benchmarks for acquiring certain rights (office holding and voting, for instance). On state-based naturalization acts before the 1789 Constitution and 1790 federal act, see Kettner, *Development*, 213–219.

68. See Bradburn, *Citizenship Revolution*, 260.

69. Before 1861, black citizens held public office, at one point or another, in New Hampshire, Vermont, Ohio, Massachusetts, Rhode Island, and possibly New York. Free blacks voted on the same basis as whites in six states in 1787 (Massachusetts, New Hampshire, New York,

Pennsylvania, New Jersey, and North Carolina). They would later gain the vote in Tennessee, Vermont, Maine, and Rhode Island. Blacks could vote under limited circumstances in Michigan. See "Appeal of Forty Thousand," 136. The "Appeal of Forty Thousand" quotes from the Articles of Confederation and Congress at length:

> The fourth of the said articles contains the following language:—"The free inhabitants of each of these States, paupers, vagabonds, and fugitives from justice excepted, shall be entitled to all privileges and immunities of free *citizens* in the several States." That we were not excluded under the phrase "paupers, vagabonds, and fugitives from justice," any more than our white countrymen, is plain from the debates that preceded the adoption of the article. For, on the 25th of June, 1778, "the delegates from South Carolina moved the following amendment *in behalf of their* State. In article fourth; between the words *free* inhabitants, insert *white.* Decided in the negative; ayes, two States; nays, eight States; one state divided." Such was the solemn decision of the revolutionary Congress, concurred in by the entire delegation from our own commonwealth. (136)

See also Ernest, *Liberation Historiography*, chap. 4.

70. "Appeal of Forty Thousand," 137. The 1837 petitioners also cite the Pennsylvania Supreme Court's 1837 decision in *Fogg v. Hobbs*, which, they note, relied on the "remembrance" of Chief Justice Gibson's father of a supposed court ruling against black suffrage "without a shred of documentation and against over 50 years of actual practice" (137).

71. James McCune Smith, "Citizenship," *AAM* (May 1859), 149 and 147.

72. *Proceedings and Debates*, 685.

73. Ibid., 685–686.

74. Ibid., 686.

75. My argument here builds on Alejandro de la Fuente's work on claims making in nineteenth-century Cuba. As de la Fuente argues, "It was the slaves, as they made claims and pressed for benefits, who gave concrete social meaning to the abstract rights regulated in the positive laws. Through these interactions with colonial authorities and judges, slaves acted (and were seen) as subjects with at least a limited legal standing" ("Slave Law," 341). Throughout this book, I argue that black citizens created the very legal standing denied them when they made their cases to the state. See especially my discussion of circulating citizenship in Chapter 2.

76. *Proceedings and Debates*, 683.

77. For a description of a similar debate around a 1797 group of Philadelphia-based former slaves protesting the 1793 Fugitive Slave Law, see DeLombard, *Shadow*, 127–128. See also Newman, "Protest in Black and White," 181, and Brooks, "Early."

78. David Ramsay, *Dissertation*, 3–4.

79. See Keyssar, *The Right to Vote*, 7–30; Bradburn, *Citizenship Revolution*, 48–49; and Rogers Smith, *Civic Ideals*, 165–167.

80. Bouvier, *A Law Dictionary*, 178–179.

81. Ibid., emphasis added.

82. Bouvier, *A Law Dictionary*, 5th ed., 281.

83. DeLombard similarly tracks additions to Bouvier's definition of "person" from the 1839 edition to the 1856 edition. Among the revisions for 1856, Bouvier restricts the definition,

initially hedging ("man and person are not exactly synonymous terms") and then linking personhood to "the rank he holds in society with all the rights to which the place he holds entitles him, and the duties which it imposes" (*Shadow*, 6–8).

84. See Nelson, *National Manhood*; Theodore Allen, *Invention of the White Race*; Dain, *Hideous Monster*; Jared Gardner, *Master Plots*, 1–24; Kazanjian, *The Colonizing Trick*; Rogers Smith, *Civic*; Roediger, *Wages of Whiteness*; Keyssar, *The Right to Vote*; Weiner, *Black Trials*; Cheryl Harris, "Whiteness as Property"; and Bradburn, *Citizenship Revolution*.

85. See *Crandall v. State* (1834); Rogers Smith, *Civic Ideals*, 257–258; and Weiner, *Black Trials*, 95–115.

86. *Crandall v. State* (1834).

87. Ibid.

88. Welke, *Law and the Borders*, 23.

89. See, for instance, Phan's argument about Douglass's constitutionalism in *Bonds of Citizenship*, 107–127.

90. See Bradburn, *Citizenship Revolution*, especially chap. 7, "White Citizen," 238 and 335–371.

91. See Mills, *Racial Contract*, and Ernest, *Chaotic Justice*, 67.

92. On potential nineteenth-century manifestations of pessimism, see Rusert, "Disappointment."

93. Scholars studying the early republic offer productive frameworks for analyzing this inverse causality. In the context of northern gradual emancipation, Melish invokes the notion of "slaves of the community," the sense that white communities assumed responsibility for free people of color as recompense for emancipation. James Brewer Stewart argues that by the 1830s, the United States was shifting into a racial modernity in which " 'color lines' that had hitherto been so sharply contested around conflicting claims of 'respectability' now had become indelibly drawn" (693). See, for instance, Bradburn, *Citizenship Revolution*, especially chap. 7, "White Citizen," 335–371; Dunbar, *Fragile Freedom*, Kettner, *Development*, 29; Melish, *Disowning Slavery*, 84–118 and "The 'Condition' Debate"; Stewart, "Modernizing 'Difference' "; Mercieca, "Irony"; Freehling, *Road to Disunion*, 450; and Welke, *Borders*, especially chap. 2.

94. Bradburn, *Citizenship Revolution*, 239–240. See also Dunbar, *Fragile Freedom*, 26–47, and Leslie M. Harris, *Shadow*, 96–133.

95. See especially Eric Gardner, *Unexpected Places*, chap. 4.

96. Loughran, *The Republic in Print*, informs my thinking throughout this project about how newspapers and print circulation can reveal fractured and dissonant communities as much as they might suggest or facilitate cohesion.

97. As Martha Jones posits and as I discuss in Chapter 2, "Place matters for any telling of race and citizenship" (*Birthright*, 12).

98. Marrs, *Nineteenth-Century*, 3.

99. My thinking here is informed by Rusert, who invokes disappointment as a way of "understanding freedom's vexed, ambivalent archive" in terms of black writers' frustrations and our own need to acknowledge their limitations ("Disappointment," 27).

100. Nelson, "Representative/Democracy," 224–230; Sklansky, *Soul's Economy*; Foner, *Free Soil*; and Appleby, *Inheriting the Revolution*.

101. Douglass, "The Kansas Nebraska Bill," in *Selected Speeches and Writings*, 299.

102. See Roediger, *Wages of Whiteness*, 119, and Hartman, *Scenes*, 32.

103. On the role of stories in constituting a political body, see Rogers Smith, "Politics of People-Building." Stancliff observes that the "ethical disposition" of enslaved women in particular guided Harper's politics and pedagogy. See Stancliff, *Harper*, 44.

104. See Wong, *Neither Fugitive nor Free.*

Chapter 1

1. "Reply," 28–29. David Walker picks up this same notion of global citizenship in addressing his *Appeal.*

2. "Reply," 29.

3. Jones, Allen, and others were engaged quite deeply in questions of self-governance and representation, as evidenced in the constitution of the Free African Society and their negotiations between the Episcopal and Methodist denominations in the late eighteenth century, and Protestant Christian and republican discourses provided useful vocabularies through which they could navigate these political problems. They formed the FAS in 1787, just a few months before the adoption of the federal constitution, "to support one another in sickness, and for the benefit of their widows and fatherless children." Du Bois famously described it as "more than a mere club" but rather the "the first wavering step of a people toward organized social life" (*Philadelphia Negro*, 19). Though Allen left the FAS in 1787 in part because of the society's increasing adoption of Quaker customs, he again worked with Jones to found the FAC in 1791. The two again parted societal ways when the majority of the FAC voted to affiliate with the Episcopal Church, with Jones remaining with the majority to become bishop of the African Church of Philadelphia at St. Thomas and Allen leading the Methodists to found Bethel Methodist Episcopal Church. See Newman, *Freedom's Prophet*; Winch, *Philadelphia*, 5–7; Nash, *Forging*, 112–133.

While civic republicanism was a more coherent concept than either liberalism or market capitalism by the late eighteenth century, how speakers and writers deployed its concepts was not. My discussion of republicanism in this chapter draws on a long historiography on republicanism from scholars including Gordon Wood, Rogers Smith, Joyce Appleby, and others who suggest that the meanings of these ideas were amorphous, more a "style" of speaking about and organizing social and political interactions than a coherent ideology. Thinking about political discourse in terms of style allows me to attend to how Jones and Allen were molding emergent republican ideals into a more inclusive citizenship practice while remembering Joanna Brooks's caution that we not read early black writers as grafting wholesale dominant discourses. See Gordon S. Wood, *Creation*, v–xiv, and *Radicalism*; Hammer, *Puritan*; Hariman, *Political Style*; Appleby, "Republicanism," 3–34, and *Inheriting the Revolution*; Kloppenberg, "Virtues," 9–33; Rodgers, "Republicanism," 11–38; Rogers Smith, *Civic Ideals*; and Kalyvas and Katznelson, *Liberal Beginnings.*

4. Allen and Jones, *Narrative*. Further references to *Narrative* refer to this imprint.

5. The stance Pratt terms "stranger humanism" was one possibility, based in "the binding strangeness of each to all" (*Strangers Book*, 6). *Narrative* provides a different, or perhaps adjacent, possibility in neighborliness that, like stranger humanism, does not attempt to replace the neighbor through acts of sentimental transfer. Where stranger humanism depends on specialized spaces and conditions and is often fleeting, neighborliness, by contrast, attempts something more lasting. It requires an internal transformation that acknowledges,

through responsiveness, the others encountered in everyday life, whether stranger, friend, or enemy. See ibid., 1–10.

6. "History before the fact," Jehlen explains, "is uncertain, apparently redundant, and contingent; only retrospectively does it take on direction and determination" (690). See Jehlen, "History Before the Fact," 688, 690–691.

7. *Narrative*, 7. *Narrative* is the first publication to be copyrighted by African Americans. See Brooks, *American Lazarus*, 168.

8. *Narrative*, 13. As the fever set in, many observers became aware that descriptions of black immunity were inaccurate, but they continued to promote the idea. Carey may have known as early as October 1793. In a letter possibly addressed to Carey, Rush explained, "The merit of the blacks in their attendance upon the sick is enhanced by their not being exempted from the disorder. Many of them had it, but in general it was much milder and yielded more easily to art than in white people." *Letters*, 29, 731. Other yellow fever narratives also admitted the error. See Lapsansky, "Abigail," 68, and Hogarth, *Medicalizing Blackness*, 17–47.

9. Knott, *Sensibility*, 295; Gould, *Barbaric*, 186–187. The scholarship on sensibility is wide-ranging. My discussion builds on Knott, *Sensibility*; Ellis, *Politics of Sensibility*; Barker-Benfield, *Abigail and John Adams*; and Garber, "Compassion," 15–27.

10. Brooks, Newman, DeLombard, and others have begun working in this direction, rethinking *Narrative* as emerging from an early black print counterpublic constructed "through black-founded, black-governed institutional venues." See Brooks, "Early," para. 21. See also Newman, " 'A Chosen Generation,' " 59–79; Saillant, "Lemuel Haynes," 79–102; the "Black Founders" forum in *William and Mary Quarterly* 64, no. 1 (January 2007); and Sinha, "Alternative," 9–30.

11. Wheatley, "On Being Brought," 5–8, and Banneker, "Copy of a Letter," in Porter, *Early Negro Writings*, 325.

12. Wheatley famously uses this turn rhetorically in "To the Right Honourable William, Earl of Dartmouth." The poem begins with praise for Dartmouth's arrival to quell factional division and to loosen the "iron chain" of "Tyranny" in British North America. Yet the poem turns midway to leverage this praise into a call for action on behalf of enslaved Africans, as the speaker draws a direct line from colonists' use of slavery as a political metaphor to her experience of kidnapping and chattel slavery (21–30). While the poem closes with a standard prayer for Dartmouth's strength in his new duties, this turn changes the nature of the "favours" and duties for which the speaker gives thanks.

13. Brooks, "Early," 87–88.

14. DeLombard, *Shadow*, 136 and 146.

15. See Newman, *Freedom's Prophet*, 107–108. See Jarrett, *Representing*, 21–47, for a longer discussion of Jefferson's *Notes* in relation to the politics of African American literature.

16. Banneker, "Copy of a Letter," 325 and 327.

17. See Pernick, "Politics," 11; and A. Kristen Foster, *Moral Visions*, 132.

18. All references to Carey's *Short Account* refer to the second edition unless otherwise noted both because this is the edition to which Jones and Allen most likely respond and because Carey alters later editions in part because of Jones and Allen's critique. For an extended treatment of Carey's publication history, including *Short Account*, see Griffith, " 'Total Dissolution,' " 45–59.

19. See, for instance, Goddu, *Gothic America*; Robert S. Levine, *Conspiracy and Romance*; Samuels, "Plague and Politics," 225–246; and Pernick, "Politics."

20. Rush, for instance, argues that this belief in a higher power and a "future state" underwrites the virtue that leads to liberty and good republican government: "Without this, there can be no virtue, and without virtue there can be no liberty, and liberty is the object and life of all republican governments." See *Plan*, 15.

21. *Account*, 11.

22. Ibid., 11. As Appleby explains, "Far from pitting merchants against farmers, rich against poor, or the commercially inclined against the self-sufficient, the Jeffersonians assumed that a freely developing economy would benefit all." See Appleby, *Liberalism*, 275.

23. *Account*, 9–10. Carey's "anarchy" resonates with federalists' fear of the spread of anarchy from the French Revolution. See Pernick, "Politics," 120–122.

24. *Account*, 11.

25. Ibid., 11–12. As Foner's discussion of price control in the 1780s suggests, many of these debates focused on merchants or other suppliers' inflating prices in times of scarcity (*Tom Paine*, 146–148).

26. *Account*, 12.

27. Ibid., 30–31.

28. The breakdown of familial ties crystalized the overall absence of "republican affection" during the crisis. The "self-love" that John Adams argued worked outward from self to family to nation turned completely inward. See Wood, *Radicalism*, 219–221.

29. *Account*, 30, 31.

30. Ibid., 31.

31. Carey's rhetoric, for instance, reproduces Publius's warning in *Federalist No. 8* of war between states, the conditions of war between individuals in Philadelphia demonstrating the potential collapse resulting from the absence of a strong federal system (61).

32. Holton, *Unruly*, 23, and 21–54 more generally.

33. *Account*, 78–79.

34. On the "band of brothers" language, see Knott, 294–295, and Otter, 27–28.

35. *Account*, 59.

36. Ibid., 59.

37. Ibid., 59–60.

38. In this discourse, virtue depended on independence from the market and was less concerned with the "private virtues" Carey outlines in *Account*'s opening (e.g., "prudence, frugality, and industry") than the "public virtues": "sacrifice of private desires and interests for the public interest . . . [, and] devotion to the commonweal" (Wood, *Radicalism*, 104). By the end of the eighteenth century, this version of republicanism had been softened to a less demanding standard of politeness or sociability. See Kalyvas and Katznelson, *Liberal Beginnings*, 3, and Ericson, *Shaping*, 3–5.

39. *Account*, 68.

40. Ibid., 95.

41. My reading of Carey is informed by Ed White's caution that we not lose sight of republicanism's "roots in the top-down managerial project of colonization" (*Backcountry*, 9–10). This two-tiered model corresponds with traditions of protective democracy that, as Marinetto explains in "Active Citizen?" "regarded the state as providing a legal and institutional framework that enabled individuals to live ordered lives whilst pursuing their selfish interests in a free market" (105). The active citizen becomes "banished" as governing is separated from the governed, allowing the citizen to pursue his or her own interests more freely.

I use two-tiered civic republicanism rather than "protective democracy" to emphasize its classed and hierarchical nature. See also Held, *Models*, 74.

42. See Wood, *Radicalism*, 189–216; and Foner, *Tom Paine*, 88–93.

43. As Held explains of Madison's logic in the *Federalist Papers*, "The theoretical focus" in this model "is no longer on the rightful place of the active citizen in the life of the political community; it is, instead, on the legitimate pursuit by individuals of their interests and on government as, above all, a means for the enhancement of those interests" (*Models*, 74).

44. Castronovo, *Necro-Citizenship*, 4.

45. *Account*, 54–55.

46. Ibid., 32–33.

47. Ibid., 33.

48. Ibid.

49. Castronovo, *Necro-Citizenship*, 3–5.

50. Ibid., 30–31.

51. Black presence became metonymically linked to white absence such that the former took moral pressure and culpability off of the latter during the fever. See Brooks, *American Lazarus*, 165–166; Gould, "Race," 172; Griffith, "Total Dissolution," 54; and Smith-Rossenberg, "Black Gothic," 252–255.

52. *Account*, 77. The same sentence appears in Carey's fourth edition but with a footnote debunking immunity theories.

53. Ibid., 77–78. See also Lining, *Essays and Observations*, 407. According to Mendelsohn, Benjamin Rush had an earlier copy of Lining's account that was published near the end of the century. See Mendelsohn, "John Lining," 278–292.

54. Hogarth, *Medicalizing Blackness*, 26–27.

55. See Goddu, *Gothic America*, 31–51, for an insightful reading of commerce as "diseased discourse" in the early nation in Charles Brockden Brown's yellow fever novel, *Arthur Mervyn* (1800).

56. Jones and Allen were aware of this tendency in public logic, explaining, "Mr. Carey pays William Gray and us a compliment; he says our services and others of their colour, have been very great &c. By naming us, he leaves these others, in the hazardous state being classed with those who are called the 'vilest' " (*Narrative*, 12–13). Carey's support of abolition, including publishing antislavery essays and works by Phyllis Wheatley and Prince Hall in *The American Museum*, might lead one to temper accusations of outright racism in this moment, but it also serves as a reminder that antislavery and antiblackness could (and often did) go hand in hand. As Lapsansky notes, if we believe that Carey's attempts to praise Jones and Allen individually may have been well intentioned, Carey's text still underwrites a larger negligence: "if the selfless efforts of this unnamed mass of most humble Philadelphians could be minimized and dismissed," Lapsanksy asks, "what hope was there for the wider acceptance of blacks as freemen and citizens?" ("Abigail," 69).

57. See also DeLombard, *Shadow*, 137.

58. See Nelson, "Representative/Democracy," for a discussion of managed democracy (330–332, 348n19) and White, *Backcountry*, 9–10, for how this management operated through republican discourse in the early United States. See also DeLombard, *Shadow*, 40, and Castronovo, *Necro-Citizenship*.

59. See Newman, *Freedom's Prophet*, 87.

60. Wood, *Radicalism*, 216, and Rogers Smith, *Civic Ideals*, 137–164.

61. *Narrative*, 8.

62. My argument builds on Otter's observation about how Jones and Allen "turn Carey's scenario and syntax against him" (*Philadelphia Stories*, 36). *Narrative*'s inversion of Carey's specific syntax provides a useful point of departure for a critique of commercial syntax more broadly.

63. *Narrative*, 7, and *Account*, 76–77.

64. *Narrative*, 7, and *Account*, 10–11.

65. *Account*, 77.

66. *Narrative*, 9.

67. Both white and black workers stood to gain political ground through their efforts during the fever, though neither did, at least not much. Pernick explains, "The white Republican mechanics who served as volunteers were ignored by the city's Federalist elite and were resented by the many voters who had fled, but their political exclusion was less severe than the scornful ingratitude shown to Richard Allen's and Absalom Jones's black followers" ("Politics," 137). Again, my argument here builds on Gould's observation that economic discourse seems to pin Jones and Allen into a corner (*Barbaric*, 186–187); however, as the next section suggests, *Narrative*'s intervention operates on a different register altogether.

68. Appleby, *Liberalism*, 275.

69. Kloppenberg, "Virtues," 22.

70. *Narrative*, 7.

71. Ibid., 8.

72. DeLombard offers a slightly different reading of these accusations in terms of Jones and Allen's use of legal culpability. See DeLombard, *Shadow*, 139–142.

73. The reference to and legal ambiguity of privateering would not have been lost on those of Jones and Allen's readers familiar with Edmond-Charles Genet's privateering activities in Charleston, South Carolina, and Philadelphia and the threat it posed to the United States' policy of neutrality. Moreover, as Otter observers, the allusion also invoked the transatlantic slave trade, expanding "their comparison to include local and systemic violations: the extortion of money and the appropriation of lives" (*Philadelphia Stories*, 37). See Patton, *Patriot Pirates*, xix–xxi, and Bradburn, *Citizenship*, 110.

74. *Narrative*, 8.

75. The letter of marque authorized the nonmilitary vessel to "capture . . . merchant ships belonging to an enemy nation" ("Privateer," *OED*).

76. Gould, "Early," 158.

77. Ibid.," 158, and Gould, *Barbaric*, 186–187. Brooks has argued that Gould's reading here is symptomatic of a larger tendency to ignore how early black writers built their own countercultures and traditions out of their collective experiences of oppression and successes in institution building ("Early"). Otter has argued similarly that Jones and Allen's discourse here was more tactical in nature (*Philadelphia Stories*, 37).

78. Carey, "Address," 5.

79. See Gould, *Barbaric*, and DeLombard, *Shadow*, 136–142.

80. Appleby notes that this protection made self-interest "a functional equivalent to civic virtue" (*Liberalism*, 275).

81. See Littlefield, "Revolutionary," 142–143, and Newman, *Freedom's Prophet*, 34.

82. Benezet, *Observations*, 4.

83. In February 1793, President George Washington signed the Fugitive Slave Act, creating a means for enforcing the constitutional right of slave owners to recover their "property." See also the Naturalization Law of 1790 and the Militia Act of 1792. See Bradburn, *Citizenship Revolution*, 260, and Nash, *Forging*, 119.

84. "Petition of Absalom Jones," in Porter, *Early Negro Writings*, 330–331. Congress overwhelmingly resolved to condemn the petition. See Bradburn, *Citizenship*, 254, and *Annals of Congress*, 6th Cong., 1st sess., House of Representatives, 229–245.

85. *Narrative*, 12, 11.

86. On the history of the FAS and FAC and an account of Allen's business ventures, see Newman, *Freedom's Prophet*; Winch, *Philadelphia*, 4–25; Nash, *Forging*, 112–133; Campbell, *Songs of Zion*; George, *Segregated Sabbaths*; Glaude and West , "Introduction," xi–xxvi; and Glaude, "Black Church," 338–365.

87. DeLombard has similarly noted that *Narrative* lays bare the "illegibility of textual performances of black virtue" (*Shadow*, 41).

88. See Haskell, "Capitalism," 156–160.

89. Nash, *Race and Revolution*, 75.

90. Saillant's reading of Lemuel Haynes's politics and theology informs the way I am reading Jones and Allen's *Narrative*. Saillant reads Haynes as combining theology with natural rights discourse to argue for black liberation and political equality more broadly. See Saillant, "Lemuel Haynes," 79–102. My use of "narrative formula" builds on Brooks, "From Edwards to Baldwin," 428. I find the term useful in this context because *Narrative* uses the parable's overall structure and tenor without explicitly referring to it. Jones and Allen's audience would have readily recognized such a narrative formula. See also Nash, *Race and Revolution*, 75, and Newman, *Transformation*. Both offer a discussion of the role that religious doctrine and the church played in African American intellectual and activist history.

91. *Narrative*, 3, 10. The word "sensible" or "sensibility" appears at least five times in *Narrative*'s first pages. *Narrative* cites sensibility as the motivation for responding to Mayor Clarkson's call for assistance and advertising their services in newspapers. The elders of the FAC join the relief efforts because they were "sensible" of their duty; later in *Narrative*, they reiterate the point: "Our services were the production of real sensibility;—we sought not fee nor reward, until the disorder rendered our labour so arduous that we were not adequate to the services we had assumed," and black citizens on the street show "more humanity, more real sensibility" than their white counterparts. See *Narrative*, 3, 4, 5, 10.

92. *Narrative*, 10–11.

93. *Account*, 32–33.

94. Ibid., 32–33.

95. *Narrative*, 11.

96. Ibid., 11.

97. Ibid., 18–19.

98. Ibid., 18.

99. Ibid., 4 (emphasis added).

100. The gentleman's reaction reflects the intermixture of two concepts: Adam Smith's logic of sympathetic identification and Edmund Burke's sense of a "natural order" structured through "decidedly theatrical and hierarchical relations." See also Julia Stern's discussion of

Adam Smith's "liberal idea that sympathy involves a dedicated imagination of the plight of the other, an act of fancy that allows both identification and compassionate transport" (*Plight*, 6–7). Stern suggests that the early American novel reflected the culture, mixing this Smithian logic with Burkean conservatism (6).

101. *Narrative*, 10.

102. Benezet, *Observations*, 92.

103. Ibid.

104. Ibid.

105. *Narrative*, 10.

106. See Ellis, *Politics of Sensibility*, 135–137, for a discussion of how sensibility could become a "specular economic voyeurism" (135) through which a rising middle class could reveal its virtue in benevolence to the "disserving poor" even as it reinscribed the capitalist practices that maintained a permanent underclass. See also Merish's discussion of "sentimental ownership" in *Sentimental Materialism* (3).

107. Phan, *Bonds of Citizenship*, 23.

108. Rush, "Oration," 32. Anthony Ashley Cooper, Third Earl of Shaftesbury, distinguished between the basic "sensible affections" all living creatures possessed and the possibility of virtue in "creatures capable of framing rational objects of moral good" when the "sensible affections" are not aligned. See Shaftesbury, *Characteristics*, 175. As Burstein posits in *Sentimental Democracy*, sensibility "was an important part of politics, at once art and strategy" (10).

109. Benezet, *Observations*, 93.

110. Edwards, *Works*, 539–540.

111. *Narrative*, 3.

112. Dunbar, *Fragile Freedom*, 29.

113. Indeed, the parable's notion of neighborliness is a common source text for *Narrative*, the FAS letter, and Benezet, *Observations*.

114. On inversion as a classic parable trope, see Cooey, *Willing and the Good*, 6.

115. Luke 10:25–27 New King James.

116. Luke 10:29–32 New King James. As Ramsey's work suggests, the parable of the Good Samaritan focuses on "neighbor-love" (rather than love for neighbor) in its attention to the subject loving rather than the identity (or restricting the identity) of the one who is loved (*Basic Christian Ethics*, 92); Waldron, "Good Samaritans," 1060.

117. See Ramsey, *Basic Christian Ethics*, 94. Contemporaneous readers familiar with the biblical narrative would have understood Jews and Samaritans as peoples from different "nations" with deep animosity toward each other. Jonathan Edwards, for instance, explains in "Long-Suffering and Kindness" (1738), "The Jews and Samaritans were bitter enemies one to another, and there was the greatest national enmity between them. . . . The Samaritans and Jews were looked upon by each other as wicked, vile and accursed, and were bitter enemies one to another." See also Edwards, *Works*, 210, 197.

118. Waldron, "Good Samaritans," 1060.

119. As Waldron explains, the parable "supposes that people can see right through the layers of convention, commonality, and difference, and respond directly—as the Good Samaritan responded—to the immediate presence of the person underlying the layers of community" (2000).

120. Burkitt, *Expository Notes*, 253. According to Newman, Allen owned a copy of *Expository Notes* at some point in his life (*Freedom's Prophet*, 116–117). While the first American printings appeared in 1794 and 1796, Allen may have had access to the text before then. Whether or not Allen read Burkitt before he and Jones crafted *Narrative*, however, Burkitt's exposition is representative of broader contemporaneous understandings of the parable.

121. *Narrative*, 5, 3, and 10.

122. Ibid., 3.

123. Delany, *Times Square Red, Times Square Blue*, 198.

124. *Narrative*, 3, 5, 20.

125. See Newman, *Freedom's Prophet*, 87.

126. Vickers, "Competency and Competition," 27–28.

127. As Pratt notes, references to the stranger in Leviticus could work for pro- or antislavery arguments, but both cases suggested a dependent other, not an equal, who was either available for enslavement or an object of sympathetic paternalism (*Stranger's Book*, 52–55). Luke's text and the rereading of the law that provides *Narrative*'s formal model, however, do different work. Jesus' response to the lawyer, rather than reaffirming the stranger-self binary, offers instead a narrative in which strangerhood is both given and irrelevant.

128. *Narrative*, 11.

129. Edwards, *Works*, 210.

130. At the same time, her request of a meal at some later point gestures toward black women's precarious position in gradual emancipation. See Dunbar, *Fragile Freedom*, 27.

131. Paine, *Rights of Man* in *Common Sense*, 279. Vickers notices a similar framework in his analysis of the early national backcountry: "On the one side, by calling on each neighboring family for unpaid help, the owner admitted that he could not survive by self-interested negotiation alone. And on the other, by voluntarily lending a hand—not only to the owner but to everyone assisting—the neighbor made quietly but in common view a simple gift to all" (27–28). These neighbors, as in Crevecoeur's account of Andrew and the "neighborhood frolic" to raise his house, literally make a neighborhood as they help each newcomer build a home and help each other over the course of the year. See Crevecoeur, *Letters*, 80–82.

132. Neighbor-love, as Ramsey observes, is not the same as the universal "love of humanity" because "it begins by 'loving the neighbor,' not mankind or manhood" (95). Ramsey goes so far as to posit, "Neighbor-love . . . stands at an opposite pole from love for mankind generally" (95) in its emphasis on the neighbor-before-us. See *Basic Christian Ethics.*

133. "Reply," 28.

134. Caroline Levine applies "affordance" to literature to describe the "potentialities [that] lie latent—though not always obvious—in aesthetic and social arrangements" (*Forms*, 6–7).

135. See DeLombard, *Shadow*, 149–150, for a similar discussion of contractualism in Johnstone's "Address."

136. Manisha Sinha traces "Golden Rule" references to Quaker antislavery writings from as early as 1657. Almost two hundred years later, the masthead for the *Liberator* from May 1850 forward would be an image with the banner: "Thou Shalt Love Thy Neighbor as Thyself." See Sinha, *Slave's Cause*, 13; Benezet, *Observations*, 2.

137. Sharpe, *Just Limitation*, 40–41.

138. Banneker, "Copy of a Letter," 325.

139. Ibid., 325.

140. Ibid. Here, I draw on Waldron's observation about the relation between the parable of the Good Samaritan and Mosaic Law ("Good Samaritans," 1060). Just as being the good neighbor summarizes the central principle of Mosaic Law, neighborliness, as Banneker, Jones, and Allen articulate it, encapsulates the central premise of fellow citizenship. Melish observes a similar connection between benevolence and the nation's responsibility for ameliorating the effects of slavery in Lemuel Haynes's 1801 "The Nature and Importance of True Republicanism." See Melish, "The 'Condition' Debate."

141. *Narrative*, 3.

142. As Otter observes, these appended addresses "underscore the fact that their entire text serves as a demonstration of character and a testament of their own sensibility" (*Philadelphia Stories*, 564–567).

143. Jefferson, *Writings*, 270. For a slightly different account of the "Address's" possible relation to *Notes on the State of Virginia* and Jefferson, see Newman, *Freedom's Prophet*, 107–108. As Newman postulates, it is not hard to imagine either Jones or Allen having Banneker's *Almanac*, printed in Philadelphia, and/or Jefferson's *Notes* in mind if not in hand as they crafted the "Address."

144. See, for instance, Otter, *Philadelphia Stories*, 35; Brooks, *American Lazarus*, 162–166; Gould, "Race," 172; Griffith, "Total Dissolution," 54; Smith-Rossenburg, "Black Gothic," 252–255; and Warner, *Letters*, 166–167.

145. As Newman aptly describes the situation, "African Americans were de facto medical examiners and notaries, telling city authorities about each day's run of dead and ill. For a brief period of time, black Philadelphian's seemed to have real power over white citizens' lives" (*Freedom's Prophet*, 91).

146. *Narrative*, 5.

147. Rush, *An Account*, 113.

148. *Narrative*, 9–10.

149. *Account*, 61.

150. *Narrative*, 9.

151. Ibid.

152. Commenting on the progress of the Free African Church in a 1791 letter to Sharpe, Rush observes, "They [the congregants] have adopted articles and a form of church government (purely republican) peculiar to themselves." See "Rush to Granville Sharp" in *Letters*, 608.

153. See Certeau, *Practice*, 37. We can think of these institutions as tactical positions, "a terrain imposed on it and organized by the law of a foreign power," but of a more permanent and secure position than Certeau suggests in the concept of a "tactic." These institutions were in constant negotiation, if not outright warfare, with racial structures, and though they never supplanted them, they did gain footholds. See also Hartman, *Scenes*, 50–51, and Newman, "'A Chosen Generation,'" 59–79.

154. See Nash, *Forging*, 109.

155. Modifying Fraser's subaltern counterpublics, Squires identifies at least four models of minority engagement with and within the public sphere: enclave, oscillating, counterpublic, and parallel. The oscillating model most directly fits the work Jones and Allen's *Narrative* does on behalf of the free Africans. It "systematically [projects] their previously enclaved ideas

toward the state and wider publics," under conditions in which legal and social barriers, while not completely rigid are still rigorously maintained, allowing only limited and circumscribed incursions. Squires, "The Black Press," 112. See also Miranda, *Homegirls*, 133, and Fraser, "Rethinking," 67–68.

156. Melish, *Disowning Slavery*, 60–61, and *Narrative*, 3.

157. Rush, letter dated October 29, 1793, *Letters*, 731, perhaps in response to Carey's request for information,

158. Jarrett, *Representing*, 37.

159. Jones and Allen would probably have had access to Banneker's pamphlet, which was printed in Philadelphia in 1792. See Newman, *Freedom's Prophet*, 107–108.

160. *Narrative*, 24.

161. Banneker, "Copy of a Letter," 327–328.

162. Ibid.

163. On early national attitudes toward education, especially its Lockean resonances, see Wood, *Radicalism*, 149. On the role of education in the overall efforts of the PAS and Philadelphia's black community, see Nash, *Forging*, 202–211.

164. *Narrative*, 23, and *Writings*, 270.

165. *Narrative*, 23.

166. Jefferson, *Writings*, 265, and *Narrative*, 23.

167. *Narrative*, 3. The two reemphasize their privileged observational position later in the text as they offer detailed descriptions of the symptoms and treatment of yellow fever and their own mortality rate (15–17).

168. Jefferson, *Writings*, 270. "Is the color of the negroes a disease?" Rush asks, in 1792, "Then let science and humanity combine their efforts, and endeavor to discover a remedy for it." See *Observations*, 19. See also, Dain, *Hideous Monster*, 24, and Jordan, *White over Black*, 517–525.

169. Rush, *Plan*, 14.

170. Ibid., 27.

171. Ibid., 14.

172. Dunbar, *Fragile Freedom*, 38–40.

173. *Narrative*, 14.

174. Raboteau has argued that the "Address" suggests that "charity must be institutionalized" (*Fire*, 96). My analysis builds on Raboteau's observation, suggesting that "Address" points toward a more radical program of national structural adjustments.

175. As David Brion Davis put it, "There can be no greater disparity of power than that between a man convinced of his own disinterested service and another man who is defined as a helpless object." As such, "Quaker reformers could not view Negroes as even potentially autonomous beings." Such a perspective short-circuits the neighborly move, as the benefactor never sees the beneficiary as morally equal. See Davis, *The Problem of Slavery*, 254, and Nash, "Absalom Jones," 245.

176. As Nash notes, Philadelphia was ahead of most of the nation in providing for the education of free Africans. See *Forging*, 203–204.

177. Rush, letter dated October 29, 1793, *Letters*, 731, perhaps in response to Carey's request for information.

178. See Phan, *Bonds of Citizenship*, 53–54.

179. White abolitionist attempts to monitor and control growing free black populations fed on and into the linkages between blackness and criminality against which Jones and Allen were writing. At the same time, the Commonwealth of Pennsylvania continued to debate and enact laws hostile to black citizens over the next decades, in part to appease the state's southern neighbors. Proposals in 1813 to sell black criminals into slavery and to require black residents to register with the state, for instance, prompted James Forten to pen his *Series of Letters by a Man of Color* (1813). A declining economy, coupled with an influx of European immigrants, increased both class and racial tensions, leaving black Philadelphians, like many black citizens in the United States, caught in a vice between class and racial oppression. By the 1830s, Philadelphia's black citizens were beset with the threat of violence, poverty, and a solidifying racial ceiling. See DeLombard, *Shadow*, 130–133 and 150–152; Dunbar, *Fragile Freedom*; and Nash, *Forging*, 203–279.

180. See Carey, *Short Account*, 4th ed., 63, and *Short Account*, 5th ed., 68.

181. *Short Account*, 4th ed., 63.

182. Easton, *Treatise*, 51–52, and "Appeal of Forty Thousand Citizens," 140.

183. Otter astutely concludes that Jones and Allen "negotiate stance and limit. Their mixture of bitterness and entreaty, sense of discursive probation, riven audiences, high rhetorical stakes, and concern with black elevation all will be echoed in the mid-nineteenth-century" (Otter, *Philadelphia Stories*, 567–570).

Chapter 2

1. Leon Litwack has argued that the New York "Reform Convention" of 1821 has "come to symbolize the expanded democracy which made possible the triumph of Andrew Jackson seven years later" and helped usher in the age of the common (white) man. See Litwack, *North of Slavery*, 82; Keyssar, *Right*, 54–59; and Nelson, *National Manhood*, 6. On rituals of consensus, see Bercovitch, *Rites*, 132–136, and Isenberg, *Sex and Citizenship*, 15.

2. Shklar, *American Citizenship*, 1.

3. Foner and Walker, introduction to *Proceedings*, xv–xvi. See also Bell, *A Survey of the Negro Convention Movement, 1830–1861*. Anyone interested in the black state conventions should begin with Foner and Walker's collection and the University of Delaware's Colored Convention's Project, *Colored Conventions: Bringing Nineteenth-Century Black Organizing to Digital Life*, http://coloredconventions.org.

4. For key historical accounts of the black state conventions and their place in antebellum black political and intellectual history, see Free, *Suffrage Reconstructed*, 33–54; Higginbotham, *Shades*; Litwack, *North*; Pease and Pease, *They Who Would Be Free*; Field, *Politics*; Swift, *Black Prophets*, 122–128; Leslie M. Harris, *Shadow*; and Wang, "Make," 118–121.

5. "Appeal," 132.

6. Ernest, *Liberation Historiography*, 252.

7. "Convention of the Colored Inhabitants of the State of New York, August 18–20, 1840," in Foner and Walker, *Proceedings*, 1:16, and http://coloredconventions.org/items/show/620. Cited hereafter as NY 1840.

8. Foreman, Patterson, and Casey, "Introduction."

9. As Moore argues of Frederick Douglass's constitutional politics, by exercising their right to sovereignty, the delegates made themselves part of the sovereign people. See Moore, *Constitutional Rights*, 8–10. See also Singh, *Black*, 18–19.

10. Shklar, *American Citizenship*, 2.

11. Welke, *Borders*, 108.

12. Waldstreicher, "Rites," 52.

13. Waldstreicher notes that local parades and similar public rituals emerged as the "very practices of nationalism" through their "reproduction in the press" in the early republic (38).

14. *Cooper & Worsham v. Mayor of Savannah*, 4 Ga. 72 (1848), quoted in Rogers Smith, *Civic Ideals*, 257–258; and Litwack, *North*, 50.

15. The U.S.-Mexican War, European revolutions, and westward expansion forced states, courts, and the federal government to articulate more explicitly policies concerning slavery and the movement of free black people, further codifying whiteness as the defining symbol of citizenship. See Bradburn, *Citizenship Revolution*, 238–240; Litwack, *North*, 82; Nelson, *National Manhood*, 6; and Rogers Smith, *Civic Ideals*, 255–268.

16. See DeLombard, *Shadow*, 30–38 and 51–62.

17. In a reversal of the national trend, Rhode Island extended the franchise to black men in 1843. For more on the elective franchise in northern states, see Field, *Politics*; Leslie M. Harris, *Shadow*; Higginbotham, *Shades*; Keyssar, *Right*; Litwack, *North*; Malone, *Between*; Pease and Pease, *They Who Would Be Free*; Quarles, *Black Abolitionists*; Rogers Smith, *Civic Ideals*; Wang, "Make"; Weiner, *Black Trials*; and Nicholas Wood, "'Sacrifice,'" 75–106.

18. See, for instance, *Crandall v. State of Connecticut*; Rogers Smith, *Civic Ideals*, 257–258; and Weiner, *Black Trials*, 95–115.

19. On the ongoing friction between groups within the national convention movement, see Rael, *Black Identity*; Litwack, *North*; Quarles, *Black Abolitionists*; and Pease and Pease, "Conventions." Each of these works to some degree argues that the many ideological and personal differences between would-be black leaders undermined any attempt at organizing the black population nationally. At the same time Leslie Alexander notes that conflicts over support of William Lloyd Garrison and the American Antislavery Society also made organizing on the national level difficult, if not impossible, in the 1840s (*African or American*, 113–114). Intrastate differences between activists, including Garnet and McCune Smith, did not necessarily disappear just because the spatial scale was smaller; indeed, they often intensified, as when Garnet and Smith's dispute over the Liberty Party threatened to dismantle New York's convention movement in the mid-1840s. See Foner and Walker, *Proceedings*, 2; "State Convention of the Colored Citizens of New York," in *Proceedings*, 32–36.

20. New Jersey joined Pennsylvania in disenfranchising black citizens in 1844. See Foner, *Free Soil*, 261; Keyssar, *Right*, 43–49; and Pease and Pease, *They Who Would Be Free*, 189–191.

21. See Alexander, *African or American*, chap. 4; Leslie M. Harris, *Shadow*, 97–101; and Hodges, *Root*, 190–202. See Dunbar, *Fragile Freedom*; Nash, *Forging*; and Nash and Soderlund, *Freedom*, for parallel examinations of gradual emancipation in Pennsylvania.

22. The Constitution of the Commonwealth of Pennsylvania, Article 3, Section 1. These requirements remained until the ratification of the Fifteenth Amendment. The previous 1790 constitution made the franchise available to "every freeman, of the age of twenty-one years" who met the residency and tax requirements. See Winch, "Free Men"; Nicholas Wood, "'Sacrifice,'" 75–106; and the 2008 special issue of *Pennsylvania Legacies* on "The Democratic Promise: Suffrage in Pennsylvania."

23. When William Howard Day argued that the Constitution was the "foundation of American liberties" during an exchange at the 1851 State Convention of the Colored Citizens of Ohio, for instance, H. Ford Douglas quipped, "The gentleman may wrap the stars and

stripes of his country around him forty times, if possible, and with the Declaration of Independence in one hand, and the Constitution of our common country in the other, may seat himself under the shadow of the frowning monument of Bunker Hill, and if the slaveholder, under the Constitution, and with the 'Fugitive Bill,' don't find you, then there don't exist a Constitution." See Foner and Walker, *Proceedings*, 262, and http://coloredconventions.org/items/show/249.

24. "State Conventions," *CA*, September 12, 1840.

25. "The Right of Suffrage in Pennsylvania," *CA*, March 13, 1841, reprinted in Stuckey, *The Ideological Origins of Black Nationalism*, 147.

26. See, for instance, Absalom Jones, "The Petition of the People of Colour," in Porter, *Early Negro Writings*, 330–333; and Forten, "Letter Addressed to . . . the Honourable George Thatcher" (1799)), in Porter, *Early Negro Writings*, 333–334, and "Series of Letters from a Man of Colour" (1813), in Newman, Rael, and Lapsanksy, *Pamphlets of Protest*, 66–74.

27. One such justification was Chief Justice Gibson's father's "remembrance" of a supposed court ruling against black suffrage. See "Appeal of Forty Thousand," 132–142.

28. I suspect that New Yorkers held conventions so often during this short period in part because the balance of political power between ostensibly prosuffrage Whigs and antisuffrage Democrats was always in flux and also because New York State held a constitutional convention in 1846. The New Yorkers did not hold a convention between 1845 and 1850, probably due to a combination of the 1846 state constitutional convention in New York, which resulted in a public vote in favor of upholding the $250 property requirement, and growing division between leading activists over participation in and endorsement of political parties.

29. While some conventions were open to the public or allowed participants to sign in on site, others required delegates to submit credentials, proving their participation in the local nomination process. The CCP has developed several fascinating exhibits tracing newspaper coverage of the conventions. See coloredconventions.org.

30. See, for instance, "A Call," *CA*, June 6, 1840.

31. The 1849 Ohio state convention met in the Hall of the House of the Representatives in Ohio, spatially linking their activities to the official state government. See "Minutes and Address of the State Convention of the Colored Citizens of Ohio, Convened at Columbus, January 10th, 11th, 12th, and 13th, 1849," in Foner and Walker, *Proceedings*, 218–240, and http://coloredconventions.org/items/show/247.

32. The organizers of the 1840 New York convention, for instance, refuted claims that they were racially exclusive by pointing out that anyone (white or black) could attend the convention, but only black citizens could be delegates, because the convention was designed to treat issues specific to black citizens. "The Convention," *CA*, June 27, 1840.

33. Ibid.

34. These proceedings appeared in whole or in part in black and abolitionist papers, including *CA*, *NASS*, *PF*, *NS*, *The Impartial Citizen*, and *Northern Republic* (Pennsylvania).

35. Where other conventions, particularly those of the American Anti-Slavery Society, featured copious speeches from individual members, printed over several weeks in the *NASS* and the *Liberator*, the early black state conventions seldom recorded addresses other than those sanctioned by the conventions.

36. The 1840 New York convention, for instance, sold pamphlets for one dollar per dozen out of the office of the *CA* in New York City. Charles B. Ray delayed reprinting the proceedings in the *CA* until those pamphlets had nearly sold out. See NY 1840, 7.

37. See, for instance, "Minutes of the State Convention of Colored Citizens of Pennsylvania, Convened at Harrisburg, December 13–14, 1848," in Foner and Walker, *Proceedings*, 125, and http://coloredconventions.org/items/show/241; and "Minutes and Address," 265; and http://coloredconventions.org/items/show/249.

38. The *CA*, for instance, records a series of smaller public meetings taking place in Manhattan and the surrounding boroughs where groups passed resolutions in approbation of the state convention's resolutions and passed form petitions. See *CA*, November 21, 1840; December 5, 1840; December 19, 1840; and December 12, 1840.

39. See Fliegelman, *Declaring Independence*, 144–151.

40. A notable exception to this trend was the 1854 National Emigration Convention. About 40 percent of recognized delegates were women, and Mary E. Bibb (wife of Henry Bibb) served as the convention's second vice president. "Proceedings of the National Emigration Convention," http://coloredconventions.org/items/show/314, and "To Stay or to Go? The National Emigration Convention of 1854," *Colored Conventions*, http://coloredconventions.org.

41. See, for instance, Harry Lewis, "'A Good Boarding Home.'"

42. The 1840 New York convention put the request this way: "We call upon that portion of the people whose influence is tender, gentle, and benign—we call upon the women," thus reinforcing normative gender assumptions (NY 1840, 22).

43. "Proceedings of the Colored National Convention, held in Franklin Hall, Sixth Street, Below Arch, Philadelphia, October 16th, 17th and 18th, 1855," in Bell, *Minutes*, 18, http://coloredconventions.org/items/show/281.

44. Waldstreicher notes a similar reciprocity between public performance and print in his study of early American nationalism. See "Rites," 41–42.

45. Field, *Politics*, 4.

46. See Leslie M. Harris, *Shadow*, 222. The petition drives began in 1837 and continued throughout the 1840s. Initially led by Charles B. Ray and Philip Bell, the drive generated a Standing Corresponding Committee of "colored young men" that expanded to the New York Association for the political Elevation and Improvement of the People of Color by 1839 and ultimately resulted in the New York State convention movement.

47. This committee included a who's who of established and up-and-coming black activists: Alexander Crummell, J. Sharp, Theodore S. Wright, Patrick H. Reason, Charles B. Ray, and Charles Lenox Remond.

48. When they appeared in the *CA*, the addresses were separated by about a month, with the address to colored citizens appearing on November 21, 1840, and the address to the state appearing on December 19, 1840.

49. Field reports that between 1837 and 1842, "the legislature received equal suffrage petitions from blacks in New York, Albany, Oneida, Dutchess, Erie, Onodaga, Schenectady, Orange, Queens, and Rensselaer counties among others" (45). See also Pease and Pease, *They Who Would Be Free*, 182–186.

50. Swift reports that the petition carried 2,093 signatures, a significant increase from the 620 collected in 1837. Garnet was invited to speak before the judiciary committee on February 18, 1841, and left confident he'd won them over, writing to the *CA* on March 13, "The God of Israel has written with his omnipotent finger upon our future prospects, those all-glorious words:—'*Hold up your heads, ye wronged and injured people, for victory is declared unto you*,'"

only to see the provision voted down (forty-six to twenty-nine) that April. Swift, *Black Prophets*, 125–127, and *CA*, March 13, 1841.

51. NY 1840, 20.

52. As Rogers Smith observes in the context of the *Crandall* ruling, states increasingly separated democratic citizenship from "political self-governance," instead insisting "citizenship had multiple classes, with only the most fortunate or worthy receiving full political privileges." Rogers Smith, *Civic Ideals*, 256. See also Bradburn's denization thesis in *Citizenship Revolution*, 335–371.

53. See Melish, *Disowning Slavery*, especially chap. 3. Douglass uses the phrase in his address to the 1848 National Colored Convention to describe the status of free black people in the putatively "free" states as having been transferred from individual ownership to community ownership (Melish, *Disowning Slavery*, 86). See also Dunbar, *Fragile Freedom*, 26–37, for a discussion of indentured servitude as a manifestation of this principle.

54. See Rogers Smith, *Civic Ideals*, 256–257.

55. NY 1840, 22. In the face of an individualizing market landscape that fostered competition more than fellow feeling, Nelson argues, the expansion of political entitlement bound white "men together in an abstract but increasingly functional community that diverted their attention from differences between them" (*National Manhood*, 6).

56. NY 1840, 20.

57. DeLombard, *Shadow*, 30.

58. NY 1840, 27.

59. Like the *Federalist Papers*, the New York convention's "Addresses" engage with developing theories of energy and power. See Kesler, "Introduction," xvii. See also Fritz, *American Sovereigns*, 236–247, for a discussion of collective sovereignty, especially in the right to "alter, reform or abolish" their government.

60. In water rights law, moving water belongs to no one (*res nullius*), belongs to the whole community (*res communes*), or is under public control (*res publica*). Even when an individual gains rights to the water for a particular purpose, it is only a "usufructory" right, contingent on that individual not wasting the resource or otherwise making it unusable for others. See Vanoni, *Sedimentation Engineering*, 378, and Anthony Scott, *Property Rights*, 63–70.

61. NY 1840, 20.

62. Then mayor of New York City, Dewitt Clinton, describes the canal in 1825 as "a bond of union between the Atlantic and Western states . . . an organ of communication between the Hudson, the Mississippi, the St. Lawrence, the Great Lakes of the north and west and their tributary rivers" that would "create the greatest inland trade ever witnessed." Clinton, quoted in Turner, *Rise of the New West*, 21.

63. NY 1840, 22.

64. As Quarles put it, "The central paradox of white American society was to think equality but to practice inequality—a succession of English monarchs had been replaced by an equally divine-right aristocracy of skin color" ("Antebellum," 229).

65. NY 1840, 10. This petition was drafted by a committee led by Patrick L. Reason, ratified by the convention as a whole, and circulated to statewide auxiliaries along with the proceedings and addresses.

66. NY 1840, 16.

67. Ibid., 16.

68. Ibid., 16.

69. Ibid., 18.

70. While New York Whigs argued to keep the property requirement for all male citizens, the more popular Democrat Party argued for universal white male suffrage. Democrats excluded black men from the suffrage in part because black voters had historically supported Whig candidates, in some places, including New York City, tipping the electoral balance. They also expressed fear that black concentrations in some districts would allow them to carry these districts entirely. Such power would inevitably result in black men running for office and participating in jury trials, which would be a "gross insult" to "southern gentleman" visiting the state with their slaves. Still others invoked white supremacy explicitly, claiming that the state's and the nation's institutions were created by and for white men and that only white men were capable of participating in them. As John G. Ross of Genesee County argues,

> all men are free and equal . . . applies to them only in a state of nature, and not after the institution of civil government; for then many rights, flowing from a natural equality, are necessarily abridged, with a view to produce the greatest amount of security and happiness to the whole community. On this principle the right of suffrage is extended to white men only.

Ross supports this exclusion by claiming that black men do not contribute significantly to the state's "common burthens" but rather exist in the same state of "dependency" as women and children. Similar arguments ignored black participation in the Revolutionary War and the War of 1812 as well as black contributions to the state's tax base. See *Reports of the Proceedings* (1821), 180–181, and *Report of the Debates* (1846), 777–786.

71. NY 1840, 18.

72. In 1848, the Pennsylvania convention would articulate this reversal more directly: that state's constitutional convention "assum[ed] *condition* as their reason, and *complexion* as the *standard*." See PA 1848, 128.

73. On the "Condition" debates, see Melish, "The 'Condition' Debate," and Rael, *Black Identity*, 193–200.

74. NY 1840, 18.

75. Ibid., 16.

76. Ibid., 18. The delegates extend this reasoning in their 1845 "Address to the People of the State of New York," arguing that the property clause has deprived them of "their check upon oppression, their wherewith to buy friends, their panoply of manhood—in short, they are thrown upon the mercy of a despotic majority." NY 1845, 39.

77. NY 1840, 22.

78. Ibid., 20.

79. Ibid., 20.

80. Rossiter, *Federalist Papers*, 92–93. As Kesler explains, the language of mathematics and physics pervaded the *Federalist*'s attempt to delineate the powers and necessities of a strong Federal Constitution. The New York convention uses this same language to outline the state government's responsibilities to all of its citizens, regardless of race. See Kesler, "Introduction," xvii.

81. NY 1840, 18.

82. Ibid., 19.

83. This rhetoric of fulfillment aligns with Bercovitch's analysis of the rhetoric of errand and the revolution as "the unfolding of a redemptive plan" that, in the hands of the Federalists and others, translated into continuing revolution as a ritual of consensus that reaffirmed rather than threatened national identity and stability or at least their ability to manage them. See Bercovitch, *Rites*, 37–49.

84. Augustine, "The Right of Suffrage in Pennsylvania," *CA*, March 13, 1841, in Stuckey, *Ideological Origins*, 146–148.

85. As Wilentz and others demonstrate, this brand of democratic practice developed in the messy back-and-forth between local, territorial, state, and national institutions, not as a necessarily coherent, coordinated movement as such. See White, *Backcountry*; Wilentz, *Democracy*; and Holton, *Unruly*.

86. The Dorrite Conventions or "Dorr War" of 1841 to 1842 and their proposed "People's Constitution" provide a potent example of these movements' potential. Isenberg cites the Dorrite Convention as installing "the convention as a new kind of public and political forum and, perhaps for the first time, [sanctioning] revolution as a constitutional rather than a natural right" (14). See also Formisano, *People*, 164–165, and Fritz, *American Sovereigns*, 246–276.

87. Isenberg, *Sex and Citizenship*, 16.

88. Ingersoll argued against entering the "Appeal of Forty Thousand Citizens" (1837) into the convention's official record because, he argued, citizens instructed their representatives; citizens did not petition or make requests of them. See *Proceedings and Debates*, 687.

89. Historians and political scientists alike have identified the inverse relation between the two. Rogers Smith, for instance, has argued that disenfranchising black men made universal white manhood suffrage possible. As Patrick Rael puts it, "In a sense, blacks paid the price for the white working class's political participation" (*Black Identity*, 202). Perhaps most dramatically, the "Dorr War" was defeated partially because the Dorrites refused black support, prompting Douglass, Garrison, and other antislavery activists to denounce the People's Constitution as a whole. The Rhode Island establishment enfranchised these same citizens, who then tipped the balance of power in their favor. The resulting political climate continued into the twentieth century as what Formisano describes as a "limited, oligarchic republicanism." Other states would use Rhode Island's strategy to justify maintaining racially exclusive voting laws. See Formisano, *People*, 164–165, 173.

90. See Isenberg, *Sex and Citizenship*, xiv, and Rogers Smith, *Civic Ideals*, 167. It might be useful here to think about these conventions in light of Fliegelman's work on the Declaration of Independence. For Fliegelman, the Declaration operates as both "the description of independence as the necessary consequence of [King] George's actions and the document's own status as a performative utterance." It is both "aggrieved narration and a proclamation of rights." Similarly, the state conventions are both a narrative of citizenship rights lost, of citizenship lost, and a performance of citizenship—a claim that citizenship rights are inherent to all men, yet a performance in need of affirmative judgment to take effect. See Fliegelman, *Independence*, 151.

91. NY 1840, 6. In some ways, the onlookers' approval mirrors tensions between narratives by formerly enslaved people and the paratextual documents surrounding them.

92. For more on the distinction between deliberative and persuasive models of civil society, see Brooke, "Consent," 207–250.

93. NY 1840, 6. Swift has read Whig politicians' regular attendance as a sign of respect. I agree with Swift in the sense that the convention provided an opportunity like no other for spectators of all stripes to see black citizens in their political element. Ray's comments, however, also suggest that black delegates felt the institutionally imposed differences even if the white attendees did not. See Swift, *Black Prophets*, 124.

94. As Isenberg argues of conventions in general and minority conventions specifically, "The conventions had a decidedly performative, staged, and theatrical quality" (*Sex and Citizenship*, 213n10).

95. McCune Smith eventually attended the 1841 convention as a delegate from New York City in accordance with his popular nomination. See McCune Smith, "Reviving the Black Convention Movement," 345–351, and "Position Defended," *CA*, August 15, 1840. Smith most likely penned this letter because the *CA* did not print his remarks in opposition to the convention in two previous meetings. See Ripley, *BAP*, 3:349n1. For a detailed account of these tumultuous meetings and competing organizations such as Thomas Van Rensellaer and David Ruggles's American Reform Board, see Alexander, *African or American?* 103–113, and Pease and Pease, *They Who Would Be Free*, 175–182.

96. *CA*, February 6, 1841. Sterling Stuckey has collected Whipper's letters with a series of responses by "Sidney" in Appendix 2, *Ideological Origins*.

97. See, for instance, "Fifteen Thousand Negro Balance-of-Power-Men Wanted, by the Whigs and Abolitionists!" reprinted in *NASS*, October 9, 1845.

98. "William Whipper's Letters No. 4," *CA*, February 13, 1841. See also Stuckey, *Ideological Origins*, 161.

99. "Samuel Ringgold Ward to Nathaniel Press. Rogers," *BAP*, 341.

100. Ibid. (emphasis added). Ward's "different medium" is a particularly apt description of how this debate positioned *Standard* against the *CA*, the major publications through which it occurred. The debate over the convention coincides with a changing of the guard at the *CA* as editorial duties shifted from Cornish to Ray and provided an opportunity for Ray to assert the paper's new direction even as he and others used the paper to frame the convention's public presence. He installs the paper as a watchdog (and preserver of black rights of oversight) over antislavery activism. See Eric Gardner, *Unexpected Places*, 5, and "Early African American Print Culture," 78–79, for another account of how black editors could leverage conventions to bolster a paper's legitimacy.

101. See Cheryl Harris, "Whiteness as Property," 276–291.

102. "Colored Convention," *NASS*, June 18, 1840.

103. "The Convention," *CA*, June 27, 1840. In a more instrumental sense, black activists could never showcase their own political acumen through these organizations because whites "will always form the majority of such Conventions, and the sentiments and opinions thus promulgated will go forth as the sentiments and opinions of white men." Over ten years later, William J. Wilson would describe a similar scene of a "hungry white crowd . . . so large that the black specs pass[ed] unobserved by the chiefs in command" (*Frederick Douglass's Paper*, April 15, 1853, quoted in Pease and Pease, *They Who Would Be Free*, 80). See also "The National Anti-Slavery Standard vs. The Convention," *CA*, July 11, 1840.

104. "The Convention."

105. See Rogers Smith, "Citizenship," 73–75.

106. Each juncture was judged by its adherence to formal cues that resemble Hariman's account of a republican style: "the manners of legislative address, seating, and the like . . .

refraining from violence, recognizing social status, observing parliamentary customs, and acting as if oneself and one's opponents always were motivated at least in part by civic virtue and the duties of public office" (122–123). See Hariman, *Political Style*, 122–123. On conventions' theatricality, see Isenberg, *Sex and Citizenship*, 213n10.

107. NY 1840, 6.

108. Ibid., 10.

109. Ibid., 12.

110. Schoenfield uses institutional heteroglossia to describe how the British periodical press managed identities by "[consolidating] distinct authorial voices into single corporate, authoritative voices" through editorial framing such that the speaker's identity was always "entwined" with the periodical's institutional structure. Because of this entanglement within the system of the bound periodical, "the periodical article—the language of which was often borrowed from prior texts, quoted from contemporary ones under review, and echoed from one article to the next—was institutionally heteroglossic" (*British Periodicals*, 3, 36–37). See also Bakhtin, *Dialogic Imagination*, 314.

111. "Mrs. Sanford's Speech."

112. NY 1840, 20.

113. "Report of the Proceedings of the Colored National Convention held at Cleveland, Ohio, on Wednesday, September 6, 1848," in Foner and Walker, *Proceedings*, 12, http://coloredconventions.org/items/show/280.

114. Peterson, *Doers*, 101.

115. "Colored Men's State Convention of New York, Troy, September 4, 1855," in Foner and Walker, *Proceedings*, 91, http://coloredconventions.org/items/show/238. On this moment, see Free, *Suffrage Reconstructed*, 42–43, and Peterson, *Doers*, 101–103.

116. As the CCP continues its recovery, transcription, and dissemination work, I suspect more moments like these will surface.

117. OH 1849, 227.

118. Ibid., 231.

119. "Mrs. Sanford's Speech."

120. Yellin, *Harriet Jacobs: A Life*, 102–103.

121. In Cary's case, at least some of the opposition might have risen from her advocacy of immigration to Canada and her participation in the 1854 Emigration Convention in Ohio. That said, her gender and some delegates' sense of the impropriety of her participation were almost certainly the central point of contention.

122. Rhodes gives an account of Cary as a delegate in *Shadd Cary*, 109–110. See also Walker, "Promoting," 280–318. Both include Cary, but both also count only two women delegates: Rhodes mentions Cary and Cliff, while Walker mentions Cary and Armstrong. The minutes list all three.

123. Wilson addressed the letter to "My Cousin M.," perhaps a reference to his wife, Mary Wilson, who was a prominent Brooklyn entrepreneur and who Ethiop mentions obliquely in several sketches.

124. "Fancy Sketches Number II," 384.

125. "Proceedings of a Convention of the Colored Men of Ohio, Held in the City of Cincinnati, on the 23d, 24th, 25th and 26th days of November, 1858," in Foner and Walker, *Proceedings*, 334, 340–341, http://coloredconventions.org/items/show/254.

126. Ward reprinted the 1848 appeals almost a year later in *Impartial Citizen* (December 5, 1849) with an article on "Progress Among Colored Men" amid a spirited debate with Douglass over the pro- or antislavery nature of the U.S. Constitution and the need for explicitly political activism.

127. This committee of seven included Whipper, Abraham Shadd (Mary Shadd's father), J. F. Dickson, J. J. G. Bias, Robert Purvis, M. W. Gibbes, and Samuel Van Brakle. Ironically, Whipper, who opposed the first New York convention of colored citizens because of its "complexional" nature, was a key member of the 1848 convention in Pennsylvania. From as early as the 1838 constitutional change in Pennsylvania, Whipper's political outlook had begun to shift. See Otter, *Philadelphia Stories*, 107–123, particularly his reading of the striking resemblances between the 1848 convention's "Appeal to the Colored Citizens" and Whipper's writing in 1839.

128. "Appeal, v.," *OED Online.*

129. PA 1848, 126.

130. Ibid., 126. In contrast to the AASS's denial of the Constitution's legitimacy, the "Appeal" uses the Constitution's guarantee of a republican government to measure the validity of Pennsylvania's franchise clause.

131. PA 1848, 123. See Nobles and Schiff, "The Right to Appeal," 676–701.

132. In *Republic of the Dispossessed*, Berthoff explains the transaction this way: "Suffrage had never been a universal right, New York and Wisconsin lawyers recalled in 1846, correctly enough, but literally a franchise, 'a privilege . . . to be conceded by all the citizens of a country to those who will exercise it best, for the common interest of all.'" "On that principle," Berthoff continues, "the New York conventions of both 1846 and 1867–1868 left the decision on enfranchisement of all black men to a referendum among the 'sovereign people'—who soundly rejected it" (163).

133. PA 1848, 127.

134. Ibid., 127.

135. This definition of "Appeal" is based on the 1839 usage in the *OED*: 1. To call (one) to answer before a tribunal; in Law: To accuse of a crime which the accuser undertakes to prove. spec. a. To impeach of treason. b. To accuse an accomplice of treason or felony. c. To accuse of a heinous crime whereby the accuser has received personal injury or wrong, for which he demands reparation.

136. PA 1848, 123.

137. Ibid., 123.

138. Ibid., 124.

139. Ibid. In referencing the recent U.S.-Mexican War in particular, the "Appeal" works its own bit of revisionist history. Where common antislavery discussions tended to read the war as a sign of the virulent expansion of the slave power, the "Appeal" appropriates the prowar rhetoric in order to invoke the nationalism upon which it fed.

140. The delegates' use of pronouns prefigures Douglass's famous invocation of "your nation" set against "fellow citizens" in his July 5, 1850, "Oration." See Douglass, "Oration," in *Selected Speeches and Writings*, 431.

141. PA 1848, 128.

142. Ibid.

143. As I mention elsewhere, Rhode Island used a similar tactic along nonracial lines when it enfranchised its black citizens.

144. PA 1848, 128.

145. Mills, *Racial Contract*, 53.

146. "Appeal to the Voters," PA 1848, 123. See Bercovitch, *Rites*, 37–49.

147. Ibid., 124. Throughout their arguments, the Pennsylvania delegates' language foreshadows notions of due process articulated in the Fourteenth Amendment.

148. PA 1848, 123.

149. Ibid., 126.

150. Ibid., 124. The "Appeal" may have been alluding to Ingersoll's comments about the "Appeal of Forty Thousand" during the 1837–1838 Pennsylvania constitutional convention. As I mentioned earlier, Ingersoll argued that the "Appeal" should not be taken as a petition from citizens of the state because citizens do not petition; citizens "command." See *Proceedings and Debates of the Convention of the Commonwealth of Pennsylvania*, vol. 3, 687.

151. "Appeal to the Voters," PA 1848, 125.

152. Isenberg, *Sex and Citizenship*, 21.

153. "An Appeal to the Colored Citizens," PA 1848, 127. The black state conventions reveal rising support for Garnet's "Address to the Slave" in the wake of the U.S.-Mexico War. Notably, the 1849 State Convention of the Colored Citizens of Ohio passed a resolution endorsing Garnet's "Address": "*Resolved*, That we still adhere to the doctrine of urging the slave to leave immediately with his hoe on his shoulder, for a land of liberty, and would accordingly recommend that five hundred copies of Walker's Appeal, and Henry H. Garnet's Address to the slaves, be obtained in the name of the Convention, and gratuitously circulated" (229).

154. "Appeal to the Voters," PA 1848, 125.

155. I discuss this document in more detail in Chapter 1.

156. Samuel Otter describes this multimodal feature as a negotiation between "stance and limit" in the context of Jones and Allen's *Narrative*: a "mixture of bitterness and entreaty, sense of discursive probation, riven audiences, high rhetorical stakes, and concern with black elevation" (*Philadelphia Stories*, 40).

157. Delany was a participating delegate at the 1841 State Convention of the Colored Freemen of Pennsylvania, and the 1848 convention made him and Lenox Remond honorary delegates (PA 1848, 124).

158. "Mary Ann Shadd Cary to Frederick Douglass," *North Star*, January 22, 1849, in Ripley, *BAP*, 32.

159. Ibid.

Chapter 3

1. See Leslie M. Harris, *Shadow*, 218.

2. See Robert S. Levine, *Representative Identity*, 5.

3. Here, I draw on two ways of thinking about the intersections of political and aesthetic representation. Dana Nelson uses representivity to signal "the subjective internalization of particular norms of representation," or how citizens come to desire a particular kind of representation. Nadia Urbinati invokes representivity to describe a political relationship of "control (on the part of the represented) and responsibility (on the part of the representatives)" in ways that are "eminently political and moral but not juridical and legal." This last part is important for my discussion of Smith and Wilson because they are looking for models of representation that can confront and circumvent the consolidation of racist state authority.

See Nelson, "Representative/Democracy: The Political Work of Countersymbolic Representation," 218, and "Representative/Democracy: Presidents, Democratic Management, and the Unfinished Business of Male Sentimentalism," 325–328; Urbinati, *Representative Democracy*, 48–50; and Harrison, *Postcolonial Criticism*, 92–103.

4. *FDP*, January 22, 1852.

5. My sense of economic citizenship draws on Nelson's analysis of a developing capitalist citizenship in which "independent, self-interested manhood will be the governing principle for capitalist citizenship, and here economy (or money) rather than familial sentiment" maintains social and political cohesion (46) and Harris's analysis of the shift in black politics in New York over the 1840s, when a new generation (including Garnet, Smith, Wilson, Douglass, and others) turned increasing attention from moral reform models and toward independence from white antislavery and other organizations and forms of economic uplift. See Nelson, *National Manhood*, and Leslie M. Harris, *Shadow*, especially 217–245.

6. Ethiop, "From Our Brooklyn Correspondent," *FDP*, "Correspondent," April 8, 1852. References to Ethiop's correspondences cited hereafter as "E., Date."

7. See Bromell, *Sweat*, 22. As this scholarship suggests, the "market revolution" was not a distinct event but rather serves as a heuristic for thinking through the host of economic, political, and cultural changes brought on through rapid industrialization. Work on the social and economic changes in the United States during these decades is expansive. I draw my understanding of the market revolution as a conceptual framework for interpreting the years between the War of 1812 and the Civil War from Sellers, *Market Revolution*, and Rael, "African Americans, Slavery" and "The Market Revolution." My understanding of class and economic citizenship more broadly draws on Appleby, *Inheriting the Revolution*; Blummin, *Middle Class*; Wilentz, *Chants Democratic*, 14–15; Glickstein, *American Exceptionalism*; Bromell, *Sweat*; Foner, *Free Soil*; Stokes, "Introduction"; and Roediger, *Wages of Whiteness*.

8. As the 1848 convention's "Address to the Colored People" put it, "A little less pride, and a little more industry on [the white employer's] part, may enable him to dispense with our services entirely." "Address to the Colored People," *North Star*, September 22, 1848. On the abolitionist front, black activists censured the Tappans during an 1854 American and Foreign Anti-Slavery Society convention for refusing to hire black clerks, while agents within the National Anti-Slavery Society continually complained that the organization refused to hire black agents for more than lecturing or other lower-level tasks. See Leslie M. Harris, *Shadow*, 226–227, and Litwack, *North*, 156.

9. Litwack, *North*, 158, and Luskey, "Jumping," 185–189.

10. Such was the case when New York City refused to grant black citizens carting licenses in the 1840s. As Harris explains, the city often policed racial boundaries and prevented black workers from more lucrative occupations by not granting them permits to do certain kinds of work and by strictly enforcing punishments for those operating without permits. See Leslie M. Harris, *Shadow*, 217–218, and Litwack, *North*, 154–159.

11. Harris offers an account of a key conflict along these lines around whether or not black waiters should unionize with white waiters for higher wages or if they should remain in black organizations such as Tunis G. Campbell's First United Association of Colored Waiters. See Leslie M. Harris, *Shadow*, 242–245.

12. As Douglass warns in "Learn Trades or Starve," "every hour sees the black man elbowed out of employment by some newly arrived emigrant, whose hunger and whose color

are thought to give him a better title to the place" (*FDP*, March 4, 1853). Leslie M. Harris, *Shadow*; Litwack, *North*, 155 and 162–166; and Foner, *Free Soil*, xviii.

13. Manning Marable explains in *Capitalism Underdeveloped*, "Capitalist development has occurred not in spite of the exclusion of Blacks, but because of the brutal exploitation of Blacks as workers and consumers. Blacks have never been equal partners in the American Social Contract, because the system exists not to develop, *but to underdevelop Black people*" (2).

14. *New York Daily Tribune*, August 25, 1843.

15. Ibid. On "condition" discourse, see Melish, "The 'Condition' Debate," 657–659.

16. Historians have documented a range of ways black communities tried to take advantage of a market that seemed to reward merit and industry indiscriminately, with sporadic success. These attempts, however, were by turns caricatured, threatened with mob violence, and thwarted by official policy, making black workers a base upon which to further clarify the whiteness of economic citizenship. See Litwack, *North*, 184–185; Leslie M. Harris, *Shadow*, especially chaps. 3 and 7 for a particularly salient account of New York; Pease and Pease, *They Who Would Be Free*, especially chap. 7; and Rael, "The Market Revolution." On the cultural demeaning of these attempts, see, for instance, Edward Clay's "Life in Philadelphia" and the "Bobolition" broadsides of the 1820s or Foster's depiction of the Five Points in *New York by Gaslight* from the 1850s. See Lott, *Love and Theft*, and Douglas Jones, *Captive Stage*, for discussions of the connection between the rise of blackface minstrelsy and the increased racial hostility of the white working class toward free blacks in the north along with chap. 4, "The Deepest Dark," of Burns, *Painting the Dark Side*.

17. This point becomes important in my later discussion of Smith's "The Boot-Black" because the sketch links narratives of domesticity and capitalist upward mobility. Scholars of the early nineteenth century have noted that "respectability" developed in response to the uncertainty the market revolution caused. In a social landscape where identities seemed indeterminate, where consumer culture allowed workingmen and women to look the part of gentry without its financial backing, where economic downturns could quickly reverse fortunes, and where opportunities for self-making and deception went hand in hand, protocols of respectability—ways of dress, habits of consumption, displays of thrift and self-control, hard work, and so on—helped make the status of economic citizens visible to each other while cloaking market antagonisms in a sheen of polite, collective striving. Cultures of "respectability" became the means by which this emerging group created and policed its own identity. Glickstein has suggested that U.S. working-class respectability developed not only in contrast to slave labor but also in contrast to "Europe's 'pauper' laborers," emphasizing the "market rewards" available to American workers. See Glickstein, *American Exceptionalism*, 34–35; Appleby, *Inheriting the Revolution*, 21; Rael, "The Market Revolution," 28 and "African Americans, Slavery," 190–193; and Luskey, "Jumping," 173–219.

Scholars have outlined and discussed both the origins of black respectability in white middle-class values and whether this politics signaled assimilation, accommodation, or varying degrees of appropriation. Evelyn Brooks Higginbotham's *Righteous Discontent* continues to be the touchstone for discussions of "bourgeois respectability" in which black elites of the early twentieth century sought to "earn" white approval by attempting to train the masses to adhere to a constellation of "middle-class values" (*Righteous*, 14–15). Even for Higginbotham, however, this dynamic was conflictual and complicated. For a summary of this debate in the antebellum context and the stakes involved for each position, see Rael's introduction to *African American Activism*, 1–38. My own sense is that the meaning of respectability and its relation to the American mainstream varies not only from context to context but also from writer to writer, with aims ranging from political and social inclusion to complete independence. *Freedom's Journal* and the *Colored American*, for instance, admonished black citizens to pursue education, seek moral and economic uplift, and live sober, decorous lives (or to at least present such lives publicly). This emphasis on the salvific of productive labor also led black activists, as other reformists, to advocate for farming and country life as healthier, more affordable, and more in keeping with notions of republican virtue. See Ball, *Antislavery Life*; McDaniel, "The Fourth and the First"; Nyong'o, "Uncommon Memory," 36–72, and *Amalgamation Waltz*, 118–119; White, "'It Was a Proud Day'"; Leslie M. Harris, "Abolitionist Amalgamators," 266–267, and "Black Wealth and the 1843 National Colored Convention."

18. *Report of the Proceedings*, 5 and http://coloredconventions.org/items/show/280.

19. *Proceedings of the Colored National Convention*, 21 and http://coloredconventions.org/items/show/458.

20. *Report* (1848), 5. See Leslie M. Harris, *Shadow*, 218–219.

21. *Report* (1848), 5. Harris's work suggests that Watson's words probably represented the views of more urban black laborers than Delany's, particularly in lieu of the dearth of work of any kind after the 1840s depression and increased competition from European immigrants. In *Condition* (1852), Delany returns to the subject in greater detail with a caveat at the beginning of chap. 23, "A Glance at Ourselves," no doubt tailored to assuage the objections of readers sympathetic to Patterson's point of view: "As an evidence of the degradation to which we have been reduced, we dare premise, that this chapter will give offence to many, very many, and why? Because they may say, 'He dared to say that the occupation of a servant is a degradation'" (200).

22. *Report* (1848), 6.

23. Ibid., 6.

24. Ibid., 13.

25. Leslie M. Harris, *Shadow*, 228–229.

26. "An Address to the Colored People," *Report* (1848), 19.

27. Ibid., 20. Douglass repeats these themes in "Learn Trades or Starve!" (*FDP*, March 4, 1853), suggesting both his role in crafting the 1848 "Address" but also how these conversations affected his own thinking: "Men are not valued in this country, or in any country, for what they *are*, they are valued for what they can *do*." He also uses the same parallelism: "When we can build as well as live in houses; when we can *make* as well as *wear* shoes; when we can produce as well as consume wheat . . . then we shall become valuable to society." By 1853, Douglass focused more on correcting what he saw as a misplaced emphasis on luxury and the appearance of respectability without attending to its material foundations. As I suggest in this chapter, I believe that Smith, Wilson, and others' debate within *Douglass's Paper* helped Douglass refine his own approach.

28. *Report* (1848), 6.

29. Ibid., 19.

30. Ibid., 20.

31. Ibid., 20.

32. Jarrett, *Representing*, 197.

33. Ball, *Antislavery Life*, 2. See also Leslie M. Harris, *Shadow*, 218. My distinction between "respectability" and "respect" attempts to get at how this strategy shifted in emphasis toward independence not only in terms of labor but also independence from tactics of persuasion. I want to separate the cultural cues of respectability from the material power suggested in "respect." They are mutually constitutive but separate issues as my discussion of Communipaw and Ethiop will make clearer.

34. Douglass reveals Smith and Wilson's identities as Communipaw and Ethiop in an 1852 review article: "Fifth Volume," *FDP*, December 17, 1852. See Vogel, "Introduction," 1; Otter, "Philadelphia Experiments," 111; and Peterson, *Black Gotham*, 218. Peterson offers the most comprehensive account of *Douglass's Paper's* pseudonymous correspondents to date. See Peterson, *Black Gotham*, 217–222.

35. Smith was appointed professor of anthropology at Wilberforce College in 1863, though the failing health that led to his death in 1865 prevented him from assuming his duties there. See Blight, "In Search of Learning." See also Rusert, *Fugitive Science*, 51–60, for a discussion of Smith's science writing.

36. See, for instance E., January 8, 1852: "If my picture has its shades, it also has its lights: indeed there are some bright spots, brighter than I can paint them." Communipaw paints "Heads" with a "Whitewash Brush": "a short brush and dry paint," with which he "cannot do these clumsy portraits without spattering some people, as I learn by their squealing" ("The Whitewasher"). That does not mean that there was not a governing order to this seeming chaos; rather, meaning in the sketch comes from the collision and the spaces between narrative and descriptive elements. See Otter, "Philadelphia Experiments," 111.

37. For more on the sketch genre, see Brand, *Spectator*.

38. See "William J. Wilson to Frederick Douglass," *BAP*, vol. 4, 144–145n11; Clytus, "Visualizing in Black Print"; Peterson, *Black Gotham*, 165–174; Wilder, *Covenant*, 72–74; and Ivy Wilson, *Specters of Democracy*, 145–168.

39. William Wells Brown, *The Black Man*, 230–235.

40. See Ivy Wilson, "'ARE YOU MAN ENOUGH?'" 265–277.

41. Ibid.

42. E., December 11, 1851.

43. Ibid.

44. E., December 20, 1851.

45. E., February 26, 1852. This categorizing move is yet another convention of the urban sketch often associated with Edgar Allan Poe. Lydia Maria Child likewise describes the city's population as "like mute actors, who tramp across the stage in pantomime or pageant, and are seen no more" ("Letters from New-York.—No. 10," *NASS*, October 21, 1841, 79). George Foster takes his readers to "Fashionable, aristocratic Broadway," to "see and hear" the various types that circulate around Broadway (*New York by Gaslight*, 70). See Brand, *Spectator*, 10.

46. E., February 26, 1852. See Hoekstra, "Hobbes," 111.

47. Here, Ethiop mocks characterizations of the "Saxon race" such as those Emerson offered in *Representative Men*: "Nobody is glad in the gladness of another, and our system is one of war, of an injurious superiority. Every child of the Saxon race is educated to wish to be first. It is our system" (625).

48. E., December 25, 1851.

49. Ibid.

50. E., January 22, 1852.

51. Rossiter, *Federalist Papers*, 184. See also Vogel, "Black Labor," 42, 37–54.

52. E., January 22, 1852.

53. Ibid.

54. Ibid.

55. E., July 1, 1852.

56. E., February 26, 1852.

57. Ibid.

58. Ibid. and E., July 30, 1852.

59. Negative blackness, as Hartman suggests, "cultivated a common sense of whiteness only as it reinforced the subjugated status of blacks" (*Scenes*, 29). See also Morrison's discussion of the Africanist presence grounding white American identity in *Playing*, 17.

60. E., February 5, 1852.

61. Hartman, *Scenes*, 4, and E., March 11, 1853.

62. E., February 5, 1852.

63. Ibid.

64. Ward's "Letters from Canada No. 1" (December 11, 1851) describes a similar scene in Philadelphia among lighter-complected black Philadelphians who "had they never been identified with the cursed negro race of the United States, this snobism would seem natural and plausible." Ward describes this "aristocracy" as "sufficiently disgusting to be sure, but its sanction and encouragement of negro-hate, makes it especially condemnable. Such folks ought to be reckoned among our enemies."

65. E., January 1, 1852. This illustration might draw on Foster's description of "painted [demons]," "magnificently attired, with their large arms and voluptuous bosoms half naked," and other salaciously drawn New Yorkers. See George Foster, *New York*, 71, 72.

66. I am grateful to Janice Simon for this insight in her commentary on a version of this chapter.

67. E., July 30, 1852.

68. E., July 30, 1852. See Emerson, *Essays and Lectures*, 625 (emphasis added). Plays such as *New York as It Is* act as one such "magnifying glass," augmented by commentaries like Foster's and Emerson's that celebrate "Saxon" enterprise.

69. Barthe, *Mythologies*, 130.

70. Du Bois, *Writings*.

71. E., July 30, 1852.

72. Ibid.

73. E., January 15, 1852. As Clytus has argued recently, "Wilson's flaneuring epistles take on a generative quality that makes it possible for black New Yorkers to see themselves according to the self-affirming logic of their own vernacular culture" ("Visualizing," 30).

74. E., December 25, 1851.

75. E., January 22, 1852.

76. Ibid.

77. Ibid.

78. Ibid.

79. Perhaps Ethiop is referencing the Society of Odd Fellows or Freemasons or he may have something like New York's Committee of Thirteen in mind. In Masonic history, the

office of Grand Conservator dates back to the biblical figure of Adam, the first Guardian and Superior Grand Conservator of the order. A black lodge of the Independent Order of Odd Fellows was organized in 1849 and was composed of men and women who were highly active in New York City's black activist circles. John Stauffer has suggested that the collection of pseudonymous writers for *Douglass's Paper*, including Ethiop and Communipaw, represents "the literary counterpart to the black masonic 'Odd Fellows.'" See Stauffer, "Introduction," in *Works*, xxxi–xxxii, and Steven, "Rise and Influence," 7.

80. E., January 15, 1852.

81. Ethiop suggests that the bonds of capitalist citizenship could supersede not only "particular ones of family, class, and region," following Nelson's reading of Federalist logic, but also of race, at least between the capitalists (*National Manhood*, 46).

82. E., January 22, 1852.

83. E., January 8, 1852. John N. Still, a fellow Brooklynite and regular attendee of state and national conventions, and others similarly argued that black-owned banks or investment firms would at least allow "our cooks, stewards, whalemen, and others" to make their earnings productive in "corporate bodies" dedicated to the benefit of the community (109). Still suggests that so-called unproductive labor, like domestic or service work, could become productive through the investment of wages. See "John N. Still to Henry Bibb," *Voice of the Fugitive*, *BAP*, February 26, 1852, 108–109.

84. E., July 1, 1852. Harris's reading of Campbell's First United Association of Colored Waiters reveals a similar strain of thought: "The association's expressed goal was to produce 'an identity of interest between the employer and the employed,'" as Campbell asked waiters to remain in the city to work during the summers to "establish a mutual feeling of confidence and good will between the employer and the employed." Leslie M. Harris, *Shadow*, 244. On "harmony of interests" rhetoric, see Wilentz, "Society," and Lang's reading of Francis Bowen in *Syntax of Class*, 1–2.

85. E., January 22, 1852. Emerson makes a similar distinction in "The Young America" (1844) between his version of nobility and an English aristocracy "incorporated by law and education" that "degrades life for the unprivileged class" (229). In Ethiop's model, the state has failed to create structures of equality for all citizens and has worked to create inequality, so "private" citizens must take over. E., January 22, 1852, and Emerson, *Essays and Lectures*, 224, 225.

86. See Peterson, "Capitalism," 578 and 558–559. For a discussion of Delany's *Blake* as a similar figure, set against the romantic individual, see Andrews, "The 1850s," 48. Peterson, however, argues that *Blake* becomes so entangled in Blake's difference from the masses that the serial leaves the question of who will govern in Cuba after the resolution largely unresolved.

87. Urbinati, *Representative Democracy*, 48–50.

88. E., January 8, 1852. In this context, Ethiop's proposal for an aristocracy follows Aristotle's binary in which an aristocracy is the constitutionally correct variant of rule by the few, and oligarchy is the deviation from that model. Ethiop's economic citizenship foreshadows what Sklansky identifies as "growing acceptance of finance capital and wage labor as the new grounds of economic democracy, not its antithesis" in the late nineteenth century (*Soul's Economy*, 3).

89. Emerson, *Representative Men*, 615.

90. E., May 27, 1852. In this particular sketch, Ethiop explicitly identifies this group as a class of capitalists: "Such is the rise of property on business thoroughfares, that I am fully persuaded that what few capitalists we have, have greatly erred" in not taking up the opportunities the real estate market presents. Unlike other reformers, who look upon the city with sentiments Lydia Maria Child describes on Moving Day as "a suppressed anathema on the nineteenth century, with its perpetual changes," or "J.T," another correspondent for *Douglass's Paper*, who argues vehemently against land monopolies and capitalism more broadly, Ethiop's critique embraces the potential this indeterminacy and constant change offers. See "Letters from New York," *NASS*, May 1, 1843, and J.T., *FDP*, June 3, 1852, and July, 30 1852.

91. E., January 22, 1852, and December 11, 1851.

92. E., January 22, 1852.

93. E., January 1, 1852. Ethiop's style invokes a host of popular theatrical, literary, and historical references playing on the theme, including Ben A. Baker's play, "New York as It Is" (1848), Edwin Williams's *New-York as It Is: Containing a General Description of the City of New-York* (1837), and Charles Dickens's *American Notes for General Circulation* (1842). As Dana Brand and others have shown, by the time Ethiop began appearing in *Douglass's Paper* in the 1850s, readers were well acquainted with this genre as a way of understanding and depicting cities from Irving's Knickerbocker sketches (1809) to Poe's "The Man of the Crowd" (1840) and Lydia Maria Child's *Letters from New York* (1843–1845) (Brand, *Spectator*, 73). See also Bank, *Theater Culture*, 85–90.

94. See Brand, *Spectator*, 7, and Clytus, "Visualizing." Originally identified by Baudelaire as "the painter of Modern Life," the flâneur became a popular journalistic narrator through which to view the diverse bustle that was the modern, industrializing city. Walter Benjamin describes the flâneur's vision as "diorama," further linking the figure and the sketch genre to visuality (35).

95. E., February 26, 1852.

96. My observations here are guided in part by Grossman's reading of the literary infusing Publius's concern with a political point of view in the *Federalist*. See Grossman, *Reconstituting*, 17–18, and Urbinati, *Representative Democracy*, 50.

97. E., January 15, 1852.

98. Ibid.

99. See Vogel, "Black Labor," 37–54, for a discussion of black periodical writers' use of republicanism. Smith drew inspiration for his "Communipaw" persona from Irving's *History of New York*, which idealized the Dutch precursor to Jersey City as a space of diversity and resilience. The characterization fit Communipaw's (the character's) focus on "mingling" and his penchant for long historical narrative. For more on Smith's use of Irving, see Peterson, *Black Gotham*, 219–222.

100. As Daniel Hack has chronicled, British novels in general, and Victorian novels in particular, were a constant presence in nineteenth-century black writing. See Hack, *Reaping Something New*.

101. Walter Scott, *The Waverley Novels*, 377. The series in general, and *Heart* in particular, was one of the most successful of its time.

102. "From Our New York Correspondent," *FDP*, February 26, 1852. References to Communipaw's correspondences cited hereafter as "C., Date."

103. Ibid. For similar contemporaneous arguments in relation to American Romanticism, see Horace Bushnell's "The True Wealth or Weal of Nations," an 1837 address at Yale, reprinted in Sklansky, *Soul's Economy*, 33–38.

104. Harris's work on black class development in New York confirms Communipaw's fears. Even as middle-class black leaders turned their eyes toward labor and labor discourse as a medium for uplift, the political gulf between them and the black workers they would lead widened. See Leslie M. Harris, *Shadow*, chap. 7.

105. C., February 12, 1852.

106. Ibid.

107. Ibid.

108. See Leslie M. Harris, *Shadow*, 255–257. As Harris notes, this district and its black entrepreneurs were made famous in accounts of the city, including Dickens's *American Notes* (1842) and Foster's *New York by Gaslight*. Both collections feature scenes of brothels and bars ostensibly owned by blacks but actually rented and leased from white owners. Still, men like dance-hall owner Peter Williams represented some of New York City's wealthiest black citizens, and they "presented a challenge to black reformers' efforts to establish morally perfect, middle-class definitions of black workers and entrepreneurs" (257). Segregation and so-called vice, ironically, provided opportunities for the development of a black professional and middle class, but it came with a price. Black restaurateurs and barbers, for instance, were compelled to bar black patrons for the sake of cultivating white clientele. See also Litwack, *North*, 178–180.

109. "Our Greatest Want," *AAM* 1, no. 6 (May 1859): 160.

110. Smith's focus on the classification of social types rather than individuals corresponds with a post-1848 drive toward social taxonomy and the birth of sociology. See Sklansky, *Soul's Economy*, particularly chap. 3, "The Birth of American Sociology." For a wide-ranging discussion of Smith's "fugitive science," particularly his responses to Thomas Jefferson and "Heads," see Rusert, *Fugitive Science*, 51–60.

111. "Civilization," *AAM* (January 1859), 8, and *Collected Works*, 251. The essay may have been drafted as early as 1844. A version of Smith's argument appeared in "The Influence of Climate on Longevity: With Special Reference to Life Insurance," printed in the May 1846 issue of *Hunt's Merchants' Magazine*. Smith follows the social statistics of Adolphe Quetelet and Prichard. In his 1835 *Treatise on Man, and the Development of His Faculties*, Quetelet claims that through careful observation, one can find the average data for any given nation. This normative curve could then be used to predict any physical or mental aspect of that nation's population. This work formed the bases of body mass index, a measure still in use today.

112. "Civilization," 15–16, and *Works*, 246 and 251.

113. *Works*, 246.

114. Just as Genesis begins with the Spirit of God passing over the waters, so will the new era begin: "by and by the spirit of God will pass over the great deep and the mountains and the dry land and the atmosphere . . . and higher laws and higher organizations will come into existence." C., February 26, 1852. On ichthyosauri and plegiosauri, see "Plesiosaurus," in *Zoological Recreations* (1849), 346, and William Buckland, *Geology and Mineralogy*, 133–166.

115. C., February 26, 1852.

116. C., February 12, 1852, and C., February 26, 1852.

117. *Politics* IV.11.1295a40-b-1

118. See Singh, *Black Is a Country*, 44.

119. C., February 26, 1852. Communipaw anticipates Du Bois in his vision of the United States as the first and perhaps the last nation through which this ideal can be realized,

but prioritizing material gain over liberty or, worse, equating the two will disrupt this development.

120. John Stauffer has anthologized ten installments of the series with an introduction and excellent footnotes, but at least one entry, printed in a now missing issue of *Douglass's Paper*, remains unaccounted for. As Stauffer notes, work "is the key to their character . . . work brings autonomy, and there is no essential difference between man and woman, black and white, rich and poor" (Stauffer, *Works*, 188). My analysis here complicates this leveling affect, but it remains strong in Smith's work. See Stauffer, *Works*, 185–242.

121. Cited hereafter as "Boot-Black."

122. This formulation of bootblacking revises the idealized image of the land-owning, self-sustaining agrarian for a modern subjectivity. The image of J. Hector St. John de Crevecoeur and Jefferson's "chosen people of God" (*Notes*, 290), whose work shelters them from the corrupting forces of the market, was a powerful formula for black activists seeking methods of political and economic empowerment that did not place their communities at the mercy of white employers. Smith, in other words, claims a sense of artisan republicanism for workers whose labor typically did not signify in such terms. See Wilentz, *Chants Democratic*, 14–17; Ostrowski, "Slavery, Labor Reform, and Intertextuality," 493–506; and Denning, *Mechanic Accents*.

123. See Roediger, *Wages of Whiteness*, 44. As Roediger suggests, the language of labor and class in the United States developed with the workers' full consciousness not only of the "dream of a republic of small producers but also against the nightmare of chattel slavery" (44).

124. "Boot-Black." Philip Livingston (1716–1778) signed the Declaration of Independence; Federalist Robert R. Livingston (1747–1813) helped oversee debates around New York's gradual emancipation act. Livingston vetoed a version of gradual emancipation that limited black citizenship rights (particularly voting), arguing that they could not be abridged based on race (Malone, *Between*, 28).

125. Of the narrative, Stauffer writes, "It is a classic tale of self-making, which McCune Smith sees as a powerful antidote to racism and caste" (James McCune Smith, *Works*, 195). See Melish, "The 'Condition' Debate," 653; Dunbar, *Fragile Freedom*; and Nash and Soderlund, *Freedom by Degrees*, for work on gradual emancipation informing my analysis.

126. See Leslie M. Harris, *Shadow*, 97–98.

127. See also my discussion of Jones and Allen's orientation to the market in Chapter 1.

128. "Boot-Black."

129. Ibid.

130. Jefferson, *Notes*, 291.

131. See Reid-Pharr's introduction to *Garies*, which describes such domestic spaces as "the center of black political life, the place at which community is formed and resistance is mounted" (xi–xii). See also Peterson's discussion of the economics of marginality in "Capitalism" and Lang's discussion of *Garies* in *Syntax of Class*, 42–58. In Communipaw's reading, maintaining the home as the central economic unit does not necessarily reinforce patriarchy as such—Smith's own history and his work in institutions, such as the Colored Orphans' Asylum, gave him an appreciation for a variety of "family" structures. See Leslie M. Harris, *Shadow*, 157–168.

132. "Boot-Black."

133. See Harris, *Shadow*, 170–172; Litwack, *North*, 214–246; and Pease and Pease, *They Who Would Be Free*, 68–93. In "The Washerwoman," Communipaw explores a more sensitive subject, the single black mother—sensitive because single working women were often viewed as promiscuous and because her child was likely her master's son's—a ready-made fallen-woman narrative. Communipaw, however, offers her narrative as a work in progress. Having a child is not the end, and neither is a marriage plot. Rather, her goal is rearing her son and earning enough money to purchase her sisters' freedom, and this departure, like the news vender's postslavery narrative, speaks to a continuum between slavery and freedom that white antislavery and moral reform tended to neglect. The narrative contributes to what Xiomara Santamarina has analyzed as "working womanhood," nineteenth-century narratives that "invoked republican rights rhetoric that emphasized the independence-producing, or character-building, potential of their wage labor" such that the characteristics originally signaling the black women's heterodoxy translate into heroism (*Belabored*, 10).

134. Delany, *Condition* (1852), 199. Delany's harsh criticism may have inspired Communipaw's sketch as much as Ethiop's articles.

135. "Boot-Black."

136. Ibid.

137. Ibid.

138. Ibid. Here, Smith is probably referencing one of the New Yorkers who took advantage of the land offered by Gerrit Smith. Unfortunately, the reality was not quite as optimistic as Smith's tone. One "shoemaker," named James Henderson, and his family, Harris notes, "attempted to make a living on Essex County land they had received from Gerrit Smith," but "when James froze to death in the forest in 1851," his family was forced to return to the city, his six children placed in the Colored Orphan Asylum for six years until his widow could "retrieve them." See Leslie M. Harris, *Shadow*, 278.

139. *Report* (1848), 13, 6.

140. C., April 15, 1852.

141. Ibid.

142. Like Wilentz's artisans, the bootblack in some ways stands against the mechanization of work. In Communipaw's framing, he is a craftsman whose art provides a critique of more "industrial" developments such as patent leather that fail to hold up ("Boot-Black"). Yet, bootblacking was still viewed as unskilled, casual labor.

143. C., February 26, 1852.

144. Even as Ethiop, Douglass, and others offered representative men as examples of black potential, they risked individualizing them so much that their political purpose as symbols for the group gets undercut. Communipaw might suggest that the link between the "hero" and the community that Andrews notes in *Blake* is disrupted as soon as the focus shifts from the hero's position as representative of a type to his difference and separation from the group.

145. "Boot-Black."

146. Ibid. This image completely upends Lydia Maria Child's description of the beggar seated in front of the slave trader's home and likewise tempers Ethiop's criticism of the lack of seriousness among black New Yorkers in the decades following emancipation.

147. "The Black News-Vender." Again, Communipaw riffs off of scripture: "I had rather be a doorkeeper in the house of my God, than to dwell in the tents of wickedness" (Psalm

84:10). In this case, the reference aligns the U.S. Senate with "tents of wickedness" and the Republic of Letters, one venue for seeking "Liberty," with the "house of my God."

148. "The Black News-Vender."

149. See Goodman, *Republic of Letters*, 1; Paine, *Common Sense*, 283–284; and Fagan, "*The North Star*."

150. Smith, "Dr. Smith's Journal," *CA*, December 2, 1837 in *Works*,12. This "transformative impulse," writes Goodman, "is the constructive result of this critical position" of betweenness (*Republic of Letters*, 2). Stauffer characterizes Smith's Republic of Letters as "an image of the nation in which blacks are neither heroes nor villains but humans—complicated men and women struggling to survive in a retrograde society that has rejected them" (*Works*, 188). This space, however, was not completely egalitarian. Rather, historically it was strongly gendered male and assumed a level of literacy and philosophical sophistication that only a small percentage of the population could obtain.

151. "The Whitewasher."

152. Ibid. This vision of the whitewasher further confirms Smith's claims in "Civilization" that "the people . . . are the source of intellectual as well as political power; they are not only bones and sinew, but also the heart and brain of a nation" (*AAM* [1859]: 8, and *Works*, 251).

153. Introduction to *My Bondage and My Freedom* in Douglass, *Autobiographies*, 132.

154. Psalm 84:10 reads, "For a day in Your courts *is* better than a thousand. / I would rather be a doorkeeper in the house of my God / Than dwell in the tents of wickedness."

155. This adaptability is in part a function of the periodical medium through which Ethiop and Communipaw wrote. As Todd Vogel has argued, the ephemeral quality of the press "made the writers nimble. They could plunge into the public conversation and get their views out immediately" ("Introduction," 2). See also Ernest, *Liberation Historiography*, 279.

156. E., May 13, 1852.

157. Here, I'm working from Lukács's differentiation between description, which "contemporizes everything," and narration, which "recounts the past" (5). Communipaw, in contrast, narrates a past that, as I will discuss in a moment, reveals a deception in Ethiop's present. Benedict Anderson describes this contemporaneous nature of the newspaper as a bedrock of imagined community. Indeed, Ethiop's descriptions connect all of Douglass's readers (imagined for him as black) as a part of a collective community sharing a concern for its development. New York operates as the center of this community or more like its epicenter, the space from whence all of its major trends and tendencies radiate and can be observed. See Lukacs, "Narrate or Describe," 130, and Anderson, *Imagined*, 63.

158. E., May 13, 1852. Ethiop was probably referring to William Morris, "rector of Trinity School" who acted as St. Philip's "officiating minister" from 1849 to 1860 but was never officially named "rector." See Townsend, *Faith*, 151–152, and Peterson, *Black Gotham*, 207–213.

159. E., May 13, 1852.

160. Ibid.

161. Downing, "St. Philip's Church and the Fugitive Slave Law," *FDP*, April 29, 1852.

162. Ibid.

163. Ibid.

164. Ibid., and E., May 13, 1852.

165. Supporters were able to purchase Preston's freedom for $1,200, and "within a month he had returned to Brooklyn" (134). See Foner, *Gateway*, 133–134.

166. See Townsend, *Faith*, 151–152; Peterson, *Black Gotham*, 147–148; and Wilder, "'Driven.'"

167. References to Cromwell recur in *Douglass's Paper* and abolitionist rhetoric, usually mentioned next to revolutionary leaders like George Washington for his "just severity." See *FDP*, October 9, 1851.

168. E., April 8, 1852.

169. Ibid.

170. Frankenstein became a common image for the destructive, frightening, or otherwise abject other. See Burns, *Painting in the Dark*, 114.

171. E., April 8, 1852.

172. C., February 12, 1852.

173. See Leslie M. Harris, *Shadow*, 266. On Seneca Village, see Alexander, *African or American*, chap. 7; and Wall, DiZerega, Rothschild, and Copeland, "Seneca Village."

174. See McShane and Tar, *The Horse in the City*, 80–81.

175. See Sklansky, *Soul's Economy*, 4.

176. See, for instance, Blumin, *Emergence*; Wilentz, *Chants Democratic*; Glickstein, *American Exceptionalism*; Bromell, *Sweat*; and Foner, *Free Soil.* As the 1848 convention predicted, Irish immigrants displaced many black New Yorkers out of those occupations forming the backbone of Communipaw's "Heads," eliminating a once stable niche in the labor market. See Harris, *Shadow*, 264–265.

177. See, for instance, Moreno's discussion of black activists' relation to white unions and the founding of the Colored National Labor Union in 1869 in *Black Americans*, 8–81, especially his discussion of the competing labor theories of value informing white union and abolitionist/Republican notions of free labor. Where the former emphasized economic independence, the latter emphasized individual ownership of the self and labor.

178. See Litwack, *North*, 164–168.

179. Many black activists and other reformers were advocating migration out of urban centers in favor of subsistence (and later market-driven) farming as a path toward elevation. Mary Ann Shadd Cary, for instance, wrote to *North Star* "that [the black population] should direct [their] attention more to the farming interest than hitherto" because, she argued, "the estimation in which we would be held in power, would be quite different, were we produces, and not merely, as now, consumers" (32). Rural life was also attractive for its perceived moral advantages. Smith himself suggested the country as preferable to the city as a part of a Committee of Three at the 1851 Convention of Colored Citizens in Rochester, New York. The report, published in Douglass's *North Star* and Greeley's *New York Daily Tribune*, describes "all city life is, after all, a kind of hot-house forcing of human beings" that forces black men to work "as servants, porters, &c." with the result that their "manhood is, in a measure, demeaned, lowered, kept down" ("Meeting of the Colored People of New York"). The committee's solution: "leave the city, its seductions, its oppressions and baleful atmosphere, and seek to expand our elbows, our lungs and our energies in the free air of the rural districts" ("Meeting").

The drop in New York City's black population began in the 1840s. Harris notes that the city's population dropped by "over 2,500" between 1840 and 1850 and by 15 percent in the five years following passage of the Fugitive Slave Law. Ethiop's Brooklyn, however, saw a rise in population over the same time. This demographic shift accounts, in part, for Ethiop's optimism. He was, after all, Douglass's "Brooklyn Correspondent." See Leslie M. Harris, *Shadow*, 275–278.

180. See Singh, *Black Is a Country*, 46–47, and Moses, *Creative Conflict*, 48.

Chapter 4

1. "What Shall We Do with the White People?" *AAM* (February 1860), 45.

2. Ibid., 41. For a discussion of Ethiop's essay in the context of a tradition of black critiques of whiteness, see Bay's chapter, "What Shall We Do with the White People: Whites in Postbellum Black Thought," in *White*, 75–77.

3. "What Shall We Do," 41.

4. Ibid., 44.

5. Ibid., 42.

6. Ibid., 43. See Loughran, *Republic*.

7. "What Shall We Do," 43.

8. On sarcasm as a "way of inflecting ideas," see Nyong'o, *Amalgamation*, 155. Ethiop's essay uses rhetorical tactics of inversion that had become standard to African American writing by the 1850s. See also Bay, *White*, 75–77. Henry Louis Gates Jr. cites Ethiop's essay as an example of signifyin(g) parody in *Signifying*, 94. In *Rhetorical Listening*, Krista Ratcliffe suggests that Ethiop's essay offers an ethnographic observation that links whiteness with consumption (115).

9. See Secor, "'There Is an Istanbul,'" 353. My analysis builds on Secor's construction by investigating how national stories, or "spatial stories" in Certeau's terms, frame and reframe these spatial practices. See Certeau, *Practice*, 29–42 and 115–130.

10. "What Shall We Do," 44. As this chapter suggests, the fractured print public Trish Loughran describes in *Republic in Print* is not antithetical to the overall sense of a cohesive, if not coherent, white citizenship.

11. Castronovo, *Necro-Citizenship*, xi. Here and throughout I draw on "police" in two senses: (1) Jacques Rancière's notion of the police as that which constrains the distribution of the sensible, what is sayable, knowable, and doable and who can say, know, or do them (*Dissenssus*, 36–41; and (2) the threat and experience of state-sanctioned violence that enforces white citizenship.

12. Caroline Levine, *Forms*, 3.

13. Here and throughout the chapter, I draw on Houston A. Baker Jr.'s concept of critical memory and John Ernest's "liberation historiography." As Baker has argued, "Critical memory compels the black intellectual . . . to keep before his eyes (and the eyes of the United States) a history that is embarrassing, macabre, and always bizarre with respect to race" (*Critical Memory*, 10). Critical memory insists on examining the discordant and disillusioning aspects of the public imaginary as a necessary process for democratic citizenship. Liberation historiography, which Ernest defines as an "African American *mode* of representing" and intervening in history, moves beyond recovery toward a "narrative method" and ways of understanding "white supremacist ideology as a systemic presence developed historically" (Ernest, *Liberation Historiography*, 41, 8, 15). Critical citizenship is about the kinds of citizens that liberation historiography and critical memory might produce and about the kinds of spaces, texts, and critical practices that might produce them.

14. *Dred Scott v. Sandford* 60 U.S. (19 Howard) 393 (1857), 537.

15. Douglass, "The Kansas-Nebraska Bill," in *Selected Speeches and Writings*, 299.

16. Ibid., 298.

17. As Gordon Barker notes, "Most of Illinois became 'enemy territory' for blacks, free or fugitive" (*Imperfect Revolution*, 27). Illinois was one among several states and territories that had instituted such codes between 1848 and 1854, including Indiana, Michigan, Iowa, Ohio, and Oregon. On how the Kansas-Nebraska Act may have contributed to the "radicalization" of Douglass, see Tekla Ali Johnson, "Frederick Douglass and the Kansas-Nebraska Act," 113–128. My own sense is that the act and rendition of Anthony Burns that same year confirmed and gave an occasion for Douglass to voice notions he had already been developing.

18. As historian Nicole Etcheson suggests of the Kansas-Nebraska Act (1854) in particular, "Settlers in Kansas accepted the premise that white voters should decide the status of black men and women. Conflict arose when the rights of white settlers to take that decision was threatened" (*Bleeding Kansas*, 4–6). The free-state/free-labor settlers had a range of attitudes toward black rights and were increasingly supportive of black equality. However, these shifts in position were always balanced against and framed by "white settlers' fears of what black rights meant for whites" (6). Rucker explains that free-soilers "indeed wanted 'free soil'—land free from slavery and, in many cases, land free of African Americans altogether." See Rucker, "Unpopular," 135–141.

19. Barker, *Imperfect Revolution*, 22.

20. Ibid., 224–225.

21. Quoted in Barker, *Imperfect Revolution*, 20. Despite Boston's affluent antislavery community, a black minister, Grimes, could not raise the funds to purchase Burns's freedom. Theodore Parker led the rally at Faneuil Hall; Lewis Hayden, Thomas W. Higginson, and others broke into the jail but were unsuccessful in their attempt to rescue Burns, in part, because the crowd that had gathered seemed more interested in the drama of the moment than taking action. For analysis of the range of responses, see Barker, *Imperfect Revolution*, 41–62. For a discussion of fugitive rendition in Boston from the perspective of black activism, see Kantrowitz, *More Than Freedom*, 184, 192–194.

22. As Nicolas Wood observes in the context of doughface politics, white democrats in particular reacted strongly as these laws and rulings "inhibited the rights of white northerners to an unacceptable degree." See Wood, "'Sacrifice,'" 106.

23. Thoreau, "Slavery in Massachusetts," in *Collected Essays*, 344.

24. Douglass, "Anthony Burns," in *Selected Speeches and Writings*, 281; *Frederick Douglass' Paper*, June 9, 1854.

25. Wood, "'Sacrifice,'" 106.

26. Before the Fugitive Slave Act, escaped slaves like Dred Scott and his family, who had taken residence or who had been taken to free states, including Ohio, had successfully sued for their freedom with the state recognizing them as citizens or at least as protected by the state's laws. See Finkelman, *Dred Scott*, v–vii, and Moore, *Constitutional Rights*, 19–30.

27. *Dred Scott*, 407. Taney connects citizenship to rights in a way that inverts the logic of the 1840s black state conventions I discuss in Chapter 2. For the range of northern press responses to the case, see the documents in Finkelman's *Dred Scott*, particularly the newspaper reactions. I do not want to understate the significance of Taney's opinion or the mass protest against it in the North; however, as McLean's opinion suggests, protest against the *Dred Scott* decision did not necessarily equate ringing support for black citizens.

28. *Dred Scott*, 529 and 538. While Justice Curtis's dissent went further than McLean's in its support of black citizenship, the Missouri Compromise, and its overall denunciation of

the Court's ruling, McLean's dissent is more useful here for its comparatively moderate tone. It, moreover, seems more in line with the discourse that follows, as the Lincoln-Douglas debates demonstrate. See Finkelman, *Dred Scott*, 100.

29. *Dred Scott*, 529.

30. Ibid., 537, and Davis and Wilson, *Lincoln-Douglas Debates*, 163.

31. See Phan, *Bonds*, 107–127. See also Crane, *Race*, 110–112, for a complementary discussion of Douglass's strict constructionism in terms of his evolving ideas of higher law constitutionalism.

32. *Dred Scott*, 529.

33. Ibid. My thinking about the consequences of separating the legal from the social is informed by Saidiya Hartman's discussion of Reconstruction in *Scenes*, 164–170. By distinguishing between taste and law, McLean sought to forestall how the Court's decision, especially Taney's "dual citizenship" theory (that one was simultaneously a state citizen and a federal citizen, and the two were separate), would negate both the restrictions on slavery outlined in the Missouri Compromise and federal power over citizenship more broadly. And since Taney did not recognize black birthright citizenship and the federal government restricted naturalization to "white" immigrants, black people had no path to federal citizenship.

34. See Phan, *Bonds*, 107–127.

35. Hartman, *Scenes*, 168.

36. Mills, *Racial Contract*, 93.

37. Castronovo, *Necro-Citizenship*, xiii and 4. DeLombard tracks this anxiety in the early national context, noting, "Whether characterized by its 'infantile citizenship,' 'necro citizenship' eager . . . incompetence,' or '*esprit de corpse*,' the normatively white, male citizen limned in legal and literary portrayals of the time is characterized by naïveté, passivity, inarticulateness, and withdrawal, if not downright silence and absence" (*Shadow*, 40). Yet, as we shall see in this section, these citizens are active participants in sustaining "fugue" citizenship for its material and psychic benefits. See also Berlant, *Anatomy*, 23–24.

38. "Anglo-Saxons, and Anglo-Africans," *AAM* (August 1859), 247. "Stops" control air circulation to organ pipes, ultimately controlling what sound the organ as a whole issues.

39. As Vogel posits in *Rewriting*, "This language served as a window into the minds and souls of the middling class and as a force to unite them" and was used as the lingua franca of any would-be reform or populist movement (34–39). Vogel reads S.S.N.'s article as symptomatic of a frustration about how this narrative foreclosed avenues to citizenship. On fugue as a form based on managed polyphony, see Adorno, *Aesthetic Theory*, 200.

40. Davis and Wilson, *Lincoln-Douglas Debates*, 131.

41. Ibid.

42. Ibid. See also Bentley, "The Strange Career," 460–485. As Bentley notes, Lincoln's "joke supports the argument of a number of scholars who contend that liberal contract doctrine served to further black subjection even when it purported to advance black liberation" (464).

43. While Lincoln's rhetoric becomes increasingly antiblack over the course of the debates, the basic premise remained the same. In the first debate, he takes the same position in very similar terms: "There is a physical difference between the two, which in my judgment will probably forever forbid their living together upon the footing of perfect equality." Lincoln's preference for writing new speeches for each debate over revising older ones suggests

that his repetition was successful enough to become a standard trope for parrying and anticipating Douglas's attempts to corner him as problack. See "First Joint Debate at Ottawa," in Davis and Wilson, *Lincoln-Douglas Debates*, 20.

44. Douglass, "Kansas-Nebraska," 298.

45. Davis and Wilson, *Lincoln-Douglas Debates*, 20.

46. DeLombard, *Shadow*, 40.

47. Davis and Wilson, *Lincoln-Douglas Debates*, 131. The "American" or "Negro School" of ethnology had gained increasing traction in mainstream public consciousness over the 1840s and 1850s thanks to the efforts of Samuel Morton (*Crania Americana*, 1839, and *Crania Aegyptiaca*, 1844), George R. Gliddon, Josiah Nott, and their collaborative efforts on *Types of Mankind* (1854). See Fredrickson, *Black Image*, 74–80; Stanton, *Leopard's Spots*, 137–173; Dain, *Hideous Monster*, 197–226; and Nelson, *National Manhood*, 115–132, for an account of the role of the American School in shaping the professional discourse of science and how this discourse (vs. naturalism or religious arguments) helped give it public legitimacy.

48. Castronovo, *Necro-Citizenship*, 8. See also Mbembe, "Necropolitics," 11–40.

49. "fugue, n." *OED* Online; Marcovitch, "Fugue," in *Black's Medical Dictionary*.

50. Butler, "Restaging the Universal," 11; Castronovo, *Necro-Citizenship*, 3; and Ivy Wilson, *Specters*, 3–4.

51. Douglass, "Kansas-Nebraska," 298.

52. Phan, *Bonds*, 4–7 and 108–112.

53. Here, I reference Toni Morrison's reading of whiteness in *Playing in the Dark*, 32–33.

54. Thomas Hamilton, "Apology," *AAM* (January 1859), 1–4. For more on Hamilton and his papers, see Fagan, *The Black Newspaper*, 119–141.

55. Hamilton, "Apology," 1.

56. *Freedom's Journal*, March 16, 1827.

57. See Fagan, *Black Newspaper*, 119–125; Penn, *Afro-American*, 83–89; Ivy Wilson, "The Brief Wondrous Life," 18–38; and Peterson, "Literary Transnationalism," 191–192.

58. "Apology," 3. As Ernest has suggested, part of the *Anglo-African*'s strength was its diversity of voices and discursive modes: "Through the multivocal forum of the *Anglo-African Magazine*, writers could respond to the ideological incoherence of the dominant culture more fully than if they were to rely solely on the discourse of scholarship and reason" (*Liberation Historiography*, 313).

59. See Joyce, *Black Book Publishers*, 119.

60. See Ernest, *Liberation Historiography*, 2–4 and 306–313; Foreman, "'Reading Aright,'" 327–354; Russell, *Legba's Crossing*, 3; and Ivy Wilson, *Specters*, 145–168.

61. Ernest, *Liberation Historiography*, 301.

62. Chiles, "Within and Without Raced Nations," 324–325.

63. It cannot "aid our cause to found an empire in Yoruba," he argues, "they might as well have built a batter at Gibraltar to destroy Sevastopol." Hamilton, "Apology," 3–4. Hamilton cites the infamous 1854 to 1855 siege in which Russia lost the city.

64. Townsend, *Faith*, 292; Holly, "Thoughts on Hayti, Number II," *AAM* (August 1859), 242–243, and "Thoughts on Hayti, Number VI," *AAM* (November 1859), 367.

65. Hamilton, "Apology," 2.

66. S.S.N., "Anglo-Saxons, and Anglo-Africans," 249. The unfixed nature of the neologism, James Clifton notes in the context of *Négritude*, "forces [readers] to *construct* readings

from a debris of historical and future possibilities." Once introduced, he continues, "no dictionary or etymology can nail down the significance, nor can an inventor's (remembered) intention." Clifton, *Predicament*, 175 and 177.

67. The series numbers twenty-seven of the pictures, but several distinct images are not numbered.

68. Ernest, *Liberation Historiography*, 325. As Ernest aptly puts it, "If one wants a quick overview of the conventional features of African American history from the early slave trade to the brink of the Civil War, one could get more from these fictional sketches than from most of the textbooks used in K-12 schools" (322). Leif Eckstrom and Britt Rusert have recently developed an edition of the series as part of the American Antiquarian Society's "Just Teach One: Early African American Print." See their Introduction to the exhibit; McHenry, *Forgotten Readers*, 130–131; and Ivy Wilson, *Specters*, 145–168.

69. See Ivy Wilson, *Specters*, 157.

70. See "Afric-American Picture Gallery," 53 and 54–55; abbreviated hereafter as AAPG. For a slightly different account of the gallery's numbering scheme, see Ivy Wilson, *Specters*, 156–157.

71. See the essays in Gerdts and Thistlethwaite's *Grand Illusions* and Patricia M. Burnham and Lucretia Hoover Giese's introduction to *Redefining American History Painting*.

72. Foucault, "Of Other Spaces," 25.

73. AAPG, *AAM* (March 1859), 87.

74. Ibid., 87. On the traditional status of history painting as educative, see Thistlethwaite, "The Most Important Themes," 8–21.

75. As Ernest observes, the gallery offers "not a singular story but a gallery of many stories, connected by a complex narrative of experience and by significant silences that push against and through that collective experience" (*Liberation Historiography*, 328).

76. AAPG, *AAM* (February 1859), 53.

77. Ibid.

78. Ruskin, *Complete Works*, 383. Turner's *The Slave Ship* depicts the 1781 *Zong* Massacre, in which over 140 slaves were thrown overboard.

79. Ruskin, *Complete Works*, 382–383.

80. AAPG, 53.

81. Ruskin, *Complete Works*, 383; AAPG, 53.

82. Frances Smith Foster, "Narrative," 718.

83. AAPG, 53.

84. Ibid., 53–54.

85. Fagan, *Black Newspaper*, 122–123.

86. McCune Smith to Smith, September 20, 1859, Gerrit Smith Papers, Syracuse University. Wilson's Ethiop sketches for *FDP* show his proclivity for placing himself and his cohort in his sketches, often as an inside joke.

87. Longinus, "On the Sublime," 27.

88. AAPG, 53.

89. See Ernest, *Liberation Historiography*, 324–325.

90. AAPG, 87.

91. William Wells Brown, *The Black Man*, 229.

92. AAPG, 88.

93. Ibid. For a discussion of the implication of Mount Vernon in larger debates over slavery, see McInnis, "The Most Famous Plantation of All," 101. See also Ivy Wilson, "The Writing on the Wall," 61–65.

94. AAPG, 88.

95. Ibid.

96. Ibid.

97. Ivy Wilson, *Specters*, 153.

98. See Castronovo, *Necro-Citizenship*, 3; Nelson, *National Manhood*, 204–205.

99. See Jones, *Captive Stage*, 99–106, for a detailed discussion of Lee's appearances in Washington paintings.

100. AAPG, 88.

101. McInnis, "The Most Famous Plantation of All," 89. More recently, Douglas Jones notes in the context of dramatic renderings of Washington that these images "functioned as cultural and 'historiographic' justification for ongoing forms of black captivity in the antebellum north." Jones, *The Captive Stage*, 106.

102. Ayers, "'Their Unfailing Friend,'" 4, and McInnis, "The Most Famous Plantation of All," 105.

103. McInnis, "The Most Famous Plantation of All," 107–109.

104. Quoted in McInnis, "The Most Famous Plantation of All," 101. See also Casper, *Sarah Johnson's Mount Vernon*, 200 and 72. Paintings including Eastman Johnson's *The Old Mount Vernon* (1857) reflected this general ambivalence toward the antislavery cause but also a radical shift in how artists and the public treated Mount Vernon.

105. Douglass, "The Meaning of July Fourth for the Negro," in *Selected Speeches and Writings*, 193.

106. AAPG, *AAM* (April 1859), 101.

107. Ibid.

108. Ibid.

109. Ibid., 103.

110. Hetherington, *Badlands of Modernity*, 40.

111. On spaces and ways of seeing the world within the African Atlantic traditions that disrupt linear notions of time and memory in a way that, following Russell, offers "a radically empowering space in which to define," see Russell, *Legba's Crossing*, 14–15, 68; Gilroy, *Black Atlantic*, 196–197; and Mbembe, *On the Postcolony*, 14–17.

112. See Peterson, "Literary Transnationalism," 190 and 196–197. For Peterson, marronage invokes the collectives that escaped slaves created and in some contexts "applies as much to populations of escaped slaves in the seventeenth-century Brazilian wilderness as it does to northern free blacks in the nineteenth-century United States; it is the foundation of black nationalist thought" (196–197). For a similar articulation of marronage in connection to print, see Baker, who describes the *New Negro* as representing "a unified community of national interests set in direct opposition to the general economic, political, and theological tenets of a racist land" (*Modernism*, 77). See also Roberts, *Freedom as Marronage*, and Thompson, *Flight to Freedom*, 13.

113. Roberts, *Freedom*, 9.

114. Ibid., 11.

115. Ibid., 11.

116. Ibid., 103.

117. AAPG, *AAM* (June 1859), 173–174.

118. Wilson and Delany seem to be developing the same type: the revolutionary artist/former slave.

119. AAPG, 174. This tablet might be a reworking of the Poe's *Narrative of Arthur Gordon Pym*, which presumably comes from a long-dead African civilization, or possibly Joseph Smith's golden tablet.

120. AAPG, 174.

121. Ibid., 174. This tablet uses the "Angry Saxon" trope that, as Mia Bay notes, had become standard to black and antislavery writing by the 1850s. See Bay, *White Image*, 108–109. This reading is also informed by Ernest, *Liberation Historiography*, 322–323.

122. AAPG, 174.

123. See Foucault, "Of Other Spaces," 26.

124. AAPG, 174.

125. Ibid., 176.

126. Ibid.

127. Ibid., 177. It is unclear whether or not "Felix" is the man's name. Given Wilson's earlier reference to Gamaliel and Paul, "Felix" might also be an allusion to Claudius Felix, the procurator of Judea, who imprisoned Paul for two years, first in hopes of a bribe from Paul and later to please influential constituents. See Acts, 21–24 KJV.

128. AAPG, 176.

129. As Matthew Cordova Frankel argues using Jefferson's *Notes*, the sublime in a Kantian sense can function as a dialectical movement from awe and rapture to harmony that mirrors the interplay between national and local interests and between actual and virtual representation in the republican citizen. Frankel explains, "It is only through the sublime . . . that each new American subject may experience nature's moral and institutional prescriptions as a single interior command, which, once complete, translates the psychic demands of citizenship into an aestheticized moment of surrender" to the state ("'Nature's Nation' Revisited," 709–710). In contrast to Jefferson's sublime, I offer Ethiop's sublime as a perspective or "attunement" in Kant's words that maintains the disharmony. I focus on the sublime here as producing a sense of agitation that leads to and is symptomatic of critique: not an end but a method and a means of not only judging other means but also (as reason) determining which ends are worthwhile.

130. AAPG, 177.

131. Morrison, *Playing in the Dark*, 39, and Goddu, *Gothic America*, 132.

132. AAPG, 177.

133. Morrison, *Playing in the Dark*, 24.

134. Goddu, *Gothic America*, 13.

135. For Kant, sublimity in nature is contingent on whether or not the viewer can face the unimaginable, threatening scene (the waterfall, for instance) without feeling threatened, without fleeing, physically or emotionally, in fear. In judging something sublime, the viewer recognizes her physical powerlessness but then finds within her mind an expanded consciousness that "calls forth our power . . . to regard those things about which are we are concerned (goods, health and life) as trivial and hence to regard its power . . . as not the sort of dominion over ourselves and our authority to which we would have to bow if it came down to our highest principles and their affirmation or abandonment" (*Critique*, 145–145).

136. Versions of this type of narrative abound throughout early black writing, from Richard Allen and Absalom Jones's yellow fever account to David Walker's *Appeal* to Harriet Jacobs's use of sentimental conventions. In each instance, the narrator normalizes the perspective of the oppressed in a way that highlights the "peculiar" nature of her surroundings.

137. AAPG, 176.

138. AAPG, 102.

139. Ibid.

140. Ibid. The exchange fits within a tradition of texts such as Daniel Coker's "A Dialogue Between a Virginian and an African Minister" (1810), which features a black man defeating a supporter of slaveholding or a slaveholder (typically Virginian) in a debate. See Coker "A Dialogue," in Newman, Rael, and Lapsanksy, *Pamphlets of Protest*, 52–65,

141. AAPG, 217.

142. Ibid.

143. Ibid.

144. Ernest, *Liberation Historiography*, chap. 5; Ivy Wilson, *Specters*, 158–160.

145. AAPG, 89–90.

146. See, for instance, AAPG, Second Paper, 89–90, and AAPG, Fifth Paper, 217.

147. Indeed, as Berlant notes, scenes like the Black Forest can become negative images upon which the National Symbolic could be made stronger. See Berlant, *Anatomy*, 54–56, and Andrew F. Wood, "Managing the Lady Managers," 291.

148. Russell, *Legba's Crossing*, 9–10.

149. Ibid., 9–11. See also Gates, *Signifying*, xx–xxi and 19–22.

150. AAPG, 100.

151. Ibid., 100. Ethiop's description of Tom echoes those of slave narrators like Henry Bibb and William Anderson, who both claim to have been "whipped up."

152. AAPG, 100.

153. Ibid.

154. Roberts, *Freedom*, 10.

155. Ibid., 10 and 13.

156. AAPG, 89–90.

157. Ibid., 90.

158. Ibid., 89.

159. Ibid.

160. AAPG, 217.

161. Ibid., 215, 219.

162. AAPG, 244.

163. Ibid.

164. Ibid.

165. Ibid.

166. Ibid., 245. She echoes "Sidney's" remonstrance during the 1840 debate over the first New York State convention: he accuses the collective of "metaphycising upon *things*, when they should be using the resistless energy of principle, to vindicate their wronged and deeply injured brethren." "William Whipper's Letters," *CA*, March 13, 1841.

167. See Lewis Hyde, *Common*, 36–38, 44. My discussion of critical citizenship in terms of commoning and beating the bounds resonates in some ways with Pratt's visualization of

stranger humanism as happening in a semiprivate room where "people discover their differences from one another, but they are barred from trying to appropriate or penetrate those differences" in a way that "facilitates the coming-into-selfhood of those who elect to enter the room" (2). I prefer the language of commoning, particularly in relation to Nelson's "vernacular democracy," for its emphasis on everyday practices that may or may not happen in print or through means that might be readily recognizable. While Ethiop engages in critical citizenship through writing, the most productive moments happen outside that context.

168. As Hyde explains in the context of premodern England, "commoners" would periodically "perambulate the public ways and common lands armed with axes, mattocks, and crowbars to demolish any hedge, fence, ditch, stile, gate, or building that had been erected without permission" (37).

169. Rancière, *Politics*, 139.

Chapter 5

1. "A Review of Ira Aldridge's *Titus*," *The Era*, April 26, 1857, in Kolin, *Titus*, 377–379.

2. Garnet, "Address," in *Walker's Appeal*, 96.

3. "The Anglo-African Magazine for 1860," *AAM* (December 1859), 400.

4. As historian Stephen Kantrowitz notes, the federal and state governments' response in 1854 with overwhelming force was a direct result of vigilance workers'—mostly, but not all, black—successful efforts earlier in the decade, including the defense of William and Ellen Craft in 1850 and the rescue of Shadrach Minkins in 1851. The show of force indicates not only the Burns rendition's importance to maintaining national political balance but also how forcefully black activists, communities, and their allies worked to thwart the Fugitive Slave Law. See Kantrowitz, *More Than Freedom*, 192–194.

5. See Reid-Pharr, "Introduction," xvii, and Fanon, *Wretched of the Earth*, 138.

6. On the role of stories in constituting a political body, see Rogers Smith, "Citizenship," 73–96.

7. Robert S. Levine, *Dislocating*, 103.

8. Frances Smith Foster, *Written by Herself*, 133 and 135.

9. Peterson, *Doers*, 3.

10. Indeed, Harper's antebellum writing has led Katherine Henry to note, "For Harper, speech is not separate from the material world of bodily existence; on the contrary, speech is most powerful precisely when it is crossing over that boundary, either from or into materiality" (*Liberalism*, 89).

11. Few literary critics have taken up "Fancy Sketches" on its own terms. My reading of the series builds on Peterson, "Literary Transnationalism," 189–208; Stancliff, *Frances Ellen Watkins Harper*; and Boyd, *Discarded Legacy*, 86–87.

12. My reconstruction of Garner's capture throughout this chapter draws on Nikki M. Taylor's *Driven Towards Madness*. For literary criticism on Harper's representations of Garner, see Wendy Dasler Johnson, "Frances Ellen Watkins Harper," 51–75, and Kristine Yole, "Enslaved Women's Resistance," 99–114.

13. Spillers, *Black, White, and in Color*, 208.

14. hooks, quoted in Wall, "Taking Positions and Changing Words," 11.15. Aristotle, *Politics*, 60, quoted in Rancière, *Disagreement*, 1.

15. Aristotle, *Politics*, 60, quoted in Rancière, *Disagreement*, 1.

16. See Bentley, "Warped Conjunctions," 292, and Rancière, "Foreword to *Politics of Aesthetics*," where Rancière defines aesthetics (following Kant) as "a delimitation of spaces and times, of the visible and the invisible, of speech and noise, that simultaneously determines the place and the stakes of politics as a form of experience" (13).

17. Here, I am indebted to Mae G. Henderson's theorizing of black women writers as entering "simultaneously into familial, or *testimonial* and public, or *competitive* discourses—discourses that both affirm and challenge the values and expectations of the reader" ("Speaking in Tongues" 20). For me, Harper's speakers *also* enter into a relationship of simultaneous identification and disidentification with readers.

18. See Stancliff, *Frances Ellen Watkins Harper*, 44.

19. See Peterson, *Doers*, 85, for a similar reading of sentimentalism in antebellum black women's writing.

20. "On Free Produce," in *Brighter*, 44–45.

21. Tillet, *Sites of Slavery*, 55.

22. Pratt, "'I Am a Stranger with Thee,'" 261.

23. Castronovo, *Beautiful*, 56.

24. "On Free Produce," in *Brighter*, 44–45.

25. Freire, *Pedagogy*, 59.

26. 2 Corinthians 7:9–11 King James Version (KJV).

27. Frances Smith Foster notes, Harper's poetry "uses the reader's familiarity with standard abolitionist scenes and blatantly appeals to sentimentality, but does not encourage self-indulgence" ("Introduction," 33).

28. "Minutes," in Foner and Walker, *Proceedings*, 229. Douglass, Garnet's most famous and vocal opponent in 1843, printed a positive notice of the document in *North Star* along with an excerpt from Garnet's sketch of Walker's life. "Sketch of the Life and Character of David Walker," *North Star*, July 14, 1848.

29. Garnet, "Address," 94.

30. Ibid., 94.

31. "Minutes," in Foner and Walker, *Proceedings*, 263.

32. See Apthecker, *American Negro Slave Revolts*, 344–350. A perusal of Apthecker's *American Negro Slave Revolts* reveals that slave states were under constant threat of an insurrection breaking out.

33. See Apthecker, *American Negro Slave Revolts*, especially chap. 14, and "Class Conflicts in the South, 1850–1860."

34. Wednesday, May 31, 1854, in *Journals*, 64.

35. For a slightly different reading of death in the context of Garner's narrative, see Gilroy, *Black Atlantic*, 64.

36. This strategy echoes the way early gallows literature could produce black legal personhood in print. See DeLombard, *Shadow*, 1–48.

37. James McCune Smith, "British West Indian Emancipation," in *Works*, 154.

38. Ibid., 154.

39. Ibid.

40. Ibid.

41. Douglass, "West India Emancipation," in *Selected Speeches and Writings*, 368.

42. Ibid., 367.

43. *AAM* (May 1869), 160.

44. As Foucault explains, *parrhesia* goes beyond simply offering an opinion. It involves speaking truth out of conviction and a sense of duty, often in the name of critique to those with relatively more power and at great risk, either of death or reputation. See Foucault, *Fearless Speech*, 14–19.

45. See also Peterson, "Literary Transnationalism," 190–191.

46. "The Two Offers," Concluded (October 1859), 311; "Home Influences, Or Fancy Sketches" No. III, 2.1 (January 1860), 8–11; "The Two Offers" (September 1859), 288–289.

47. "Home Influences, Or Fancy Sketches" No. III (January 1860), 9.

48. "Chit Chat," 342.

49. See Peterson, "Literary Transnationalism," 190–191.

50. "Town and Country, or Fancy Sketches" No. II, 385.

51. Ibid., 384–385.

52. Wordsworth, *Lyrical Ballads* (1802), quoted in Peterson, "Literary Transnationalism," 195.

53. On the pseudonymous correspondents for *Douglass's Paper*, see Peterson, *Black Gotham*, 217–222. On "Magawiska," see Bruce, *Origins*, 199.

54. Readers familiar with the economic debates in *Douglass's Paper* and the economic discourse in the *Anglo-African Magazine*, including Harper's own "Our Greatest Want" (*AAM*, May 1859) and the last installment of the "Afric-American Picture Gallery," would recognize several key terms from that argument: "wealth" and "position" on one side and "whitewash" on the other.

55. "Chit Chat," 341.

56. Ibid.

57. Ibid.

58. Ibid.

59. Ibid.

60. See also Peterson, "Literary Transnationalism," 198, and Stancliff, *Frances Ellen Watkins Harper*, 44–47.

61. "Chit Chat," 341–342.

62. See Kantrowitz, *More Than Freedom*, 238.

63. *WAA*, January 26, 1861.

64. As Peterson aptly observes, "Coming from parlor men of privilege," the notion of emigration or slave rebellion "smack[s] of hypocrisy, of a fundamental lack of sympathy." Peterson, "Literary Transnationalism," 198.

65. "Chit Chat," 341.

66. See Caleb, "A Note on Leaders," *WAA*, May 4, 1861. Caleb was joining several readers who were frustrated with the several-months'-long debate in public and in print between Garnet, Smith, Delany, and others over various emigration plans. At points, the debate devolved into name calling with Garnet describing Smith as "Dr. Smith, the autocrat of the West Broadway drug shop," and Smith purportedly arguing that for Garnet and his supporters, "next to God is the white man." See, for instance, McCune Smith, "Emigration," *WAA*, January 5, 1861; "A Note from Mr. Garnet," *WAA*, January 12, 1861, 78; "The Emigration Question: Letters from the People," January 26, 1861; and "Dr. Delany's Letter," February, 2 1861. See also Pease and Pease, *They Who Would Be Free*, 296.

67. Peterson, "Literary Transnationalism," 198.

68. "Chit Chat," 340.

69. In Plato's thought experiment in Book VII of the *Republic*, people sitting in a dark cave watch the shadows of a pantomime and mistake this pantomime for reality because they, trapped in their seats, know no other representation. One escapes outside and realizes that the world inside the cave is a lie built on shadows and, moreover, recognizes the mechanisms that maintain the illusion. Upon reentry, the philosopher tries to reveal the truth to his fellows only to be shunned. See also Heidegger, "Plato's Doctrine," 251–270.

70. "Chit Chat," 341.

71. Halttuen, *Confidence*, 107.

72. "Town and Country, or Fancy Sketches. Number II," 383.

73. Hamilton, "Apology," *AAM* (January 1859), 3.

74. See Kantrowitz, *More Than Freedom*, 192–194.

75. See Foster, "Introduction," 25–35.

76. Reid-Pharr, "Introduction," xi.

77. "Zombi, or Fancy Sketches," *AAM* (February 1860), 35.

78. See Peterson, "Literary Transnationalism," 202. Peterson suggests that Robert Southey's *History of Brazil* (1821) was most likely the source for Harper's account of the Palmares. A version of the narrative also appears in Lindley, *Narrative of a Voyage to Brasil*, 176–186, and Child, *An Appeal*.

79. See Callahan, *Between the Lines*, 44.

80. "Zombi, or Fancy Sketches. Number IV," *AAM* (February 1860), 36.

81. Ibid. Callahan notes that Zombi was most likely captured, but the suicide narrative remains in circulation (*Between*, 46).

82. "Home Influences," 11. As Pease and Pease observe, by 1860, such lists and the call for free black citizens to find inspiration in them was "commonplace" (*They Who Would Be Free*, 237).

83. "Zombi," 35. See Peterson, "Literary Transnationalism," 196–197, and Callahan, *Between*, 44–50.

84. Hahn, *The Political Worlds*, 29.

85. Peterson, "Literary Transnationalism, 196–197.

86. "Home Influences," 10.

87. Ibid., 11.

88. See Peterson, "Literary Transnationalism," 206, and Holly, "Thoughts on Hayti," *AAM* (September 1859), 299.

89. "Zombi," 36.

90. "Home Influences," 10.

91. Harper, "An Appeal for the Philadelphia Rescuers," in *Brighter*, 52.

92. I am mindful here of Sylviane A. Diouf's caution not to collapse the distinction between marronage as autonomous separation and looser definitions of marronage as flight or resistance. See Diouf, *Slavery's Exiles*, 1–3.

93. "Home Influence," 11.

94. Callahan, *Between*, 48.

95. Kant, *Critique*, 527.

96. "Zombi," 36–37.

97. As Peterson has argued, Jane's sketches "blur the lines between public an domestic spheres, and challenge traditional views of men and women's proper spaces" in a way that also allows for a more capacious definition of revolutionary work ("Literary Transnationalism," 197).

98. Peterson, "Literary Transnationalism," 190 and 196–197.

99. On the role of the black press in cultivating its own particular mode of reading, see Ernest, *Liberation Historiography*, 297, and McHenry, *Forgotten Readers*, 130–140.

100. Carol Wilson, "Active Vigilance," 111.

101. Ibid., 114, and Kantrowitz, *More Than Freedom*, 185.

102. Carol Wilson, "Active Vigilance," 118.

103. Harper, "The Triumph," in *Brighter*, 115–116.

104. See Stancliff, *Frances Ellen Watkins Harper*, 34–35.

105. Greenspan, *William Wells Brown*, 70

106. "Triumph," 116.

107. Ibid., 116.

108. Ibid., 117.

109. See Boyd, *Discarded Legacy*, 86–87.

110. Harper, "To John Brown," November 25, 1859, in *Brighter*, 49–50.

111. Harper, "Miss Watkins and the Constitution," in *Brighter*, 47–48.

112. Ibid., 117.

113. Ephesians 6:12 KJV.

114. McKivigan and Harrold, "Introduction" to *Antislavery Violence*, 2.

115. Bacon, *The Humblest*, 66–68.

Conclusion

1. "Samuel Ringgold Ward to Nathaniel P. Rogers," *BAP*, 341.

2. Secor, "Citizenship," 353.

3. Levine, *Forms*, 3–5.

4. Jarrett, *Representing*, 26.

5. "Herstory," *Black Lives Matter*, https://blacklivesmatter.com/about/herstory/ (accessed February 15, 2018). See also Taylor, *From #BlackLivesMatter*.

6. Quoted in Lee, *For Freedom's Sake*, 89. As Hamer biographer Chana Kai Lee notes, "Their attendance was its own challenge to convention nonbelievers who had all but dismissed the possibility that a meaningful contest would take place." Partway through the speech, Johnson, fearing the loss of southern Democrats, scheduled an impromptu press conference in an attempt to distract from Hamer's testimony. See Lee, *For Freedom's Sake*, 86.

7. Quoted in ibid., 99.

8. Warner, *Letters*, 11. See, for instance, Santamarina, "Thinkable Alternatives"; Otter, "Philadelphia Experiments"; and Brooks, "Early American."

9. See Henderson, "Speaking in Tongues"; Peterson, *Doers*; Baker, *Blues*; Spillers, "Mama's Baby," in *Black, White, and in Color*; and Gates, *Signifying Monkey*.

10. See, for instance, the *MELUS* special issue on African American print cultures, edited by Joycelyn Moody and Howard Rambsy II, *MELUS: Multi-Ethnic Literature of the U.S.* 40, no. 3 (2015).

11. Fagan, *Black Newspaper*, 10.

12. Wright, *Black Girlhood*, 8–9. Wright builds her argument through P. Gabrielle Foreman's "'Reading Aright.'" For a slightly different articulation of this principle, see Brooks, "The Early American Public Sphere."

13. Rusert, *Fugitive*, 19 and 5.

14. See Gardner, *Unexpected Places*. Work including Peterson, *Doers*; Wright, *Black Girlhood*; Foreman, *Activist Sentiments*; and McCaskill and Gebhard, *Post-Bellum, Pre-Harlem* has helped us break from this narrative.

BIBLIOGRAPHY

Adorno, Theodor. *Aesthetic Theory*. Trans. Robert Hullot-Kentor. Minneapolis: University Minnesota Press, 1997.

Alexander, Leslie. *African or American? Black Identity and Political Activism in New York City, 1784–1861*. Urbana: University of Illinois Press, 2008.

Allen, Theodore. *The Invention of the White Race: Racial Oppression and Social Control*. Vol. 2. *The Origin of Racial Oppression in Anglo-America*. New York: Verso, 1994.

Anderson, Benedict. *Imagined Communities: Reflections on the Origin and Spread of Nationalism*. New York: Verso, 2006.

Anderson, Elijah. "Black Shadow Politics in Midwestville: The Insiders, the Outsiders, and the Militant Young." *Sociological Inquiry* 42, no. 1 (January 1972): 19–27.

Andrews, William. "The 1850s: The First Afro-American Literary Renaissance." In *Literary Romanticism in America*, ed. William Andrews, 38–60. Baton Rouge: Louisiana State University Press, 1981.

Appleby, Joyce. *Inheriting the Revolution: The First Generation of Americans*. Cambridge, Mass.: Harvard University Press, 2000.

———. Appleby, Joyce Oldham. *Liberalism and Republicanism in the Historical Imagination*. Cambridge: Harvard University Press, 1992.

———. "Republicanism in Old and New Contexts." *William & Mary Quarterly* 43 (January 1986): 3–34.

Aptheker, Herbert. *American Negro Slave Revolts*. 1943. New York: International Publishers, 1983.

Arendt, Hannah. *The Origins of Totalitarianism*. New York: Schocken, 1994.

Aune, James Arnt. "Democratic Style and Ideological Containment." *Rhetoric & Public Affairs* 11, no. 3 (2008): 482–490.

Ayers, Linda. " 'Their Unfailing Friend' Edward Everett and the Mount Vernon Ladies' Association." Paper presented at the Annual George Washington Symposium. Mount Vernon, Va., November 8, 2003.

Bacon, Jacqueline. *The Humblest May Stand Forth: Rhetoric, Empowerment, and Abolition*. Columbia: University of South Carolina Press, 2002.

Baker, Houston A. "Archaeology, Ideology, and African American Discourse." In *Redefining American Literary History*, ed. A. LaVonne Brown Ruoff and Jerry W. Ward Jr., 157–199. New York: Modern Language Association of America, 1990.

———. *Blues, Ideology, and Afro-American Literature*. Chicago: University of Chicago Press, 1984.

———. *Critical Memory: Public Spheres, African American Writing, and Black Fathers and Sons in America*. Athens: University of Georgia Press, 2001.

———. *I Don't Hate the South*. New York: Oxford University Press, 2007.

———. *Modernism and the Harlem Renaissance*. Chicago: University of Chicago Press, 1987.

Bakhtin, Mikhail. *The Dialogic Imagination: Four Essays*. Ed. Michael Holquist. Trans. Caryl Emerson and Michael Holquist. Austin: University of Texas Press, 2006.

Ball, Erica. *To Live an Antislavery Life: Personal Politics and the Antebellum Black Middle Class*. Athens: University of Georgia Press, 2012.

Bank, Rosemarie K. *Theater Culture in America, 1825–1860*. New York: Cambridge University Press, 1997.

Barker, Gordon S. *The Imperfect Revolution: Anthony Burns and the Landscape of Race in Antebellum America*. Kent, Ohio: Kent State University Press, 2010.

Barker-Benfield, G. J. *Abigail and John Adams: The Americanization of Sensibility*. Chicago: University of Chicago Press, 2010.

Barthe, Roland. *Mythologies*. Trans. Richard Howard and Annette Lavers. New York: Hill and Wang, 2012.

Bascom, Benjamin. "Citizens as Verbs: The Politics of Belonging in Nineteenth-Century and Contemporary American Citizenship." *Kritik* (blog). *Unit for Criticism and Interpretative Theory*, March 8, 2016. https://unitforcriticism.wordpress.com/2016/03/18/unit-faculty-fellows-symposium-panel-3-derrick-spires-j-david-cisneros-response-by-ben-bascom/.

Batstone, David, and Eduardo Mendieta, eds. *The Good Citizen*. New York: Routledge, 1999.

Bay, Mia. *The White Image in the Black Mind: African-American Ideas About White People, 1830–1925*. New York: Oxford University Press, 2000.

Bell, Howard Holman. *Minutes of the Proceedings of the National Negro Conventions, 1830–1864*. New York: Arno Press and the *New York Times*, 1969.

———. *A Survey of the Negro Convention Movement, 1830–1861*. New York: Arno Press and New York Times, 1969.

Benezet, Anthony. *Observations on the Enslaving, Importing, and Purchasing of Negroes*. Philadelphia: Henry Miller, 1766.

Benhabib, Seyla. "Models of Public Space: Hannah Arendt, the Liberal Tradition, and Jürgen Habermas." In *Habermas and the Public Sphere*, ed. Craig Calhoun, 73–98. Cambridge, Mass.: MIT Press, 1992.

Bentley, Nancy. "The Strange Career of Love and Slavery: Chesnutt, Engels, Masoch." *American Literary History* 17, no. 3 (2005): 460–485.

———. "Warped Conjunctions: Jacques Rancière and African American Twoness." In *American Literature's Aesthetic Dimensions*, ed. Cindy Weinstein and Christopher Looby, 291–312. New York: Columbia University Press, 2012.

Bercovitch, Sacvan. *The Rites of Assent: Transformations in the Symbolic Construction of America*. New York: Routledge, 1992.

Berlant, Lauren. *Anatomy of National Fantasy: Hawthorne, Utopia, and Everyday Life*. Chicago: University of Chicago Press, 1991.

———. "Citizenship." In *Keywords for American Cultural Studies*, ed. Bruce Burgett and Glenn Hendler, 37–42. New York: New York University Press, 2014.

———. *Cruel Optimism*. Durham, N.C.: Duke University Press, 2011.

Bertoff, Roland. *Republic of the Dispossessed: The Exceptional Old-European Consensus in America*. Columbia: University of Missouri Press, 1997.

Blight, David W. "In Search of Learning, Liberty, and Self Definition: James McCune Smith and the Ordeal of the Antebellum Black Intellectual." *Afro-Americans in New York Life and History* 9, no. 2 (July 1985): 7–25.

Blumin, Stuart M. *The Emergence of the Middle Class: Social Experience in the American City, 1760–1900*. New York: Cambridge University Press, 1989.

Bouvier, John. *A Law Dictionary, Adapted to the Constitution and Laws of the United States of America, and of the Several States of the American Union with References to the Civil and Other Systems of Foreign Law*. Philadelphia: T. and J. W. Johnson, 1839.

———. *A Law Dictionary, Adapted to the Constitution and Laws of the United States of America, and of the Several States of the American Union with References to the Civil and Other Systems of Foreign Law*. 5th ed. Philadelphia: Deacon & Peterson, 1857.

Boyd, Melba Joyce. *Discarded Legacy: Politics and Poetics in the Life of Frances E. W. Harper, 1825–1911*. Detroit: Wayne State University Press, 1994.

Bradburn, Douglass. *Citizenship Revolution: Politics and the Creation of the American Union, 1774–1804*. Charlottesville: University of Virginia Press, 2009.

Brand, Dana. *The Spectator and the City in Nineteenth-Century American Literature*. New York: Cambridge University Press, 1991.

Broderip, W. J. *Zoological Recreations*. London: Henry Colburn, 1849.

Bromell, Nicholas K. *By the Sweat of the Brow: Literature and Labor in Antebellum America*. Chicago: University of Chicago Press, 1993.

Brooke, John L. "Consent, Civil Society, and the Public Sphere in the Age of Revolution and the Early American Republic." In *Beyond the Founders: New Approaches to the Political History of the Early American Republic*, ed. Jeffrey L. Pasley, Andrew W. Robertson, and David Waldstreicher, 207–250. Chapel Hill: University North Carolina Press, 2004.

Brooks, Joanna. *American Lazarus: Religion and the Rise of African-American and Native American Literatures*. New York: Oxford University Press, 2003.

———. "The Early American Public Sphere and the Emergence of a Black Print Counterpublic." *William and Mary Quarterly* 62, no. 1 (2005): 67–92.

———. "From Edwards to Baldwin: Heterodoxy, Discontinuity, and New Narratives of American Religious-Literary History." *American Literary History* 22, no. 2 (2010): 439–453. http://muse.jhu.edu.

Brown, Thomas Allston. *A History of the New York Stage from the First Performance in 1732 to 1901*. Vol. 1. New York: Dodd, Mead and Company, 1903.

Brown, Vincent. *The Reaper's Garden: Death and Power in the World of Atlantic Slavery*. Cambridge, Mass.: Harvard University Press, 2008.

Brown, Wendy. "The Humanities and the Crisis of the Public University." *Representations* 116, no. 1 (Fall 2011): 19–41.

Brown, William Wells. 1863. *The Black Man, His Antecedents, His Genius, and His Achievements*. New York: Thomas Hamilton, 1863. *Documenting the American South*. Chapel Hill: University Library, University of North Carolina, 1999. http://docsouth.unc.edu/neh/brownww/brown.html.

Buccola, Nicholas. "'Each for All and All for Each': The Liberal Statesmanship of Frederick Douglass." *Review of Politics* 70 (2008): 400–419.

Burkitt, William. *Expository Notes, with Practical Observations upon the New Testament of Our Lord and Saviour Jesus Christ*. Birmingham: J. Thompson, 1789. Eighteenth Century Collections Online.

Burnham, Patricia M., and Lucretia Hoover Giese, eds. *Redefining American History Painting*. New York: Cambridge University Press, 1995.

Burns, Sarah. *Painting the Dark Side: Art and the Gothic Imagination in Nineteenth-Century America*. Berkeley: University of California Press, 2004.

Butler, Judith. "Restaging the Universal: Hegemony and the Limits of Formalism." In *Contingency, Hegemony, Universality: Contemporary Dialogues on the Left*, ed. Judith Butler, Ernesto Laclau, and Slavoj Žižek, 11–43. New York: Verso, 2000.

Bruce, Dickson D. *Origins of African American Literature*. Charlottesville: University of Virginia Press, 2001.

Caleb. "A Note on Leaders." *Weekly Anglo-African* 2, no. 42 (May 1861): 94.

Calhoun, Craig, ed. *Habermas and the Public Sphere*. Cambridge, Mass.: MIT Press, 1992.

Callahan, Monique-Adelle. *Between the Lines: Literary Transnationalism and African American Poetics*. New York: Oxford University Press, 2011.

Campbell, James T. *Songs of Zion: The African Methodist Episcopal Church in the United States and South Africa*. New York: Oxford University Press, 1995.

Carey, Matthew. "Address of M. Carey to the public Philadelphia April 4, 1794. or Reply to a printed attack, signed Argus, and to Absalom Jones and Richard Allen's Narrative of the proceedings of the Black people, both regarding Carey's conduct during the yellow fever epidemic." In *Pamphlets and Papers by M. Carey*. Vol. 3. Philadelphia: Joseph R. A. Skerrett, 1826.

———. *A Short Account of the Malignant Fever, Lately Prevalent in Philadelphia: With a Statement of the Proceedings that Took Place on the Subject in Different Parts of the United States*. 2nd ed. Philadelphia: Matthew Carey, 1793.

Casper, Scott E. *Sarah Johnson's Mount Vernon: The Forgotten History of an American Shrine*. New York: Hill and Wang, 2008.

Castronovo, Russ. *Beautiful Democracy: Aesthetics and Anarchy in a Global Era*. Chicago: University of Chicago Press, 2007.

———. *Necro-Citizenship: Death, Eroticism, and the Public Sphere in the Nineteenth-Century United States*. Durham, N.C.: Duke University Press, 2001.

Certeau, Michel de. *The Practice of Everyday Life*. Trans. Steven Rendall. Vol. 2. Los Angeles: University of California Press, 1984.

Child, Lydia Maria. *An Appeal in Favor of That Class of Americans Called Africans*. Boston: Allen & Ticknor, 1833.

Chiles, Katy. "Within and Without the Raced Nations: Intratextuality, Martin Delany, and *Blake; or the Huts of America*." *American Literature* 80 no. 2 (2008): 323–352.

Clifton, James. *The Predicament of Culture: Twentieth-Century Ethnography, Literature, and Art*. Cambridge, Mass.: Harvard University Press, 1988.

Clytus, Radiclani. "Visualizing in Black Print: The Brooklyn Correspondence of William J. Wilson aka 'Ethiop.'" *J19: The Journal of Nineteenth-Century Americanists* 6, no. 1 (Spring 2018): 29–66.

Cohen, Lara Langer. "Democratic Representations: Puffery and the Antebellum Print Explosion." *American Literature* 79, no. 4 (December 2007): 643–672.

Condit, Celeste Michelle, and John Louis Lucaites. *Crafting Equality: America's Anglo-African World*. Chicago: University of Chicago Press, 1993.

Cooey, Paula M. *Willing the Good: Jesus, Dissent, and Desire*. Minneapolis: Augsburg Fortress, 2006.

Countryman, Edward. *The American Revolution*. New York: Hill and Wang, 1985.

———. *A People in Revolution: The American Revolution and Political Society in New York, 1760–1790*. Baltimore: Johns Hopkins University Press, 1981.

Crandall v. State of Connecticut. 10 Conn. 339 (1834).

Crane, Gregg. *Race, Citizenship, and Law in American Literature*. New York: Cambridge University Press, 2002.

Crèvecoeur, J. Hector St. John. *Letters from an American Farmer*. Ed. Susan Manning. New York: Oxford University Press, 1997.

Dain, Bruce. *A Hideous Monster of the Mind: American Race Theory, 1787–1859*. Cambridge, Mass.: Harvard University Press, 2002.

Davis, David Brion. *The Problem of Slavery in the Age of Revolution, 1770–1823*. New York: Oxford University Press, 1999.

Davis, Rodney O., and Douglas L. Wilson. *The Lincoln-Douglas Debates*. Urbana: Knox College Lincoln Studies Center and the University of Illinois Press, 2008.

Delany, Martin R. *Condition, Elevation, Emigration, and Destiny of the Colored People in the United States Politically Considered*. Philadelphia: King and Laird, 1852. archive.org.

———. *Martin R. Delany: A Documentary Reader*. Ed. Robert S. Levine. Chapel Hill: University of North Carolina Press, 2003.

Delany, Samuel. *Times Square Red, Times Square Blue*. New York: New York University Press, 1999.

DeLombard, Jeannine Marie. "Apprehending Early African American Literary History." In *Early African American Print Culture in Theory and Practice*, ed. Jordan Alexander Stein and Lara Cohen, 93–106. Philadelphia: University Pennsylvania Press, 2012.

———. *In the Shadow of the Gallows: Race, Crime, and American Civic Identity*. Philadelphia: University of Pennsylvania Press, 2012.

———. *Slavery on Trial: Law, Abolitionism, and Print Culture*. Chapel Hill: University of North Carolina Press, 2007.

Denning, Michael. *Mechanic Accents: Dime Novels and Working Class Culture*. New York: Verso, 1998.

Dennison, George M. *The Dorr War: Republicanism on Trial, 1831–1861*. Lexington: University Press of Kentucky, 1976.

Douglass, Frederick. *Autobiographies*. New York: Library of America, 1994.

———. "Make Your Sons Mechanics and Farmers—Not Waiters, Porters, and Barbers." *Frederick Douglass's Paper*, March 18, 1853.

———. *Frederick Douglass: Selected Speeches and Writings*. Ed. Philip S. Foner. Chicago: Lawrence Hill Books, 1999.

———. "A Trip to Hayti." *Pine and Palm*, May 11, 1861.

Douglass, William. *Annals of the First African Church in the United States of America, Now Styled the African Episcopal Church of St. Thomas, Philadelphia*. Philadelphia: King & Baird, 1862.

Du Bois, W. E. B. *The Philadelphia Negro: A Social Study*. Philadelphia: University of Pennsylvania Press, 1899.

———. *The Souls of Black Folk*. New York: Bantam, 1989.

———. *W. E. B. Du Bois: Writings*. New York: Library of American, 1986.

Dunbar, Erica Armstrong. *A Fragile Freedom: African American Women and Emancipation in the Antebellum City*. New Haven, Conn.: Yale University Press, 2008.

Easton, Hosea. *A Treatise on the Intellectual Character, and Civil and Political Condition of the Colored People of the U. States.* Boston: Isaac Knapp, 1837.

Eckstrom, Leif and Britt Rusert. "Introduction." "Afric-American Picture Gallery." *Just Teach One: Early African American Print.* American Antiquarian Society. http://jtoaa.common-place.org/introduction-afric-american-picture-gallery /.

Edwards, Jonathan. *Works of Jonathan Edwards.* Vol. 8, *Ethical Writings.* Ed. Paul Ramsey. New Haven, Conn.: Yale University Press, 1970.

Ellis, Markman. *The Politics of Sensibility: Race, Gender and Commerce in the Sentimental Novel.* New York: Cambridge University Press, 2004.

Emerson, Ralph Waldo. *Essays and Lectures.* New York: Literary Classics of the United States, 1983.

Engels, Jeremy. "Some Preliminary Thoughts on Democratic Style." *Rhetoric & Public Affairs* 11, no. 3 (2008): 439–440.

Ericson, David F. *The Shaping of American Liberalism: The Debates over Ratification, Nullification, and Slavery.* Chicago: University of Chicago Press, 1993.

Ernest, John. *Chaotic Justice: Rethinking African American Literary History.* Chapel Hill: University of North Carolina Press, 2009.

———. *Liberation Historiography: African American Writers and the Challenge of History, 1794–1861.* Chapel Hill: University of North Carolina Press, 2004.

Estes, J. Worth, and Billy G. Smith, eds. *A Melancholy Scene of Devastation: The Public Response to the 1793 Philadelphia Yellow Fever Epidemic.* Canton, Mass.: Science History Publications, 1997.

Etcheson, Nicole. *Bleeding Kansas: Contested Liberty in the Civil War Era.* Lawrence: University Press of Kansas, 2004.

Fagan, Benjamin. *The Black Newspaper and the Chosen Nation.* Athens: University of Georgia Press, 2016.

———. "*The North Star* and the Atlantic 1848." *African American Review* 47, no. 1 (2014): 51–67. https://muse.jhu.edu/.

Fanon, Frantz. *The Wretched of the Earth.* Trans. Constance Farrington. New York: Grove Weidenfeld, 1991.

Field, Phyllis. *The Politics of Race in New York: The Struggle for Black Suffrage in the Civil War Era.* Ithaca, N.Y.: Cornell University Press, 1982.

"Fifteen Thousand Negro Balance-of-Power-Men Wanted, by the Whigs and Abolitionists!" *Daily (N.Y.) Globe.* Reprinted in *National Anti-Slavery Standard,* October 9, 1845.

Finkelman, Paul. *Dred Scott v. Sandford: A Brief History with Documents.* Boston: Bedford, 1997.

Fliegelman, Jay. *Declaring Independence: Jefferson, Natural Language, and the Culture of Performance.* Stanford, Calif.: Stanford University Press, 1993.

Foner, Eric. *Free Soil, Free Labor, Free Men: The Ideology of the Republican Party Before the Civil War.* 2nd ed. New York: Oxford University Press, 1995.

———. *Gateway to Freedom: The Hidden History of America's Fugitive Slaves.* New York: Oxford University Press, 2016.

———. *Tom Paine and Revolutionary America.* New York: Oxford University Press, 1976.

Foner, Philip S., and George E. Walker, eds. *Proceedings of the Black State Conventions, 1840–1865.* Vol. 1, *New York, Pennsylvania, Indiana, Michigan, Ohio.* Philadelphia: Temple University Press, 1979.

Foreman, P. Gabrielle. *Activist Sentiments: Reading Black Women in the Nineteenth Century.* Urbana: University of Illinois Press, 2009.

———. "'Reading Aright': White Slavery, Black Referents, and the Strategy of Histotextuality in *Iola Leroy.*" *Yale Journal of Criticism* 10, no. 2 (1997): 327–354.

Foreman, P. Gabrielle, Sarah Patterson, and Jim Casey. "Introduction to the Colored Conventions Movement." *Colored Conventions: Bringing Nineteenth-Century Black Organizing to Digital Life.* http://coloredconventions.org/introduction-to-movement.

Formisano, Ronald P. *For the People: American Populist Movements from the Revolution to the 1850s.* Chapel Hill: University of North Carolina Press, 2008.

Forten, James. "Letter Addressed to the Honourable George Thatcher, Member of Congress." In *Early Negro Writing, 1760–1837,* ed. Dorothy Porter, 333–335. Baltimore: Black Classic Press, 1995.

Foster, A. Kristen. *Moral Visions and Material Ambitions: Philadelphia Struggles to Define the Republic, 1776–1836.* Lanham, Md.: Lexington, 2004.

Foster, Frances Smith. Introduction to *A Brighter Coming Day: A Frances Ellen Watkins Harper Reader,* ed. Frances Smith Foster, 3–40. New York: Feminist Press, 1990.

"A Narrative of the Interesting Origins and Somewhat Surprising Developments of African-American Print Culture." *American Literary History* 17, no. 4 (Winter 2005): 714–740.

———. *Written by Herself: Literary Production by African American Women, 1746–1892.* Blacks in the Diaspora. Bloomington: Indiana University Press, 1993.

Foster, George. *New York by Gaslight and Other Urban Sketches.* Ed. Stuart M. Blumin. Berkeley: University of California Press, 1990.

Foucault, Michel. *Fearless Speech.* Ed. Joseph Pearson. Los Angeles: Semiotext(e), 2001.

———. "Of Other Spaces." Trans. Jay Miskowiec. *Diacritics* 16 (Spring 1986): 22–27.

———. *The Order of Things: An Archaeology of the Human Sciences.* New York: Vintage, 1994.

Frankel, Matthew Cordova. "'Nature's Nation' Revisited: Citizenship and the Sublime in Thomas Jefferson's Notes on the State of Virginia." *American Literature* 73, no. 4 (December 2001): 695–725.

Fraser, Nancy. "Rethinking the Public Sphere: A Contribution to the Critique of Actually Existing Democracy." *Social Text* 25–26 (1990): 56–90. http://www.jstor.org/stable/466240.

Fredrickson, George M. *The Black Image in the White Mind: The Debate on Afro-American Character and Destiny, 1817–1914.* New York: Harper & Row 1971.

Free, Laura E. *Suffrage Reconstructed: Gender, Race, and Voting Rights in the Civil War Era.* Ithaca, N.Y.: Cornell University Press, 2015.

Freehling, William H. *The Road to Disunion: Secessionists at Bay, 1776–1854.* New York: Oxford University Press, 1991.

Freire, Paulo. *Pedagogy of the Oppressed.* Trans. Myra Bergman Ramos. 30th anniversary ed. New York: Continuum, 2005.

Fritz, Christian G. *American Sovereigns: The Constitutional Legacy of the People's Sovereignty Before the Civil War.* New York: Cambridge University Press, 2008.

Fuente, Alejandro de la. "Slave Law and Claims-Making in Cuba: The Tannenbaum Debate Revisited." *Law and History Review* (Summer 2004): 339–369.

Galtung, Johan. *The True Worlds: A Transnational Perspective.* New York: Free Press, 1980.

Garber, Majorie. "Compassion." In *Compassion: The Culture and Politics of An Emotion,* ed. Lauren Berland, 15–27. New York: Routledge, 2004.

Gardner, Eric. *Black Print Unbound: The Christian Recorder, African American Literature, and Periodical Culture*. New York: Oxford University Press, 2016.

———. "Early African American Print Culture and the American West." In *Early African American Print Culture in Theory and Practice*, ed. Jordan Alexander Stein and Lara Cohen, 75–92. Philadelphia: University Pennsylvania Press, 2012.

———. *Unexpected Places: Relocating Nineteenth-Century African American Literature.* Jackson: University Press of Mississippi, 2009.

Gardner, Jared. *Master Plots: Race and the Founding of an American Literature, 1787–1845.* Baltimore: Johns Hopkins University Press, 1998.

Garnet, Henry Highland. *Walker's Appeal, with a Brief Sketch of His Life by Henry Highland Garnet and also Garnet's Address to the Slaves of the United States of America.* New York: J. H. Tobitt, 1848.

Gates, Henry Louis, Jr. *The Signifying Monkey: A Theory of African-American Literary Criticism.* New York: Oxford University Press, 1988.

Gentleman, Marvin E. *The Dorr Rebellion: A Study in American Radicalism, 1833–1849.* New York: Random House, 1973.

George, Carol V. R. *Segregated Sabbaths: Richard Allen and the Emergence of Independent Black Churches, 1760–1840.* New York: Oxford University Press, 1973.

Gerdts, William H., and Mark Thislewaite, eds. *Grand Illusions: History Painting in America.* Fort Worth, Tex.: Amon Carter Museum, 1988.

Gilroy, Paul. *The Black Atlantic: Modernity and Double Consciousness.* Cambridge, Mass.: Harvard University Press, 1993.

Glaude, Eddie S., Jr. "Of the Black Church and the Making of a Black Public." In *African American Religious Thought: An Anthology*, ed. Cornel West and Eddie S. Glaude Jr., 338–365. Louisville, Ky.: John Knox, 2003.

Glaude, Eddie S., Jr., and Cornel West. "Introduction." In *African American Religious Thought: An Anthology*, ed. Cornel West and Eddie S. Glaude Jr., xi–xxvi. Louisville, Ky.: John Knox, 2003.

Glickstein, Jonathan A. *American Exceptionalism, American Anxiety: Wages, Competition, and Degraded Labor in the Antebellum United States.* Charlottesville: University of Virginia Press, 2002.

Goddu, Teresa A. *Gothic America: Narrative, History, and Nation.* New York: Columbia University Press, 1997.

Goodman, Dena. *The Republic of Letters: A Cultural History of the French Enlightenment.* Ithaca, N.Y.: Cornell University Press, 1994.

Gould, Philip. *Barbaric Traffic: Commerce and Antislavery in the Eighteenth-Century Atlantic World.* Cambridge, Mass.: Harvard University Press, 2003.

———. "Race, Commerce, and the Literature of Yellow Fever in Early National Philadelphia." *Early American Literature* 35, no. 2 (2000): 157–186.

Greenspan. Ezra. *William Wells Brown: An African American Life.* New York: W. W. Norton, 2014.

Griffith, Sally. "'A Total Dissolution of the Bonds of Society': Community Death and Regeneration in Matthew Carey's Short Account of the Malignant Fever." In *A Melancholy Scene of Devastation: The Public Response to the 1793 Philadelphia Yellow Fever Epidemic*, ed. J. Worth Estes and Billy G. Smith, 45–59. Canton, Mass.: Science History Publications, 1997.

Grimke, Charlotte Forten. *The Journals of Charlotte Forten Grimke*. Ed. Brenda Stevenson. Schomburg Library of Nineteenth-Century Black Women Writers. New York: Oxford University Press, 1998.

Grossman, Jay. *Reconstituting the American Renaissance: Emerson, Whitman, and the Politics of Representation*. Durham, N.C.: Duke University Press, 2003.

Gruesz, Kirsten Silva. *Ambassadors of Culture: The Transamerican Origins of Latino Writing*. Princeton, N.J.: Princeton University Press, 2002.

Habermas, Jürgen. *The Structural Transformation of the Public Sphere: An Inquiry into a Category of Bourgeois Society*. Trans. Thomas Burger and Frederick Lawrence. 1962. Cambridge, Mass.: MIT Press, 1991.

Hack, Daniel. *Reaping Something New: African American Transformations of Victorian Literature*. Princeton, N.J.: Princeton University Press, 2017.

Hahn, Steven. *The Political Worlds of Slavery and Freedom*. Boston: Harvard University Press, 2009.

Halttunen, Karen. *Confidence Men and Painted Women: A Study of Middle-Class Culture in America*. New Haven, Conn.: Yale University Press, 1986.

Hamer, Fannie Lou. "To Praise Our Bridges." In *Mississippi Writers: Reflections of Childhood and Youth*, vol. 2, *Nonfiction*, ed. Dorothy Abbott, 321–330. Center for the Study of Southern Culture Series. Jackson: University Press of Mississippi, 1986.

Hammer, Dean. *The Puritan Tradition in Revolutionary, Federalist, and Whig Political Theory: A Rhetoric of Origins*. New York: Lang, 1998.

Hariman, Robert. *Political Style: The Artistry of Power*. Chicago: University of Chicago Press, 1995.

Harper, Frances Ellen Watkins. *A Brighter Coming Day: A Frances Ellen Watkins Harper Reader*. Ed. Frances Smith Foster. New York: Feminist Press, 1990.

Harris, Cheryl. "Whiteness as Property." *Harvard Law Review* 106, no. 8 (1993): 1707–1791.

———. "Whiteness as Property." In *Critical Race Theory: The Key Writings That Formed the Movement*, ed. Kimberlé Crenshaw, Neil Gotanda, Gary Peller, and Kendall Thomas, 276–291. New York: New York University Press, 1996.

Harris, Leslie M. "From Abolitionist Amalgamators to 'Rulers of the Five Points': The Discourse of Interracial Sex and Reform in Antebellum New York City." In *African-American Activism Before the Civil War*, ed. Patrick Rael, 250–271. New York: Routledge, 2008.

———. *In the Shadow of Slavery: African Americans in New York City, 1626–1863*. Chicago: University of Chicago Press, 2003.

Harrison, Nicholas. *Postcolonial Criticism: History, Theory, and the Work of Fiction*. Malden, Mass.: Blackwell, 2003.

Hartman, Saidiya. *Scenes of Subjection: Terror, Slavery, and Self-Making in Nineteenth-Century America*. New York: Oxford University Press, 1997.

Haskell, Thomas L. "Capitalism and the Origins of Humanitarian Sensibility, Part 2." In *The Antislavery Debate: Capitalism and Abolitionism as Problems of Historical Interpretation*, ed. Thomas Bender, John Ashworth, and David Brion Davis, 109–160. Los Angeles: University of California Press, 1992.

Heidegger, Martin. "Plato's Doctrine of Truth." In *Philosophy of the Twentieth Century: An Anthology*, vol. 3, ed. William Barrett and Henry D. Aiken, 251–270. New York: Random House, 1962.

Held, David. *Models of Democracy*. Stanford, Calif.: Stanford University Press, 2006.

Henderson, Mae G. "Speaking in Tongues: Dialogics and Dialectics and the Black Woman Writer's Literary Tradition." In *Changing Our Own Words: Essays on Criticism, Theory, and Writing by Black Women*, ed. Cheryl Wall, 16–37. New Brunswick, N.J.: Rutgers University Press, 1989.

Henry, Katherine. *Liberalism and the Culture of Security: The Nineteenth-Century Rhetoric of Reform*. Tuscaloosa: University of Alabama Press, 2011.

Hetherington, Kevin. *The Badlands of Modernity: Heterotopia and Social Ordering*. London: Routledge, 1997.

Higginbotham, Leon A., Jr. *Shades of Freedom: Racial Politics and Presumptions of the American Legal Process*. New York: Oxford University Press, 1996.

Hodges, Graham Russell. *Root & Branch: African Americans in New York and East Jersey, 1613–1863*. Chapel Hill: University of North Carolina Press, 1999.

Hoekstra, Kinch. "Hobbes on the Natural Condition of Mankind." In *The Cambridge Companion to Hobbes's Leviathan*, ed. Patricia Springborg, 109–127. New York: Cambridge University Press, 2007.

Hogarth, Rana A. *Medicalizing Blackness: Making Racial Difference in the Atlantic World*. Chapel Hill: University of North Carolina Press, 2017.

Holton, Woody. *Unruly Americans and the Origins of the Constitution*. New York: Hill and Wang, 2007.

Horton, Lois E. "From Class to Race in Early America: Northern Post-Emancipation Racial Reconstruction." In *Race and the Early Republic: Racial Consciousness and Nation-Building in the Early Republic*, ed. Michael A. Morrison and James Brewer Stewart, 55–74. Lanham, Md.: Rowman and Littlefield, 2002.

Hyde, Carrie. *Civic Longing: The Speculative Origins of U.S. Citizenship*. Cambridge, Mass.: Harvard University Press, 2018.

Hyde, Lewis. *Common as Air: Revolution, Art, and Ownership*. New York: Farrar, Straus & Giroux, 2011.

Isenberg, Nancy. *Sex and Citizenship in Antebellum America*. Chapel Hill: University of North Carolina Press, 1998.

Jarrett, Gene Andrew. *Representing the Race: A New Political History of African American Literature*. New York: New York University Press, 2011.

Jefferson, Thomas. *Writings*. New York: Library Classics of America, 1984.

Jehlen, Myra. "History Before the Fact: Or, Captain John Smith's Unfinished Symphony." *Critical Inquiry* 19, no. 4 (Summer 1993): 677–692.

Johnson, Tekla Ali. "Frederick Douglass and the Kansas-Nebraska Act: From Reformer to Revolutionary." In *The Nebraska-Kansas Act of 1854*, ed. John R. Wunder and Joann M. Ross, 113–128. Lincoln: University of Nebraska Press, 2008.

Johnson, Walter. "On Agency." *Journal of Social History* 37, no. 1 (Autumn 2003): 113–124.

Johnson, Wendy Dasler. "Frances Ellen Watkins Harper, Black Poet Ventriloquist." In *Antebellum American Women's Poetry: A Rhetoric of Sentiment*, ed. Wendy Dasler Johnson, 51–75. Carbondale: Southern Illinois University Press, 2016.

Jones, Absalom, and Richard Allen. *A Narrative of The Proceedings of the African American People, During the Late Awful Calamity in Philadelphia, in the Year 1793: And a Refutation of Some Censures, Thrown upon Them in Some Late Publications. By A.J. And R.A.* Philadelphia: William W. Woodward, 1794.

Jones, Douglas A., Jr. *The Captive Stage: Performance and the Proslavery Imagination of the Antebellum North.* Ann Arbor: University of Michigan Press, 2014.

Jones, Martha S. *Birthright Citizens: A History of Race and Rights in Antebellum America.* New York: Cambridge University Press, 2018.

Jordan, Winthrop. *White over Black: American Attitudes Toward the Negro, 1550–1812.* Chapel Hill: University of North Carolina Press, 2012.

Joyce, Donald F. *Black Book Publishers in the United States: A Historical Dictionary of the Presses, 1817–1990.* New York: Greenwood, 1991.

Kalyvas, Andreas, and Ira Katznelson. *Liberal Beginnings: Making a Republic for the Moderns.* New York: Cambridge University Press, 2008.

Kant, Immanuel. *Critique of the Power of Judgment.* Ed. Paul Guyer. Trans. Paul Guyer and Eric Matthews. New York: Cambridge University Press, 2000.

Kantrowitz, Stephen. *More Than Freedom: Fighting for Black Citizenship in a White Republic, 1829–1889.* New York: Penguin Press, 2012.

Kazanjian, David. *The Colonizing Trick: National Culture and Imperial Citizenship in Early America.* Minneapolis: University of Minnesota Press, 2003.

Kesler, Charles R. "Introduction." In *The Federalist Papers*, ed. Clinton Rossiter, vii–xxxi. New York: Signet, 2003.

Kettner, James H. *The Development of U.S. Citizenship, 1608–1870.* Chapel Hill: University of North Carolina Press, 2005.

Keyssar, Alexander. *The Right to Vote: The Contested History of Democracy in the United States.* New York: Basic Books, 2000.

Kloppenberg, James T. "The Virtues of Liberalism: Christianity, Republicanism, and Ethics in Early American Political Discourse." *Journal of American History* 74, no. 1 (June 1987): 9–33.

Knott, Sarah. *Sensibility and the American Revolution.* Chapel Hill: University of North Carolina Press, 2009.

Lamb, Kevin. "Foucault's Aestheticism." *Diacritics* 35, no. 2 (Summer 2005): 52.

Lang, Amy Schrager. *The Syntax of Class: Writing Inequality in Nineteenth-Century America.* Princeton, N.J.: Princeton University Press, 2003.

Lapsansky, Phillip. "'Abigail, a Negress': The Role and the Legacy of African Americans in the Yellow Fever Epidemic." In *A Melancholy Scene of Devastation: The Public Response to the 1793 Philadelphia Yellow Fever Epidemic*, ed. J. Worth Estes and Billy G. Smith, 61–78. Canton, Mass.: Science History Publications, 1997.

———. "Afro-Americana: From Abolition to Bobalition." In *The Library Company of Philadelphia 2003 Annual Report*, 36–49. Philadelphia: Library Company of Philadelphia, 2003.

Lawson, Andrew. *Walt Whitman & the Class Struggle.* Iowa City: University of Iowa Press, 2006.

Lee, Chana Kai. *For Freedom's Sake: The Life of Fannie Lou Hamer.* Urbana: University of Illinois Press, 1998.

Levine, Caroline. *Forms: Whole, Rhythm, Hierarchy, Network.* Princeton, N.J.: Princeton University Press, 2015.

———. "Strategic Formalism: Toward a New Method in Cultural Studies." *Victorian Studies* 48, no. 4 (Summer 2006): 625–657.

Levine, Robert S. *Dislocating Race and Nation: Episodes in Nineteenth-Century American Literary Nationalism.* Chapel Hill: University of North Carolina Press, 2008.

———. *Martin Delany, Frederick Douglass, and the Politics of Representative Identity.* Chapel Hill: University of North Carolina Press, 1997.

———. *Conspiracy and Romance: Studies in Brockden Brown, Cooper, Hawthorne, and Melville.* New York: Cambridge University Press, 1989.

Levine, Robert S., and Ivy Wilson. "Introduction." In *The Works of James M. Whitefield:* America *and Other Writings by a Nineteenth-Century African American Poet*, 1–27. Chapel Hill: University of North Carolina Press, 2011.

Lewis, Harry. "'A Good Boarding Home Greatly Needed by the Colored Citizens': Black-Owned Boarding Houses in the Post-Bellum Colored Conventions Movement." Ed. Jenn Briggs. *What Did They Eat? Where Did They Stay? Black Boardinghouses and the Colored Conventions Movement.* Curators, Jenn Briggs, Anna Lacy, and Psyche Williams-Forson. Instructor, P. Gabrielle Foreman. *Colored Conventions: Bringing Nineteenth-Century Black Organizing to Digital Life.* http://coloredconventions.org/exhibits/show/williams-forson-exhibit/conclusions/---a-good-boarding-home-greatl.

Littlefield, Daniel C. "Revolutionary Citizens, 1776–1804." In *To Make Our World Anew: A History of African Americans to 1880*, ed. Robin D. G. Kelley and Earl Lewis, 103–168. New York: Oxford University Press, 2000.

Lindley, Thomas. *Narrative of a Voyage to Brasil.* London: Printed for J. Johnson, 1805.

Lining, John. *Essays and Observations, Physical and Literary. Read before a Society in Edinburgh, and Published by Them.* Vol. 2. Edinburgh: G. Hamilton and J. Balfour, 1756.

Litwack, Leon F. *North of Slavery: The Negro in the Free States 1790–1860.* Chicago: University of Chicago Press, 1961.

Longinus. "On the Sublime." In *The Sublime: A Reader in British Eighteenth-Century Aesthetic Theory*, ed. Peter De Bolla and Andrew Ashfield, 22–29. Cambridge: Cambridge University Press, 1996.

Looby, Christopher. *Voicing America: Language, Literary Form, and the Origins of the United States.* Chicago: University of Chicago Press, 1996.

Lott, Eric. *Love and Theft: Blackface Minstrelsy and the American Working Class.* New York: Oxford University Press, 1993.

Loughran, Trish. *The Republic in Print: Print Culture in the Age of U.S. Nation Building, 1770–1870.* New York: Columbia University Press, 2007.

Lukacs, Georg. "Narrate or Describe." In *Writer and Critic and Other Essays*, ed. and trans. Arthur D. Kahn, 110–148. New York: Grosset and Dunlap, 1970.

Lummis, C. Douglas. *Radical Democracy.* Ithaca, N.Y.: Cornell University Press, 1996.

Luskey, Brian. "Jumping Counters in White Collars: Manliness, Respectability, and Work in the Antebellum City." *Journal of the Early Republic* 26 (Summer 2006): 173–219.

Malone, Christopher. *Between Freedom and Bondage: Race, Party, and Voting Rights in the Antebellum North.* New York: Routledge, 2008.

Marable, Manning. *How Capitalism Underdeveloped Black America: Problems in Race, Political Economy and Society.* Boston: South End Press, 1983.

Marcovitch, Harvey. "Fugue." In *Black's Medical Dictionary*, ed. Harvey Marcovitch. 42nd ed. London: A&C Black, 2010.

Marie, Miranda. *Homegirls in the Public Sphere.* Austin: University of Texas Press, 2003.

Marinetto, Michael. "Who Wants to Be an Active Citizen? The Politics and Practice of Community Involvement." *Sociology* 37, no. (February 2003): 103–120.

Marrs, Cody. *Nineteenth-Century American Literature and the Long Civil War*. New York: Cambridge University Press, 2015.

Mbembe, Achille. "Necropolitics." Trans. Libby Meintjes. *Public Culture* 15, no. 1 (Winter 2003): 11–40.

———. *On the Postcolony*. Berkeley: University of California Press, 2001.

McCaskill, Barbara, and Caroline Gebhard, eds. *Post-Bellum, Pre-Harlem: African American Literature and Culture, 1877–1919*. New York: New York University Press, 2006.

McDaniel, Caleb. "The Fourth and the First: Abolitionist Holidays, Respectability, and Radical Interracial Reform." *American Quarterly* 57, no. 1 (March 2005): 129–151.

McGuir, Ian. "'Who Ain't a Slave?': Moby Dick and the Ideology of Free Labor.'" *Journal of American Studies* 37, no. 2 (2003): 287–330.

McHenry, Elizabeth. *Forgotten Readers: Recovering the Lost History of African-American Literary Societies*. Durham, N.C.: Duke University Press, 2002.

Mills, Charles W. *The Racial Contract*. Ithaca, N.Y.: Cornell University Press, 1997.

McInnis, Maurice. "The Most Famous Plantation of All: The Politics of Painting Mount Vernon." In *Landscape of Slavery: The Plantation in American Art*, ed. Angela D. Mack and Stephen G. Hoffius, 86–114. Columbia: University South Carolina Press, 2008.

McKivigan, John R., and Stanley Harrold, eds. *Antislavery Violence: Sectional, Racial, and Cultural Conflict in Antebellum America*. Knoxville: University of Tennessee Press, 1999.

McShane, Clay and Joel A Tarr. *The Horse in the City: Living Machines in the Nineteenth Century*. Baltimore: Johns Hopkins University Press, 2007.

Melish, Joanne Pope. "The 'Condition' Debate and Racial Discourse in the Antebellum North." *Journal of the Early Republic* 19, no. 4 (Winter 1999): 651–672. http://www.jstor.org/stable/3125137.

———. *Disowning Slavery: Gradual Emancipation and "Race" in New England, 1789–1860*. Ithaca, N.Y.: Cornell University Press, 1998.

Mendelsohn, Everett. "John Lining and His Contribution to Early American Science." *Isis* 51, no. 3 (September 1960): 278–292.

Mercieca, Jennifer R. "The Irony of the Democratic Style." *Rhetoric & Public Affairs* 11, no. 3 (Fall 2008): 441–449.

Merish, Lori. *Sentimental Materialism: Gender, Commodity Culture, and Nineteenth-Century American Literature*. Durham, N.C.: Duke University Press, 2000.

Minutes of the State Convention of Coloured Citizens of Pennsylvania, Convened at Harrisburg, December 13th and 14th, 1848. Philadelphia: Merrihew and Thompson, 1849. Library Company of Philadelphia.

Miranda, Marie. *Homegirls in the Public Sphere*. Austin: University of Texas Press, 2003.

Moody, Joycelyn. *Sentimental Confessions: Spiritual Narratives of Nineteenth-Century African American Women*. Athens: University of Georgia Press, 2001.

Moore, Wayne D. *Constitutional Rights and Powers of the People*. Princeton, N.J.: Princeton University Press, 1996.

Moreno, Paul D. *Black Americans and Organized Labor: A New History*. Baton Rouge: Louisiana State University Press, 2006.

Morgan, Thomas M. "The Education and Medical Practice of Dr. James McCune Smith 1813–1865, First Black American to Hold a Medical Degree." *Journal of National Medical History* 95, no. 7 (July 2003): 603–614.

Morrison, Toni. *Playing in the Dark: Whiteness and the Literary Imagination*. Cambridge, Mass.: Harvard University Press, 1992.

Moses, William J. *Creative Conflict in African American Thought?: Frederick Douglass, Alexander Crummell, Booker T. Washington, W. E. B. Du Bois, and Marcus Garvey*. New York: Cambridge University Press, 2004.

Mowry, Arthur May. *The Dorr War; or, The Constitutional Struggle in Rhode Island*. 1901. New York: Chelsea House, 1970.

"Mrs. Sanford's Speech at the 1848 Ohio National Convention." *Colored Conventions: Bringing Nineteenth-Century Black Organizing to Digital Life*. Accessed September 27, 2017. http://coloredconventions.org/items/show/429.

Nash, Gary. "Absalom Jones and the African Church of Philadelphia: 'To Arise out of the Dust.'" In *The Human Tradition in the American Revolution*, ed. Nancy L. Rhoden and Ian K. Steele, 241–266. Wilmington, Del.: SR Books, 2000.

———. *Forging Freedom: The Formation of Philadelphia's Black Community, 1720–1840*. Cambridge, Mass.: Harvard University Press, 1988.

———. *Race and Revolution*. Lanham: Rowman & Littlefield, 1990.

Nash, Gary B., and Jean R. Soderlund. *Freedom by Degrees: Emancipation in Pennsylvania and Its Aftermath*. New York: Oxford University Press, 1991.

National Emigration Convention of Colored People. "Proceedings of the National Emigration Convention of Colored People Held at Cleveland, Ohio, On Thursday, Friday, and Saturday, the 24th, 25th, and 26th of August, 1854." ColoredConventions.org. http://coloredconventions.org/items/show/314.

Nelson, Dana D. *Commons Democracy: Reading the Politics of Participation in the Early United States*. New York: Fordham University Press, 2016.

———. *National Manhood: Capitalist Citizenship and the Imagined Fraternity of White Men*. Durham, N.C.: Duke University Press, 1998.

———. "Representative/Democracy: Presidents, Democratic Management, and the Unfinished Business of Male Sentimentalism." In *No More Separate Spheres*, ed. Cathy N. Davidson and Jessamyn Hatcher, 325–354. Durham, N.C.: Duke University Press, 2002.

———. "Representative/Democracy: The Political Work of Countersymbolic Representation." In *Materializing Democracy: Toward a Revitalized Cultural Politics*, ed. Dana D. Nelson, Russ Castronovo, 218–247. Durham, N.C.: Duke University Press, 2002.

Newman, Richard. "'A Chosen Generation': Black Founders and Early America." In *Prophets of Protest: Reconsidering the History of American Abolitionism*, ed. Timothy Patrick McCarthy and John Stauffer, 59–79. New York: New Press, 2006.

———. *Freedom's Prophet: Bishop Richard Allen, the AME Church, and the Black Founding Fathers*. New York: New York University Press, 2008.

———. "Protest in Black and White: The Formation and Transformation of an African American Political Community During the Early Republic." In *Beyond the Founders: New Approaches to the Political History of the Early American Republic*, ed. Jeffrey L. Pasley, Andrew W. Robertson, and David Waldstreicher, 180–204. Chapel Hill: University of North Carolina Press, 2004.

———. *The Transformation of American Abolitionism: Fighting Slavery in the Early Republic*. Chapel Hill: University of North Carolina Press, 2002.

Newman, Richard, Patrick Rael, and Phillip Lapsansky, eds. *Pamphlets of Protest: An Anthology of Early African American Protest Literature, 1790–1860*. New York: Routledge, 2001.

Newman, Richard S., and Roy E. Finkenbine. "Forum: Black Founders in the New Republic: Introduction." *William and Mary Quarterly* 64, vol. 1 (January 2007): 83–94.

Nobles, Richard, and David Schiff. "The Right to Appeal and Workable Systems of Justice." *Modern Law Review* 65, no. 5 (September 2002): 676–701.

Nwankwo, Ifeoma. *Black Cosmopolitanism: Racial Consciousness and Transnational Identity in the Nineteenth-Century Americas.* Philadelphia: University of Pennsylvania Press, 2005.

Nyong'o, Tavia. *The Amalgamation Waltz: Race, Performance, and the Ruse of Memory.* Minneapolis: University of Minnesota Press, 2009.

———. "Uncommon Memory: The Performance of Amalgamation in Early Black Political Culture." PhD diss., Yale University, 2004.

Ostrowski, Carl. "Slavery, Labor Reform, and Intertextuality in Antebellum Print Culture: The Slave Narrative and the City-Mysteries Novel." *African American Review* 40, no. 3 (Fall 2006): 493–506.

Otter, Samuel. "Philadelphia Experiments." *American Literary History* 16, no. 1 (Spring 2004): 103–116.

———. *Philadelphia Stories: America's Literature of Race and Freedom.* New York: Oxford University Press, 2010.

Paine, Thomas. *Common Sense, Rights of Man, and Other Essential Writings of Thomas Paine.* Ed. Sidney Hook. New York: Signet Classics, 2003.

Patterson, Orlando. *Slavery and Social Death: A Comparative Analysis.* Cambridge, Mass.: Harvard University Press, 1982.

Patterson, Sarah, Nathan Nikolic, Gwen Meredith, Caleb Trotter, Gerti Wilson, and Ariana Woodson, eds. "Black Wealth and the 1843 National Colored Convention." *Colored Conventions: Bringing Nineteenth-Century Black Organizing to Digital Life.* http://coloredconventions.org/exhibits/show/exhibit-1843.

Patton, Robert H. *Patriot Pirates: The Privateer War for Freedom and Fortune in the American Revolution.* New York: Pantheon, 2008.

Pauly, Thomas H. "The Literary Sketch in Nineteenth-Century America." *Texas Studies in Literature and Language* 17, no. 2 (Summer 1975): 489–503.

Pease, Jane H., and William H. Pease. "Negro Conventions and the Problem of Black Leadership." *Journal of Black Studies* 2, no. 1 (September 1971): 29–44. http://www.jstor.org/stable/2783698.

———. *They Who Would Be Free: Blacks' Search for Freedom, 1830–1861.* New York: Atheneum, 1974.

Penn, Irvine Garland. *The Afro-American Press and Its Editors.* Springfield: Willey, 1891.

Perez v. Brownell, 356 U.S. 44 (1958).

Pernick, Martin S. "Politics, Parties, and Pestilence: Epidemic Yellow Fever in Philadelphia and the Rise of the First Party System." In *A Melancholy Scene of Devastation: The Public Response to the 1793 Philadelphia Yellow Fever Epidemic*, ed. J. Worth Estes and Billy G. Smith, 119–146. Canton, Mass.: Science History Publications, 1997.

Peterson, Carla. *Black Gotham: A Family History of African Americans in Nineteenth-Century New York City.* New Haven, Conn.: Yale University Press, 2011.

———. "Capitalism, Black (Under)Development, and the Production of the African-American Novel in the 1850s." *American Literary History* 4, no. 4 (Winter 1992): 559–583.

———. *"Doers of the Word": African-American Women Speakers and Writers in the North 1830–1880.* New York: Oxford University Press, 1995.

———. “Literary Transnationalism and Diasporic History: Frances Watkins Harper’s ‘Fancy Sketches,’ 1859–1860.” In *Women’s Rights and Transatlantic Antislavery in the Era of Emancipation*, ed. Kathryn Kish Sklar and James Brewer Stewart, 189–208. New Haven, Conn.: Yale University Press, 2007.

Phan, Hoang Gia. *Bonds of Citizenship: Law and the Labors of Emancipation.* New York: New York University Press, 2013.

Portelli, Alessandro. *The Text and the Voice: Writing, Speaking, and Democracy in American Literature.* New York: Columbia University Press, 1994.

Porter, Dorothy, ed. *Early Negro Writing, 1760–1837.* Baltimore: Black Classic Press, 1995.

Pratt, Lloyd. “‘I Am a Stranger with Thee’: Frederick Douglass and Recognition After 1845.” *American Literature* 85, no.2 (2013): 247–272.

———. “The Stranger and the City of New Orleans: Racialization, Americanization, and Literary Print Culture.” In *Early African American Print Culture in Theory and Practice*, ed. Jordan Alexander Stein and Lara Cohen, 253–274. Philadelphia: University Pennsylvania Press, 2012.

———. *The Strangers Book: The Human of African American Literature.* Philadelphia: University of Pennsylvania Press, 2016.

Proceedings and Debates of the Convention of the Commonwealth of Pennsylvania to Propose Amendments to the Constitution, Commenced and Held at Harrisburg, on the Second Day of May, 1837. Harrisburg, Pa.: Packer, Barrett, and Parke, 1837. Historical Society of Pennsylvania.

Proceedings of the Colored National Convention, Held in Rochester, July 6th, 7th and 8th, 1853. Rochester, N.Y.: Office of Frederick Douglass’s Paper, 1853.

Pryor, Elizabeth Stordeur. *Colored Travelers: Mobility and the Fight for Citizenship before the Civil War.* Chapel Hill: University of North Carolina Press, 2016.

Purvis, Robert. “Appeal of Forty Thousand Citizens, Threatened with Disfranchisement, to the People of Pennsylvania” (1837). In *Pamphlets of Protest: An Anthology of Early African American Protest Literature, 1790–1860*, ed. Richard Newman, Patrick Rael, and Phillip Lapsansky, 133–142. New York: Routledge, 2001.

Quarles, Benjamin. “Antebellum Free Blacks and the ‘Spirit of ’76.’” *Journal of Negro History* 61, no. 3 (July 1976): 229–242.

———. *Black Abolitionists.* New York: Oxford University Press, 1977.

Quetelet, Adolphe. *A Treatise On Man And the Development of His Faculties.* Edinburgh: W. and R. Chambers, 1842. https://catalog.hathitrust.org/api/volumes/oclc/8333229.html.

Raboteau, Albert J. *A Fire in the Bones: Reflections on African-American Religious History.* Boston: Beacon, 1995.

Rael, Patrick. “African Americans, Slavery, and Thrift from the Revolution to the Civil War.” In *Thrift and Thriving in America: Capitalism and Moral Order from the Puritans to the Present*, ed. Joshua J. Yates and James Davison Hunter, 183–206. New York: Oxford University Press, 2011.

———. *Black Identity & Black Protest in the Antebellum North.* Chapel Hill: University of North Carolina Press, 2002.

———. “Introduction.” In *African American Activism Before the Civil War: The Freedom Struggle in the Antebellum North*, ed. Patrick Rael, 1–38. New York: Routledge, 2008.

———. “The Market Revolution and Market Values in Antebellum Black Protest Thought.” In *Cultural Change and the Market Revolution in America, 1789–1860*, ed. Scott Martin, 13–45. Lanham, Md.: Rowman and Littlefield, 2004.

Ramsay, David. *A Dissertation on the Manners of Acquiring the Character and Privileges of a Citizen*. Charleston, S.C.: AAS, 1789.

Ramsey, Paul. *Basic Christian Ethics*. Louisville, Ky.: Westminster/John Knox, 1993.

Rancière, Jacques. *Disagreement: Politics and Philosophy*. Trans. Julie Rose. Minneapolis: University of Minnesota Press, 1999.

———. *Dissensus: On Politics and Aesthetics*. Ed. and trans. Steven Corcoran. New York: Continuum, 2010.

———. *The Politics of Aesthetics: The Distribution of the Sensible*. Trans. Gabriel Rockhill. New York: Continuum, 2006.

Ratcliffe, Krista. *Rhetorical Listening: Identification, Gender, Whiteness*. Carbondale: Southern Illinois University Press, 2005.

Reid-Pharr, Robert F. *Conjugal Union: The Body, the House, and the Black American*. New York: Oxford University Press, 1999.

———. "Introduction." In *The Garies and Their Friends*, ed. Robert F. Reid-Pharr, vii–xvii. Baltimore: Johns Hopkins University Press, 1997.

Report of the Debates and Proceedings of the Convention for the Revision of the Constitution of the State of New York: 1846. Albany, N.Y.: Evening Atlas, 1846.

Reports of the Proceedings and Debates of the Convention of 1821 Assembled for the Purpose of Amending the Constitution of the State of New York: Containing All the Official Documents Relating to the Subject, and Other Valuable Matter. Albany, N.Y.: E. and E. Hosford, 1821.

"A Review of Ira Aldridge's *Titus* at the Britannia, Huxton [1857]." *The Era* (1857): 10. Rpt. in *Titus Andronicus: Critical Essays*, ed. Philip C. Kolin. New York: Garland, 1995.

Rhodes, Jane. *Mary Ann Shadd Cary: The Black Press and Protest in the Nineteenth Century*. Bloomington: Indiana University Press, 1998.

Richardson, Gary A. "Plays and Playwrights: 1800–1865." In *The Cambridge History of American Theatre*, vol. 1, *Beginnings to 1870*, ed. Don B. Wilmeth and Christopher Bigsby, 330–417. New York: Cambridge University Press, 1998.

Ripley, Peter C, ed. *The Black Abolitionist Papers*. Vol. 3, *The United States, 1830–1846*. Chapel Hill: University of North Carolina Press, 1991.

———. *The Black Abolitionist Papers*. Vol. 4, *The United States, 1847–1858*. Chapel Hill: University of North Carolina Press, 1991.

Roberts, Neil. *Freedom as Marronage*. Chicago: University of Chicago Press, 2015.

Rodgers, Daniel T. "Republicanism: The Career of a Concept." *Journal of American History* 79, no. 1 (June 1992): 11–38.

Roediger, David. *The Wages of Whiteness: Race and the Making of the American Working Class*. New York: Verso, 1991.

Rossiter, Clinton, ed. *The Federalist Papers*. New York: Signet, 2003.

Rousseau, Jean Jacques. *Of the Social Contract*. In *The Social Contract and Other Later Political Writings*, ed. and trans. Victor Gourevitch. New York: Cambridge University Press, 1997.

Rucker, Walter C. "Unpopular Sovereignty: African American Resistance and Reactions to the Kansas-Nebraska Act." In *The Nebraska-Kansas Act of 1854*, ed. John R. Wunder and Joann M. Ross, 129–158. Lincoln: University of Nebraska Press, 2008.

Rusert, Britt. "Disappointment in the Archives of Black Freedom." *Social Text* 33, no.4 (December 2015): 19–33.

———. *Fugitive Science: Empiricism and Freedom in Early African American Culture*. New York: New York University Press, 2017.

Rush, Benjamin. "An Oration, Delivered before the American Philosophical Society, held in Philadelphia on the 27th of February; Containing an Enquiry into the Influence of Physical Causes upon the Moral Faculty." Philadelphia: Charles Cist, 1786.

———. *An Account of the Bilious Remitting Fever, As It Appeared in Philadelphia in the Summer and Autumn Of The Year 1780*. Philadelphia: Dobson, 1794. American Antiquarian Society.

———. *A Plan for the Establishment of Public Schools and the Diffusion of Knowledge in Pennsylvania; to Which Are Added Thoughts upon the Mode of Education, Proper in a Republic. Addressed to the Legislature and Citizens of the State*. Philadelphia: Dobson, 1786. American Antiquarian Society.

———. *Letters of Benjamin Rush*. Ed. L. H. Butterfield. Princeton, N.J.: Princeton University Press, 1951.

Ruskin, John. *The Complete Works of John Ruskin: Poetry of Architecture, Seven Lamps, Modern Painters*. Vol. 1. New York: National Library Association, 1873. http://www.gutenberg.org/files/29907/29907-h/29907-h.htm.

Russell, Heather. *Legba's Crossing: Narratology in the African Atlantic*. Athens: University of Georgia Press, 2009.

Shachar, Ayelet. *The Birthright Lottery: Citizenship and Global Inequality*. Cambridge Mass.: Harvard University Press, 2009.

Saillant, John. "Lemuel Haynes and the Revolutionary Origins of Black Theology, 1776–1801." *Religion and American Culture* 2, no. 1 (Winter 1992): 79–102.

Samuels, Shirley. "Plague and Politics in 1793: Arthur Mervyn." *Criticism* 27, no. 3 (Summer 1985): 225–246.

Santamarina, Xiomara. *Belabored Professions: Narratives of African American Working Womanhood*. Chapel Hill: University of North Carolina Press, 2005.

———. "Thinkable Alternatives in African American Studies." *American Quarterly* 58, no. (1 March 2006): 274.

Schiller, Friedrich von. *Essays*. Ed. Walter Hinderer and Daniel O. Dahlstrom. New York: Continuum, 2005.

Schoenfield, Mark. *British Periodicals and Romantic Identity: The "Literary Lower Empire."* New York: Palgrave Macmillan, 2009.

Scott, Anthony. *The Evolution of Resource Property Rights*. Oxford: Oxford University Press, 2008.

Scott, Walter. *The Waverley Novels, by Sir Walter Scott, Complete in 12 Vol., Printed from the Latest English Ed., Embracing the Author's Last Corrections, Prefaces & Notes*. Philadelphia: Lippincott, Grambo, and Co., 1852.

Secor, Anna. "'There Is an Istanbul That Belongs to Me': Citizenship, Space, and Identity in the City." *Annals of the Association of American Geographers* 94, no. 2 (2004): 352–368.

Sedgwick, Eve Kosofsky. *Touching Feeling: Affect, Pedagogy, Performativity*. Durham, N.C.: Duke University Press, 2003.

Sellers, Charles. *The Market Revolution: Jacksonian America, 1815–1846*. New York: Oxford University Press, 1991.

Shaftesbury, Anthony Ashley Cooper. *Characteristics of Men, Manners, Opinions, Times*. Ed. Lawrence Eliot Klein. 1771. Cambridge: Cambridge University Press, 1999.

Sharp, James Roger. *American Politics in the Early Republic: New Nation in Crisis*. New Haven, Conn.: Yale University Press, 1995.

Sharpe, Granville. *The Just Limitation of Slavery in the Laws of God, Compared with the Unbounded Claims of the African Traders and British American Slaveholders*. London: Printed for B. White, and E. and C. Dilly, 1776. http://www.archive.org/details/justlimitationofooshar.

Shklar, Judith N. *American Citizenship: The Quest for Inclusion*. Tanner Lectures on Human Values. Cambridge, Mass.: Harvard University Press, 1991.

Shoenfield, Mark. *British Periodicals and Romantic Identity: The "Literary Lower Empire."* New York: Palgrave Macmillan, 2009.

Sidney. "William Whipper's Letters No. 4." *Colored American*, February 13, 1841.

Singh, Nikhil Pal. *Black Is a Country: Race and the Unfinished Struggle for Democracy*. Cambridge, Mass.: Harvard University Press, 2004.

Sinha, Manisha. *The Slave's Cause: A History of Abolition*. New Haven, Conn.: Yale University Press, 2016.

Sinha, Manisha. "An Alternative Tradition of Radicalism: African American Abolitionists and the Metaphor of Revolution: Freedom, Race, and Power in American History." In *Contested Democracy: Freedom, Race, and Power in American History*, ed. Manisha Sinha and Penny Von Eschen, 9–30. New York: Columbia University Press, 2007.

Sklansky, Jeffrey P. *Soul's Economy: Market Society and Selfhood in American Thought, 1820–1920*. Chapel Hill: University of North Carolina Press, 2002.

Smith, Eric Ledell. "The End of Black Voting Rights in Pennsylvania: African Americans and the Pennsylvania Constitutional Convention of 1837–1838." *Pennsylvania History* 65, no. 3 (Summer 1998): 279–299.

Smith, James McCune. "Civilization: Its Dependence on Physical Circumstances." *Anglo-African Magazine* 1, no. 1 (1859): 5–17.

———. "Citizenship." *Anglo-African Magazine* 1, no. 5 (May 1859): 8–16.

———. "Position Defended." *Colored American*, August 15, 1840.

———. "Reviving the Black Convention Movement." In *Black Abolitionist Papers*, vol. 3, *The United States, 1830–1846*, ed. Peter C. Ripley, 345–351. Chapel Hill: University of North Carolina Press, 1991.

———. *The Works of James McCune Smith*. Ed. John Stauffer. New York: Oxford University Press, 2007.

Smith, Rogers. "Citizenship and the Politics of People-Building." *Citizenship Studies* 5, no. 1 (2001): 73–96.

———. *Civic Ideals: Conflicting Visions of Citizenship in U.S. History*. New Haven, Conn.: Yale University Press, 1997.

Smith-Rossenberg, Carroll. "Black Gothic: The Shadowy Origins of the American Bourgeoisie." In *Possible Pasts: Becoming Colonial in Early America*, ed. Robert Blair St. George, 243–269. Ithaca, N.Y.: Cornell University Press, 2000.

Somers, Margaret. *Genealogies of Citizenship: Markets, Statelessness, and the Right to Have Rights*. Cambridge Cultural Studies. New York: Cambridge University Press, 2008.

Spillers, Hortense. *Black, White, and in Color: Essays on American Literature and Culture*. Chicago: University of Chicago Press, 2003.

Squibbs. Richard. "Civic Humorism and the Eighteenth-Century Periodical Essay." *ELH* 75, no. 2 (Summer 2008): 389–313.

Squires, Catherine. "The Black Press and the State: Attracting Unwanted (?) Attention." In *Counterpublics and the State*, ed. Robert Asen and Daniel C. Brouwer, 111–136. Albany, N.Y.: SUNY Press, 2001.

S.S.N. "Anglo-Saxons, and Anglo-Africans." *Anglo-African Magazine* 1, no. 8 (August 1859): 247–251.

Stancliff, Michael. *Frances Ellen Watkins Harper: African American Reform and the Rise of a Modern Nation State*. New York: Routledge, 2010.

Stanton, William. *The Leopard's Spots: Scientific Attitudes Toward Race in America, 1815–59*. Chicago: University of Chicago Press, 1960.

Stein, Jordan Alexander, and Lara Cohen, eds. *Early African American Print Culture in Theory and Practice*. Philadelphia: University Pennsylvania Press, 2012.

Stepto, Robert B. *From Behind the Veil: A Study of Afro-American Narrative*. 2nd ed. Urbana: University of Illinois Press, 1991.

———. "Teaching Afro-American Literature: Survey or Tradition, the Reconstruction of Instruction." In *Afro-American Literature: The Reconstruction of Instructions*, ed. Dexter Fisher and Robert Stepto, 8–24. New York: Modern Languages Association of America, 1978.

Stern, Julia A. *The Plight of Feeling: Sympathy and Dissent in the Early American Novel*. Chicago: University of Chicago Press, 1997.

Steven, Craig. "The Rise and Influence of the New York African Society for Mutual Relief, 1808–1865." *Afro-Americans in New York Life and History* 22, no. 2 (July 1998): 7–18.

Stewart, James Brewer. "Assessing Abolitionism: 'So What's New?'" *Reviews in American History* 27, no. 3 (1999): 397–405.

———. "Modernizing 'Difference': The Political Meanings of Color in the Free States, 1776–1840." *Journal of the Early Republic* 19, no. 4 (Winter, 1999): 691–712.

Stokes, Melvyn. "Introduction." In *The Market Revolution in America: Social, Political, and Religious Expressions, 1800–1880*, ed. Melvyn Stokes and Stephen Conway, 1–20. Charlottesville: University of Virginia Press, 1996.

Stuckey, Sterling, ed. *The Ideological Origins of Black Nationalism*. Boston: Beacon, 1972.

Swift, David E. *Black Prophets of Justice: Activist Clergy Before the Civil War*. Baton Rouge: Louisiana State University Press, 1989.

Taylor, Diana. *The Archive and the Repertoire: Performing Cultural Memory in the Americas*. Durham, N.C.: Duke University Press, 2003.

Taylor, Keeanga-Yamahtta. *From #BlackLivesMatter to Black Liberation*. Chicago: Haymarket Books, 2016.

Taylor, Nikki M. *Driven Towards Madness: The Fugitive Slave Margaret Garner and Tragedy on the Ohio*. Athens: Ohio University Press, 2016.

Thistlethwaite, Mark. "The Most Important Themes: History Painting and Its Place in American Art." In *Grand Illusions: History Painting in America*, ed. William H. Gerdts and Mark Thislewaite, 7–58. Fort Worth, Tex.: Amon Carter Museum, 1988.

Thompson, Alvin O. *Flight to Freedom: African Runaways and Maroons in the Americas*. Kingston: University of the West Indies Press, 2006.

Thoreau, Henry David. *Collected Essays and Poems*. New York: Literary Classics of the United States, 2001.

Tillet, Salamishah. *Sites of Slavery: Citizenship and Racial Democracy in the Post–Civil Rights Imagination*. Durham, N.C.: Duke University Press, 2012.

Tocqueville, Alexis. *Democracy in America*. New York: Library of America, 2004.

Townsend, Craig D. *Faith in Their Own Color: Black Episcopalians in Antebellum New York City*. New York: Columbia University Press, 2005.

Turner, Frederick Jackson. *Rise of the New West.* New York: Collier, 1962.
Urbinati, Nadia. *Representative Democracy: Principles and Genealogy.* Chicago: University of Chicago Press, 2006.
Vanoni, Vito A., ed. *Sedimentation Engineering.* 2nd ed. Reston, Va.: American Society of Civil Engineers, 2006.
Vickers, Daniel. "Competency and Competition." *William and Mary Quarterly* 47, no. 1 (January 1990): 3–29.
Villa, Dana. *Socratic Citizenship.* Princeton, N.J.: Princeton University Press, 2001.
Vogel, Todd, ed. Introduction to *The Black Press: New Literary and Historical Essays,* 1–14. New Brunswick, N.J.: Rutgers University Press, 2001.
———. "The New Face of Black Labor." In *The Black Press: New Literary and Historical Essays,* ed. Todd Vogel, 37–54. New Brunswick, N.J.: Rutgers University Press, 2001.
———. *Rewriting White: Race, Class, and Cultural Capital in Nineteenth-Century America.* New Brunswick, N.J.: Rutgers University Press, 2004.
Waldron, Jeremy. "On the Road: Good Samaritans and Compelling Duties." *Santa Clara Law Review* 4, no. 4 (2000): 1053–1103.
Waldstreicher, David. "Rites of Rebellion." *Journal of American History* 82, no. 1 (June 1995): 31–61.
Walker, Juliet E. K. "Promoting Black Entrepreneurship and Business Enterprise in Antebellum America: The National Negro Convention, 1830–1855." In *A Different Vision: Race and Public Policy,* ed. Thomas D. Boston, 280–318. London: Routledge, 1997.
Wall, Diana DiZerega, Nan A. Rothschild, and Cynthia Copeland. "Seneca Village and Little Africa: Two African American Communities in Antebellum New York City." *Historical Archaeology* 42, no. 1 (2008): 97–107.
Wall, Cheryl A. "Taking Positions and Changing Words." In *Changing Our Own Words: Essays on Criticism, Theory, and Writing by Black Women,* ed. Cheryl A. Wall, 1–15. New Brunswick, N.J.: Rutgers University Press, 1989.
Wang, Xi. "Make 'Every Slave Free, and Every Freeman a Voter': The African American Construction of Suffrage Discourse in the Age of Emancipation." In *Contested Democracy: Freedom, Race, and Power in American History,* ed. Manisha Sinha and Penny Von Eschen, 117–133. New York: Columbia University Press, 2007.
Warner, Michael. *The Letters of the Republic: Publication and the Public Sphere in Eighteenth-Century America.* Cambridge, Mass.: Harvard University Press, 1990.
———. *Publics and Counterpublics.* New York: Zone Books, 2002.
Weheliye, Alexander G. *Habeas Viscus: Racializing Assemblages, Biopolitics, and Black Feminist Theories of the Human.* Durham: Duke University Press, 2015.
Weiner, Mark S. *Black Trials: Citizenship from the Beginnings of Slavery to the End of Caste.* Ann Arbor: University of Michigan Press, 2004.
Weinstein, Cindy. *Time, Tense, and American Literature: When Is Now?* New York: Cambridge University Press, 2015.
Welke, Barbara Young. *Law and the Borders of Belonging in the Long Nineteenth Century United States.* New York: Cambridge University Press, 2010.
Wheatley, Phillis. *Complete Writings.* Ed. Vincent Carreta. New York: Penguin Books, 2001.
Whipper, William. "To the Colored American." *Colored American,* February 6, 1841.
White, Ed. *The Backcountry and the City: Colonization and Conflict in Early America.* Minneapolis: University of Minnesota Press, 2005.

White, Shane. "'It Was a Proud Day': African Americans, Festivals, and Parades in the North, 1741–1834." *Journal of American History* 81, no. 1 (June 1994): 13–50.

White, Shane, and Graham White. *Stylin': African American Expressive Culture from Its Beginnings to the Zoot Suit.* Ithaca, N.Y.: Cornell University Press, 1998.

Wilder, Craig Steven. *A Covenant with Color: Race and Social Power in Brooklyn 1636–1990.* New York: Columbia University Press, 2000.

———. "'Driven . . . from the School of the Prophets': The Colonizationist Ascendance at General Theological Seminary." *New York History* 93, no. 3 (Summer 2012): 157–185.

Wilentz, Sean. *Chants Democratic: New York City and the Rise of the American Working Class, 1788–1850.* 20th anniversary ed. New York: Oxford University Press, 2004.

———. *The Rise of American Democracy: Jefferson to Lincoln.* New York: Norton, 2005.

———. "Society, Politics, and the Market Revolution." In *The New American History*, ed. Eric Foner, 51–71. Philadelphia: Temple University Press, 1990.

Wilson, Carol. "Active Vigilance Is the Price of Liberty: Black Self-Defense Against Fugitive Slave Recapture and Kidnapping of Free Blacks." In *Antislavery Violence: Sectional, Racial, and Cultural Conflict in Antebellum America*, ed. John R. McKivigan and Stanley Harrold, 108–127. Knoxville: University of Tennessee Press, 1999.

Wilson, Ivy. "'ARE YOU MAN ENOUGH?' Imagining Ethiopia and Transnational Black Masculinity." *Callaloo* 33, no. 1 (Winter 2010): 265–277.

———. "The Brief Wondrous Life of the *Anglo-African Magazine*, or, Antebellum African American Editorial Practice and Its Afterlives." In *Publishing Blackness: Textual Constructions of Race Since 1850*, ed. George Hutchinson and John Young, 18–38. Ann Arbor: University of Michigan Press, 2013.

———. "Periodicals, Print Culture, and African American Poetry." In *A Companion to African American* Literature, ed. Gene Andrew Jarrett, 133–148. Malden, Mass.: Wiley-Blackwell, 2010.

———. *Specters of Democracy: Blackness and the Aesthetics of Politics in the Antebellum U.S.* New York: Oxford University Press, 2011.

Winch, Julie. "Free Men and 'Freemen': Black Voting Rights in Pennsylvania, 1790–1870." *Pennsylvania Legacies* 8, no. 2 (November 2008): 14–19.

———. *Philadelphia's Black Elite: Activism, Accommodation, and the Struggle for Autonomy.* Philadelphia: Temple University Press, 1988.

Wong, Edlie L. *Neither Fugitive nor Free: Atlantic Slavery, Freedom Suits, and the Legal Culture of Travel.* New York: New York University Press, 2009.

Wood, Andrew F. "Managing the Lady Managers: The Shaping of Heterotopian Spaces in the 1893 Chicago Exposition's Woman's Building." *Southern Communication Journal* 69, no. 4 (Summer 2004): 289–302.

Wood, Gordon S. *The Creation of the American Republic, 1776–1787.* Chapel Hill: University of North Carolina Press, 1998.

———. *The Radicalism of the American Revolution.* New York: Knopf, 1992.

Wood, Nicholas. "'A Sacrifice on the Altar of Slavery': Doughface Politics and Black Disenfranchisement in Pennsylvania, 1837–1838." *Journal of the Early Republic* 31, no. 1 (2011): 75–106.

Wright, Nazera. *Black Girlhood in the Nineteenth Century.* Urbana: University of Illinois Press, 2016.

Wright, Richard. "Blueprint for Negro Writing." In *Within the Circle: An Anthology of African American Literary Criticism from the Harlem Renaissance to the Present*, ed. Angelyn Mitchell, 45–53. 3rd ed., 1937. Durham, N.C.: Duke University Press, 1993.

———. *White Man, Listen!* New York: Harper Perennial, 1995.

Yellin, Jean Fagan. *Harriet Jacobs: A Life.* New York: Basic Civitas Books, 2004.

Yole, Kristine. "Enslaved Women's Resistance and Survival Strategies in Frances Ellen Watkins Harper's 'The Slave Mother: A Tale of the Ohio' and Toni Morrison's *Beloved* and Margaret Garner." In *Gendered Resistance: Women, Slavery, and the Legacy of Margaret Garner*, ed. Mary E. Frederickson and Dolores M. Walters, 99–114. Urbana: University of Illinois Press, 2013.

Zafar, Rafia. *We Wear the Mask: African Americans Write American Literature, 1760–1870.* New York: Columbia University Press, 1997.

Zarefsky, David. *Lincoln, Douglas, and Slavery: In the Crucible of Public Debate.* Chicago: University of Chicago Press, 1990.

INDEX

Page numbers in italics indicate illustrations.

ACKNOWLEDGMENTS

Many people cultivated this work before it was a project. My thanks go to Jerry W. Ward Jr. for first suggesting I read Dorothy Porter's *Early Negro Writings* when I expressed an interest in black print culture. As is so often the case, he was prescient. Thanks also to Elizabeth Heitman and Kathy Willingham; to Dana Nelson for helping me learn to know when to fish and when to cut bait; to Teresa Goddu for reminding me to just "do good work" (Goddu-ism #1); to Carla Peterson for responding to an email from a stranger looking for Jane Rustic and for continuing to be a model for scholarship. I am also grateful to Ifeoma Nwankwo for her encouragement and presence. Thanks to Houston A. Baker, Jr., Vereen Bell, Richard Blackett, Matt Duques, Sean Goudie, Katherine Schwarz, Shawn Salvant, Hortense Spillers, and Cecilia Tichi.

Thanks to the Reclaiming Citizenship Reading Group—Sarah Passino, John Morrell, Sarah Kersh, and Amanda Hagood—for expanding my understanding of citizenship and social movements, and to the Fellows at the Robert Penn Warren Center for the Humanities—Jeff Edmonds, Donald Jellerson, Sonalini Sapra, Laura Taylor, Jonathan Wade, and David Wheat—for the timely and careful reading. I workshopped portions of this manuscript at the McNeil Center for Early American Studies, the Southern California Americanist Group, and the Caltech Brownbag Series. I appreciate the prodding, questioning, and critiques from them all.

At a crucial stage in the writing process, James Grady was a lifeline. The lessons I learned from working with him serve me to this day. Participants in the Unit for Criticism and Interpretive Theory Junior Faculty Fellow Workshop read significant portions of the manuscript, and I cannot express my gratitude for their time and their generosity: Ivy Wilson, John Ernest, Susan Koshy, Justine Murison (hallmate!), Ikuko Asaka, and Gilberto Rosas. Others to whom I am grateful for eyes, ears, and insight include Lisa Calvente, Aaron DeRosa, Nell Gabiam, Octavio González, Sarah Levine-Gronningsater, Monica Martinez, and Sarah Mesle, Michele Navakas. My gratitude goes as well to John Levi Barnard, Lara Cohen, Jeannine DeLombard, John Ernest, P. Gabrielle Foreman, Eric Gardner, Ben Fagan, Koritha Mitchell, Zita Nunes, and Richard Yarborough for invaluable guidance, generative conversations, and examples of good citizenship.

I also want to thank my colleagues at the University of Illinois. I could not have wished for a better place to write this book. Chris Freeburg, Trish Loughran, Bob Parker, Dale Bauer, and Candice Jenkins all read the manuscript in part or in whole. Their attention to detail and questions were invaluable. My thanks go to Lindsay Rose Russell, Andy Gaedtke, Andrea Stevens, and Catherine Gray, for the happy hour camaraderie. Thanks to Nancy Abelman, Craig Koslofsky, Maria Gillombardo, and the First Book Writers Group for your insight, persistence, and patience. My thanks also to my other California family: Stefanie Sobelle, Chris Hunter, Jennifer Jahner, Cindy Weinstein, Bert Emerson, and the faculty and staff at Caltech and the Huntington Library.

Research for this project was conducted at the American Antiquarian Society, the Library Company of Philadelphia, the Historical Society of Pennsylvania, the Schomburg Center for Research in Black Culture, New York Historical Society, Historical Society of Pennsylvania, the Brooklyn Historical Society, the Oberlin College Archives, University of Michigan archives, and the Huntington Library. It has been generously supported by the National Endowment for the Humanities, the Unit for Criticism and Interpretative Theory, a Mellon Caltech-Huntington Instructorship, Mellon Mays Initiatives, the Social Science Research Council, the Ford Foundation, the Robert Penn Warren Center for the Humanities, the Robert M. Greenfield Fellowship at the Library Company of Philadelphia and Historical Society of Pennsylvania, the Kate B. & Hall J. Peterson Fund at the American Antiquarian Society, the Frederick Binkerd Artz Research Grant at the Oberlin College Archives.

I am grateful to Gail and Rufus Thompson for your ongoing support. Nafissa Thompson-Spires, you continue to inspire me. Merlene Walker and Tony Spires, you have taught me so much. I want to thank my mom, Daisy I. Spires, for her unconditional love and for teaching me to love reading. Finally, I thank God for grace.

Portions of Chapter 3 appeared in *Early African American Print Culture in Theory and Practice* (University of Pennsylvania Press, 2012).